Human Evolution, Reproduction, and Morality

Human Evolution, Reproduction, and Morality

LEWIS PETRINOVICH

A Bradford Book
The MIT Press
Cambridge, Massachusetts
London, England

First MIT Press edition 1998.

Originally published by Plenum Press, New York.

1995 Plenum Press, New York

Printed and bound in the United States of America.

Library of Congress Cataloging-in-Publication Data

Petrinovich, Lewis F.
    Human evolution, reproduction, and morality / Lewis Petrinovich
      p. cm.
    Includes bibliographical references and index.
    ISBN 0-262-66143-8 (pbk. : alk. paper)
    1. Ethics. Evolutionary. 2. Human evolution—Moral and ethical aspects
  I. Title
  BJ1311.P48 1998
  171'.7—dc21   98-24298
                                                CIP

Preface

My initial interest in the issues considered in this book was triggered by questions regarding animal rights. I took my Ph.D. in physiological psychology at the University of California at Berkeley and began academic research studying brain function and learning. Specifically, I studied the effects of drugs that stimulate the nervous system on the characteristics of maze and discrimination learning by rats and expanded that research to study the effects of various types of brain lesions on the retention of learned responses. I continued this line of research for a number of years until I realized that the constraints of the laboratory often made it difficult to generalize the principles I had developed beyond the laboratory, and that the specific conditions of the experiments often prevented generalization to the universe of events I intended to understand at the outset of the research program.

I decided that it would be useful to study behaviors that organisms are designed by nature to perform and chose the development of language as a likely candidate. Normal human brains do not require specific training to develop a language. It is only necessary for an infant to be exposed to a language community at an appropriate time, and the infant comes to comprehend and express the language of that community without any conscious training on the part of adult models. This state of affairs, it seemed to me, could provide the royal road to an understanding of what brains need to do and how they do it.

I read in the psycholinguistic and child development literature to gain some understanding of how human language is used and how it develops. Because it is not possible to manipulate systematically the sensory input received by infants to investigate the operation of the biological and cognitive systems, I cast about for another languagelike system to study. The system that seemed to possess many of the characteristics in which I was interested was that involved in the development of song dialects by birds; specifically the white-crowned sparrows (*Zonotrichia leucophrys* that are located along the west coast of the United States. Young birds develop a distinctive and stable vocal pattern as a result of mere exposure to singing adults. These young birds develop the vocal characteristics of the prevailing "language" environment much in the way that human infants do, and I decided that the song system would be much easier to understand because it consists of only a single two-second-long song.

Because this species of bird does not breed readily in captivity it was necessary to collect young birds in the field before they had experience with adult song in order to study song development in the laboratory. To find nests and remove the nestlings for study, I had to make extensive field observations of breeding populations of white-crowned sparrows.

Alas, a true "slippery slope" developed. The more field experience I accumulated, the more questions regarding the functional significance of song dialects came to interest me, and to approach these questions it was necessary to understand the principles of evolutionary biology. These questions led me to conduct field studies of the distribution of song types, the stability of dialect systems through time, and studies of the transmission of song from bird to bird across generations of singers. These concerns led to studies of mating patterns and population structure and to thoughts of how to place these findings in a perspective that included population genetics and sociobiology.

While teaching my undergraduate course in comparative psychology, I came to realize that those of us who engage in laboratory and field studies of animals have an extensive set of implicit assumptions that justifies our research. However, we seldom bother to make these assumptions explicit, either to ourselves, to our colleagues, or to the public. This realization was quickened by the virulent and destructive attacks of members of the animal rights movement on the animal research community at our university. I decided that it was incumbent upon me to examine the underlying implicit presuppositions on which much of my academic life's work had been based. I began to read moral philosophy to develop an understanding of what is generally referred to as bioethics. I have now negotiated that slippery slope and arrived at a stopping place. This book is the result of a piece of that extensive journey.

I approach the development of a personal ethic from the perspective of a behavioral scientist who has had an active research career in psychology and biology. I hope to develop an understanding of the implicit and unexamined beliefs professional scientists have regarding underlying moral issues because I believe firmly that the unexamined life is not worth living, and that one's own most basic beliefs and values should be subjected to critical scrutiny. Nobel laureate George Snell (1988) adopted what he called the principle of self-interest as the starting point in his search for a rational ethic to guide the scientist and the layperson attempting to deal with modern ethical dilemmas. He argued that one can recognize a truly enlightened choice when one comes to understand the dictates of self-interest. When faced with a choice between alternative courses of action, pure self-interest must be acknowledged in order to develop an acceptable rational ethics. I intend to examine and describe some of the underlying beliefs and intuitions that people have regarding moral and biological issues involved in human life, and to use this descriptive base to develop an ethic based on what I call a rational liberalism.

In earlier writings I have devoted considerable attention to an examination of the implicit assumptions involved when scientists measure, experiment, and perform logical and statistical analyses of data (Petrinovich 1979, 1981). I have tried to identify problems that occur when scientists decide to observe certain events in certain ways and then bring the results of these observations to bear on theoretical concerns (Petrinovich 1989, 1990).

I began the present inquiry by analyzing the moral positions that behavioral scientists use, or at least should consider, when they decide to experiment using animals as subjects. These analyses led me to the realization that any adequate moral position would have to be broader than those concerning only nonhuman animals. Moral principles should be framed broadly enough to provide guidelines for all issues pertaining to life, whether it be plant, animal, or human. I agree with the moral philosopher Michael Tooley (1983) who argued that it is essential to discuss morality in terms that are broad enough to cover the widest variety of substantive issues under a uniform set of principles. The same principles should apply to issues regarding contraception, abortion, infanticide, death of humans, and keeping, killing, and consuming nonhuman animals. It is not tenable, rationally, to use a number of different moral systems, each specially designed to apply to a specific case. It is important to develop consistent moral principles, especially if they are to justify arguments regarding decisions that influence reproductive practices, the termination of life, and the pursuit of biomedical research. We should examine these moral positions carefully in regard to a broad range of related issues pertaining to life and its quality on earth, and I begin such an examination in this book.

This enterprise is not only the pursuit of a personal quest; it can be argued that humanity stands at a crossroads that makes it necessary for such inquiry to be approached in depth. The philosopher and social ethicist John Harris (1992, p. 2) began his book *Wonderwoman and Superman* by pointing out that "for the first time we can literally start to shape not only our own destiny in terms of what sort of world we wish to create and inhabit, but in terms of what we ourselves wish to be like. We can now, literally change the nature of human beings."

The arguments that I develop attempt to bring to bear the thinking of biologists (both organismic and evolutionary), moral philosophers, cognitive scientists, and social and developmental psychologists. I believe it is essential to consider matters at this multidisciplinary level. I have encountered the argument that, given the immense complexity involved in such things as human morality, it is neither possible nor profitable for any one individual to present a multidisciplinary perspective. This argument might have some merit if the goal is to present a comprehensive philosophical treatise that considers the various extant philosophical positions, arguing the merits and demerits of each, and bringing the available evidence to bear in evaluating the various positions. The force of that argument is diminished if the intent is to provoke a community of scholars (including biological and social scientists, philosophers, and policymakers) to consider these issues with a broad intellectual scope. The specialists can straighten out the problematic details later, philosophers can take delight in pointing out that their favored positions were not discussed, and scientists can bring more and different substantive data to bear. The advantage of having one person make the presentation is that it avoids the unevenness inherent in edited volumes and has the advantage (one hopes) of being argued in a consistent voice. I agree with Tooley (1983, p. 425), who concluded that "there is unfortunately a tradition of splendid isolation that has grown up between philosophy and the sciences. While that endures, there is little hope that these issues can be completely resolved." I hope I have been able to reduce that splendid isolation.

I acknowledge the valuable assistance of several colleagues and friends. Taylor Stoehr, Professor of English at the University of Massachusetts at Boston, professional writer, and a friend for 40 years, read the first draft of the manuscript and scolded me into developing a more consistent voice. Dr. A. J. Figueredo, one of my Ph.D. students and now professional collaborator, read the next two complete drafts and improved the organization, coaxing me to greater clarity. The penultimate draft received a careful critical reading by Joel Feinberg and Bruce Sales. I also received helpful comments on some of the chapters from Marc Bekoff, Paul Bloom, Martin Daly, Joel Feinberg, Grete Haberman, Patricia O'Neill (another of my Ph.D. students who has gone on to bigger and better things). I have profited from the excellent treatment of the principles of moral philosophers by John Fischer and Mark Ravizza (1992), and I am pleased to acknowledge my deep indebtedness to both of them for listening to my wonderings and wanderings and guiding me to this writer and to that thought. I recommend their book of critical essays, especially their introductory chapter, which is a concise discussion of some of the relevant basic philosophical principles. I would like to say that all the good stuff was my doing and that any faults that remain are due to the bad advice given by the above individuals. However, that statement would be untrue; so to serve the interest of honesty, I conclude they did good and I tried my best.

Contents

3. Basic Concepts: Evolutionary Mechanisms. 43

4. Evolutionary Mechanisms and Human Behavior. 67

5. The Evolved Human Social Condition 95

PART II. ISSUES IN REPRODUCTION

8. Contraception, Abortion, and Infanticide: Issues and Arguments

9. The Critical Nature of Personhood

I

Basic Principles

1

The Basic Approach

INTRODUCTION: THE NATURE OF THIS ENTERPRISE

The purpose of this book is to present some basic principles of evolutionary theory, neurophysiology, and cognitive science and illustrate how they can be brought to bear on some issues that moral philosophers have considered carefully for many years. My hope is that I will convince moral philosophers, as well as others interested in understanding the human condition, that the evolutionary model is a useful one and that there is a great deal of empirical data which can provide insights regarding human nature. This enhanced insight might assist philosophers, humanists, and social and biological scientists who want to frame a view of morality that respects the biological and cognitive nature of the human organism. I will argue that a knowledge of the principles of biological and cognitive development constitutes the *is* that can be useful in framing a reasonable, attainable, and intuitively satisfying *ought*. I will examine the factual evidence bearing on a series of issues related to human life, especially reproduction and abortion, and will suggest some reasonable and moral social policies based on this evidence.

One of the most successful approaches toward understanding morality within the framework of evolutionary principles has been that of the University of Michigan evolutionary biologist R. D. Alexander (1987) who developed a clear and concise argument regarding the possible evolutionary contribution to an understanding of morality in *The Biology of Moral Systems*. In that book he discussed the importance of evolved biological traits dominated by natural selection and argued that these traits underlie our conception of moral behavior. He demonstrated that it is reasonable to inquire into the nature of these basic evolved traits. Not only has he shown that the undertaking is a reasonable one, but he has pushed it far enough along to suggest that insights regarding the development of a moral social policy might well result. My intent, here, is to develop the relevant factual base on which morality can be grounded using evolutionary principles, and to discuss the relevance of these principles to the development of social policy. The arguments I will present are not so much concerned with individual choices given specific circumstances, but with the development of a set of bioethical principles that can be used to help shape social policies regarding life. I have taken considerable pains to acquaint myself with the thinking and insights of moral philosophers who work within the Western intellectual tradition. I hope to demonstrate the value of considering this philosophical tradition within an evolutionary framework, and to demonstrate how this perspective can be extended to enable social scientists and public policymakers to develop just and moral social policies.

I want to emphasize that I am not in anyway implying that the views developed here replace those of the philosophical traditions that exist. I am only arguing that the evolutionary perspective, and the facts on which it is based, will be a useful methodological addition to the armamentarium that philosophers have available. The major differences, as I see them, between the methods used by moral philosophers and those used by psychologists of my ilk is that the former develop a set of basic principles based on assumptions regarding the nature of the universe with which they are concerned. They then proceed to examine a set of consistent and logical arguments and counterarguments regarding the nature of morality and delineate those actions that should be permissible given the initial assumptions. My method is to begin with a similar set of basic assumptions, to frame them as testable hypotheses, and to make observations that bear on, and can support or refute, those assumptions. Using what is basically the scientific method and framing the hypotheses using accepted methods, theories, and data accepted by the biological and social sciences, I intend to demonstrate how such a scientific perspective can provide a useful way to consider the nature of the realities on which views of morality can be based. I believe that this naturalistic realism provides a useful way to begin argumentation regarding the way people are, and that it can help us develop a system of morality regarding how we would like things to be in a humane universe. One of the greatest researchers and theorists in the history of neuropsychology, Karl Lashley (1958/1960, p. 531), expressed similar views in a discussion of cerebral organization and behavior: "I was forced to the conclusion that philosophers have been unreliable observers and that much of the difficulty of the mind–body problem is due to their incompetence as psychologists. The phenomena to be explained, as studied by psychologists, are mostly not what the philosophers have claimed them to be."

My intention is not to reinvent moral philosophy, and I hope I will not raise the hackles of philosophers who might be inclined to consider this to represent an attempt at a "hostile takeover." I hope too, that the philosophical and evolutionary perspectives developed here will prove useful to social scientists and policy makers who are trying to foster their own humane and just world.

GUIDELINES FOR ARGUMENT

At the risk of boring the philosophically sophisticated reader, I will discuss a few basic issues in argumentation that are not often brought to the attention of scientists and policy makers. I want to develop these issues explicitly because they have guided me in my attempts to arrive at a reasonable, informed, and consistent set of principles to be applied to an understanding of issues in human reproduction. The first set of questions concerns how arguments about moral issues might be framed and evaluated. What criteria should be used to establish and evaluate the adequacy of moral beliefs in relation to issues regarding life? An excellent and concise discussion of these concerns has been provided by Tom Regan (1983), a moral philosopher who has written extensively on the topic of animal rights, and who has suggested several standards that should be used to arrive at moral judgments (although I disagree with his analysis of some of the substantive issues concerning animal rights).

Six Standards for Argument

Conceptual Clarity

The first standard is that of conceptual clarity. One lack of clarity is due to the fact that words have a range of different meanings when different people use the same words to apply to different things. When words are used in widely different senses the central distinctions involved in a dispute are often blurred, and no progress can be made, even if the participants in the argument are of good will. For example, many arguments regarding the question of when abortion is permissible have turned on the issue of whether the fetus is a person at a particular time. If this is a central question, then there must be a clear and agreed upon idea of what a "person" is—of the criteria to be used to determine the existence of personhood. Does the fertilized egg possess the essential quality of a person at conception? Does a person come into being only when brain activity can be recorded? Do we bestow personhood at some given arbitrary age, such as 40 days, 80 days, or 6 months after conception? Does personhood commence when the fetus can survive outside the womb, or does it start at birth? If the criterion for personhood is the ability to survive outside the womb, then the existence of a person would depend on the status of available medical technology. Is it reasonable philosophically to base a moral criterion on technological grounds? Is the fetus a nonperson until it is born and can survive without direct attachment to the mother? Does personhood commence with the appearance of sentience, or does it require demonstrable consciousness? Might personhood begin only when the infant appears as a public social entity?

Without agreement on the criteria used to signify personhood, arguments over abortion cannot proceed very profitably, even though everyone might agree on the basic premise that it is not proper to kill an innocent person; that is, a person who is not currently doing harm, nor is a threat to do so in the near future. These issues are discussed at length in Chapters 8 and 9. Much fruitless debate can be avoided by being clear about the basic concepts involved in arguments. At least, with such understanding we can agree to disagree and know what it is we disagree about.

Factual Information

The second standard is factual information. Moral positions should be based on a foundation that is verifiable, or at least one that has consensual agreement. There are facts regarding the efficacy of biomedical research using animals in order to prevent and to treat disease, and a scholarly review of the research literature can quiet a great deal of nonsense and fruitless charge and countercharge. On a number of volatile issues there are observations that most people accept as valid, and these can be brought to bear on points of argumentation. For example, there are arguments that capital punishment is not justified morally because it involves killing a person. On the other hand, some people justify capital punishment on the grounds that the fear of the death penalty deters would-be murderers from killing innocent people. Although this proposition is not easy to evaluate one could attempt to estimate its likelihood by examining homicide records of countries that do and do not have the death penalty, or by examining the change in homicide rates of countries when they change their policy regarding capital punishment. It would be appropriate to know if paroled killers do or do not tend to kill again. Although the interpretation of such statistics is difficult, information can be brought to bear, and arguments can be made based on public interpretation of the available data.

There has been controversy regarding the value of behavioral research using animals. The biomedical research community is convinced that behavioral research using animals is of major value, while some animal rights organizations label such research as being nothing more than "fraud." One can examine data regarding what has been accomplished as a result of biomedical research on animals, and decide whether the theoretical principles derived from animal research have any practical value in such endeavors as the practice of psychotherapy, the alleviation of chronic pain, or the management of ulcers. If, in fact, such psychologically oriented research does have value, as many writers have argued, (Fox, 1986; Miller, 1983) the continuation of such research would be justified. If the psychological research has led to information that has been of little or no value, as argued by many writers, (Regan, 1983; Singer, 1990), then it could be more difficult to justify its continuation. It should be acknowledged, however, that it is difficult ever to establish what aspects of basic research are going to have useful applications in the future. A practical application of basic research data is only one justification for pursuing ideas that bear on the nature of reality. It can be argued that the interest of pursuing knowledge and understanding, in and of themselves, is sufficient justification to engage in basic research.

The point I am developing is that some of the basic premises on which moral judgments are based can be supported or challenged by evidence; some of the premises will have a factual basis and others must remain at the level of beliefs and intuitions that should be debated. It is important to know the basis on which such premises stand. As the moral philosopher Sumner (1981) indicated, science is an established procedure of publicly confirming or disconfirming beliefs about the world. Factual claims, therefore, should be subject to some form of empirical evaluation and, perhaps, disconfirmation. I will, in Chapter 7, discuss some studies that examine the structure of the moral intuitions that people have and will argue that these intuitions are organized into a coherent pattern that could be considered to be universal. If this argument is accepted, then the structure of these intuitions might provide a basis for us to begin framing ideas regarding the moral *ought* in a manner that takes into consideration the reasons why people have developed these underlying belief systems.

Rationality

A third standard is that of rationality. Arguments can be evaluated in terms of internal logic. The logic that links basic, major premises to observations that have been generally accepted, can be evaluated, and the minor premises used to develop arguments leading to conclusions regarding the nature of moral behavior can be analyzed. It is important to decide whether or not accepted observations support the premises, whether the arguments are based on conceptually clear terms, and if the logic used to arrive at a conclusion is tight and compelling. The example of capital punishment, again, can be used to illustrate this point. A major premise could be that it is wrong to kill persons, which leads to the conclusion that society will ensure that no person is killed by any other agent, except in the special circumstance where a person willfully has killed some innocent person. The special circumstance is justified by supporters of capital punishment on the factual ground that capital punishment is a deterrent to murder. In fact, even murder might be considered to be justified if it prevented more murders of innocents. We could agree that the reasoning is logical and consistent and we need not be concerned further with the formal nature of the argument. What should be considered are the reasons to support the major premise, and whether there is adequate factual support for the special circumstances that permit killing.

An important test of the rationality of such arguments is the basis on which a special circumstance is established. For example, if a man is morally opposed to abortion based on the major premise that the killing of persons should not take place, and accepts the minor premise that a fetus meets the test of personhood, but still encourages his wife to have an abortion based on special circumstances relating to the financial needs of his family, then the rationality of the special circumstance as a permissible exception to the major premise should be questioned. There seems to be an internal contradiction between the basic moral principle stated in the major premise and his particularized special circumstance. In this instance one could question the rationality of his argument on logical grounds. Most philosophical schools of thought agree that there must be rational argument to justify moral conclusions and the manner in which such justification is argued will be considered below when discussing John Rawls' principle of reflective equilibrium (1971).

Impartiality

A fourth standard is impartiality, which involves a requirement of universality. This standard is at the heart of any formal principle of justice; to be "just" similar individuals must be treated similarly in the face of similar circumstances. All persons should be accorded the same privileges and opportunities, and these privileges should apply across an extensive range of situations. It is not acceptable arbitrarily to guarantee life and liberty only to some people in some circumstances but not to other people in similar circumstances. Arguments have been made that such justice should be extended to species other than humans as well. The importance of applying a basic moral system concerning life, liberty, and freedom from harm in a consistent manner is evident when one considers issues of animal welfare, abortion, contraception, infanticide, euthanasia, capital punishment, and suicide. The principles applied must be used consistently for all individuals, rich and poor, male and female, privileged and commoner.

Valid moral principles should require all moral agents (those who are accorded full moral standing with its freedoms, duties, and responsibilities) to act in certain ways. Such rules should specify how one *ought* to act, and should have adequate scope. Ideally, such principles should be universal, and at the very least apply to everyone who is a moral agent. These principles should also have precision in the sense of conceptual clarity. For example, the Commandment "Thou shalt not kill" remains a useless moral principle unless we can agree to whom "thou" refers, and how broadly "kill" is to be construed. "Thou" does not refer to everyone under all circumstances. Even those guided by this Commandment engage in warfare in which the enemy is killed. Many who accept the Commandment approve of killing in the form of capital punishment, and they kill animals for food. When self-defense is involved it is considered legitimate to kill. The point is that for such a simple statement to carry any moral weight the meaning of the basic terms must be unpacked with care.

A great deal of disagreement occurs because of confusion regarding the organisms to be included under moral guidelines. It has been argued that "Animals have rights." Without arguing the case here it is clear that no agreement can be reached until we agree concerning the class of beings that "animal" includes, and what is meant by and included under the term "rights." Are the rights and responsibilities of all animals, vertebrate and invertebrate, equal to those of humans, and if not, how and why are they limited? Only after such issues have been resolved is it possible to engage in fruitful discussion regarding the rights of animals.

Coolness

A fifth standard that Regan (1983) suggested is coolness, by which he means that discussions and debates concerning moral positions should take place in emotionally calm circumstances. It is difficult enough to work through the logical bases of moral beliefs when we are in a calm, rational state. Most of our moral beliefs have been developed gradually through the years, and are mapped onto a specific set of cultural traditions within a given societal structure. These beliefs tend to remain unanalyzed and to bear a strong emotional load. Often the intent of individuals on one side or another of a policy argument is to obtain publicity and to draw dramatic attention to their own belief system. One way to do this is to confront those who have different beliefs and to disrupt their pursuance of whatever behaviors these beliefs entail. While such a political circus certainly is a conventional and acceptable part of political advocacy, it should have no part in the development of moral principles sufficient to guide practical behavior and regulate social policy.

Moral issues should be discussed openly and freely, and should not be pursued through raw demagoguery, scare tactics, distortion, or the use of political might. Activists should be constrained to exhibit respect and to practice tolerance, and academics should be constrained to present and discuss issues in a balanced manner. I will attempt to follow such an admonition throughout, probably with varying degrees of success.

Intuitive Acceptability

A sixth standard, intuitive acceptability, is difficult to codify, but is appropriate to consider. Not only should arguments meet the five standards outlined above, they should not violate our basic intuitions concerning morality. This is an arguable position because morality characteristically develops much as one learns language as a child; not through formal instruction, but by participation in the common life of a society. John Rawls (1971) in his monumental book, *A Theory of Justice*, suggested that there is a similarity between the development of grammar in our natural language and the development of moral capacities (a point I will argue further in Chapter 4). He proposed that everyone has an internal sense of the whole form of moral conceptions, and I will argue that these moral intuitions have evolved to enhance the likelihood that an individual organism will contribute genes to succeeding generations. This intuitive sense of morality might well be a reflection of biological imperatives that have developed during human evolutionary history. If this sense does reflect an imperative, then discomfort or acceptance, at the level of intuitions, should at least be analyzed to identify possible underlying biological (or cultural) imperatives that may be manifest, and that lead to the feelings of discomfort or acceptance.

The moral philosopher, Thomas Nagel (1979), in the preface to a collection of essays that is highly accessible to the nonphilosopher, characterized moral theory in terms of a contest between extravagances and repression, imagination and rigor, expansiveness and precision. While trying to avoid one horn of each dilemma it is easy to be impaled by the excesses of the other. He stated his own philosophical sympathies in the following terms (Nagel, 1979, p. *x*), "I believe one should trust problems over solutions, intuition over arguments, and pluralistic discord over systematic harmony. Simplicity and elegance are never reasons to think that a philosophical theory is true: on the contrary, they are usually grounds for thinking it false."

Nagel argued that one should always have great respect for the intuitive sense of an unsolved problem given that philosophical methods are themselves in question. Because it is possible that the methodology used is faulty, one should be prepared to abandon a given method of analysis at any point. He counseled (Nagel, 1979, p. xi–xii) that, "All one can do is to try to maintain a desire for answers, a tolerance for long periods without any, an unwillingness to brush aside unexplained intuitions, and an adherence to reasonable standards of clear expression and cogent argument."

A cautionary note in this regard has been extended by yet another leading moral philosopher, James Rachels (1986), who suggested that one should, at the same time, be suspicious of concessions to intuition. Every such concession should be examined with suspicion, not because it is an intuition, but because intuitions can be trusted too loosely.

One example of where I encountered "intuitive discomfort" regards the conclusion reached by Tooley (1983) who, after a carefully reasoned, rational, and factually based argument concerning abortion, arrives at what I consider the counterintuitive position that infanticide is permissible until an infant is 3 months old. This position is counterintuitive to many who agree with most of the sound basic premises and compelling logic of Tooley's argument. Such discomfort should lead to a reexamination of the system Tooley developed. I make such an examination in Chapter 9, and suggest a modification in terms of an additional premise that makes his conclusions intuitively more acceptable, to me at least.

Rawls and Methodology

Veil of Ignorance

An important methodological point is made by John Rawls who suggested that, as far as possible, one should develop principles under a "veil of ignorance," by which he means that one should develop principles of justice without considering whether one will be the actor or the recipient in any recommended course of action. Rawls (1971) argued that moral principles should be considered as though one did not know one's class or social status, nor how one will fare in the distribution of natural assets and abilities. Principles should be chosen to be those that would be acceptable whatever position one is to assume in the scenario. Clearly, people *do* know their relative positions in the morality game, but it should be possible to "role play" the different positions, and to reflect on whether or not one might feel violated by the application of the different principles proposed.

Reflective Equilibrium

The general method used to generate moral principles should involve what Rawls calls the method of reflective equilibrium. With this method one starts the analysis with a set of general moral principles, applies these principles to resolve moral dilemmas, and makes recommendations regarding the proper actions people should take when making practical decisions. Rawls (1971, p. 51) argued that, "There is a definite if limited class of facts against which conjectured principles can be checked, namely, our considered judgments in reflective equilibrium." In criticism, Hare (1989) noted that Rawls thinks of a theory of justice as analogous to a theory in empirical science. I propose to "objectify" what Hare considers Rawls' essential subjectivism. It is not necessary for the description of moral intuitions to remain at an anecdotal and subjective level. The principles of empirical science can be brought to bear in order to place the study of moral intuitions on a more substantial empirical footing, and, as described in Chapter 7, I have attempted to do so. As Hare noted, it must be possible to "check" the philosophical theory against people's views so that any disagreement between the theory and those views can be identified objectively. The aim is to provide a naturalistic base for intuitionism in order to escape the specter of subjectivism. Hare noted, and I agree, that moral theories should be checked against people's actual moral judgments in terms of what people *think* ought to be done, not against moral principles about what one ought to do. If problems appear, either because the basic principles lead to intuitively intolerable recommendations or result in logically incompatible recommendations in different circumstances, it may be necessary to reconsider the terms of the basic moral system. This reflection can suggest guidelines that can be used to revise the moral principles, and enable one to generate principles which do not violate intuitions.

Rawls' idea of wide reflective equilibrium has been considered by the philosopher Norman Daniels (1979) to be a method that can provide coherence to a set of beliefs held by an individual. Daniels argued that one should begin by collecting the individual's initial moral judgments and sift through them to develop some understanding of that individual's moral intuitions (the procedure that will be followed in the studies discussed in

Chapter 7). When a set of arguments has been constructed from the observed intuitions, then Daniels suggested that one should work back and forth, making adjustment between the judgments, moral principles, and the accepted background principles. Ronald Dworkin (1989) added that this structure of principles must explain moral judgments by showing the underlying assumptions they reflect, and that the structure must provide guidance in those cases about which we have either no, weak, or contradictory convictions. Viewed in this manner moral reasoning in philosophy is considered to be a process of reconstructing the fundamental principles of morality by assembling concrete judgments in a way that reveals the nature of those fundamental principles.

Wide reflective equilibrium, as Daniels has described it, allows for theory-based revision of the principles thought to underlie moral judgments. Plausibility judgments are made and revised in light of theoretical considerations, with no one type of considered moral judgment being immune to revision. Thus, moral judgments are taken as starting points for theory construction, and these are subjected to exhaustive review and testing against a relevant body of theory. This general process will be discussed further in Chapter 7, where the studies of peoples' moral intuitions are described in order to develop some understanding of the basic principles that regulate moral judgments.

The interaction between the application of general moral principles and the relation of these principles to evidence (moral judgments) involves the same procedures as those used in science. Scientists begin with theoretical principles that have been developed to account for a universe of events that are part of what I have called the universe of generalization. The principles involved in developing scientific theories must meet the same standards I outlined above as guidelines for arguments concerning moral issues. When discrepancies appear between expectations based on theory and the evidence based on observations, the theory is examined and revised until it seems to explain the observed outcomes more adequately. This revised theory is then applied to a new set of observations to determine whether or not the theory performs better (in terms of explaining known phenomena), and leads to a better understanding of novel aspects of the world to which it has not yet been applied (has predictive efficiency).

What Rawls refers to as wide reflective equilibrium can be used in the same way as the general scientific method. There is a wide range of possible principles that must be considered to arrive at a rationale on which to base moral decisions. The reflective evaluation of the various policies that are recommended using one (or some) of the principles, with differing patterns of emphasis, should lead to an increasingly adequate set of consistent principles to guide behavioral choices. The data base that the philosopher has available is a more difficult and amorphous one than that available to the scientist, but the basic principles, procedures, and argumentation are the same. At least, that is the assumption on which I proceed in the analyses to follow.

Rachels (1986) suggested a similar view of philosophical argumentation. He divided such arguments into three categories. The strongest is when there is a contradiction within the theory that cannot be tolerated; if a contradiction appears the theory must be modified or rejected. The second category is when the theory leads to a conclusion or consequence that is not inconsistent, but is contradicted by independent evidence; such contradiction weakens the theory to the extent that it should be revised. The third is when a consequence of the theory is counterintuitive; in this case the theory should be examined carefully, and defended in the light of the counterintuitive consequence, or revised to avoid that consequence. When the basic arguments have undergone this reflective evaluation and adjustments have been made, then a new stage of equilibrium between basic principles, derived consequences, and moral intuitions will have been established, and these adjusted arguments should once again be tested by another round of derivations, applications, and evaluation of consequences.

When a rational set of general principles has been developed, and it is suggested that these principles can serve to ground a universal moral system, then Tooley (1983) suggested that one should search for counterexamples consisting of some conceivable situation in which the principle would lead to an intuitive judgment that the recommended course of action is morally wrong. When such a situation occurs this might indicate that some aspect of the suggested moral system should be revised, or that the particular counterexample is not a true exemplar that should be included in the universe of events to which the principle can be generalized. This method of counterexamples provides an important tool to examine the consistency and power of a moral system and helps us to understand the consequences of adopting the system as outlined.

Strategy of the Present Scheme of Argument

In broad strokes, I will sketch some basic considerations which will be brought into play in what follows.

1. Issues pertaining to life should be considered using a universal and consistent set of moral principles. (To develop these principles I will begin with the issues of abortion, contraception, and infanticide. After developing the argument within this arena I will then apply them in turn to another set of issues concerning reproduction.)

2. These moral principles should be comprehensive and conceived broadly enough to apply to all life forms. It should be emphasized that the range of practical moral problems considered cannot be derived from any single basic source. I will, therefore, appeal to principles based on several scientific, philosophical, and methodological perspectives and disciplines. I will be concerned here with issues relating to human life, particularly those involving reproduction.

3. Guidelines should be developed clearly enough to resolve conflicts between beings who are qualitatively different, and between different individuals with similar qualities. (At the level of premises, *ceteris paribus* clauses will be developed which set constraints under which the general principles must operate, and these constraints ["other things" which must be equal] should be identified and considered carefully as the specific arguments proceed.)

Several steps will be taken to realize these goals.

1. A cost–benefit analysis of the relative value of the outcomes of the various behavioral decisions will be made when any conflict between circumstances or organisms exists. (This proposition provides a wedge for evolutionary principles to enter because all evolutionary systems can be conceived to operate at the level of the type of cost–benefit trade-offs involved in consequentialism.)

2. Whenever possible, positions will be identified that are acceptable to all (or almost all) rational observers, as well as positions which all find unacceptable. Such bases of total agreement will make it easier to approach the gray areas where observers beginning with different moral premises disagree, as well as those that are problematic for any rational observer.

3. Whenever a gray area is found between the two poles of acceptability-unacceptability it can be explored, using a sorites-style argument, until the range of questionable or disputable exemplars is defined. The sorites argument is useful to clarify conceptual and definitional issues. The style of argument proceeds from a clearly agreed upon starting point, the classic one being, when does one have a heap of sand. If one has one grain of sand and adds one to it, that does not constitute a "heap," and adding one more grain to those two will not result in a recognizable heap either. Can one conclude, then, that the addition of one grain of sand can never result in a heap? Not really, because if one adds one grain, again and again, there will sooner or later be a point where everyone agrees that there is a heap of sand. This sorites argument can be used to discuss basic processes, to identify clear points of agree-

ment regarding presence or absence of a quality, and to identify the
gray area where it is not possible to arrive at complete agreement
whether or not a "heap" exists.

4. Evidence can be brought to bear that will enable one to narrow the
range of the gray area, and subsidiary arguments can be developed
to aid policymakers to arrive at decision rules that can be used
when there is a lack of clear agreement.

5. Any "trumps" should be carefully identified and justified. (A
trump is any factor that takes precedence over all others when it is
present.)

Some Additional Considerations

Assertion vs. Argumentation

There will be several undercurrents throughout much of the argument to be developed, and it will be useful to signal them at the outset.
First of all, *assertion is not a substitute for argumentation*. I will point out,
especially in the section where the arguments regarding abortion are considered, that slogans are asserted regularly with almost nothing in the way
of argumentation. Here, I refer to such things as assertions that "abortion
is murder," and references to the "sanctity of life." It is difficult for such
slogans to bear the weight they must to sustain the philosophical arguments that rest on these assertions. The basic arguments fail because the
premises asserted cannot withstand careful analysis when applied to specific instances. If such moral assertions are to prevail they must be
grounded by basic arguments sufficient to establish them as moral principles.

Slippery Slope Arguments

In discussions regarding the wisdom of implementing new policies
regarding matters of life and death, the slippery slope argument appears
quite frequently. Any such arguments should be examined closely because
many proposed changes in social policy have been greeted with an expression of fear that, once some first step is taken, it will start one down
a slippery slope that leads to the inevitable depths of an unacceptable end.
I will discuss this problem at greater length in Chapter 2, and will identify
the occurrence of this argument, and challenge its validity, in specific
contexts in which it occurs.

In his book, *Slippery Slope Arguments*, Douglas Walton (1992) discussed the use and abuse of such arguments and pointed out that, while

they can be abused, they do not necessarily involve a fallacy. Indeed the use of the causal or the sorites style of argumentation can sharpen distinctions through sound Socratic or adversarial dialogue, thereby narrowing the range of disagreement. Here I will only point out that, unless there is a specification of the causal mechanisms that produce the inevitable slide, the slippery slope demon often represents little more than an unfortunate metaphor used to justify and maintain the status quo.

Evolutionary Perspective

The value of an evolutionary perspective will be considered and argued throughout. This presentation is, essentially, the extension of evolutionary principles to issues in human morality that usually are considered from a cultural perspective or are argued on the basis of philosophical premises, rather than on the foundation of evolutionary biology. Because all of the issues to be considered refer to life, it is appropriate, indeed necessary, to bring to bear this most powerful and general set of biological principles. The modern synthetic theory of evolution has been applied successfully to an understanding of the nature and functioning of a comprehensive range of organic systems. I will argue in Chapters 3, 4, and 5 that it is possible to gain insight and understanding of the nature of human behavior and morality through the application of the conceptual framework of evolutionary biology. As argued in Chapter 2, the consideration of naturalistically based principles is a useful early step in the development of views regarding what moral behavior should be—the *ought*. The nature of the *ought* should be examined in the context of what *is*, if the interest is to understand the structure of the *ought* of moral codes. Basing moral principles on what *is*, and understanding the *ought* in terms of what *can* be does not constitute a naturalistic fallacy.

Anthropocentrism.

I will employ throughout this book an anthropocentric viewpoint. It will be argued that moral systems reflect the social and legal codification of basic human needs, interests, values, and desires. Such codification is an inherently anthropocentric enterprise. To develop, understand, and apply a normative system of morality it is necessary for individuals to be able to comprehend the complex contingencies that such systems entail. Those who do not possess the cognitive capacities to understand rules obviously cannot be expected to regulate their behavior in accordance to rule-bound dictates. This uniquely human perspective will be used to define full moral standing, called moral agency, and it will be argued that the power of an avowed anthropocentrism can be used to advantage to gain understanding of the nature and extent of moral obligations and responsibilities.

The value of anthropocentrism was defended by the moral philosopher John Kleinig (1991) who argued, in his book *Valuing Life*, that one should recognize and appreciate the richness of human experience as a major contributor to the value of diverse forms of life. The diversity of organic life and the complexity humans associate with this diversity enriches the world, but this richness is accessible only to human moral agents. He contended that the very conceptualization of experience in terms of its richness reflects the perspective of the valuer, and this anthropocentric perspective cannot, and should not, be avoided.

Empirical Naturalism

The extensive development and use of theory based scientific evidence drawn from the different disciplines seeking to understand the nature of biological and psychological reality, is one of the major differences between this presentation and the usual philosophical treatise. I hope that the bodies of scientific literature I will bring to bear will be of interest to philosophers and can be used by them to develop philosophical arguments more effectively, and with greater argumentative precision, than I am trained to do. I believe the arguments I have developed are justified in light of the evidence available, but have no doubt that the seasoned philosopher will be able to produce more philosophically nuanced and compelling arguments. What I offer here is a body of evidence regarding the nature of biological and psychological realities that philosophers should take into consideration. I also have taken steps to develop a sketch of a philosophical position compatible with that evidence. I believe that social scientists, humanists, and those who construct and implement social policies should be aware of the relevant data that have been provided by the evolutionary and cognitive sciences. These data provide a deep understanding of the human condition and of the forces that drive human actions and thoughts.

Above I argued that, to ground moral positions, factual information regarding the human condition should be brought to bear as much as possible. Much biological, medical, and demographic information has been gathered, and this information can be used to consider issues in morality. Also relevant are empirical data regarding the structure of people's moral intuitions, the nature of cognitive functioning, and basic evolutionary constraints. These latter three sources of information are not often brought to bear when considering morality, but all three will be used to develop the arguments to follow.

Fantasy Dilemmas

Philosophers often resolve arguments by examining hypothetical situations and reaching conclusions regarding the nature of morally permissible behavior, given the hypothetical circumstances. The use of this method is based on the assumption that the philosophers' moral intuitions are ones that reasonable people share. The bioethicist Arthur Caplan (1992a, p. xiv) characterized the popular operating procedure of moral theorists as follows: "[They] climb into an armchair and imagine as hard as one can what human beings would choose to do with respect to the division of resources or the recognition of rights if they were put in a position of disinterested, disembodied, and disengaged existence." The criteria moral theorists use to establish this pattern of moral intuitions are subjective clarity and intuitive acceptability. Philosophers state and then argue for an explicit set of premises, and from these premises, follow a chain of logic to justify general conclusions, with care being taken to speak to possible alternative arguments.

Another mode of approach widely used by philosophers is to create fantasy dilemmas that pit different possible moral positions against one another to consider what would be the better thing to do to resolve the dilemmas (see Fischer & Ravizza, [1992], for a discussion of these methods and a collection of some of the important papers using this approach). The relative importance of different moral positions can be estimated in terms of which ones are applied consistently, and which are seldom used in the resolution of the dilemmas.

I will describe, in Chapter 7, a series of empirical studies involving two moral dilemmas—the trolley and the lifeboat problem that were used to probe the structure of peoples' moral intuitions (Petrinovich, O'Neill, & Jorgensen, 1992, 1993; Petrinovich & O'Neill, 1995; unpublished manuscript). Dilemmas were constructed so that several dimensions that philosophers and biologists have argued to be of major importance were included, and this was done in such a way that the relative importance of these dimensions in the resolution of the dilemmas could be determined empirically.

The moral philosopher F. M. Kamm (1992), in her book *Creation and Abortion*, made good use of what she refers to as "farfetched hypothetical cases." She developed these cases in order to reason without the burden of the preconceived commitments and emotional responses that real life situations entail. I believe that the results of studies of fantasy dilemmas provide a factual basis to determine what people believe, and that this determination of the nature and structure of moral intuitions provides a tool to understand the moral *oughts* that people have developed and accepted. The procedures used in these studies will be described in Chapter 7, and the results will be brought to bear whenever they are appropriate to the issues discussed throughout this book.

PLAN OF ATTACK

Part I of this book is composed of seven chapters that contain the background, principles, and evidence on which the later substantive arguments are based. Chapter 2 contains a discussion of the use of naturalism and a refutation of the argument that the use of naturalism in moral theory necessarily constitutes a "fallacy." That chapter also contains a discussion of the slippery slope fallacy, a discussion of when and when it is not a fallacy, and some observations regarding the problem of reductionism. Chapter 3 is a nontechnical sketch of some of the basic concepts of evolutionary theory which can be applied to understand reproduction. In Chapter 4 these principles, as well as some based on studies in ethology and cognitive science, are brought to bear on issues relating to human nature. It should be emphasized that the evolutionary argument developed is not the only possible one that could be offered. Chapter 5 extends the evolutionary argument to aspects of human social behavior that are often considered to be produced by cultural factors, and to be relatively free of biological influences. The view presented is *an* evolutionary argument regarding human behavior that, although there could be differences in particulars, is soundly based on generally accepted evolutionary theory.

Chapter 6 contains a discussion of the basic philosophical arguments that will be encountered in this book. Although the discussion might seem elementary to philosophers, it should be useful to those from other disciplines when they consider issues regarding morality. Chapter 7 begins with a discussion of some sociobiological views of morality, followed by a summary of the basic moral principles examined in this book. This discussion provides a framework for the empirical study of moral intuitions described in the remainder of the chapter.

Part II deals with issues involved in reproduction. In Chapter 8 there is a discussion of some basic arguments that must be faced when considering the morality of contraception, abortion, and infanticide. Abortion has been the subject of extensive discussion, it is an issue that concerns and divides members of human societies, and a variety of views have been presented with force and clarity. The arguments concerning abortion will be developed at a level of generality adequate to deal with contraception and infanticide as well—all issues relating to the beginning of life. In Chapter 9, I argue for the central importance of the concepts of personhood and moral agency as the bases to establish moral standing, obligation, and responsibility. The basic restrictive and permissive positions argued regarding abortion will be presented and discussed in Chapter 10. In Chapter 11, a set of policy recommendations will be developed regarding contraception, abortion, and infanticide. These policy recommendations follow from the analyses of each of the problems considered. The moral issues involved in the use of newly developed reproductive technologies, such as artificial insemination, in vitro fertilization, and fetal tissue research will be considered in Chapter 12. Chapter 13 is a restatement of the essential steps of the argument and a summary of the policy recommendations.

2

The Naturalistic and Slippery Slope Fallacies

In this chapter I discuss three problems that arise when one attempts to understand the nature of morality. The first concerns what is known as the naturalistic fallacy and it must be addressed if the principles of morality are to be related to biological principles. The second concern is one that basically involves the issue of causation, known as the slippery slope fallacy, and it is frequently raised when innovative interventions in current policies are proposed. The third is the fear that the use of biological explanations leads to an undesirable reductionism, a concern that results from a failure to recognize the contrast between event and theory reduction.

I will consider, and reject, an objection that has been made to the idea of grounding moral decisions on a construction of the nature of reality. Critics phrase this objection in terms of the "Naturalistic Fallacy." I argue that it is valuable to understand the nature of underlying reality if we want to understand human behaviors, intentions, and ethics in the light of biological and behavioral principles. It is essential that the theories and data bearing on the realities of life be developed in detail, and I will develop some ideas that will be applied later when speaking of issues in morality. The biological considerations that will be presented in the next three chapters are those at the level of the evolutionary propensities and biases that influence the propagation of life. To understand these biological considerations it is necessary to understand the principles of evolution and the behavioral strategies that have developed to enhance the survival and selection of organisms in order that they can transmit their genes to succeeding generations.

THE NATURALISTIC FALLACY

I believe that understanding the nature of what *is* provides a reasonable first-step to the question of what *ought* to be. There is no necessary fallacy involved in considering the nature of reality, the *is*. One commits a fallacy only if it is argued that the *ought* is determined by the *is*. It is appropriate to consider the *is–ought* relationship whenever it is suspected that there are biasing tendencies (either biological or cultural) that could influence behavior patterns. If such biasing tendencies exist they should not be denied or ignored, but should be taken into consideration, especially in attempts to develop a system of morality. Thus, there are two fallacies to be wary of: One is the much discussed naturalistic fallacy and the other could be called a cultural fallacy that uncritically evokes universal cultural factors that determine the *ought*.

Caution has been expressed by some philosophers, social scientists, and humanists that one should not commit the naturalistic fallacy, which is moving from a consideration of what *is* the state of nature to a decision regarding what *ought* to be the state of nature. G. E. Moore (1903) accused evolutionists of committing the naturalistic fallacy, and as the historian and philosopher Robert Richards (1987) documented, this accusation has been endorsed by many subsequent philosophers. The claim has been made that no moral statement can be deduced from empirical statements alone. The fallacy is invoked when factual observations are accepted and then used to establish a conclusion regarding moral value. The psychologist Allen Waterman (1988) pointed out that such a value claim requires the use of reasoning that goes beyond a statement of the facts, thereby making it impossible for empirical science to settle questions of moral values. He argued that if one relies on a philosophical analysis of morality, and if this reliance is combined with (grounded by) empirically justified statements, then the naturalistic fallacy is circumvented.

The only assumption that a biologically oriented view need involve is that people have evolved tendencies that enhance the community good; no particular social arrangement or set of values has to be specified as being better than others. This assumption leaves the question open regarding how that enhancement might be realized given the specific conditions of life that prevail. As Richards (1987) affirmed, it is appropriate to raise questions concerning the internal logic of moral principles, to consider the terms of discourse used within the context of a given moral system, and to examine three kinds of empirical assumptions: The nature of the formal framework assumptions about human nature; the objects, events, and conditions that are peculiar to different human societies (which may vary across societies); and the empirical methods used to justify the moral system. When the above procedures are brought into play, arguments can be arrived at (quite properly) that derive normative moral conclusions based on factual propositions.

In Richards' (1993) view, the justification of basic moral principles and inference rules should rest on an empirical appeal to the beliefs and practices of people. He drew an important distinction between the empirical and moral justification of behavior. The empirical justification is a factual description of the actions, beliefs, and intentions that people have. One can move beyond this descriptive enterprise and seek a normative moral justification by trying to understand the rules which seem to ground and drive the factual aspects. He emphasized that moral principles can be justified only by facts—a view that insists that it is necessary to understand the *is* if one is to understand *oughts*.

A similar distinction was made by the philosopher Alan Gewirth (1993) between descriptive and normative ethics, and he invoked intentionality as an important aspect of morality. It can be denied that the naturalistic fallacy necessarily exists when propositions are justified using a rational strategy that appeals to actions based on common beliefs and practices in order to understand moral positions. When this distinction is maintained, the idea that the naturalistic fallacy is a fallacy can be rejected. An example of the proper style of argument can be found in R. D. Alexander's *Biology of Moral Systems* (1987) in which he described, at the empirical level, behaviors that characterized humans in the past and which are still appropriate at present. He then moved to the normative level and suggested that these behaviors all involve a morality based on enlightened self-interest. This style of argumentation honors the distinction between descriptive and normative concerns that must be observed.

The nature of what *is* should be understood as a factor to enable us to frame the *ought* in better terms. Much of the discussion regarding what people actually believe often rests at the level of anecdotal evidence whereby logical conclusions are based on what "people" are reputed to do and say. In the philosophical literature, one frequently encounters statements of the type, "people agree that . . .," or, "given the choice between action X and Y, pertaining to individuals of the class A and B, people will. . . ." In such instances the basis for the represented consensus is usually left unspecified, and inferences are accepted solely on the basis of their intuitive appeal. I will, in Chapter 7, present the results of studies of the structure of people's moral intuitions in order to establish some factual bases regarding the structure of moral beliefs.

I do not assume that any particular social arrangement is best, nor that naturalism will reveal anything resembling the "noble savage" that characterized some earlier philosophical construals. Nor is it assumed that the bestial nature of humans must be overcome because there are innate tendencies that impel people to become territorial, to engage in warfare, or to exploit all other beings. Rather, it is assumed that people will seek (and have sought throughout evolutionary time) social arrangements that tend to enhance inclusive fitness (defined in Chapter 3), either directly or through reciprocation. Social arrangements can be justified on the basis of enhancing the good of the community, however that good should be defined. Because the definition of what is "good" and "bad" will differ in the light of ecological and cultural constraints, the objects, events, and conditions that are conceived to be good might differ for different societies, whether these are past or contemporary societies. Yet, community welfare can be argued to be the basis of the highest moral good, with the particular cultural apparatus differing for different societies. These differences occur because the ultimate cause of reproduction can be furthered by any of a number of proximate behavioral mechanisms. The exact nature of the cultural traditions that develop can be influenced by the nature of the ecology, the characteristics of the founder population, and the nature of accidental occurrences, all of which can have profound influences on the development of society. It should be recognized, however, that actions enhancing the welfare of a community of people may be perverted to evil ends when these actions lead to intergroup competition, as has happened all too frequently based on nationalistic, racial, religious, or other ideological grounds.

Richards (1987, 1993) argued, and I agree, that evolution has provided human beings with a number of sociobiological tendencies; among them are those leading one to care about one's own welfare, to protect offspring, to provide for the general welfare of members of the community, and to defend the helpless members of the community against violence and aggression. All of these tendencies and dispositions serve to define what most people consider to be a moral creature. Richards (1993) defined the moral good in terms that include actions based on an altruistic motive operating at the level of kin and community selection. He believed that these actions are performed intentionally in the service of those interests, and are justified by the actor through an appeal to an altruistic motive. The proximate mechanisms that have evolved to further this moral sense require an intelligence sufficient to weigh the outcomes of decisions and to support the development of cultural traditions that provide an enduring basis for morality. Richards wrote (1987, pp. 623–624), "evolution has, as a matter of fact, constructed human beings to act for this community good; but to act for the community good is what we mean by being moral. Since, therefore, human beings are moral beings—an unavoidable condition produced by evolution—each ought to act for the community good."

It was argued by the philosopher Rachels (1990) that to accept a position that extols community values does not entail any idea that humans are special per se. It is important to treat all individual organisms, not by considering group (or species) membership, but by considering the particular characteristics that individuals possess, whether they are humans or nonhumans. This individual moralism is consistent with the thinking of evolutionary biologists who emphasize principles based on reproductive success at the level of individual organisms. Treating organisms differently is not necessarily objectionable, as long as there is a relevant difference between them that justifies a difference in treatment.

In a review in *The New York Review of Books* Robert Nozick (1983), professor of philosophy at Harvard, suggested that members of any species legitimately give their fellows more weight than a neutral view would grant them, and he added that if lions had the capacities of moral agents we should not criticize them for putting the interests of other lions above those of the human community. Similarly, we should not criticize an alien species with "superior" attributes who use mere humans for their own ends in order to facilitate the welfare of their community, if these attributes, whatever they may be, do entitle them to a higher level of moral standing than we are able to enjoy.

One should have empirical evidence regarding what *is* (a description of moral intuitions, for example) and this descriptive base should be used, as Rodd (1990) has suggested, to argue about the way in which these facts should be interpreted. Alexander (1979) observed, quite sensibly, that whatever biologically based constraints there might be on the modifiability of human behavior, such constraints could be effectively bypassed or superseded by humans if they were aware of them, and were able to understand undesirable implications of existing constraints. He continued (Alexander, 1979, p. 95), "If there is one thing that natural selection has given to every species it is the ability to adjust in different fashions to different developmental environments. This is what phenotypes are all about, and all organisms have phenotypes."

The Humean point that morality emerges from our "brute nature" was argued by one of the leading philosophers of biology, Ruse (1993), who insisted that cooperation is a good biological strategy for individual organisms to follow in order to enhance their reproductive success (the payoff in ultimate evolutionary terms). He emphasized the importance of intelligent calculation in order to enable one to think about the possible returns that might be realized by alternative possible actions, and stressed the importance of social contracts that regulate the exchanges between the members of nonhuman and human communities—points that I will emphasize throughout this book.

Alexander (1993) also argued that it is important to consider those acts done after a calculation of perceived temporary net cost (risks) to the actor in order to provide benefits to others. Alexander's arguments imply a strong element of intentionality similar to that used by Richards and Gewirth. In Alexander's view social cooperation evolved as a method to regulate intraspecific and intragroup competition. This contractarian view of morality emphasizes the importance of considering the contrasting effects of intragroup amity and intergroup enmity. It is notable that humanity has developed a common set of moral rules to govern the behavior of our own group, but that these rules are not necessarily extended to other groups. He pointed out that one barrier to the development of a universal morality is that decisions involving right and wrong sometimes are group decisions made by majority or consensual opinion, but sometimes they are made by powerful leaders who may represent a minority, and it is here where the biases that are intended to enhance the reproductive success of a community are often used to exploit other people who are "different."

Although there are different expressions of permissible behavior considered to be ethical by different cultures, the ethics of all peoples involve a set of similar concerns. The ability to recognize the realms of ethical consideration can be considered to be a common property of all humans, even though the specifics of right and wrong differ for different cultures. All human societies have a system of morality that imposes a degree of social control over the actions of the individual members of the community.

The emphasis should be on the fact that there are biological biases that have arisen during the course of evolutionary history, but that these biases, once recognized, can be modified by channeling the actions of the members of society to satisfy biological tendencies in a culturally acceptable manner. Williams (1993) needlessly worries that, if one accepts any theories of prescriptive evolved ethics, then one must accept constraints on behavior that deny free will because they constitute external and internal coercions on behavioral decisions. This worry is occasioned by her belief that morality must rest on free will. In her view, to be an ethical being one must be free to be praised or blamed and to be held responsible for actions, and evolved predispositions would provide internal coercion, which denies people the ability to choose ethical first principles, leading to a restricted ethical life.

A few comments are in order regarding considering moral issues in the terms suggested by Williams. If we are going to reject evolved predispositions because they restrict ethical lives, then what are we going to do with the various cultural influences that clearly restrict our ethical lives? I refer to influences, mentioned by Gewirth (1993), regarding aspects of our family background, religious beliefs, national identity, economic status, and sexual orientation. It would seem that, if we cannot be free ethically because of constraints due to evolved influences, we cannot be free in the face of cultural constraints either. I suggest, as does Gewirth, that influence is not the same as causal determination. What we have evolved is not a tendency to choose ethical behavior but a tendency to *choose*, and it might be at this level that an evolved moral *ought* appears.

Williams' statements embody an unhelpful contrast between nature and nurture. In Chapter 3 I will introduce the ideas of experience-expectant, experience-dependent, and activity-dependent structures and discuss how they provide a conceptual model for behavioral development that permits the analysis of inherited predispositions without an attendant loss of plasticity or a harmful distinction between learned and inherited influences on behavior. The type of thinking represented by Williams implies the exclusion of a middle position that emphasizes the continual dynamic interaction of experience and structure from the moment of conception, that continues throughout development.

I believe that Williams exemplifies views that are produced by the biophobia I will discuss in Chapter 4, and which Alexander (1993) attributed to a lack of formal education concerning biological science that persists among the members of the human-oriented disciplines. This indifference and hostility to evolutionary principles on the part of social scientists and humanists is likely to persist, in Alexander's view, as long as it is possible to obtain the highest possible academic degree in any of these disciplines without taking so much as a single course in the biological sciences. In the field of medicine one can be degreed, residenced, and highly specialized with no training or knowledge regarding evolutionary biology. Insisting that organisms have evolved to possess certain predispositions in no way diminishes the plasticity of behavior development nor takes away the capacity to develop a humane normative system of morality. Such fears on the part of humanists and social scientists are baseless ones.

Empathy and Ought

A good overview and summary of the philosophical positions discussed above are provided in an article by Gillett (1993). He presented an interesting argument concerning the *ought* and what he calls "well-being." I will discuss this article at length because I believe it introduces a sound perspective regarding the relationship between the *is* and the *ought*, and can be extended to include the biological dimension supporting the argument that a naturalistic based *ought* does not necessarily produce a fallacy.

Gillett addressed the problem of why a person acts morally, asking three questions: Is there an internal relationship between morality and well-being, are moral claims objective in any sense, and what are the respective places for moral theory and moral actions in the realm of moral reasoning. He first argued that there is a nonindividualistic conception of human good—one that involves a concept of empathic understanding of the desires and interests of others. This empathic understanding provides an incentive to obey the moral *ought*. It is possible to derive statements about human needs from purely factual information about what humans *are*, and the conceptions should encompass not merely biological nature, but the nature of rational social beings as well. Mental ascriptions with morally relevant content rest on rules that arise in the course of inter-personal conduct and relations.

These relevant rules are based on an enlightened self-interest that links morality to one's own future interests and arises from the human need to form "peaceable" societies. These shared rules are conveyed in communicative interactions and their employment depends on an appreciation of how and why certain things matter to others. Thus, the meaning of moral concepts is built on a foundation of empathy which is based on our shared human nature as biological organisms. The shared rational rules which govern our use of concepts "emerge" as ingredients of the moral sense.

On the basis of this shared appreciation of reality and feeling, people are able to appreciate how they ought to treat others, and this appreciation is based on the acquisition of a shared set of rules that govern relations and interactions involving empathy and reciprocity. Gillett concluded that one functions as a participant in a community of beings who share concerns regarding things that matter to them, leading to a reciprocity with others that is intrinsic to the mental economy of a rational social being.

I will paraphrase Gillett's summary of his argument to this point: An individual is moved by concerns that are central to its being; central concerns are articulated in conceptual terms that provide reasons for action; these terms have shared meaning; the grasp of their content depends on an empathic recognition of what matters to others; and this empathic recognition provides the force required to understand what matters to the others. This all results in an internal relationship between conceptualizing one's own interests and those of others, leading to a moral incentive based on one's nature as a conceptualizing and rational social being. I will argue below that one can take this argument one step further and base this "incentive" on the biological realities involved in reproduction; it is the biological episode involved in reproduction that drives evolutionary mechanisms.

Gillett noted that people can have a grasp of moral predicates, yet still fail to feel the moral force they ought to feel and this failing makes them able to act in vicious ways. One must master moral concepts in order to appreciate implicit moral incentives and to be able to understand conflicting self-directed motives. One must be able not only to conform to rules, but also to choose whether or not to follow them. It is possible that, in some circumstances and for some people, the inherent force of the moral *ought* does not prevail, and these people act in a manner that disregards the influences of empathy and reciprocity. How is the likelihood of such a perversion of the moral *ought* enhanced? The simplest way is to pervert the *is-related ought* by distorting the perceived reality on which the rules are based. Thus, the idea of humanity is redefined so that it does not include an outgroup (e.g., blacks, Jews, women, peasants) and this definition is used to justify decisions to disregard moral obligations to those of the outgroup on the grounds that they are not equal humans of our kin, kind, or community. This is permissible, argue the perverters, because "they" do not feel as we do, they do not have our fine sensibilities, and it is improper to have empathic feelings regarding such essentially different beings. In this view, the fault lies not in the fact that the *ought* is redefined, but in the fact that we have redefined the reality on which we base the *is*. Within this perspective the conceptual or ideological rules that characterize a rational social being have not been violated. However, the grounds have been laid for self-deception and immoral behavior to occur.

Restatement of the Biological *Ought*

I believe this general argument can be used to incorporate the biological reality, as well as the conceptual one. The biological reality to which I refer is based on the assumption that the primary purpose of organisms (not in any conscious or intentional sense—a point that will be developed below) is to reproduce in order to contribute genes to succeeding generations. Gillett emphasized the importance of achieving some general understanding of human function in order to arrive at an objective understanding of moral claims. He noted that it is possible to determine what makes for excellence in a hawk or in a surgeon because we know what function they serve. He goes on to argue that if we had a conception of excellence of activity in accordance with reason, we would have some positive conception of good for a human being. I will argue that, in terms of moral *oughts*, we do have such a biological conception—excellence relates to those actions that increase the likelihood of reproductive success. When this likelihood is considered at the level of human interactions (as Gillett has argued regarding conceptual structures) it is expressed at the level of the formation of mating pairs, the establishment of family and kin systems, and the development of communities of cooperating and reciprocating individuals.

The act of human reproduction is, in this view, an act in conformity with a virtue that is pleasant to engage in (a view of function Gillett attributes to Aristotle), and such a basis is the necessary foundation for a nonindividualistic conception of human good, providing the incentive for the individual to develop and obey the moral *ought* that will serve us well the majority of the time. I agree that such biological "virtue" has, as Gillett phrased it, an integral role in one's mental life, and that it is intrinsic to "human flourishing." We are able to satisfy Gillett's claims that we have an *is* that is inherent in humanity (the intuitive awareness and appreciation of the moral properties of situations), and have dispositions to act and react in accordance with this intrinsic sense of human well-being. Gillett argues that the structure of moral reasoning rests on the human propensity to cognize one's own needs and interests, to appreciate that others experience the same needs, and, in certain situations, to recognize that other human beings experience similar needs and feelings. The body of evolutionary theory to be developed in the next three chapters is based on the development of just such a system of sharing and reciprocation among biologically and community-related individuals.

The Value of Naturalism

If it is accepted that a naturalistic description of behavior is a good place to begin when considering principles of morality, then it will be profitable to consider the value of naturalistic observations. Many moral philosophers and social scientists have expressed pessimism and suspicion regarding the value of attempts to base moral principles on the nature of observed reality. However, careful naturalistic description has provided the most useful base on which to form ideas about complex entities in other contexts. I am referring to the use of naturalistic description in those sciences—such as ethology and the psychology of perception, learning, and memory—that deal with aspects of biology and behavior.

Many writers from a variety of disciplines have argued the value of naturalistic description. The literary scholar, Don Gifford (1990), in a book dealing with influences that have shaped human civilization, developed the position that all attempts at literary, poetic, and scientific understanding should begin with a consideration of the natural history of the phenomena under consideration. Such a natural history should focus on the objects and images immediately available to the senses. His analyses begin with a discussion of the writings of Gilbert White (1789) who published an epistolary journal, *The Natural History of Selbourne*. White's writings are valuable because of his ability to observe and record what he saw and experienced, all with a simplicity and exceptional clarity that was not lost on such later observers as Coleridge, Darwin, Thoreau, or, more recently, Stephen Jay Gould. White, an untutored amateur naturalist, used no particular conceptual biases to distinguish between trivial and significant observations, and was faced each day with the problem of deciding which bits of data were worth recording. Gifford (1990, p. 11) wrote, "[White] encouraged his eye and ear in the discipline of turning his back on the wisdom of the closet naturalists and starting from scratch. . . ."

Darwin cited White's observations several times in *The Origin of Species* (1859) and, in his *Autobiography* (1887/1958, p. 45), acknowledged his debt to White: "From reading White's *Selbourne* I took much pleasure in watching the habits of birds, and even made notes on the subject." As I have discussed elsewhere (Petrinovich, 1973b) part of Darwin's immense contribution can be attributed to the fact that he was a careful and thoughtful observer who took pains to gather all available evidence on whatever question was under consideration before evaluating the adequacy of a conclusion. This careful attention to observation characterized all of Darwin's writings, and the continual moving back and forth from observation to deduction was a major strength of the Darwinian theory of evolution.

The most direct line of Darwinian influence on the study of behavior was his influence on the procedures used by those zoologists who studied the complex behavior of animals in their natural environment. I will outline some of these naturalistically based contributions in Chapter 3, under the heading "Ethological Mechanisms," where I will discuss the importance of imprinting as a general mechanism influencing the biological and social development of many species. I will discuss the development of human speech and language in Chapter 4, the understanding of which owes much to the solid base provided by descriptive linguists. The principles that have been derived from observations of speech and language development provide a useful analogue to the processes involved in moral development, as will be argued in Chapter 5. For all of these instances the initial insights, as well as the predictive power of current theoretical positions, were made possible by the depth and detail of the naturalistic foundation that was constructed through many years of patient observation.

The Study of Perception

It has been argued that much of what we understand about perceptual processes is based on the careful description of people's experience: This study of human experience has been "ologized" as phenomenology. Through the centuries, philosophers, literary people, and scientists of all kinds have observed and described events, have pondered about the ways these events are organized, and how they come to comprise our versions of reality. Gifford (1990, p. 15) eloquently expresses it:

> But the history of perception offers a third possibility that mediates between change in the physical world and change in the realm of ideas. I assume that perception takes its shape from the givens of the physical world while creatively shaping the physical world in turn. I also assume that the capacity of perception to shape and reshape is both influenced by and gives rise to those more formal historical presences we call ideas. In an elaborate choreography of turn and counterturn, perception functions as both foretaste and aftereffect in our physical and mental worlds.

One of the most powerful theories of perception was developed in the first part of the twentieth century by the German Gestalt psychologists, the best known of whom are Wolfgang Kohler, Kurt Koffka, and Max Wertheimer. Gestalt theory was based on the codification of the observations of phenomena based on ordinary perceptions that could be experienced by any normal observer. More powerful analytic models were developed using such phenomenological bases, as was outlined by J. J. Gibson (1950, 1986), who developed what he called ecological psychology. His approach stressed the importance of the structure of the natural environment within which perception took place, and his ideas flourish at the present time. Egon Brunswik (1952, 1956) developed a cognitively based perceptual psychology that he called probabilistic functionalism, and it has had a powerful revival of late (e.g., Gigerenzer and Murray, 1987). The perceptual theories of Brunswik and Gibson were powerful because they were based on a strong observational description that led to an understanding of the nature of perceptual events, and this descriptive *is* led to a series of effective synthetic theories.

Another good example of how naturalistic, observational principles can lead to deeper understanding can be found when the study of visual perception is considered in historical perspective. Julie Hochberg (1988), an American Brunswikian and Gestalt-influenced psychologist, made the persuasive argument that major advances in our understanding of the neurophysiological mechanisms involved in perception have been forced by considerations of the data based on the way things appeared to the casual observer. Physiological views about visual phenomena such as lateral inhibition, hue, and contrast were designed to account for these phenomenological facts of perception, and physiological mechanisms were proposed to allow direct comparisons and calculations based on the relations between different aspects of the proximal stimulation. Hochberg

(1988, p. 232) summarized: "But the historical facts seem clear: phenomenology has predicted more of recent neurophysiology than vice versa, and indeed if we wish eventually to be able to predict perceptual experience, then some explicit relationship between appearances and physiology must be provided."

Don Hebb's successful development of a heuristically valuable theory (1949) couched at the level of the neurophysiological and psychological mechanisms involved in learning and perception can be attributed to three strategies. First, he started with phenomenology, then considered known neurophysiological mechanisms, and from these two viewpoints speculated about their probable relationships. He and his colleagues continually revised this phenomenologically based theory as the understanding of neurophysiology advanced (e.g., Milner, 1957; Goddard, 1980). The study of the physiology of visual perception, as well as the power of Hebb's theoretical formulations, can be counted as scientific success stories. I attribute much of this success to the recognition that observational and factual constraints must be respected at all levels of analysis.

I could continue citing examples from a variety of fields, all of which would support the argument that a solid observational basis regarding what *is* enables us to understand psychological realities. If one is interested in developing behavioral and philosophical theories that "cut nature closer to the joints," then care must be taken to study the anatomy of behavior and thought by seeking to understand what things *are*.

I find it difficult to understand the arguments of those who object to certain lines of inquiry on the grounds that we should not seek to know the nature of reality because what we discover might not be to our liking. It has been argued that we should not study any possible relationship between race and intelligence, or genes and criminality, or gender and cognitive ability because what might be found may not be socially or politically acceptable. Such thinking seems to be motivated by the paranoid view that those who seek such understanding are motivated by evil intentions, or that their well-intentioned knowledge will be taken from them and used by members of some evil entity or another to diminish human dignity.

These concerns are two-edged, as Vicedo (1992) noted when discussing the ethical implications of the human genome project, which is an attempt to map and sequence the entire human genome. Doubts have been raised whether the project should be pursued, even though the resulting knowledge might bring some benefits, because it is clear that potential misuses could be enormous. On the other hand, doubts have been raised regarding whether it is ethical to deny access to knowledge simply because that knowledge might be misapplied, even though the potential benefits could be enormous. Vicedo concluded that the challenge is to find a way to assess the risks and benefits rationally and to make decisions accordingly.

I conclude that naturalism provides one of the best tools for understanding behavioral systems, and that such understanding will provide the foundation on which to develop a humane set of moral principles. When the biological realities that drive the evolutionary system—principally cooperation, communication, and helping behavior—are understood, one might better understand some of the universal moral principles that are evident in all known societies. Having such knowledge does not mean that one has to accept nature as it is. Rather, that knowledge can help to frame the *ought* in a way that will respect the interests and welfare of members of society and provide institutional safeguards to avoid the perversions that can appear due to such things as the nepotistic tendencies of humans because of their evolved biological and cognitive natures. There is no necessary fallacy involved in using naturalism in the manner discussed in this section.

THE SLIPPERY SLOPE FALLACY

Concern is often expressed that, when the first step is taken in pursuit of certain kinds of research or to institute certain social policies, we will be led inevitably down a "slippery slope" to an inevitable and unacceptable end. I mentioned such slippery slope arguments in Chapter 1 and will develop some points about them at greater length here. Slippery slope arguments are encountered regularly in social and political discourse. These arguments assume that one should not take some initial step, or accept some first principle, because a dangerous precedent would be set which will lead to an inevitable and morally unacceptable end point. The progression from step to step proceeds according to an implied, relentless causal mechanism, whereby one kind of action is causally instrumental in producing the next one, and that action, yet the next one, and on and on to the depths of doom. It is often argued that if we tolerate some minimal action, which may be acceptable in itself, the result will be a plausible and unacceptable outcome; one that not only is plausible, but which the slippery slope arguer considers to be implicitly inevitable once the first step is taken.

Walton (1992), who has written extensively on informal logic and argumentation, devoted a book to the problems inherent in such slippery slope arguments, and I will highlight only a few of them. So far as the metaphor is concerned, it could be argued that it is just as proper to consider a series of events to be more like staircases than slippery slopes. At each step we can decide whether we want to take the next step or not, and at each such step we can decide to make it impermissible for anyone to continue any further down by erecting a barrier. There is no necessity to conceive of decisions in terms of a continual slide which, once entered, permits no turning back before reaching the bottom, wherein lurks the horrible outcome. Kleinig (1991) took the slippery slope metaphor to task and argued that slopes are only as slippery as you make them. Skilled and sensitive skiers can stop even on steep and slippery slopes. The essential point is that the reasonableness of a slippery slope argument should depend on the statements made in the argument and not on the thoughts, ideas, motives, and metaphors that might exist.

It is important to understand the nature and operating characteristics of the causal mechanisms that are said to propel us inevitably from one level to the next, all the way to the unacceptable conclusion. Are we dealing with necessity, plausibility, high (or low) probability, or merely possibility? My suspicion is that seldom is logical necessity involved because complex reality is seldom absolutely determined by a single factor acting in isolation. Complex behavioral outcomes tend to be caused by multiple factors interacting with aspects of changing environmental circumstances, which make it difficult to predict future states with any degree of certainty.

Even if there is a slippery slope it is not necessary to slide down it to the depths. The action that comprises the first step can be modified so that it will not have the harmful effect. This modification can be done by eliminating or counteracting any causal harmful factor that has been identified.

To paraphrase Walton (1992, pp. 260–261), there are conterarguments to the slippery slope, and he suggested six inquiries that should be made whenever a slippery slope argument is encountered: (1) Are the negative consequences possible outcomes at all?; (2) What is the probability that the certain future outlined will follow?; (3) Can we modify the goal in such a way that the negative consequences are eliminated?; (4) Do the positive consequences that can be expected outweigh the negative ones?; (5) Is there an alternative means to achieve the goal that does not have the negative consequences?; (6) Could failing to take the course of action in question have even worse negative consequences?

The point is that all slippery slope arguments should be viewed with great skepticism and should be examined closely before they are accepted. There should be strong arguments to support the contention that knowledge about the nature of the universe should not be sought for its own sake, unless it can be demonstrated that the actual steps taken are harmful or unjust in themselves. Ignorance might be bliss, but only knowledge can make us free!

The naturalistic fallacy is an argument based on just such a scare tactic as the slippery slope argument entails. Rather than revealing truths that we would be better off not knowing, it is just as likely that understanding the nature of existing reality will allow us to engineer that reality for the better because the knowledge of what is will make it easier to cause changes in the consequences that follow, given reality. In the area of morality, if we know what human behavioral tendencies, or biological predispositions, exist (be they physiological, anatomical, genetic, or what have you) it will be possible to develop oughts that are feasible and to formulate social and legal policies that are just. I will identify (and quarrel with) the slippery slope argument in Chapter 12 which is a discussion of policies involved in regulating the reproductive technologies that are being so rapidly developed.

REDUCTIONISM

Some philosophers and social scientists have worried that, when considerations of human morality are based on naturalism, there is too great a reliance on reductionist principles, and these commentators imply that one cannot reduce complex sympathies and motivations to the level of simple, mechanistic processes. It should be noted, however, that there are two types of reductionism, and they are quite different. I have characterized these two types of reductionism at some length elsewhere (Petrinovich, 1976), referring to them as molecular and molar reductionism. When adopting the principles of molecular reductionism the intent is to achieve a reductionism in terms of events. Events at a more complex level are to be reduced to those of a more basic level with the hope that this will enable one to understand the complex level better through the application of the laws that have been developed to understand the simpler events of which the complex events are composed.

This molecular reductionist position argues that complex behavioral events, for example those involved in learning and memory, can be understood and explained if they are reduced to the level of the neurophysiological events that take place when the behavioral event occurs, and this neurophysiological level can be further reduced to the level of the biochemical level, and it in turn to that of biophysics. The defense that is made against there being an infinite regress to lower and lower levels to obtain a complete and cosmic understanding, can be countered by the argument that one is not seeking to obtain complete understanding, but only to reduce the events to a level at which the scientific laws have been established, in order to permit the manipulation of the relevant underlying variables regulating the processes of interest.

The major objection to this type of reductionism is that the redefinition of events that occurs when moving from one level to a lower one results in an undesirable redefinition of the processes of interest. The events involved in a complex event (e.g., problem solving) can be redefined in terms of more basic principles involving concepts of learning, retention, and recall, and these lower level behavioral events can be reduced to the level of the neurophysiological changes that occur at the level of the functional connections of neurones, the synapse. However, it is unlikely that, even if we understood the biochemical and biophysical events that take place at synapses, we would be able to make very meaningful inferences regarding the characteristics of problem solving. Another way to express this is that there seem to be emergent properties that appear in complex behaviors that cannot be captured completely, even though we understand the operation of the simpler events involved. One such emergent property, discussed in Chapter 4, is the discovery that human problem solving is radically different, being much more efficient, when the problems involve a social contract than when they are logically equivalent but no social contract is involved.

A clear instance of this argument was suggested by Morton Beckner (1974), who discussed the events involved in executing a last will and testament. There are two events involved: One can be described as "executing a will" (D1) and the other "moving the hand in a certain way" (D2). Both events occur at the same time, but the context can make them not identical at all. D1 could be done by making an X or by writing with the other hand, or by dictating to a notary if both hands are nonfunctional—the precise hand movements used to make the signature is not necessary to D1. The precise aspects of D2 could occur when signing any number of things, such as a love letter, which (one hopes) should not be confused with a last will and testament. Both D1 and D2 determine a class of events, and the event in either class may or may not be the same as an event in the other. In this view D1 is a sociolegal concept embodying a theoretical structure that is not entailed in D2. The events involving hand movements constitute a descriptive set which is neutral regarding the functional achievement of executing a will. Neither D1 nor D2 is more or less "real" than the other; they entail different theoretical structures.

The conclusion to be drawn is that the description of the event (either in terms of D1 or D2) fails to give sufficient evidence to establish an identity between them or to identify the function of the event. Thus, we have events which are quite separable from the theories that are involved. It is arguable that a molecular event reductionism of moral principles to the level of proximate evolutionary processes is possibly a waste of time.

The goals of molar reductionism are quite different. The aim is to obtain a theoretical reduction to a set of unifying functional principles that have broad generality. I believe that evolutionary theory, with its populational emphasis on relative reproductive success, provides a set of unifying principles shown to be applicable at every level involving the interaction of simpler and more complex organic systems. The hope is that this unifying framework will be applicable to the evolution of social systems and to the development of morality, just as it has been to other aspects of organismic functioning. An important characteristic of the types of explanation involved is that they rely on a probabilistic model that permits the vicarious expression of events in order to attain a common goal, and are able to accommodate the reality that the different ways desired functional outcomes can be achieved are influenced by learned and inherited predispositions, as well as by the structure of the environment in which the events are taking place.

There are many ways to achieve a functional goal: If I want to get from here to there, and it is not far, I can choose to crawl, walk, or run. What I choose to do will depend on the terrain: If it is glare ice I might crawl; if there are deep pits in the roadway I might walk; if the way is flooded I might make a raft and float there; or I might choose to float across the flood on my back or to swim across. The choice I make will also depend on my abilities: If I cannot swim, then that eliminates the swimming option and lessens the likelihood of the unassisted floating option; if I am in dreadful physical condition that would lessen the likelihood that I would run if I could walk. Another set of factors involves my intentions: If I want to enjoy the outing I would likely walk; if I want to observe the insects along the way I might crawl; if I am eager to get there I would run. Yet another set of factors would be the distance involved: If the distance is not long, then any of the aforementioned ways might be the likely ones I would choose; if the distance is longer I might choose to bicycle; if the distance is even longer I might take a bus or drive a car; and if the distance is extensive I might choose to fly in an airplane. Given the complex set of circumstances, plus my (fallible) psychological estimations of what the realities are, there is a strong likelihood that I will somehow get there, especially if I consider it important to do so. No one, at the outset (including myself) will be able to predict precisely what I will do, and circumstances might change in such a way that I move to a different mode of approach than I intended or started with. Because there is a level of unpredictability in how I achieve the functional goal, however, does not mean that the likelihood of reaching the goal is low or that the reasons for the particular acts used cannot be understood after the fact.

The important lesson to be drawn from all of this is that, given an ultimate goal, there are many different proximate actions that will permit the attainment of that goal. In terms of achieving a stable and reproductively successful society there are many proximate mechanisms that will support that attainment. Thus, a diversity of proximate societal rules might exist, but the common goal should be to achieve the ultimate end of a high level of relative inclusive fitness, and this common ultimate goal might constitute the evolved component of morality.

SUMMARY

A study will be described in Chapter 7, the purpose of which is to understand the nature of people's moral intuitions; to discover what is the nature of intuitive oughts. If the structure of intuitions is understood, then it might be possible to develop further understanding of the underlying moral principles on which these intuitions are based. Such understanding might make it easier to consider the nature of the moral imperatives that influence people's beliefs, especially when there is a legitimate conflict of interest between different living beings. One basic factor that might modulate moral value is the necessity to survive, reproduce, and transmit genes to succeeding generations, and this basic factor might be one on which the ought of moral systems could be based (and, I believe, should).

Ruse (1993) observed that we can learn a lot about human nature by appealing to people's feelings and asking them to examine these feelings deeply and carefully, much as has been done in the study of moral intuitions discussed in Chapter 7. Ruse noted that people do seem to have a consistent differential sense of moral obligation such that they do tend to favor the interests of kin and members of their own community over those of strange humans, and those of humans over nonhumans, as will be demonstrated in our research.

People do have a uniform sense of moral obligation as revealed by the example that I might pay lip service to my equal obligation to all the starving unknown people in the Third World. However, as Ruse noted, if I contributed 90% of my income to a charity to feed large numbers of those starving individuals, while my own children suffered from malnutrition as a result, I would not be hailed as a moral giant, but might well be prosecuted for child neglect, even though I could be saving the lives of hundreds of nameless children. It is clear that there are deep moral imperatives and that a great deal can be learned about the bases of normative morality by examining and describing deep intuitions that might exist, and this examination could well lead to an understanding of the course a normative ethics could take.

3

Basic Concepts

Evolutionary Mechanisms

In this chapter I will develop some basic concepts concerning evolutionary biology that should be understood to consider bioethical issues at what I believe is an adequate level of complexity. In the next two chapters these concepts will be applied to consider issues in human evolution, behavior, and psychology. Much of what follows in later chapters concerns the nature of the defining characteristics of life: When does life begin, when is moral standing attained, when is one bound by rules of morality, and when is one justified in intervening in the natural stream of life events? Most of the issues to be considered involve sexual reproduction, the process by which a significant proportion of plants and animals propagate themselves. It has been demonstrated that many aspects of the social life of plant and animal species are related to traits that developed to further the reproductive success of organisms, and that these traits can only be understood within the context of the environmental pressures to which organisms must adapt in order to survive.

BASIC BIOLOGICAL PHENOMENA

The principles of evolutionary biology provide the most powerful set of unifying ideas that have been developed to deal with organic systems. To gain an adequate perspective concerning the relationships between organisms within an ecological context, it will be helpful to discuss some of the principles on which evolutionary theory is based. Briefly, to understand the theory of evolution, there are five biological phenomena that should be considered, inheritance, mutation, natural selection, isolation, and genetic drift.

Inheritance

This concept requires an understanding of what genes are, their mechanisms of action, and how they interact to influence the characteristics of organisms. To understand the action of genes at an adequate level one must understand the structure and characteristics of the environments in which particular genes are expressed because environmental influences determine the range of reactions that are possible, in terms of phenotypic expression. There is no simple relationship between genes and morphological, physiological, or psychological traits. Without genetic inheritance there can be no cumulative change in the traits of successive generations of organisms.

Mutation

There is some spontaneous change that takes place in genes, and these changes can be heritable as well. These mutations are not predictable and most of them have little effect; they either are not expressed in the phenotype, or they are deleterious to the organism because organisms consist of sets of coadapted gene complexes. In the former case the genes could be present in the genotype of some organisms but not be evident in the phenotype (the appearance of the organism), while in the latter case the organism dies, and the mutated gene disappears with it.

Natural Selection

This overriding principle includes the external processes and pressures that act on an organism. Natural selection acts on the phenotypic variation presented by different organisms in the population, to destroy that variation through a process of favoring some phenotypes (and their underlying genetic structure) at the expense of others. It has been suggested that, whenever a relatively rapid directional change occurs in the characteristics of a given species, natural selection might well be involved. Sober (1987), cautioned that no evolutionist should hold that natural selection is the only cause of a trait appearing in a population, because other factors, such as mutation and genetic drift, play a crucial role. Yet, it can be argued that selection is the most powerful force at work in directing change.

Isolation

All genetic lines do not interbreed freely because of geographic or reproductive isolation. If all species were free to interbreed, eventually there would be but a single species inhabiting the biosphere. If a number of organisms from a given species remain geographically isolated from the others for a considerable period of time, then they might well develop characteristics that make them so different from the others both genotypically and phenotypically that they cannot interbreed with those others and would be considered to be a new biological species.

Genetic Drift

Genetic materials are sometimes lost by random or nonrandom accidents. When drift occurs it reduces the direct influence of selection and provides some uncertainty regarding the direction that selection might take. Recent arguments (e.g., Kaufman, 1993) have stressed the importance of spontaneous sources of order; the self-organized properties of biological systems which act to permit, enable, and limit the effectiveness of natural selection. In Kaufman's view organisms should be considered to involve a collaboration between the actions of natural selection and the existing balance that organisms have achieved. This view directs attention to the role of intrinsic sources of order in organisms that add to those extrinsic sources producing natural selection.

These five phenomena have all been demonstrated in many contexts and with many plant and animal species. They can be demonstrated at will in both the field and the laboratory, and the relative importance of each, as well as the mode of some of their interactions, are understood for a variety of specific instances. Alexander (1979), argued that these five phenomena can be considered to be the *factual basis* of evolution. In contrast, he pointed out, there is the *theory* of evolution, which is the proposition that the effects and interactions of these five phenomena account for the traits and history of all forms of life in the succession of environments in which organisms have lived throughout geological time.

It cannot be stressed too strongly that evolutionary theory operates at two distinct levels, the proximate and ultimate. At the *proximate level* the concern is with how processes work, and with the mechanisms within the organism and the environment that drive evolutionary processes. At the *ultimate level* the currency is differential reproductive success, which is cashed in by counting the number of genes put back into the gene pool, relative to the performance of others in the population—counting at least as far as the number of grand offspring produced. Evolutionary explanations are not complete unless they address both levels, and a consideration of each can lead to insights regarding the nature of the other. Also, a great deal of confusion can result when explanations are framed at one level and uncritically extended to explain events at the other level.

Another useful way to organize thinking about evolution is in terms of two general underlying classes of factors, intrinsic and extrinsic. These two classes of factors, along with the overriding principle of natural selection, provide the tools required to understand most evolutionary processes.

INTRINSIC FACTORS

Intrinsic factors concern the basic material, the genotype, on which evolution depends and natural selection must influence. The genotype can be defined as the totality of the genetic attributes of an individual. When we think at the level of a species, we refer to the gene pool, which is the population of genes that exist in any individual who is a member of the species; the sum total of different alleles (alternative genes that appear at the same locus of paired chromosomes) in the population. Any given individual has a genotype which is but a sample of the total gene pool.

The phenotype, on the other hand, is the totality of characteristics that are evident in the appearance of the individual. The phenotype is the physical expression of the underlying genotype, and it will be influenced by other factors (such as nutrition, climate, pollutants) than the purely genetic. It should also be emphasized that natural selection acts on the phenotype, but that the effects of selection are transmitted (inherited) through the underlying genotype.

Consider twins: There are two types, fraternal and identical. Fraternal twins are produced when two different eggs are independently fertilized by two different sperm, while identical twins are produced when a single egg, fertilized by one sperm, splits into two separate organisms prior to implantation in the uterine wall. Speaking in simple Mendelian terms, two individuals, say fraternal twins, might display a similar phenotype, that is related to some underlying dominant genes, but still they will have a different genotype. At the simplest level one of the individuals might have two dominant genes for a trait, while the other might have one dominant and one recessive. The result would be a similar phenotypic appearance of the dominant in both instances, but the underlying genotype would be quite different for the two individuals. Given such circumstances the contribution of the two identically appearing individuals to the next generation could be quite different: If a double-dominant individual mated with a double-recessive person, then the trait would appear in all offspring; if the individual with a dominant–recessive combination mated with a double-dominant, the trait would also appear in all offspring; but if the dominant–recessive mated with a double-recessive, for half of the progeny the trait would not be expected to appear.

A widespread misconception is that if a trait appears at birth as a result of genetic instructions, it is unmodifiable. This misunderstanding commonly appears in the thinking of many social scientists and humanists, as evidenced by assertions that any discussion of a universal human nature denies the uniqueness of individuals. Such assertions imply a biological or genetic determinism considered by some to be antithetical to a belief in fundamental human dignity. Tooby and Cosmides (1990a) argued that the concept of a universal human nature is a valid one, but that such universality does not deny genetic or biochemical uniqueness. They noted that even a basic universal human nature would permit variable manifest psychologies, traits, and behaviors between individuals and across cultures. They view such variable states as the product of a common, underlying psychology that operates under different environmental circumstances, drawing a useful distinction between heritability (the process of transmission of characteristics) and adaptation (the modification of behavior to cope with the demands of the environment). This distinction leads them to adopt the evolutionarily solid argument that one function of sexual reproduction and genetic variation is to establish evolved defenses against pathogens (a view developed by Hamilton and his colleagues, discussed below).

Without going into the arguments in any depth at this point, it is clear that there seem to be characteristics we all share by virtue of the fact that we are humans rather than members of another species. If so, an understanding of the organization of existing variation between individuals should be considered within the framework of the universally shared biological and psychological mechanisms that characterize humans. Major differences in behavioral tendencies might appear between males and females, for example, because the differences in their reproductive physiologies and organismic structures favor the use of different reproductive strategies and these, in turn, lead to a different set of parental responsibilities, as discussed in the next two chapters.

EXTRINSIC FACTORS

In addition to intrinsic factors there are extrinsic ones, such as the nature of the food supply, the structure of the environment, and the type and prevalence of predators—all of which influence the development of behavior patterns. These extrinsic factors influence the course of evolution through their effect on the differential survival rate of differing phenotypes; they provide the selection pressures.

Natural Selection

Natural selection refers to the processes that favor certain phenotypes over certain others, and it is the mechanism that causes differential perpetuation of different genotypes. More properly, the effect of natural selection is expressed as the difference in the number of surviving, reproducing offspring produced by individuals that is caused by variation in appearance, behavior, physiology, or other traits. The individual organism arises as a unique temporary genotype formed (in many species of organisms) through sexual reproduction which combines two samples of gametes (the mature sexual reproductive cells: the eggs or the sperm) from the gene pool that defines the species. The genotype of the individual is a set of instructions for producing an interactor, the fitness of which will be determined by the nature of the environment it encounters during development (Williams, 1992).

Because no two individuals (with the possible exception of identical twins) are the same genetically, there is an immense amount of possible genetic diversity that can be influenced and operated on by extrinsic factors. Natural selection must be considered to be a statistical phenomenon, and its effects can be understood in terms of selective sampling of individual genotypes from a large population (the gene pool). The effects of natural selection are not rigorously predictable, especially in changeable environments in which the types of ecological factors and their modes of interaction will vary from one time period to another. Individuals with similar fitness also may have quite dissimilar reproductive success because of chance environmental events that impinge on one and not the others.

Evolution is a two-stage phenomenon: the production of phenotypic variation, and the sorting of these variants by natural selection. The genotype is an interacting and integrated system, and the existence and relative success of differing phenotypes can only be understood in terms of a compromise between sets of opposing selection pressures—through analyses of costs and benefits. It might well be that, say for a given species of bird, an increase in the size of display plumage will enhance the probability that a male bird will attract a breeding female. This is an instance of sexual selection by the female; a male that has the preferred plumage will also have an enhanced reproductive success, and the genotype he has that produced the plumage characteristics will be perpetuated—the benefit. However, an overdevelopment of such plumage might also make it much easier for a predator to locate him and hasten his demise. This negative natural selection will cause the loss of the male's somewhat unique genotype—the cost. Therefore, some compromise between these two alternatives of conspicuous display to attract females and nondistinctive plumage to be inconspicuous to predators is often found. In some instances the display plumage can be hidden when not used in courtship, or the display plumage might be developed only during the breeding season, and we have an otherwise drab male animal that is highly conspicuous only during the courtship period.

It is a general principle that evolution tends to preserve the functional germ cells, at least as far as successful species are concerned. Because an existing genotype represents at least a satisfactory adjustment to the environment on the part of the species of which the parents are a part, any drastic genotypic deviation will quite likely be a less satisfactory solution to the problems involved in survival and will be of negative value. In general, individuals that mate with members of an alien species tend to produce fewer fertile offspring than do those that mate exclusively with individuals of their own species. Thus, gene combinations which lead to phenotypic differences favoring mating between individuals of the same species will have a positive value and will be selected (as long as there is no inbreeding depression due to extensive mating between closely related individuals). The result will be a certain amount of evolutionary constancy, with species tending to maintain themselves. However, there will usually be some outbreeding mechanisms that will serve to promote incest avoidance between the members of breeding communities.

The observed variability in genotypes and phenotypes that appears in different individuals should not be conceived to represent unwanted errors that occur in the process of sexual recombination. Individual differences between different organisms are necessary in order to produce continually varying genotypes from the gene pool. It is essential to maintain this genetically based variability in order to produce individuals who might survive if extrinsic factors change radically in ways that make it difficult or impossible for those individuals located near the norm to survive. Some of the individuals with highly distinctive characteristics, the outliers, might be able to survive and reproduce, and they will then reconstitute the gene pool with an altered set of gene frequencies from that now characterizing the species. Through this process a degree of variability is encouraged and maintained through sexual recombination each generation. I suggest that it might be a good social strategy to encourage, tolerate, and maintain individual differences in the physiological and behavioral characteristics of the people making up the human social community as well.

The above processes can be summarized by quoting Stebbins (1971, p. 162):

> In order to survive and evolve, populations of organisms need a pool of genetic variability which enables them to establish successful relationships with certain factors of their immediate environment. Depending both on the nature of the organism–environment relationship present at one time, and on the way in which the environment changes relative to the qualities and potentialities present in the available gene pool, an evolutionary line of populations may progress either rapidly or slowly, may become extinct, or may remain constant for long periods of time.

Fitness

Fitness is defined in terms of differential survival and reproductive success of individuals in the population. As mentioned above, the outcome currency is not at the level of the survival, fertility, or fecundity of a given individual, but at the ultimate level at which one counts at least as far as the number of grand offspring produced. It matters not that a healthy and fertile offspring is produced if it, in turn, is unable, for any of a variety of reasons, to raise its own offspring. It is entirely possible that, due to chance occurrences, a very fit organism will perish while a less fit one will survive. However, the fact that good and bad luck can have an influence does not lessen the value of the concept of fitness when it is viewed from a probabilistic perspective.

Keller (1992) developed a point that is important to remember when fitness is considered for sexually reproducing organisms. She reminds us that fitness is always context dependent, with the fitness of a particular organism depending on the availability of a member of the opposite sex and on the fertility of that mate. Although fitness is often discussed in terms of individuals, it is not an individual property for sexually reproducing organisms, but is a composite characteristic of the entire interbreeding population. She argued that sex "undermines" the reproductive autonomy of the individual organism and makes it difficult to locate specific causal mechanisms producing individual changes. Natural selection and the concept of fitness must be considered to be factors that are distributed throughout the entire population of interbreeding organisms. As Cosmides and Tooby (1987) pointed out, for social and reproductive behaviors the favored strategy will depend on the distribution of other behaviors in the population. They identified a number of domains of human activity that should have Darwinian algorithms associated with them: Aggressive threat, male choice, sexual behavior, pair-bonding, parenting, parent–offspring conflict, friendship, kinship, resource accrual, resource distribution, disease avoidance, predator avoidance, and social exchange. These domains will be discussed at length in the next two chapters.

SEXUAL RECOMBINATION

The fact that sexual reproduction exists so widely poses problems that have concerned evolutionists for some time. If the game of life is played to maximize one's contribution to the genes of succeeding generations, then why doesn't the female just clone herself so that all of her offspring's genes are the same as her own? Why do we have sexual reproduction, thereby sharing half of the genetic makeup of offspring with a sexual partner? An understanding of why these costs are acceptable in terms of the genetic ledger balance is best achieved through an economic analysis of cost and benefit (Williams, 1975).

It is agreed that heritable variation is the fuel that powers evolutionary change. There must be a wide range of genotypes present to enable the gene pool to respond to changes in selection pressures, and sexual recombination is one way to assure that continual variation is present in each generation.

Crow (1988) pointed out that there are at least three distinct evolutionary advantages to sexual recombination. These involve an increased ability to adjust to environmental changes, to incorporate beneficial mutations, and to remove deleterious mutation. The most important factors seem to be the first and third, because the incorporation of beneficial mutation seems not to occur often. Most mutations are not beneficial, and as mentioned above, those beneficial mutations that might occur do not appear readily within the context of the coadapted genetic systems that characterize individuals of a thriving species. For these reasons mutations usually are deleterious or have no phenotypic effect at all.

Environments often change suddenly, especially in the frame of geological time, as the result of radical alteration of the physical characteristics of the ecology or the introduction of infectious diseases, such as through the action of parasites. Some general differences have been identified between those species that utilize sexual, compared to those that employ asexual, modes of reproduction. Sexual species generally are found in old, stable, and complex environments, and the organisms tend to be relatively large and complex. Asexual species tend to occupy recent, novel, or disturbed environments, and have simpler genomes and larger population sizes. It has been demonstrated, in both laboratory and field, that with sexual reproduction a few generations of selection can produce individuals with a genetic complement quite different from that of the original population. It is recognized that the production of a variable array of propagules will buffer the system from extinctions that might be brought about by these rapid changes in ecology or through the introduction of new infectious vectors. An asexual system is not capable of such rapid response to change, and is at great risk of extinction in response to such change. George Williams (1992) argued that asexual reproduction leads to a degeneration of the genome, in the sense that it acquires a heavier and heavier load of mutations which will always lead to rapid extinction on an evolutionary time scale.

The insightful British evolutionary theorist Hamilton and his colleagues have championed the parasite model very convincingly (Hamilton, Axelrod, & Tanese, 1990; Seger & Hamilton, 1988; Zuk, 1992). The parasite model assumes that hosts usually have generation times that are longer than those of parasites, whose generation times are sometimes many orders of magnitude shorter than those of their hosts. When this asymmetry exists, parasites can evolve improved methods of attack much faster than their hosts can evolve improved methods of defense. Under such circumstances the host's best defense will be to maintain a broad range of genetic diversity. If there is sexual recombination in each generation, as Seger & Hamilton (1988, p. 176) vividly state, the host organisms "can present to the parasites what amounts to a continually moving target." Continual recombination will occur in organisms with a wide range of genetic diversity and this recombination will make it difficult for parasites that specialize in current host characteristics to exploit the diverse host offspring, and such failure could lead to the extinction of that particular set of parasites in but one host generation. There will be a benefit to hosts that have genotypes that vary from generation to generation because they will be less exploitable by parasites.

Another function of sexual recombination is to remove the deleterious effects of mutations, especially in large and complex organisms. Recombination will make it possible to effect exogenous repair of deleterious mutations because most evolutionarily important traits are polygenic. In general, extinction is less likely for those genetic systems that practice sex than would otherwise be the case. I want to emphasize that this is not an argument that involves group selection; all effects are at the level of changes in gene frequencies of individuals, but their effects can be detected, and are effective, at the level of breeding populations. It is not necessary (nor acceptable in terms of basic mechanisms) to think at the level of effects being for "the good of the species."

PHYLOGENY AND ONTOGENY

It is important to have an adequate conception of the nature of phylogenetic development, especially if the interest is to relate ontogeny (the biological development of an individual organism) to phylogeny (the evolutionary development of species). One of the most influential, and incorrect, ways of viewing phylogeny was that of Aristotle who proposed the *Scala Naturae*, or Great Chain of Being. This view conceived of animal species as arranged in a linear, ladderlike fashion, ranging upward from "lower," simpler organisms at the bottom of the ladder (such as the one-cell protozoans). The series progresses up through worms, insects, and fish, continuing to mammals (such as rats, cats, and dogs), increasing to the primates, to reach the top of the ladder at humans. (Theologians placed angels yet higher, with God at the pinnacle, and all other creatures considered to be progressively less perfect copies of God. While this might be an adequate theological model, biologically it is questionable.)

In one sense it is not the case that humans are the most highly evolved species, with "lower" organisms less so. The lower species are more highly evolved in the sense that they have been doing it for a much longer time, and those that are still in existence have been more successful than humans, who represent the new kids on the block. The evolutionary time differential is even greater given the fact that most species require much less time per generation than do humans.

A better way to conceive of phylogeny is that species are genetically different, with these genetic differences having developed in response to ecological and behavioral factors. The proper scheme is not that of a sequential ladder, but of a divergent, treelike structure. No fish should ever be considered to be the ancestor of any reptile, bird, or mammal, and no chimpanzee should be considered to be the ancestor of humans. Some species existed millions of years ago, so they are ancestral in the sense of having been present long ago, but most of the animal species that exist today represent different evolutionary lineages that split off from one another at different times and then continued their separate lines of development.

It might be helpful to concentrate on the primate lineage to illustrate phylogenetic relationships. An analysis of the structure of deoxyribonucleic acid (DNA), the gene-bearing double helix molecule that is the primary hereditary molecule, indicates that about 30 million years ago the old world monkeys diverged from the line that developed into the rest of the primates, with the monkey line continuing its separate course to the present time. The other primate line diverged once again about 20 million years ago into two lines, one into gibbons and the other with yet another divergence into orangutans. The continuing primate line then diverged about 10 million years ago when gorillas branched off, with humans branching off about 6 million years ago (see Diamond, 1992b, Fig. 1, p. 21). This primate line kept developing, with pygmy chimpanzees diverging about 3 million years ago, and the major line continuing to the common chimpanzee.

The DNA story indicates that, about 6 million years ago the human line branched off, and at this point the story can be continued using archaeological evidence. Beginning at that time, evidence appears for the existence of an upright hominid and of apes (see Diamond, 1992b, Fig. 2, p. 35). Three million years ago the hominid line seemed to split into *Australopithecus (A.) africanus* and *A. robustus*. The latter line did not survive, but *A. africanus* again split into *Homo (H.) habilis* and perhaps another line that disappeared. About 1.7 million years ago *H. erectus* was present with *H. sapiens* appearing about 500,000 years ago. By 100,000 years ago the Neanderthal was present, as was an Asian line, and the anatomically modern *africanus* which developed into the Cro-Magnon. According to Diamond there were no Neanderthals 40,000 years ago. He believes they became extinct because they could not compete with Cro-Magnon. The original Asian line had disappeared as well; Diamond suggests that their disappearance was due to interbreeding with the Cro-Magnon line which continues as the present human line, *H. sapiens*.

There has been no phylogenetic change that would support the construction of a ladder running from lower to higher species. There has been a branching of lineages into different forms, some of which survived to the present, and most of which did not. What happened, as Gould (1977) documented, is that there have been two phylogenetic adaptations that characterize the evolution of characteristics important in ontogenetic change. One is that new characteristics are introduced at given stages of development with varying effects upon subsequent stages. The second is that characteristics that are already present undergo changes in developmental timing. The implication is that no complex animal repeats any adult stage of simpler ones, but that development proceeds from undifferentiated, general stages to differentiated, special stages. Gould focuses on the significance of the acceleration of development at some stages and the retardation of development at others, with the timing of these two processes being of special importance. He considers neoteny (the retardation of the development of selected organs) to be a major determinant of human evolution. Neoteny permits such things as the gradual increase in the development of the cerebral cortex by prolonging into later life the rapid brain growth that characterizes the developing fetus, neonate, and infant.

One should be wary of arguments based on the assumption that ontogeny recapitulates phylogeny, when that statement is taken to mean that the developing fetus moves through the adult stages that are characteristic of "lower" species. For example, Tooley (1983, p. 383) interprets the pattern of myelination of nerve tracts to "illustrate the general principle that ontogeny recapitulates phylogeny." He believes this to be the case because, "Those regions of the brain that were the last to emerge in the development of species leading up to man . . . are also the ones that myelinate last in the development of the individual. . . ." Elsewhere, Tooley speaks of animals "very far down the evolutionary scale," which invokes the idea of the Scala Naturae. The philosopher Roger Wertheimer (1971) embraced both recapitulation and the Scala Naturae in his discussion of abortion arguments. He suggested that the higher the evolutionary stage of a species, or the later the developmental stage of a fetus, the more restricted the permission to kill. While such statements may reflect people's convictions, they do not reflect sound biological thinking and their factual bases should be examined carefully.

ETHOLOGICAL MECHANISMS

In Chapter 9, when considering issues regarding abortion, it will be argued that the point at which a mammal is born, or a bird or invertebrate is hatched, is of signal importance in most species. I argue that the point of birth should be emphasized, even though there have been demonstrations that prenatal experience influences the development of such basic processes as the functional development of the central nervous system (see Kalil, 1989) and the development of aggressive behaviors in rats (vom Saal, Grant, et al., 1983).

Despite the fact that prenatal experience can have strong effects, the critical aspects for socialization begin at the point at which the neonate is exposed to the specific environmental events that characterize the social milieu in which it finds itself. At that point, not only does an independent existence commence, but the matrix of social factors critical to the development of the entire social system that prevails for the members of the species exerts a strong influence. There are some behavioral interactions that seem almost universal among vertebrates (as well as many invertebrate species). I discuss these mechanisms under the heading "Ethological Mechanisms" because it was those zoologists (ethologists) who studied animals in their natural environment, identified the mechanisms involved, and developed an understanding of the operating characteristics of those mechanisms. In addition, the ethologists demonstrated the importance of the contribution of these mechanisms to the ultimate reproductive success of the individuals involved. I will develop some of these characteristics and outline their importance in regulating the development of the social aspects of crucial interactions involved in later mating, courtship, and parental behaviors.

Parental Strategies

The ethological mechanisms that will be discussed here are ones that ensure that young recognize their parents in order to assure they acquire behavior patterns that will be crucial for their later survival and reproduction. It will be emphasized that it is important, in certain social systems, for parents to recognize and nurture their own young if the young are to prosper. In the case of those birds that lay eggs in the nests of other species it will be pointed out that, in some instances, the young must recognize those of the opposite sex of their own species that have been raised by the proper host species. In general, display mechanisms exist (usually visual or acoustic in birds, and extending to olfaction in mammals) that serve to identify species membership, to signal gender, to signal reproductive status, and to indicate overall quality of individuals in terms of the likelihood of being a reliable and hardy mate able to foster high quality young.

Not only is it important to recognize the qualities of different individuals, but it is important to use strategies that will increase the likelihood that a breeding attempt will lead to reproductive success. Trivers (1972) developed the argument that the parental investment of male and female members of a number of species can be quite different at different stages of a pregnancy. For mammals (and birds to a lesser extent) the costs of reproduction—the effort required to successfully produce viable young—become quite high after fertilization. The female mammal has to carry the young inside her body for a considerable period of time, has to provide adequate sustenance for herself and the developing fetus, and has to forego any other opportunity for reproduction during this considerable period of time. Almost from the point of fertilization the female has incurred a considerable parental investment. Such is not the case for the male. He loses relatively little by the act of copulation with the female; the metabolic investment in sperm is small, so his initial parental investment is low. The strategies of males and females should be quite different, and the type of strategy adopted will be influenced by the quality of environmental resources sufficient to produce and raise the young.

If the female needs no help from the male throughout the breeding episode and is able to provide adequately for the young by herself, then the important consideration concerns her choice of a studly male—one who has good quality genes, because that will be his only contribution to the quality of the offspring.

However, if the ecological conditions are such that the female requires assistance, either to protect the turf on which she will live and raise the young, to help her to avoid predators, to feed her during the gestation of the progeny, or to assist her in the care and feeding of the young, she has to assure herself of several things. She should make sure that the male has no other filial attachments and commitments, that he is a strong enough individual to perform the parental tasks that might be required, and that he can be depended upon to stay and help as long as needed. It should be emphasized that when reference is made to the reproductive strategies that evolve this does not imply conscious strategy on the part of individual organisms. All that is implied is that individuals who have genetically based tendencies that lead to certain reproductive behavioral strategies will have a higher fitness, given the nature of the environment, than those who do not use those strategies. In cases such as the above the breeding system likely will be monogamous (at least relatively so for the breeding season).

The male strategy should be to seek out as many females as he can and attempt to inseminate them, especially if he is not required to assume any parental obligations. However, if none of the females he inseminates are successful at raising viable young he has wasted his sperm, his time, and much of a breeding season. In such situations the male should enter into a stable pair-bond to ensure that the primary female will succeed, and he should be alert that she has qualities that indicate she will be a good mate and mother. He should be willing to copulate with other females who might be around, however. The effort involved in such extrapair copulations is minimal for the male and the responsibility for the consequences are nil. He should engage in these extrapair copulations if there is any possibility that the inseminated female will be able to raise viable young. If the female who appears has not been impregnated yet, but is paired with another male, all the better. The male who sneaks the extrapair copulation will benefit from any efforts the cuckolded male might expend in raising any offspring that result from the copulation.

Females in situations where monogamy tends to be the rule should prefer loyal, high-quality males, while males should prefer younger and larger females (assuming that, other things being equal, larger females are healthier and stronger). These young and large females will have a higher reproductive value in the sense that they will be expected to produce more viable young for a longer period of time. If monogamy is the prevailing system, then the male would do better to invest in a female with a high reproductive value. Males should value quality in a female but also invest in quantity of copulations, while females should value quality above all— one successful sperm is all that is necessary. Let me caution that this scenario is oversimplified, the range of scenarios is much more extensive, and the interaction of factors can be quite complicated. Many other variables and considerations come into play, but the scenario I have described highlights some of the important principles involved in sexual selection, parental investment, and to determine reproductive value.

Imprinting

The early ethologists, such as Lorenz (1935/1970), considered instance after instance where the phenomenon of imprinting occurred shortly after birth or hatching. Lorenz was impressed by the similarities between the developmental processes of what he called instinctive behavioral systems and processes which had been identified in morphological development. He pointed out that if, at a certain time in development, cell material was grafted from one location to another in a frog embryo, the cells would become a constituent part and would function in a manner appropriate to its new location. He interpreted this to indicate that the cells are influenced by organizational aspects of the biological environment, and sought evidence to implicate the same principles in behavioral development. These and many later studies (see Immelmann & Suomi, 1981) indicated that adult behavior can be crucially influenced through exposure to stimuli during specific times in early development. If a freshly hatched gosling is exposed to a moving object, and if this is the first thing the gosling has seen, it "imprints" on this object and behaves toward it as if the moving object were a parent—which it usually is in nature.

The general phenomenon of imprinting has been demonstrated in many species, for many stimuli, and for a wide range of behaviors. Shortly after birth there does seem to be a time when those stimuli that appear are accorded crucial roles in the regulation of complex behaviors. The appropriate stimuli almost invariably appear in the course of normal development: The first object experienced is usually the mother; the first animal sounds heard are usually those of the parents, of members of the immediate family, or singers of the same species. The first tastes experienced are usually those of the food-types available in the immediate environment—either taken directly or through maternal feeding. There are hundreds of instances that have been identified throughout the animal kingdom to attest to the generality of this tendency to be sensitive to certain classes of stimuli for a considerable time after birth. The course of later development often is influenced profoundly, and sometimes unalterably, by the nature of these early interactions. Almost always the crucial stimuli are certain to be present during normal developmental episodes, thereby ensuring that the neonate will develop normal patterns of behavior. Experimental manipulation of the stimuli made available to the neonate have demonstrated the power of the process because it is possible, for example, to imprint a gosling's parental following response to a human (e.g., Lorenz) if the portly, bearded Lorenz was the first moving stimulus to which the gosling was exposed. If there are a host of competing stimuli that might interfere with normal development (such as a lot of different sounds that could serve as biologically inappropriate standards on which development would be based), it has been demonstrated that genetic tuning of receptor systems can occur. This increases the likelihood that only stimuli with the proper characteristics will be selected, and that attention will preferentially be directed to those stimuli.

Experience-Expectant Structures

I have discussed elsewhere the nature of the physiological theories that have been invoked to account for imprinting behavior, especially as it relates to the development of bird song (Petrinovich, 1988) The early ideas were based on models of control systems that had been developed to account for visual–motor adjustments that insects use to catch prey. These mechanistic models were extended beyond the visual–motor system to account for sensory events as well, with the development of the idea of a sensory template (Marler, 1976). This template was considered to provide a structural base for the perceptual analyses of stimuli and to be located somewhere in the auditory neural system. The template was considered to impose constraints on processes of vocal learning by focusing attention, during a relatively early and brief sensitive period, on sounds that met the innate specifications of the template. In addition to this sensory gating mechanism a centrally located template was postulated that held both innate and experiential information. Unfortunately, little direct neurological evidence exists that makes it possible to determine the locus, or to understand the functional characteristics, of the presumed template mechanisms, and I suggest that the ideas involved in the sensory template idea are too mechanistic and inflexible to encompass the dynamics that are evident in either physiological or behavioral development. As I noted (Petrinovich, 1988, p. 264), "It confuses the issue to use the construct of a template variously as a sensory filter, a genetic blueprint 'to focus the learning bird's attention upon conspecific song models . . . ,' a long-term memory system, and the model in a match-to-sample process."

Alexander (1993) insisted that it is time to replace notions of inherited, genetic, genetically determined, innate, and instinctive behaviors, as well as notions of templates or substrates, with concepts of epigenetic pre-programming. He argued this because he believes the earlier phraseology is vague and leads to erroneous thinking about the interactions of heredity and development, and the nature of phenotypic plasticity.

If an argument is made against a proposed mechanism, then there should be some idea of how the matter might be better conceptualized. Greenough, Black, and Wallace (1987) proposed a classification of the ideas of a sensitive period in a manner that provides a better concept-ualization of the physiological mechanisms involved in regulating the behavior of the developing organism. They introduced the concept of experience-expectant structures designed to utilize environmental infor-mation that is so ubiquitous that it is universal; it invariably occurs in the developmental history of individual organisms, and probably throughout the evolutionary history of the species. These experience-expectant sys-tems are regulated by intrinsically governed generation of an excess of functional connections (synapses) among neurons, with experiential input subsequently determining which of the synapses survive. They suggest there is a second experience-dependent system that involves the storage of information depending on the unique experiences of the individual orga-nism and involving the generation of new synaptic connections in re-sponse to the occurrence of a "to-be-remembered" event.

Greenough, et al. discussed a wide range of behavioral and neurolog-ical evidence supporting their conceptualization, much of it bearing on the development of the visual system in various species, including humans. They considered the advantage of the experience-expectant system to be that sensory systems are free to develop much greater performance capa-bilities by responding to stimulation that would be available in the normal course of the development of all young animals of the species. In this way the genes need only roughly outline the pattern of neural connectivity in a sensory system, leaving the specific details to be determined through the organism's interactions with its environment.

Another fact that plays an important role in this conceptualization is that there is an overproduction of synapses early in development, many of which are lost as development proceeds, with the successful competitors being those that were the most actively utilized by experience-generated neural activity. This competitive retention allows for a great deal of plas-ticity to occur in the course of development. Such developmental plasticity in central neural representation is observed in many species when one sensory modality suffers damage or the organism is deprived of sensory input to the modality.

A further important aspect of this conception of experience-expectant systems is provided by evidence that the maturation of different brain regions takes place at different times for different modalities, allowing an experience-expectant developmental system to provide a basic framework for a subsequent experience-dependent system. John Locke (1993), Direc-tor of the Neurolinguistic Laboratory at Massachusetts General Hospital, has applied these ideas with great success to account for the development of human speech and language, as discussed at length in Chapter 4. Locke adds what he calls an activity-dependent system, by which the activity of the developing organism causes sensory impressions that further the development of critical intermodal associations that are critical to the development of speech and language.

It should be emphasized that the general viewpoint of an experience-expectant system allows for the action of both inherited and experiential influences, but renders meaningless the notion of innate versus learned influences. What is taking place is a continual dynamic interaction between some biased perceptual and motor dispositions that are almost certain to be activated if the human infant is in the nurturant environment necessary for its survival. If the usual array of stimulation is not available completely, because of a defective sensory system, for example, the developing organism is able to use stimulation from other modalities to continue along the path of development. As Locke (1993) emphasized, it is difficult to defeat the specializations for human language development. If an infant cannot hear it can use visual and motor stimulation and still develop a normal language system (sign language) based on the functioning visual and motor modalities.

The Development of Bird Song

Many of the imprinting studies have been concerned with the development of simple behavioral tendencies, such as the following of moving objects and the preference for certain kinds of general stimuli. There are studies in which neonatal experience determines the course of development of more complex behaviors involved in social interactions. One of the most actively studied developmental sequences has been the acquisition of song by young birds. It has been found that many young of many species of birds learn their songs from older birds of the same species (see Kroodsma & Baylis, 1982). Many bird species develop regional song dialects, defined as stable differences in the song types of birds of the same species that are located in particular geographic regions. Among the most intensely studied birds are the European Chaffinch (*Fringilla coelebs*) (Thorpe, 1961) and the White-crowned Sparrow (*Zonotrichia leucophrys*) (Marler, 1970; Petrinovich 1988, 1990). In a number of studies it was found that young White-Crowned Sparrow nestlings that had been raised in acoustic isolation could learn a wide variety songs. The learning could occur during an extensive period of time early in life, given the appropriate conditions. The most effective way to teach a young bird a song is to allow it to have visual interaction with a live bird, permitting some social interaction (Petrinovich, 1990).

When the birds were studied in nature, it was found (Petrinovich, 1988) that young sparrows almost always sing the appropriate song of their species, that their regional dialects change slowly through the years, and that the song of the young birds that settled in the region resembled many aspects of the persisting dialects. It is apparent that early social interactions between young birds and adults provide critical events in the development of this complex behavior that is important in the regulation of social interactions for this territorial species.

Avian Brood Parasites

Among the most fascinating studies of behavioral development are those which have investigated the developmental history of what are known as avian brood parasites. Birds of these parasitic species do not build nests or care for their young but locate the nest of a breeding pair of birds of another species and deposit one or more eggs in that nest. The birds of the host species undertake the chores of incubating the eggs and providing for the care and feeding of the parasite's young.

For example, the parasitic Widow bird (Ploceidae) found in Africa parasitizes different species of finch. An interesting aspect of the social behavior of the young Widow birds involves the ability to recognize not only their own species but the song of the proper host species as well. The recognition of the proper host is important because the young must have physical and behavioral characteristics that resemble several of those pos-sessed by the host young: They must have the proper beak markings, begging calls, juvenile plumage, and they must have a digestive system similar to that of the host species because they are dependent on the type of food the host species parent feeds its young. If the physical resemblance is not close enough the host parents will reject the parasitic young. The problem is that all of the information that must be coded genetically is too complex to be carried on the Y-chromosome of the female, so the male with which the female mates must have the proper genes as well—which means that he was reared by the same host species as was the female.

The parasitic birds' ability to recognize their own species seems to be based on the song of the host species. When the young female parasite is being raised by the hosts she accepts the host song as part of the proper courtship display. When she comes to be of breeding age she hears the host male sing the proper courtship song and observes the host female prepar-ing her nest. When the host male sings, and the host female builds her nest, the female parasite is stimulated to ovulate in synchrony with the host. The male Widow bird, having been raised by the same host species, is stimu-lated by the song of the host male and copulates with the female Widow bird, who is receptive and is performing the proper Widow bird courtship displays in response to the activities of the finch foster father. In this way the parasitic egg is ready at about the time the host female produces her second or third egg. The entire sequence is set off by the host song which starts the courtship behavior of the parasitic species at the proper time, and both the parasite male and female use the song of the host species to regulate their courtship and reproduction. This responsiveness to the specific characteristics of the host song provides a barrier to hybridization with other Widow-Bird populations, the members of which would have specialized on some other host species. The members of this other Widow-Bird population would not have the appropriate genes or the proper early song experience to enable them to be successful parasites of the local host species.

The brood parasites provide an instance in which a female is primed by early social experience to search for a male as a mate who sings the same song as the female's foster father, which signifies that the male was raised with the same host species, but the mate must have the copulatory displays of her own species. Once again complex neonatal social experience directs the course of adult social behavior.

Most of the instances described above illustrate that neonates often imprint on the characteristics of objects that appear early in their life and the neonates behave toward those objects as they would toward a parent or a conspecific. The same phenomenon has been shown for many instances of sexual imprinting, in which a young organism fixates on some characteristic of its own species, and that characteristic determines the qualities the appropriate sexual partner must have. Often the time course of sexual imprinting is different from that for parental imprinting but a similar process in involved.

Instances of Adult Imprinting

Not only do young imprint on the characteristics of adults but it has been demonstrated that adults of some species imprint on the characteristics of the young. I studied the ability of Northern Elephant Seal (*Mirounga angustirostris*) mothers to recognize the distress barks of their own neonate pups, both by making observations and using the playback of tape-recordings of pup calls (Petrinovich, 1974). During the pupping season the pregnant females gather together in a harem controlled by one bull, with a few others hanging around. These peripheral males are able to approach the harem if the harem is large enough to allow the dominant bull to be distracted on some other front. Harem life involves a great deal of turmoil, with males crashing in and out, and a large number of mothers and pups grouped closely together. Observations indicated that there was a strong tendency for a mother to respond positively to her own pup's vocalization and almost no tendency to respond to her pup's call negatively. When tape recordings were played of the distress vocalization of her own pup versus those of alien pups it was found that the mother emitted a pup attraction call to the vocalization of her own pup, but not to the playback of the vocalization of an alien pup.

The adaptive significance of this differential response to the different pup vocalizations can be understood given the social organization of the elephant seal herd. If the neonatal pup is separated from the mother it will be attacked and likely killed by another female, be crushed by a marauding male, or die of starvation because mothers do not usually suckle strange infants. Therefore, it is valuable for the mother to be able to recognize the distress vocalization of her own pup, if the pup is to survive. How could she come to recognize her own pup? Observations suggested that immediately after the pup is born the mother turns to it and emits a pup attraction call which elicits a vocal response from the pup. It is likely that this results in a quick imprinting which enables the mother to recognize her own pup. There is a high probability that when the infant issues its distress call the mother, who is almost always in close contact, will make a pup attraction call and the pup will then move toward the calling mother and survive for the time being. This type of recognition has been demonstrated in other species which tend to live in herds, such as the fur seal (Bartholomew, 1953), and the reindeer (Espmark, 1971). There are many instances in which young imprint on parental characteristics, and others in which the adults also imprint on characteristics of their young, given the proper adaptive conditions.

SUMMARY

In Chapter 2 I argued that the value of employing a naturalistic stance to view the behavior of organisms need not involve committing the naturalistic fallacy. Rather, such a perspective permits an understanding of the problems facing organisms in their efforts to survive and reproduce and gives some insight into the behavioral strategies that are employed to pursue survival, reproduction, and transmission of genes to succeeding generations. Some of the basic concepts that have been developed by evolutionary biologists to understand the development and functioning of organic systems have been sketched in this chapter. The basic factors involved in evolutionary processes and in reproduction have been described and some of the basic ethological mechanisms have been discussed that will be considered, in the next two chapters, to influence the behavior of humans. It has been suggested that the practice of thinking of physiological and behavioral development in terms of nature versus nurture is not a useful mode of approach. An alternative conceptualization was described that utilizes the ideas of experience-expectant, experience-dependent, and activity-dependent systems. The advantage of this conceptualization is that it emphasizes the complex interplay of influences at all stages of development rather than artificially typifying them as independent entities.

4

Evolutionary Mechanisms and Human Behavior

The major question to be addressed in this and the next chapter is, how the basic biological mechanisms described in Chapter 3 influence the development and functioning of the complex types of behavior that characterize human beings and form the foundation for human social behavior.

EVOLVED PROCESSES IN HUMAN BEHAVIOR

How far can basic evolutionary ideas be extended to help us to understand the human condition? Are we, the people, so emergent that we have transcended the basic rules that govern other organic systems, and do we have an essence that, although it might have evolved, has become free to manifest itself through cultural rules that are uniquely independent of biology?

Some Games Reproduction Plays

It has been proposed (Parker, 1982), that the male ejaculates a large number of sperm to enhance the competitive success of that male's sperm, with the male producing the largest number of sperm at each ejaculation being the most successful fertilizer of the female's eggs. However, as Williams (1992) pointed out, with this strategy most of the nearby sperm that will be excluded would be from the same male providing the successful sperm. Arguments have been advanced that Parker's view is too simplistic. The English researchers Baker and Bellis (1988, 1989, 1992) presented evidence obtained in studies of humans, suggesting that a large number of sperm do not function as "egg-getters" (specialized to fertilize eggs), but are either "kamikaze" sperm (specialized to seek and destroy the sperm of other males), or "blocking" sperm (specialized to block out alien sperm from gaining access to the eggs).

The idea that there is competition among sperm has been subjected to empirical test with humans by Baker and Bellis (1993a). They reviewed the research evidence for species ranging from butterflies and beetles to non-human primates and humans and noted that all of the evidence is consistent with the predictions of sperm competition theory: Males inseminate more sperm into the female when the risk of sperm competition is higher. The evidence also suggests that males invest more sperm when the female's reproductive value is higher. They considered four models that have been suggested to account for sperm investment: a fixed inseminate model that proposed there is a fixed number of sperm inseminated during a fixed interval; a physiological constraint model that assumes that males inseminated all of the stored sperm mature enough to be ejaculated at each copulation; a partitioning model that assumes the male allocates sperm to maximize the likelihood of inseminating the female during each fertile phase; a "topping-off" model that assumes the total number of sperm inseminated during a given time interval is not fixed but that males attempt to maintain an optimum-sized population of sperm in their partner's reproductive tract as a defense against sperm competition. The latter view suggests that successive in-pair copulations become "toppings-off" to replace sperm lost since the last insemination.

They concluded that the evidence is most consistent with the topping-off model, with males strategically adjusting the number of sperm ejaculated as a function of the time since last insemination. According to their model the primary trade-off that determines ejaculate size is between the probability that the male will fertilize the female if the insemination does or does not encounter sperm competition, with the optimum number of sperm for each insemination determined simply by the risk of sperm competition. They argue that the male reproductive system has been tuned evolutionarily to maximize the likelihood of reproduction given varying conditions surrounding the copulatory episode.

Baker and Bellis (1993b) argued that the female is not just a passive receptacle in which males play out their sperm competition games. They found, in their studies of the function of female orgasm, that females also have the potential to influence the outcome of the contest in several ways. Female orgasms occur in humans, but there has been little understanding (and until recently not much interest) regarding their function in reproduction. Bellis and Baker (1990, 1992) suggested that the female orgasm can effectively regulate the number of sperm retained at both the current and a succeeding copulation. Their view implicates a hitherto unsuspected active female role that could have major influences on the effectiveness of sperm from different males. The sequence and frequency with which a female copulates with different males, as well as the time interval between in-pair and extrapair copulations, can have a major influence on the outcome of sperm competition in many different species of birds and mammals, including humans.

They identified two favored hypotheses concerning the function of copulatory orgasms in females: the "poleaxe" hypothesis, which suggests that, because it is important for the female to lie down after copulation to reduce sperm loss due to flowback, the orgasm functions to induce fatigue and sleep; the "upsuck" hypothesis, that the orgasm functions to suck up sperm during copulation. Neither hypothesis accounted for the data, and they proposed that the timing of female orgasm is the mammalian female's key instrument in male–female conflict and cooperation, and that it works within the female reproductive tract. They consider nocturnal, masturbatory, and copulatory orgasms to be the primary mechanisms by which the female influences the ability of sperm inseminated in different copulations to remain in, and travel through, her reproductive tract. Their data on the retention of male sperm after copulation led them to conclude that the female strategy is to influence sperm retention differently at successive copulations. Females are able to regulate the number of sperm retained in such a way that the sperm from a first copulation are retained less well than those from a subsequent copulation, and one mechanism producing this regulation is the frequency of intercopulatory orgasms. These organisms would be cryptic to the males, even though the same level of overt copulatory orgasms would be obvious to the males. Thus, the female is able, on any given occasion, to negate the male strategy through her implementation of different extracopulatory orgasm regimes to manipulate the male's sperm. It should be emphasized, again, that these various competitive strategies have developed through the natural selection of characteristics that enhance the reproductive success of individuals who possess such heritable traits, and no conscious intent is implied.

Trivers (1972) developed the argument that the interests of males and females might be quite different depending on the amount of parental investment each has at any given time during the course of a pregnancy. As discussed in Chapter 3, for many bird and mammal species a female has a larger investment than does the male from the moment of insemination. This greater investment should lead the female to engage in different behavioral strategies than the male, and these strategies should be related to the characteristics of the breeding ecology. Trivers (1974) also argued that there should be a conflict between parents and offspring, a conflict that occurs because it is to the benefit of offspring to receive more parental care than parents are prepared to give. The parents should act to benefit their lifetime reproductive success as much as possible, even if the actions are at the expense of the existing young, while the young should act to receive a maximum amount of care and resources for a maximum length of time.

Haig (1993), suggested that there is a complex relationship between a woman and her fetus. Haig's premise is that the evolutionary interests of a mother and her offspring can differ greatly. The fetus benefits by extracting as many resources as possible from the mother, while the mother must strike a balance between nourishing the fetus and keeping some resources for herself, as well as providing for her existing and future children. Maternal genes pay the present cost of pregnancy to gain a future benefit, and natural selection acts to increase the benefit per unit cost. There is, therefore, conflict between what is best for the "mother's genes" and what is best for the "fetal genes." This conflict is also marked by a high degree of interdependence, what Haig has called a conflict of interest within a basically peaceful society.

If the fetus has a genetic or developmental defect that will make it unlikely to survive, then it will be in the interest of the mother's overall reproductive success to miscarry and try to conceive again. However, the interest of the fetus is to survive at all costs, so it should try to prevent the woman's body from miscarrying, because that occurrence would result in a total loss to the fetus. Haig has identified a large number of hormonal and metabolic events in human reproduction that support his interpretation. Analyses in terms of cost-benefit are applicable, even at the earliest stages of fetal development, and the web of interactions is complex indeed.

The phenomenon of pregnancy sickness has been examined from an adaptationist perspective by Profet (1992), who argued that it evolved as a deterrent to the maternal ingestion of teratogens. There is a great deal of evidence indicating that food aversions, nausea, and the vomiting that occurs during pregnancy sickness evolved during the course of human evolution, and Profet interpreted the evidence to support the argument that the function is to protect the embryo against internal ingestion of teratogens and abortifacients, which are abundant in natural foods. She noted that many foods can be safely ingested by adults, but they contain compounds that can be adaptively costly or fatal to embryos; women with pregnancy sickness selectively avoid such things as coffee, bitter tasting food, and strong cooking fumes that emit cues associated with toxicity. Pregnancy sickness begins when the embryo becomes vulnerable to these toxins and ends when the embryonic need for calories becomes greater than its vulnerability to these toxins. The mother's olfactory perceptual system changes during pregnancy in ways that promote selective avoidance of toxins. Women who have moderate or severe pregnancy sickness have a higher pregnancy success rate than those who have mild or no pregnancy sickness. Profet noted that pregnancy sickness is universal across cultures, and interpreted this universality to support the idea that pregnancy sickness conferred a strong and consistent selective advantage on ancestral humans. The environmental cues that elicit pregnancy sickness at the present time are those that would have been associated with toxins in the Pleistocene, suggesting that the taste aversion and sickness mechanisms are evolved adaptations.

To summarize, the available evidence suggests that, starting at the basic level of egg and sperm interactions, processes in both males and females have been selected to enhance both individual and common reproductive interests. Further, the mother and the fetus have both common and conflicting interests, and have evolved mechanisms to serve their particular interests, starting early in fetal development and continuing into later development, when parental investment strategies are brought into play to enhance the lifetime reproductive success of both parents. In addition, there seem to be a set of hormonally triggered mechanisms that influence maternal food choices (and the retention of those foods) in order to protect the young fetus from teratogens and abortifacients, and these mechanisms are active during the time the fetus is most susceptible. These feeding and sickness mechanisms are switched off during the second and third trimesters when the nutritional needs of the fetus become greater and the mother needs nutrients to sustain them both. Even these basic levels of evolved reproductive functioning events can best be understood within the perspective of cost–benefit analyses of the functional interests and strategies of the different players. These basic mechanisms operate in most species, and their manner of operation has been studied carefully within many organic systems.

THE INTERACTION OF BIOLOGICAL AND
EXPERIENTIAL INFLUENCES

Many ethologists and psychologists have argued that species have evolved biological constraints that are appropriate to the ecological features to which that species was adapted evolutionarily. One such universal process is a general associative mechanism. Gallistel, Brown, Carey, Gelman & Keil (1991) more appropriately suggested that learning in animals should be thought of as the product of behavioral mechanisms with elaborated internal structures that have evolved to guide the learning of species-relative features of the environment. In their view it would be productive to consider the nature of general mechanisms that have evolved to regulate the course of development, to examine the functional specializations that are evident, and to identify the underlying mechanisms that produce these specializations.

Cosmides and Tooby (1987) suggested that evolution should have worked its way with underlying behavioral and psychological mechanisms, and not with expressed manifest behaviors. Based on the study of biology and psychology we know that vicariousness of expression is favored so that if one action does not result in a successful outcome, or if it is not possible even to perform that action, other actions can be used. Shepard (1987) agreed that the most important evolutionary structures will be found at the level of underlying cognitive structures rather than at the level of particular, observable responses issuing from those underlying structures. He suggested one general psychological law to be the probability that a response learned to one stimulus will generalize to another, and that the probability of such generalization decreases with the distance between these stimuli, according to an invariant and universal mathematical function. Such a mechanism would support an animal's need to detect differences between the present and an earlier situation in order to appreciate any differential outcomes that might follow one or the other stimulus, and also to enable the animal to decide that two stimuli are similar enough to belong to a single class of objects that predict the same consequences. However, as will be seen when language acquisition is considered, there are powerful content-specific generalization processes that are used to categorize objects in the world.

Evolved cognitive mechanisms could embody knowledge of the enduring regularities of the world and would be engaged in contexts that resemble the natural conditions to which perceptual–representational systems were adapted. These evolved cognitive mechanisms could provide organisms with experience-expectant systems that can be influenced by experience-dependent and activity-dependent systems that function much the same as will be outlined for speech and language development.

I will argue below that the principles applicable to the development of cognition, speech, and language also can be applied to the development of the principles of morality. Perhaps people have a predisposition to adopt some set of principles (not any particular set) that will define the moral system of society and that the exact nature of the system depends on early experience, with these principles reflecting the coordinated influence of the evolved genome and early social interactions.

Some Basic Evolved Processes

Almost everyone accepts the fact that many physiological processes, perceptual mechanisms, and basic aspects of learning involve the operation of innate tendencies. One of the basic behavioral adaptations that almost all animals have is a tendency to orient toward a suddenly appearing stimulus and, if the stimulus is repeated over and again, and is not followed by any particular consequence, the response to the stimulus wanes with repetition—a process called habituation (see Petrinovich [1973a], for a review of this literature). No one seems distressed when it is suggested that this complex mechanism is an evolved process.

Some organisms have receptor elements that react preferentially to selected types of stimulation and are difficult to habituate. For example, frogs have retinal cells that react preferentially to small, fast moving objects (called "bug detectors" by Lettvin, Maturana, McCullough, and Pitts, 1959), and there seems little doubt, or disagreement, that this enhanced responsiveness to prospective food stimuli evolved as an adaptation to environmental conditions. Frogs that sensed insects more efficiently would be likely to be better nourished and able to reproduce more than those that lack the enhanced bug sensitivity. All that remains is to demonstrate that the behavioral disposition is heritable and that reproductive success is enhanced. Animals of many species, including humans, have specialized retinal cells that respond positively or negatively to such things as edges, to lines of certain types, figures of particular shape, objects moving in certain directions; depth of field is perceived without experience.

Humans have mechanisms that "automatically" process certain kinds of visual stimuli preattentively. Such stimuli are said to "pop out" of displays, and the time required to detect these stimuli is independent of the number of elements (Treisman, 1988). Detection of other stimuli requires the use of an attention mechanism that checks each item in the display using a serial search: If there are more elements to be checked, then search time is longer. It can be seen that these simple sensory and perceptual mechanisms could have undergone strong selection and would have conferred a survival advantage in the environment of evolutionary adaptation—for humans the Pleistocene era, during which time humans were organized into small, nomadic hunter–gatherer bands with decentralized authority, generalized reciprocity, little wealth, adult male status equality, and diffuse, flexible interband alliances (Knauft, 1991). At simple functional levels few people reject the argument that these simple processes are evolved content-specific information processing adaptations. Social scientists and humanists, however, become increasingly resistant to extend such arguments much beyond these simple perceptual processes.

Comparative psychologists and ethologists have developed an enormous body of evidence showing that animals of many species not only have specialized detection systems, allowing them to adapt to the demands of the environment, but that they also have content-specific learning mechanisms that enhance the likelihood that certain kinds of events will be learned quickly. It has long been known that insects, for example wasps, require only one exposure to learn the characteristics of the complex gestalt of stimuli surrounding nests containing the larvae they are provisioning. These wasps can learn such characteristics better than members of most avian and mammalian species, but can hardly be characterized as mental giants.

There is evidence for such content-specific learning mechanisms in a wide variety of situations that are critical to the survival of organisms, and that can be presumed to have existed throughout the period of their evolutionary adaptation. These mechanisms include species-specific defense reactions (Bolles, 1970), learned food aversions mediated by taste in rats and vision in birds (Garcia & Brett, 1977), and selective learning of certain sounds by birds (Petrinovich, 1990). When learning mechanisms are studied within the context of the ecology within which organisms exist and cope, it is obvious that searching for content-general "intellectual" mechanisms is not of use in understanding an animal's functioning, any more than trying to understand language development by studying the way humans process nonsense syllables captures the essence of language acquisition and utilization.

THE DEVELOPMENT OF HUMAN SPEECH AND THE BEGINNINGS OF LANGUAGE

Most of the examples of evolutionary mechanisms discussed to this point were based on nonhuman animals. I suggested that one might consider that humans acquire the tendencies on which moral principles are based in much the same way they acquire the ability to comprehend and produce language, especially in the development of speech. There are aspects of human language development that are similar to those outlined above for nonhuman animals.

One of the defining characteristics of all normal human beings is the ability to acquire spoken language, and the development of speech occurs with mere exposure to the sounds of a human language community. The development of the ability to speak a human language does not require any elaborate or systematic teaching, but occurs spontaneously and rapidly, with a strong chronological regularity across languages in the rate of development of speech sounds and the acquisition of various syntactical and grammatical forms. In an insightful review of the role that natural selection plays in the development of natural language, Pinker and Bloom (1990) made the heretical suggestion that the ability to use natural language belongs more to the study of human biology than to human culture, and that the best way to explain the origin of language is through the theory of natural selection. Pinker (1994) has developed and expanded this argument in his book, *The Language Instinct*, adding the comment that language is the most accessible part of the mind; knowledge regarding the working of language will provide insights about human nature.

Ann Fernald (1992) summarized the extensive investigations of the effect of human maternal vocalization to infants. She centered her discussion on the argument that the development and use of these vocalizations (called "motherese," even though fathers use the same vocal patterns) should be viewed as biologically relevant signals that can be understood most adequately from an evolutionary perspective. Fernald noted that, in order to support the argument that this special form of speech is an instinctive caretaking behavior, it is crucial that there be cross-cultural universality in the modulation of the sounds used in infant-directed vocalizations. She reviewed a large number of studies conducted in her laboratory, and those of other researchers, demonstrating that infant directed vocalizations are similar across all cultures examined. These language communities included Latvian, Japanese, Comanche, Sinhala, French, Italian, German, British English, and American English. The infant-directed speech of mothers from all of these language communities have similar characteristics: They have a higher mean fundamental frequency, greater variability of the fundamental frequency, longer pauses, shorter utterances, and more stereotyped, exaggerated, and repetitive fundamental frequency contours. These characteristics of infant-directed speech are evident when mothers address newborns, which argues that the speech patterns are not shaped in response to the reactions of the newborn infants. The use of motherese persists for more than 12 months, and by 18 months of age the infant is beginning to acquire the ability to identify familiar words equally well if presented in either adult-directed or infant-directed speech, although exaggerated intonation patterns are still important and used when the infant is acquiring new words.

Among the illuminating studies of the processes involved in speech development are those conducted by Janet Werker (1989). She noted that adults easily perceive the differences in the speech sounds used to contrast meaning in their own language better than they can perceive the critical sounds in a different language. Infants are able to discriminate all possible phonetic contrasts soon after birth, even though they have never heard them before. By the time they are one year old, they group speech sounds as do the adults of their own language community and have lost the ability to discriminate those sounds that may be critical in other languages.

Werker used a head-turning response to test both babies and adults, and obtained a differential response to repeated versus nonrepeated sounds for both babies and adults. If the sound is repeated the infant habituates to it and a different sound results in a reinstatement of the response. Because infants cannot respond to a question with a "yes" or "no," or understand the instructions to do so, this testing procedure was developed to permit them to indicate whether one sound was the same as another.

Werker and Lalonde (1988) tested babies raised in the English language community with sound contrasts used by both the Hindi and English languages, as well as with sound contrasts used in Hindi but not in English. For the Hindi contrasts 100% of Hindi-speaking adults could discriminate between the sounds that signified important Hindi phonetic distinctions while only about 10% of English-speaking adults could. The interesting fact is that 90% of the 6- to 8-month-old infants also could make the discriminations for both the Hindi and English contrasts. Although almost all of these young "English-hearing" infants could recognize the Hindi contrasts, only 60% of 8- to 10-month-old infants could do so, and only 10% of 10- to 12-month-old infants could—the same percentage as for English-speaking adults. Thus, by 10 to 12 months of age the infants have lost their general ability to discriminate Hindi contrasts, and have begun to respond appropriately to the intonation patterns used in the language community in which they are immersed. It was also found that this loss of the ability to make the fine discriminations between contrasts was specific to speech sounds and did not occur to non-speech sounds. When adults were given several hundred training trials on the Hindi contrasts there was no improvement in their ability to discriminate them. Early in life there is a general sensitivity to all phonemic contrasts that are typical of some existing language, but the auditory system loses its initial plasticity to make auditory discriminations of those speech sounds not important to the language community to which the infant has been exposed.

It has been known for some time that the characteristics of the native language have little influence on the quality of vocal output during the early portion of the babbling stage (Petrinovich, 1972), but have large effects around the time the first word is acquired (again, at about 10 to 12 months of age). Congenitally deaf infants initially babble normally, but their babbling ceases at the age at which normal infants begin echoing sounds they hear. Such findings indicate that the speech system involves an early developmental sequence little influenced by specific experience until a later developmental age has been reached.

Kuhl, Williams, Lacerda, Stevens, & Lindblom (1992) found that, by 6 months of age, infants from two countries (the United States and Sweden) gave evidence they had learned some critical information about their native language. Such research results have been interpreted to mean that, through exposure to the sounds of the local speech community, infants develop a tendency to produce sounds that will be important in the later production of whatever language they have heard, and that, initially, they have a general ability to distinguish between a wide range of potentially significant speech contrasts. This general ability is soon lost and they become specialized in their native language very early, even before they have uttered any meaningful words.

It has been shown that these early developmental effects are not peculiar to speech sounds, also occurring in the language acquisition of deaf children who have been exposed to American Sign Language (ASL) from birth. Petitto and Marentette (1991) found that manual babbling occurs at the appropriate time in these deaf children. By the time the signing infants are 10 months of age, the form, developmental sequence, and organization of their signed babbling is similar to that involved in spoken babbling by hearing children. The babbling structure they observed was tied to the abstract linguistic structure of the native language, just as it was for hearing infants' spoken babbling.

Elissa Newport and her colleagues (Newport, 1991; Meier, 1991) studied children who had learned ASL, and found that the earlier they had been exposed to ASL the better they scored on tests involving the meaning of the advanced, morphologically complex signs in ASL. They also found that those whose native language was ASL did better than those who did not learn ASL until they were a bit older, and they, in turn, were better than those who learned ASL even later in life. Late learners did not entirely lack control over ASL morphology but they did lack the grammatically consistent use of ASL, and were not as skilled at analyzing the structures displayed by native signers.

Newport (1991) studied the ultimate competence achieved in the acquisition of a second language in relation to the age at which people were first exposed to that language. The control over word order and some simple aspects of grammar were the same for native and second language learners who began to learn the language late in life. However, late learners were poorer than early learners in using most aspects of English morphology and syntax, with a gradual decline in performance across the ages of 3 to 17, to a maximally low ability which persisted as far as it was tested (age 39). Newport concluded that language learning abilities are not spared from maturational decline by exposure to another language early in life. As for many other evolved adaptations, language learning ability does not persist throughout the lifetime of the organism.

Pinker (1994, p. 294) described language learning as a "one-shot skill. Once the details of the local language have been acquired from the surrounding adults, any further ability to learn (aside from vocabulary) is superfluous." Pinker also argued that the adaptive language-acquisition circuitry might be expected to be disconnected once it has served its function because having "greedy" neural tissue lying around beyond its point of usefulness incurs too great a cost to be tolerated.

At the 1992 meetings of the American Psychological Association, Newport and Singleton presented an interesting case history of a 9-year-old boy, Simon, who had been born to deaf parents who had not learned to sign as children, and who had acquired ASL imperfectly as teenagers (Kolata, 1992a). The sentences signed by these parents were highly ungrammatical, and almost seemed to be a word salad. Pinker (1994) characterized their signing as similar to that of speakers of pidgin—the type of language that develops when people speaking two different languages come into contact and develop a primitive language in which to communicate. Bickerton (1990) described pidgin languages as having no articles, no prepositions, no complementizers, and no markers of tense or aspect. The few grammatical items that exist are relatively rich in meaning and the language lacks elements whose primary function is structural. Bickerton noted that pidgin languages exist for only a single generation. When the language is acquired by locally born children it becomes a fully developed language with a complete grammar, and is then called a creole language.

Simon was exposed to the parents' grammatically flawed system of sign language, but he came to sign and to understand sentences with correct grammar, even though the only people he had seen signing in ASL signed incorrectly. Pinker (1994) commented that the boy's superiority to his parents represents an example of creolization by a single living child— although the language input the child received was essentially a signed pidgin language he converted it into the proper grammatical forms typical of creole languages.

Pinker (1994) also discussed a region in Nicaragua in which deaf children, who had not learned to sign, had been raised in different villages that were isolated from one another. When a deaf school was opened the children were drilled in lip reading and speech. However, the children invented their own sign system, pooling the idiosyncratic gestures each had developed at home to communicate with their hearing families. This system of signs had all the characteristics of a pidgin language. However, when young deaf children around the age of 4 began joining the school they learned the existing pidgin signing system, but, in addition, created a creole system which all the young shared and which contained many grammatical devices that were absent in the pidgin system. Pinker, once again, considers this to be a true language born before our eyes.

These cases support some of the ideas of the linguist Noam Chomsky (e.g., 1986) who argued that there is an underlying linguistic component in language acquisition (what he called a language acquisition device), and that all languages share universal features. Children are surrounded by errors and incompleteness when learning language, but they display the rich grammatical structure of language correctly, and their competence goes beyond the models to which they were exposed. The cases presented by Newport and Singleton, and discussed by Pinker, are based on normal, rather than feral or abused children, and provide important evidence supporting the idea that there is a universal grammatical structure that will emerge if a developing child is exposed, at an early age, to a natural language, be it signed or spoken.

Pinker and Bloom (1990) noted that parents provide their children with sentences of English, not rules of English, and suggested that natural selection is the programmer. Psycholinguist Studdert-Kennedy (1990) added that the conditions of language acquisition are quite different from those under which language evolved, because contemporarily the child is guided into language by speakers of a fully evolved system.

Studies of deaf users of ASL who had left or right hemisphere brain damage, were done by Poizner, Klima, and Bellugi (1987). Their results indicated that the pattern of loss for these individuals, who communicated using visual–manual modalities, was the same as that found for those who depend on auditory–spoken modalities. Thus, the development of hemispheric specialization for normal language does not depend on auditory input or mode of production, but is specific to the communicative-social abilities that language involves.

The effects discussed here are not peculiar to language systems, but could apply to many kinds of social communication. Pinker and Bloom (1990) pointed out that grammar is a poor medium with which to convey subtle patterns of emotion and that facial expressions and tones of voice are more informative. They based this view on research such as that done by Etcoff and Magee (1992) who studied the categorical perception of facial expression. Etcoff and Magee identified the contrast boundaries between facial expressions that signified happiness, sadness, fear, anger, disgust, and surprise. A century of cross-cultural research, as well as systematic research with human infants, has shown that the same facial movements are used universally to signal emotions. It was demonstrated that the perceptual system is tuned to the particular facial movements that signal these emotions, and that there are boundaries at which a graded series of expressions will be judged suddenly to signal one emotion rather than another. Such boundaries are well established for speech perception and are called phonemic boundaries: A sound is perceived as a *p* over a range of physical sounds and, at the phonemic boundary, is suddenly perceived as a *b*. There is no intermediate state when a person hears something between a *p* and a *b*. Similar results were found with facial expressions, suggesting that the results found with verbal and visual language systems might apply to many kinds of communicative systems, both cognitive and emotional.

The Development of Spoken Language

Two exciting books have appeared that present a comprehensive view of speech and language development in humans, both of which support, extend, and consolidate some of the views I have been suggesting here and which I will extend in Chapter 9. The first book, *The Child's Path to Spoken Language* (1993), is an insightful treatise by Locke, who has summarized and organized a vast body of research and conceptions concerning the salient factors guiding the development of human speech and early aspects of language. The second book, *The Language Instinct* (1994), is by Pinker, and presents a wise, argumentative, and witty discussion of psycholinguistics and language development which has a strong emphasis on the insights of Noam Chomsky. Pinker extended Chomsky's arguments by developing an evolutionary hypothesis that language is an instinct that has developed as an expression of "mentalese," which he defines as the hypothetical language of thought that is couched in the brain.

Locke considered data regarding normal human development, development in humans with impaired processing systems, and information regarding the nature of the underlying neurophysiological systems. Because his views are congruent with those I am developing here, I will present a detailed summary of those arguments. I will only touch on the major points of his presentation and consider a few general conclusions. Those interested in pursuing the complete arguments, and the research evidence on which these arguments are based, should consult Locke's scholarly discussion.

Both Locke and Pinker emphasize a crucial distinction between the principles involved in the development of speech (which initially serves social communication) and those involved in the development of language (which involves the grammatical analysis of words and the development of syntax). I will emphasize the development of speech, because it is these phonological aspects that are central to my arguments regarding the emotional attachments that form between the developing infant and the social community, especially as represented by the mother. This analysis emphasizes the importance of the developing pattern of sound production and comprehension by the infant, and is only secondarily involved in the development of grammar or syntax—aspects of language that deal with meaning. The development of syntax has received the most attention by and elicited extensive disputes among psycholinguists. For example, the review of the development of natural language by Pinker and Bloom (1990) was 20 pages long, elicited 31 commentaries in response (38 pages), and their response to these commentaries occupied 12 pages. Both Studdert-Kennedy (1990) and Lieberman (1990) remarked that the review by Pinker and Bloom placed a heavy emphasis on syntax and relatively little on phonology. I intend to shy away from the conceptual minefield involving the development of syntax because my concerns are the early processes involved in the development of phonology which, as Studdert-Kennedy noted, is logically prior to syntax, perhaps evolved earlier, and still develops earlier in the child.

Lieberman (1990) noted that the preadaptations basic for the brain mechanisms underlying human syntactic ability involve the precise motor control required for speech. Whenever meaning does not determine word order, it is necessary to examine articulatory events to understand the order in which many words are produced in speech (Pinker, 1994). The underlying mechanism seems to be based on how the tongue produces vowels; the mind does not just "flip a coin" when ordering words. For example, there is a uniformity in saying compound words such as "razzle-dazzle," "superduper," "hocus-pocus," "namby-pamby," and the like. Why are these words pronounced in this order by everyone, Pinker asks. The answer is that the word obstructing the flow of air the least always comes before the word beginning with the more obstruent consonant. There is uniformity in pronunciation, although no one is taught it, no cognitive decision is required, and when new compound words are formed everyone will form them the same way. This could be an instance of an evolved process which was not a primary adaptation produced by natural selection, but which occurred due to structures that developed for other reasons.

I will focus most of the following discussion on those events that support the development of a social contract between the infant and the community. It is the public establishment of social bonds that I argue, in Chapter 9, signals the beginning of personhood, and the regularity involved in the development of phonology provides the stable and universal input required to sustain this important biological event.

The processes involved in speech begin to develop prenatally, with the fetus being especially sensitive to tones that are in the range of the fundamental frequencies of the mother's voice. Studies have shown that, beginning at about 26 weeks, the fetus is responsive to sounds in the frequency range around 250 Hz. The mother's voice rises about 24 dB above background noise in that portion of the sound spectrum when the mother speaks at a normal, conversational volume, and voices produced ex utero at the same intensity exceed background sound levels in the uterus by about 8 to 12 dB. In the last trimester the heart beat of the fetus habituated to a vocal stimulus (e.g. [babi]) but responded once again with a heart beat deceleration when the stimulus was changed (e.g., to [biba]). Such dishabituation indicates that the observed habituation is not due to a general decrement in sensitivity or to a fatigue of the motor response system, but is a stimulus specific decrease.

Some prenatal experiences influence the neonate's early postnatal behavior. Newborns prefer the sound of the maternal heart beat, which would have been experienced prior to birth, to the sound of the father's voice, which would have been experienced little, if at all, and prefer the mother's voice over strange male and female voices which, in turn, are preferred over quiet. Neonates can discriminate between the mother's voice and that of another mother, and can discriminate between sounds of the language spoken by the mother and other languages.

In general, a picture emerges that human infants enter life with strong perceptual biases and motoric dispositions which represent both experience-expectant and experience-dependent systems, and that the infant's own behavior prompts caregivers (especially the mother) to provide physical, social, and vocal information that will form the linguistic system that Locke considers to be the very definition of what it means to be human. The newborn's preference for the mother's voice selectively orients it to the source of that voice, which leads to an emotional attachment between the neonate and coarse visual characteristics of the primary caregiver, almost always the mother. As mentioned above, it has been suggested that the vocal motherese used by both males and females when interacting with infants, is quite similar across a number of disparate languages and cultures.

Pinker and Bloom (1990) reasoned that, within a group of interdependent and cooperating individuals, the states of other individuals are among the most significant things in the world that the infant and its caretakers must know about. They also noted that such communication should involve minimal ambiguity as a function of context, encoding and decoding should be done rapidly by these young creatures that have developed only a limited capacity for short-term memory, and the code used should be one that is shared by an entire community of potential communicants.

Locke also argued that the function of the early speech system is to develop an emotional attachment between the neonate and the mother, a point whose significance I discussed in the preceding chapter. The beginnings of this social attachment are evident at birth, and the critical events involve an interaction between visual stimuli and the sounds of speech.

When the mother vocalizes it has been demonstrated that the neonate fixates on the talking face, which responds to the fixation by engaging in vocal behaviors having a higher fundamental frequency and exhibiting more exaggerated frequency variations than does the mother's ordinary adult speech. There appear to be universal speech patterns that are used to express praise, soothing, and disapproval, and infants respond to these prosodic differences in an appropriate manner (see, Bloom, [in press], for a review of this literature). It has also been suggested that the patterns of exaggerated intonation might give infants clues as to how to parse adult utterances, which could help them acquire the syntactic structure of their language. Bloom noted that the speech mothers direct to children is virtually perfect from a grammatical standpoint, which supports the idea that motherese provides children with a reliable source of positive grammatical tokens. Locke cited data indicating that synthetic sound contours, which have the extreme pitch variations typical of motherese, evoke pleasant emotions, even in adult subjects. These adults associated the sounds with happiness, interest, and surprise.

Locke reviewed data showing that newborns as young as 9 minutes old, and before they saw any human faces without surgical masks, looked significantly longer at simple drawings of human faces that represented reasonably normal, though stylized, facial features than they did at drawings in which the features were scrambled, and faces with scrambled features were preferred to the unfilled outline of a face. At an average age of 37 minutes it was shown that a moving facelike pattern elicited more visual following than a nonfacelike pattern. At 45 hours of age newborns looked longer at the face of the mother than at the face of other adult females, and the preference was even stronger if they also heard the mother's voice. These strong visual effects appeared even though the neonate is visually alert only about 3% of the time, indicating that the learning of the characteristics of the mother's face and the association of that voice with its sound take place rapidly. Locke noted that, by the end of the second day of life, most neonates recognize the face, voice, and odor of their mother, which ensures that the infant bonds with the mother under the normal nurturant circumstances that prevail in early life.

At 45 minutes of age infants who have not yet seen their own face can imitate at least three facial gestures: protruding the lips, opening the mouth, and sticking out the tongue. Locke invoked the idea that this "contagious" effect is a social process by which behaviors spread, and that this is the beginning of a developmental progression that eventuates in the capacity to share in group life.

When the mother speaks, 3- to 5-week-old infants fixate mainly on the edges of her face, somewhat on the eyes, and much less on the nose and mouth. At 7 weeks the infants mostly fixated on the eyes, then edges, and still very little on the nose and mouth. Locke interpreted these data to mean that the eyes become "social organs" that convey interest, excitement, and other basic emotional states. From the standpoint of the adult speaker the mother's vocal behavior is talk in the sense of language, but from the standpoint of the infant the thing conveyed is emotion (much as it is for adults who do not understand a given language, or for the family dog who responds to vocalizations as signals).

In Locke's view, these young infants are not acquiring language but are displaying a number of communicative behaviors, and are using this communicative foundation to identify people by voice. Tooby and Cosmides (1990b) noted that these innate aspects of speech perception exploit standard and recurrent statistical regularities and universal properties of pronunciation and word formation across human languages, and that these universals are produced by such factors as the properties of the human articulatory apparatus, as noted above when discussing Pinker's views. Tooby and Cosmides emphasized that it is important to activate these human information processing mechanisms during the early interaction between mother and child. The events that occur following birth are universal, and they reliably identify situations that would have occurred throughout human evolutionary history, with all participants making similar construal of the situation and responding to them in similar ways.

These early discriminations precede learning the identity of vowels or the development of the ability to discriminate between different vowels. Learning about vowel sounds represents developmental additions piled on top of the prosodic (the natural changes in vocal pitch, intensity, and timing), affective, and speaker-identifying cues that form the infralinguistic core of vocal messages.

Fernald (1992) outlined a four stage model that summarizes the multiple developmental functions of intonation in adult speech that is directed to infants throughout the first year of life. Her model provides a concise summary of the communicative functions of infant-directed speech in all known spoken languages. A first level has the prelinguistic function of using the infant's predisposition to respond differentially to certain prosodic characteristics of infant-directed speech. These maternal vocalizations function as unconditioned stimuli to alert (high frequency sounds with a gradual rise-time in intensity) or to soothe (continuous, low frequency sounds, especially white noise, such as "shhh").

At a second level the melodies of maternal speech are increasingly effective to direct infant attention and to modulate arousal and emotion. Over the first 6 months of life the infant's visual capabilities and motor coordinations improve, the infant can recognize individual faces and voices more quickly, and the social smile in response to voices and faces appears more frequently. The infants prefer infant-directed to adult-directed speech sounds, whether they are natural or artificially generated.

At this level the mother's speech not only captures attention, but also evokes emotion in the infant. For the first 6 months infants are more responsive to voices than to faces, but, at about 7 months of age, they reliably recognize happy and angry facial expressions. By 5 months infants from monolingual English-speaking families respond only to infant-directed speech used in approval and prohibition, but respond to this infant-directed speech if it is spoken in any of several languages, which argues that it is the prosodic elements, rather than the meaning, that are important.

A third level involves the communication of intention and emotion, with the vocal and facial expression of the mother providing the infant initial access to the feelings and intentions of others. The infant begins to interpret the emotional states of others and to make predictions about the future actions of others, using vocal and facial expression.

At a fourth level prosodic elements are accepted as markers to help the infant identify linguistic units within the stream of speech. As Fernald phrased it, words begin to emerge from the melody. At 15 months of age infants recognize familiar words better in infant-directed speech, but by 18 months can identify familiar words equally well in adult-directed and infant-directed speech, although the exaggerated tone of infant-directed speech can aid the acquisition of new words.

Locke invoked a domain-specific mechanism he called a Specialization in Social Cognition (SSC) which plays an enabling role in the development of spoken language. Neonates orient to facelike stimuli just minutes after birth and fixate on the expressive face.

Infants and their mothers tend to gaze together at the same things, which leads to a shared reference because the mothers tend to name whatever the infant is looking at. In the first week of life infants demonstrate a preference for the mother's voice and for patterns of maternal prosody capable of distinguishing between languages. They also learn the art of vocal turntaking which provides a frame within which vocal dialogue can develop. The utterances by a child at this developmental stage are formulaic in the sense that they represent associations mechanically built up, are noncomputational (unlike the computational nature of true linguistic structures), and are nonrule governed. Long stretches of speech might be produced by infants, but these are based on the infant's love of melody and prosody, and not on the expression of an underlying grammar. Up to this point, the pattern of development seems to unfold uniformly and a set of emotional relationships and expectations have been developed which set the state for the development of language.

Early Stages of Language Development

Locke argued that a major step toward the development of language and syntax occurs when a Grammar Analysis Module (GAM) becomes active at about 28 months of age. The signs that this stage has been reached are that children string words together in novel and variable combinations, they overregularize verbs, and display regressions in the use of plural and past tense forms. Locke regards these regressions to represent the beginning of new ways of doing linguistic business. This view differs a bit from that of Pinker (1994), who argues that the universal language module is hard-wired at the outset, and that infants are equipped with basic linguistic skills, being able to put words together at 18 months of age.

Locke considers the GAM to have no data acquisition device but to construct grammar and rules from the utterances that are heard. When the GAM becomes active a multiplicity of categorical phonetic cues are piled on top of the prosodic, affective, and speaker-identifying cues the individual has developed under the guidance of the SSC. The GAM makes it possible for the listener to know both what a speaker is saying and what is intended in the saying. As Locke (1993, p. 355) phrased it, "The listener is thus able to hear conflicts between 'the words' and 'the music' of spoken language."

In Locke's view, the SSC is a mechanism humans share with many other animal species, but the GAM is a uniquely human attainment and is based on a series of neurological developments that do not occur in other species. I will consider some of the relevant neurological data in Chapter 9. Locke argued that this conception of two different systems in humans permits the SSC to share pseudolinguistic behaviors with the other primates (and perhaps dolphins; Herman, Kuczaj, and Holder, 1993), but the GAM is left in the clear "to do with purity the only language things that it does at all—grammatical analysis and computation." Both Locke's and Pinker's models avoid viewing nonhuman language systems as representing only some proportion of a language module—a view they find nonsensical and nonparsimonious.

An interesting aspect of Locke's view of the development of the speech system is that executive control over the precursors of language acquisition reside primarily in the child rather than being entrusted to the environment. He refers to this control system as the activity-dependent system. Infants are preadapted to process phonetic cues and only a brief early experience with speech is sufficient to activate and stabilize the pre- and neonatal biases that are present. Human infants are preadapted to indexical and effective communication, and under the direction of the activity-dependent system; babies tend to look and listen when family members speak.

Locke (1993, p. 107) summarized the linguistic significance of mother–infant interactions as follows:

> When infants become *attached* to their mothers many language-critical processes are encouraged: the desire to engage in playful vocalization, including vocal exploration, the emergence of turn taking and dialogue structure, and the desire to imitate vocal patterns. In turn, mothers who are attached to and feeling nurturant toward their infants provide them with a number of opportunities to learn. Among the other processes encouraged by attachment are the use of eye gaze and manual gestures to signal attentional focus and convey labels, and the use of voice to designate and convey. Attachment is a powerfully enabling construct that conspires with other factors to set it all in motion.

There is a long period during which the infant is able to sense the world, but to do little in the way of direct manipulation of it. This period is characterized by an active vocal and visual interaction of infants and caregivers with one another. These interactions establish the foundation for general social behavior. The set of experiences involved in this early period of life will be experienced by all infants in the normal course of development of the language system. The critical genetic influences and environmental events are available to all normal members of the species. The research evidence indicates that, even if adequate stimulation is lacking, infants engage in behaviors (such as babbling more in the quiet) that provide self-stimulation sufficient to overcome the lack of externally provided stimulation. The model being described here is one that conceives the role of the infant as an active one, involving an active participation in the structuring of its environment. This view is highly preferable to a passive one, in which parents are considered as providing their children with both genes and an environment conducive to the development of a particular trait, or to a reactive one, in which other people are considered as producing an environment for the child that reinforces endogenous tendencies.

The result of these universal and active processes is that the speech and language systems are robust and are buffered against physical, physiological, and environmental interference, as any system must be if it is to constitute the foundation of the uniqueness of human communication and culture. As long as an infant has access to nurturant talkers (or signers) the capacity for spoken (or signed) language will be realized, and such access is almost inevitably provided if the infant is to survive.

All natural languages are preferentially spoken rather than signed if the developing individuals have normal hearing and speech capabilities. No human culture has developed anything other than spoken language because there are early biases toward vocal and visual modalities. If the auditory channels are not available to the developing individuals, then a signed language is learned as rapidly as a spoken one, and the signed language carries information that is as complex as the spoken one. Locke attributes this ability to develop an alternative signed language to reflect the tendency of all infants to assimilate environmental stimulation using the channels available to them. In the usual situation communication, as well as the underlying neural development, is biased toward sound.

THE EVOLUTION OF HUMAN LANGUAGE

The studies discussed in this chapter indicate that, with both spoken and signed languages, a child easily can gain native competence in a language if it is exposed to that language early in life. These conclusions are supported by the results of studies of the perception of socially significant facial expressions and by studies of the development of many social behaviors observed in nonhuman animals in the laboratory and field. Thinking of behavioral development as a continuous pattern of interactions that exploit predispositions between genetic instructions, experience-expectant, experience-dependent, and activity-dependent systems is compatible with Williams' (1992) argument that one should think of biological development in terms of a whole, active organism in a constant material flux with its environment, and that the organism is not an object, but a region in which certain processes take place.

Pinker (1994) has made some major advances toward identifying the processes in language that constitute the human Universal Grammar. He has argued his model in enough detail to strengthen the position that complex language is an adapted evolutionary mechanism selected during the period of evolutionary adaptation. It is clear that language development (except for learning vocabulary) cannot be characterized as a process regulated by content-general learning mechanisms. No human-made computer model can match a human in decoding speech because, as Pinker noted, the artificial systems are frustrated by a trade-off: If a system has to be able to listen to many different people, then it can recognize only a small number of words, and if it is to recognize a large number of words, then it has to be trained to the voice of one single speaker.

Speech is not only the fastest way of "getting information into the head through the ear," as Pinker phrased it, but it also takes a continually graded phonemic system and converts it automatically into a series of discrete phonemes with very sharp boundaries. The difference between the computer and people is that the computer excels at the memory part of language learning, the part that is hard for people but which is of little use in language acquisition. The part that is easy for people, and hard for a computer, is to make the decisions required to understand a sentence. This process requires a determination of what to use next and when to use it in order to build additional parts of a developing sentence. These decisions require a strategy whereby an analysis that seems to be working is pursued as long as possible, but when it cannot be fitted into the developing tree of the sentence, the sentence parser must backtrack and start over with a different possible tree. The computer has great difficulty with this process. These considerations all argue that there must be specialized processors in the untutored human mind that do not depend on mere computing power in order to succeed.

The content-general learning models that have been suggested to account for language learning require that the child be presented with models to copy, and be reinforced for proper utterances but not for improper ones. A process of generalization is invoked whereby categories of "correctness" are constructed on the basis of the similarity of new utterances to those already encountered. This idea is not adequate to the task. Some innate computational mechanisms are required that use a fixed set of mental categories to define which sentence is similar to which others. Part of these computations involve the grammatical category of noun, verb, and auxiliary, which will be discussed below when considering the word "fish."

I pointed out that one of the most effective ways to communicate with infants is through the use of motherese, even at the late developmental periods when new, meaningful words are being acquired. Yet, motherese is a lousy grammatical model: It doesn't display many aspects of grammar, lacking such things as compounds that contain plurals. The idea that children acquire grammar by being differentially reinforced when they copy utterances of various types boggles the mind, given that children whose parents speak nongrammatical pidgin are able to develop a grammatical creole language; and it makes no difference whether the language is spoken or signed.

Pinker developed another argument that poses difficulties for a content-general learning mechanism. There are three ways to inflect a noun: for example, dog, dogs, dog's. It has been estimated that a typical child in high school has learned something like 20,000 nouns. If all of the possible combinations had to be learned separately it would require about 140 million exemplar sentences which, at the rate of one sentence every 10 seconds, 10 hours a day, would take a century. Not a likely scenario. However, if the child is programmed to label all nouns as such, and all noun phrases as such, the child only has to hear about 25 different kinds of noun phrases, learn the nouns one by one, and the millions of possible combinations become available automatically. Through simple innate programming the child is able to gain the ability to produce an infinite number of sentences. Pinker notes that this ability is one of the quintessential properties of grammar and characterizes first-language learning.

To be understandable, words must be couched as grammatical categories, such as noun, verb, and auxiliary, rather than as actual words. Pinker argues that the word "fish" as a noun, and "fish" as a verb must be kept in separate categories. If they are categorized separately there is no confusion between "Jane likes fish" and "Jane might fish." These categories are built into the vehicles of memory and context, and people have a tendency to look for phrases and use them as the basic element of analysis.

What are some of the important preadaptations that would have made it possible for a Universal Grammar to evolve? Among them would be the ability to record which element comes before which others, and the ability to define and identify the elements through the use of a cognitive module. Such abilities are shared with other people in the community, enabling children to learn the variable parts of language in a manner ensuring that their grammars are synchronized with that of their community. Different languages have appeared because communities of speakers become isolated. The differences between languages include such things as the elimination of ambiguity by developing a strong reliance on word order in some, others use case markers, and still others use different phrase structure rules. Chomsky suggested that children are born knowing super-phrase structure rules, and they only have to learn whether their particular language uses a rule that considers the head of the sentence first, as in English, or last, as in Japanese. This they can do merely by noticing whether a verb comes before or after its object in any sentence that appears in their parents' speech. As Pinker noted, huge chunks of grammar are available to the child all at once, which means that they are not acquiring dozens or hundreds of rules; they are just setting a few mental switches.

The next question concerns the possibility that such complex mental machinery could have arisen through the process of natural selection. This is similar to the question Darwin considered regarding whether it was possible for an organ as complex as the eye to have arisen through the gradual steps required by the evolutionary process. Darwin reasoned that the very excellent eye descended from those possessed by a long line of ancestors that saw a bit better than their rivals, which allowed them to outreproduce those rivals. Those random variants in the quality of vision that improved seeing (providing they were heritable) were retained and improved over the ages, leading to better and better eyes. As Pinker (1994, p. 361) expressed it, "The ability of *many* ancestors to see a bit better in the past causes a single organism to see extremely well now." In Pinker's view, natural selection is the only respectable alternative to a view relying on divine creation, because none of the alternative explanations that have been proposed can do much more than suggest such things as the importance of the random grouping produced through genetic drift. The idea that the complexity of the eye could have come about by such a happy grouping of coincidences is infinitesimally small. The only viable alternatives are Darwin or Deity.

Language is another highly complex "organ system" composed of many parts with an adaptive complexity. Pinker (1994, p. 362) identifies a number of these complexities: syntax, with its discrete combinatorial system, building phrase structures; morphology, a second combinatorial system building words; a capacious lexicon; a revamped vocal tract; phonological rules and structures; speech perception; parsing algorithms; and learning algorithms. These parts are physically realized as intricately structured neural circuits, laid down by a cascade of precisely timed genetic events. It seems highly unlikely that "the pitiless laws of physics" could have done us the favor of hooking up that circuitry so that we could communicate with one another in words. Pinker argues that selection favored those speakers in each generation that the hearers could best decode, as well as those hearers who could best decode the speakers. This process of natural selection led to the development of a Universal Grammar.

Innateness and Social Cognition

The evidence discussed above pertains to language acquisition, and was developed through a great deal of experimentation and theorizing by those who work within psycholinguistics, one of the most active branches of the cognitive sciences that deal with natural behavior. Those scientists have quite effectively utilized the power of the principle of natural selection to generate testable alternative hypotheses. Many social scientists, however, display a tendency toward biophobia and intellectual isolationism, which Tooby and Cosmides (1992) argue has become more extreme with time. What Tooby and Cosmides characterize as the Standard Social Science Model insists that genetic variation is not able to explain the claimed fact that many behaviors are shared within groups of people, but not between groups. This standard model argues that inputs are everywhere the same, although adults everywhere differ in behavioral and mental organization. It is argued that these differences are produced by cultural events that are extragenetic. The generators of complex and meaningful organization in human life are considered to be emergent processes whose determinants are realized at the group level of sociocultural events. Thus, human nature is an empty vessel waiting to be filled, another tabula rasa on which the hand of experience can write. The standard model argues that human evolution has progressed to a point where, although natural selection was involved at one time, the influence of genetically determined systems of behavior has now been removed and replaced with general-purpose learning mechanisms using content-independent cognitive processes.

The arguments of this standard model should be challenged: It is clear that organ systems, physiological mechanisms, reproductive strategies, sensory and perceptual mechanisms, and even emotional responsiveness and human language can be considered as adaptations that have appeared through natural selection. They might well be secondary adaptations of Gould's exaptations that developed to serve other purposes, or as functionless concomitants of developments that were adaptations to other demands.

Cosmides and Tooby (1992), as well as Gigerenzer and Hug (1992), have conducted a series of studies indicating that, when cognitive behaviors are representative of those that would be adaptive within the human natural ecology, the standard, domain-general model of problem solving fails. One of the most important processes used to explain the evolution of social cooperation and competition is that of inclusive fitness, on which is built the idea that one contributes one's genes to succeeding generations, not only by enhancing direct genetic contributions, but by behaving in ways that enhance the genetic contribution of relatives, and even of members of the social community who could reciprocate any aid given them should the need arise. The centrality of this process leads to the prediction that cognitions involving social exchanges, having undergone selection pressure for many thousands of years, should display design features that are particularly appropriate in dealing with problems involving social exchange. Individuals should be especially adapted to reason in certain ways when social contracts are involved, and should be especially attuned to detect cheating, which is a violation of a social contract. People should be able to reason more efficiently when solving problems that require the detection of rule violations involving social contracts than when the same formal rule violations do not involve social contracts.

Social contract theory was the only one of several alternatives evaluated that was able to account for the consistently better performance on problems involving social contracts. The alternative theories considered, and rejected, were those involving pragmatic reasoning schemas and availability, appealing to the amount of experience people have with the content involved (see Gigerenzer and Hug, [1992], for a description and discussion of these theories). People have inference procedures that are specially applied to social contract problems. They are especially able to detect cheaters, leading them to perform much better on those tasks than on problems that involve the same formal logical steps but which do not involve social contracts. They also perform well on problems that are posed in a perspective in which the person is in a position where a cheater should be detected than in one in which the person is only searching for information regarding the operative rule.

An interesting report that was published by Damasio, Grabowski, Frank, Galaburdo, & Damasio (1994) provides some speculative support for the idea that social contracts might have an anatomical modularity, and that these social contracts involve one unit of what we consider ethical behavior. These investigators used computer imaging techniques to reconstruct the brain damage suffered by a patient who has fascinated researchers for many years. In 1848, Phineas Gage suffered an industrial accident in which a metal rod that was an inch and a quarter in diameter was propelled into his face just under his left cheek, entering behind his left eye, and exiting through the top of his skull. Mr. Gage survived and recovered with his speech, memory, and intellectual functioning intact; however, he was characterized as irreverent and capricious. Before the accident he was described as a socially responsible person who was well liked by those who knew him, while afterward he began using profane language, lied to his friends, and could not be trusted to honor social commitments.

Damasio et al. reconstructed the damage to Gage's brain and showed that it involved the ventral and medial sectors of both frontal lobes. This pattern of damage has been noted by Damasio et al. to produce behaviors in the living patients they have studied that were similar to Gage's: problems making rational decisions in personal and social matters, difficulty processing emotions, and becoming generally untrustworthy. It can be speculated that there is an anatomical system that could have developed as the result of evolutionary selection to enable people to more efficiently solve problems involving social contracts. This ability to engage in social communication and to understand social obligations could well be evolved mechanisms that are involved in the development of human moral systems.

There undoubtedly are domain-general mechanisms as well, such as those used in rote memory (for example, a short-term memory load of seven plus or minus two) and in the attribution of cause, and these mechanisms are deployed generally. However, there are also a multitude of domain-specific mechanisms that have been selected to enhance the adaptation of organisms coping with evolutionarily significant problems. The significance of these mechanisms can best be understood as adaptations to the representative environments in which animals developed and adapted, and with which they now cope. Once we understand the functional significance of behaviors and cognitions we can better move to analytic studies to discover the ways in which they accomplish their function.

SUMMARY

The theory and data discussed in this chapter support the argument that some of the basic mechanisms outlined in Chapter 3 can be brought to bear in order to gain an understanding of the functioning of humans. There is little doubt that the basic processes in reproduction can be understood using an evolutionary cost–benefit analysis, and that sensory and perceptual systems have evolved specializations that would enhance the reproductive success of those who have those specializations. Such basic processes as habituation, attention, and content-specific learning mechanisms clearly are evolved adaptations.

The major portion of this chapter was devoted to a consideration of the development of human speech and language because these developmental process are a universal characteristic of all humans and represent rather unique attainments. The mechanisms that are involved in the development of speech and language can provide a useful model to understand the evolution of complex behaviors, extending from the general processes involved in the communication of emotion and specialized adaptations enabling complex grammar to develop, to context-specific cognitive systems that are activated whenever social contracts are involved. It was suggested, and will be discussed further in the next chapter, that such social contracts are involved in basic human socialization and could well be the evolved foundations of moral systems.

5

The Evolved Human
Social Condition

In this chapter I will extend the argument begun in Chapter 4 to aspects of
human behavior that involve the interaction of organisms with other organisms, all coping with the demands of the environment. These aspects
often are considered to require a set of emergent cultural mechanisms
freed from biology.

BASIC THEORY AND DATA

The Environment of Evolutionary Adaptation

There seems to be a consensus that the early human communities
consisted of relatively small breeding populations of related individuals.
If so, chance historical factors would be expected to have played an important role in determining the characteristics of the different breeding
groups (demes) due to sampling variability from the pool of available
genotypes on which the forces of selection could work. Because of such
sampling variability, the pioneers constituting each deme should have a
different response to any new ecological niches they come to occupy. It
might be expected, then, that the contemporary human gene pool would
have survived the tests of a wide range of environmental factors; the norm
of reaction should have been established and tested within a wide range
of ecological circumstances.

As mentioned in Chapter 3, sexual reproduction tends to prevail in
old, stable environments, especially if the organisms involved are large

and complex, as is the case with *Homo sapiens*. Because humans have a relatively long generation time, diversity would be important to defeat short-lived parasites, and sexual recombination would permit the intergenerational repair of deleterious mutations. Many factors seem to favor sex for humans and it would seem that sex is here to stay.

When reflecting on the nature of human biological predispositions it is important to reconstruct the nature of the probable social environment of evolutionary adaptation for humans. It is generally agreed that at the time human nature evolved, the reproductive system was one in which mateships were predominantly monogamous, paternal investment was important to enhance the survival of young, and the variance in reproductive success was slightly greater among men than among women. Such a system is found in almost all relict human societies occupying nonagricultural ecological niches, with a similar pattern characterizing the reproductive system throughout the wide diversity of cultural and technological situations that now exist. Wilson and Daly (1992, p. 254) suggest that this affords "windows on the sociosexual milieu in which the human mind evolved and on the adaptive problems to which our species-typical social and sexual motives, emotions, and way of thought constitute the solutions."

The complex agricultural and industrial societies humans now occupy are very different from the environments of evolutionary adaptation. Yet, no matter what the structures of current societies there seem to be common threads concerning aspects of sociosexuality. Some of these universal structural characteristics concern such things as the existence of a pair bond with mutual obligation which persists over prolonged periods of time, it is blessed by the rest of society, and there are codes to legitimize the offspring of the pair. Halliday (1980) suggested that even anatomical characteristics such as the sturdier physique of men could have developed to enable a man to fulfill his parental role in a mating alliance, as well as for the usually emphasized reason that these physical characteristics exist in the interests of competition between men for the possession of women. Recent anthropological evidence indicates that the size dimorphism for our precursors, *A. africanus*, was very great (men being as much as twice as large as women) which argues that these tendencies were of even greater importance in the early developmental history of humans.

Not only are universal structural characteristics found within human societies but there are universal behavioral tendencies as revealed by patterns of homicide (Daly & Wilson, 1988, 1990), different patterns of jealousy shown by men and women (Wilson & Daly, 1992), sex differences in the characteristics preferred for mates (Buss, 1989, 1994), and in differential reproductive strategies employed by males and females (Kenrick & Keefe, 1992).

Patterns of Homicide

Daly and Wilson (1988) developed a selectionist argument to understand patterns of human homicide. They analyzed extensive police files for Canada and the city of Detroit, supplemented by available data from other cities and countries, and examined existing ethnographic data. Without going into detail, their extensive and detailed analyses support the hypothesis that, as an evolutionist would expect, there are few instances where close genetic kin are killed, because such killing would lower inclusive fitness. Conflicts tended to be increasingly severe and dangerous the more distantly related were the principals. When homicides did occur between cohabitants the victims were seldom genetic kin.

In general, their analyses supported several conclusions. Selection shapes behavioral control mechanisms to increase fitness, to enhance nepotism, and to enable individuals to be effective reproductive competitors. Species-typical motives have evolved to promote genetic posterity such that murder is rare among genetic relatives. When infanticide occurs by males it is generally when paternity is uncertain, when the child is of poor phenotypic quality, or it is unlikely to survive. The risk of infanticide is greater at all ages when there is a stepparent than when there are two natural parents. When infanticide occurs by natural parents the rate is greater early in the infant's life (when parental investment is still low). There is also a sex difference in human competition and violence in terms of reproductive competition. When homicide occurs between individuals of the same sex there is an extremely high incidence of male–male homicide as compared to female–female (a ratio of about nine to one). The pattern of male–male homicide supports the hypothesis that men compete for control over reproductive capacities of women and that children are the currency regulating the competition.

Daly and Wilson examined alternative explanations that have been offered by social scientists and psychoanalysts to account for their data, and found the alternative explanations inadequate to account for more than the specific instances they were designed to explain. If social scientists are to offer plausible alternatives to evolutionary explanations, then the alternatives they employ must be developed to accommodate a broad range of relevant facts. Similarly, evolutionary psychology should be developed at a depth to encompass more than the few aspects of behavior (usually reproduction) with which it deals. David Buss (1989) argued that the task for evolutionary psychologists is to identify psychological mechanisms, to specify the adaptive problems they solve, and to study overt behavior within the context of important features of the ecology. He has summarized the available data regarding sexual strategies in his book, *The Evolution of Desire* (1994), and places all of it within a framework that emphasizes the significance of behavioral traits within the environment of evolutionary adaptation.

Age Preferences for Mates

Buss (1989) studied sex differences in human mate preferences using questionnaire data based on 37 samples from 33 countries, located on six continents and five islands; a sample of 10,047 people. Buss predicted that men should prefer as mates women who are in their midteens to early twenties, and men should value youth and physical attractiveness in prospective partners. Women should prefer men with greater resources, and because male fertility is less steeply age graded from puberty, women should value physical appearance that could be used to gauge mating value and indicate the man has the ability to protect her. These predicted differences should transcend cultural variations.

As predicted, women valued males who had "good financial prospects," were ambitious, and industrious. Men preferred younger mates and women preferred older ones. Buss (1989, p. 42) summarized the results as follows:

> (1) All 37 societies in this study placed tremendous value on *kindness-understanding and intelligence* in potential mates . . . and it is reasonable to characterize them, provisionally, as species-typical mate preferences; and (2) males and females in all (in the case of preferred age differences), or nearly all, societies showed significant differences in the value they attached to physical attractiveness (males valuing it more) and good financial capacity (females valuing it more).

He interpreted these findings to support the contention that human psychology is not sexually monomorphic.

Kenrick and Keefe (1992) used several ingenious approaches to examine sex differences in the preferred age of mates based on hypotheses derived from evolutionary theory. They hypothesized that two factors should be important in determining mate choice. The first was the partner's reproductive potential, given that the goal of mating is reproduction, and the second was the partner's similarity to the individual's own age, which would enhance the likelihood of common and cooperative parental effort. They hypothesized that men would overvalue youth and physical attractiveness in women and that this would lead them to prefer younger women. This latter hypothesis is based on the assumption that younger women have a greater reproductive value and that physical attractiveness is a marker of health and vigor. In addition, they hypothesized that women would overvalue the ability of men to provide economic resources, which would lead them to prefer older men.

Although men should prefer women with higher reproductive potential there should be some modulation due to pressures favoring a similarity in ages. Because the reproductive potential of women declines more rapidly than does that of men, the age of the preferred partner should change as the man ages, with teenage men showing little or no discrimination against women older than they, middle-aged men showing a greater bias, and older males preferring progressively older women who are somewhat similar in age, but still ones who are younger than themselves. Women should begin with a preference for older men and, compared to men, show less change in that preference over the life span.

These hypotheses were tested in several studies using three basic types of data. The first was an analysis of classified personal advertisements in singles newspapers in Arizona, Germany, Holland, and India: Indicators of preference. The second was an examination of marriage age statistics in Seattle (1986), Phoenix (for both 1923 and 1986), and an isolated island in the Philippines (1913 to 1939): indicators of behavioral choice. The third method involved an analysis of those personal ads in the *Washingtonian* magazine, published in Washington DC, that provided information regarding the wealth and social status of the advertiser.

All of these analyses supported all of the major hypotheses and were the same for individuals of high and low socioeconomic status. Kenrick and Keefe (1992, p. 16) concluded:

> [A]ge preferences are more complex than earlier social psychological models led us to expect. Earlier studies suggested a simple relationship: males seek younger females, and females seek older males. Our results are consistent with half of that generalization: females tend to seek males who are slightly older than they are. For males, however, the preference for younger females is weak or nonexistent during early years, but becomes increasingly pronounced with age.

These analyses of homicide and of mate preference support a framework that is consistent with that expected on the basis of evolutionary predictions. It seems difficult to account for all of them with any single competing hypothesis. It should also be emphasized that all of these studies considered the data at the level of the individuals involved, as must be done if evolutionary mechanisms are to be used in manner that will permit the identification of the underlying processes.

Gender Differences in Partner Preferences

Alan Feingold (1992) conducted a meta-analysis of 28 studies in the research literature published after 1960 on differences in mate selection preferences. He inquired into some characteristics of mate preferences that were based on evolutionary hypotheses regarding parental investment, reasoning that men should be attracted to women primarily because of those visible cues that signal capacity to reproduce. These cues would be those related primarily to qualities of attractiveness, which could be used to signify health and vigor. Women should seek nonappearance-related factors that signal the capacity to acquire resources because these resources would maximize the survival prospects of offspring. This argument leads to the expectation that men should value physical attractiveness in a partner more than should women. Women should value socioeconomic status (SES) and ambition highly, because these are highly observable cues. A woman should also value both intelligence and character of men because these traits would be important for the survival of the woman's offspring, and she should value those traits more highly than should men. Because the traits of intelligence and character are not as directly observable, these gender differences should be smaller than those for SES and ambition. Finally, Feingold reasoned that traits of personality and humor should have little or no effect on the survival of progeny and there should be no gender differences in preferences for these traits.

His results supported all predictions, and he concluded that the research data support strongly the hypothesis that women, more often than men, seek characteristics in a partner that maximize survival prospects of offspring. These conclusions should be approached with caution, however, because the basic conceptual terms (intelligence, character, personality, and SES) are imbued with an intrinsic cultural bias. This analysis has been presented because it is congruent with the conclusions of the other studies that examined the issues at the level of individual behaviors and expressed direct preferences.

There are a host of other studies, all consistent with the expectations based on evolutionary biology. These studies are, however, more difficult to interpret because they are analyses of data from the Human Relations Area Files which contain information regarding many aspects of the culture of more than 200 different societies. These data are from a collection of studies that were done through the years by anthropological field researchers, and are maintained at Yale University. Also available are ethnographies for societies in the Standard Cross Cultural Sample developed by Murdock and White (1969), which contain data for 186 societies. The evolutionary conclusions derived from such data are more difficult to evaluate because critical information is not available for all societies, the ethnographic records are sometimes incomplete, and different anthropologists studied only certain aspects of cultures, while ignoring others that would be critical to an evaluation of evolutionary expectations. Despite such limitations, these studies support evolutionary expectations quite well. Among the excellent studies that exist using those files are ones by Betzig (1986) on despotism and differential reproduction, and by Thornhill (1991) on rules regulating human inbreeding and marriage.

Sexual Strategies Theory

Buss and Schmitt (1993) proposed what they called a contextual-evolutionary theory of human mating strategies which effectively organized and codified many of the points discussed here under the headings of "Age Preferences for Mates," and "Gender Differences in Partner Preferences." They defined strategies as behavioral solutions to adaptive problems (remember, there is no implication of consciousness or awareness on the part of the strategist). Buss and Schmitt developed nine specific hypotheses and a series of 22 predictions derived from these hypotheses. The hypotheses were based on a consideration of the adaptive problems and different constraints on reproductive success that men and women have faced throughout human evolutionary history. They emphasized the basic principles included in Trivers' (1972) theory of parental investment and sexual selection, which stressed that women's initial investment in progeny is greater than that of men, and that these differences would lead women to employ different strategies in terms of courtship, sexual preferences, and mate selection than those employed by the men, for whom the consequences of short-term sexual activity could well be less considerable. They also used Fisher's (1930) idea of reproductive value, which emphasizes the difference between fertility (referring to the probability of reproducing at the present time), and reproductive value (referring to the expected future contribution to future generations).

Many of the studies discussed above were evaluated by Buss and Schmitt who also generated new data, mainly attitudinal, to evaluate the specific predictions. The evidence supported the contentions of Sexual Strategies Theory. The adaptive logic of men and women was different when pursuing short- versus long-term mating strategies. In general, when pursuing short term mating strategies, men were more willing to engage in sexual activity on a briefer acquaintance and with more women, a high emphasis was placed on the woman's physical attractiveness, and a low emphasis was placed on resource commitment to these women. Women, on the other hand, were cautious in terms of length of acquaintance before sexual activity took place, were interested in having a smaller number of sexual partners, and sought high initial levels of resource commitment on the part of the man, who was also valued more if he was physically stronger.

When long-term mating strategies were considered, men valued faithfulness, preferred younger women (who would have a higher reproductive value), and avoided women who showed evidence of promiscuity or who were sexually experienced. Women sought men who were willing to commit economic resources and who had a high probability of being successful as providers in the future: they wanted men who were both willing and able.

It was also found that both men and women were interested in a mate who would be a good parent to any offspring because these progeny need intensive nurturance for a considerable period of time by both parents. Both males and females want, for a long-term mate, a committed ally who is kind and understanding and who shows evidence of good parenting skills, including such things as intelligence, kindness, and nurturance. Buss and Schmitt considered the available attitudinal and behavioral data regarding mating patterns, they evaluated large-scale sociological studies of marriage decisions in a variety of cultures, cross-cultural studies of the causes of divorce, as well as patterns of homicide and sexual jealousy. They also discussed the tactics used by men and women in intrasexual competition. All of these sources of data supported the hypotheses of Sexual Strategies Theory. A couple of alternative hypotheses were examined briefly (Freudian theory and the structural powerlessness hypothesis), and neither was as adequate to explain the existing data as was the evolutionary-based hypotheses based on the parental investment theory they explicated.

Buss (1994) has summarized the research investigating human sexuality in his book, *The Evolution of Desire*. When he examined his data for all the continents, political systems, religious, and systems of mating included in his cross-cultural study he noted that women place about twice as much value than do men on good financial prospects when they consider a marriage partner. Also, women's marriage decisions, worldwide, often match their mating preferences, with the average age of brides being about three years less than that of grooms. Women valued intelligence more than men in 10 of the 37 cultures, with both sexes placing a high premium on intelligence in the remaining 27 cultures.

Men who are in a position to get what they want, due to their wealth and status, often marry young, attractive women and very strongly abhor promiscuity and infidelity by their wives. Buss makes the observation that evolutionary psychology offers the possibility that key psychological mechanisms on which behavior is based can be identified and that some of the crucial contexts that activate those mechanisms can be understood.

Buss (1994, p. 159) wrote, "The message of evolutionary psychology is not that these problems are biologically determined, unmodifiable, or inevitable. Rather, by identifying key contexts that foster the occurrence of such things as sexual harassment, evolutionary psychology offers hope for understanding and intervention." One of his central messages regarding human sexual strategies is that mating behavior is enormously flexible and sensitive to social context, with no proximate sexual behavior inevitable or genetically preordained. However, there are general strategies toward which people are predisposed and there are differences between the sexes that appear to be universal features of our evolved selves.

The standard social science interpretation of the data bearing on the primacy of experience in establishing patterns of socialization has been challenged by Rowe (1994). He reviewed the extensive behavior genetic literature that used research designs to separate genetic and environment effects on the development of traits and behaviors. These studies considered the development of separated monozygotic and dizygotic twins, as well as the adoption of nontwins. The effects of environment and genetic factors on such things as personality traits, psychopathology, social attitudes, and intelligence as measured by IQ was evaluated. Rowe interprets these data to indicate that parent–child resemblances in natural families are due primarily to biological rather than environmental influences. His argument stands the usual interpretation of socialization on its head, arguing that genetic influences have a greater effect on socialization than does variation in family environment, which he argues has almost no effect. While the argument is occasionally overdrawn, given that he attributes benefit of the doubt (and tends to assign shared variance) to genetic influences, the point of view serves to counteract the usual uncritical acceptance of explanations framed in terms that concentrate on the family environment to the exclusion of biological influences.

The results of a study by Simpson and Gangestad (1992) offer a cautionary note to Feingold's sweeping conclusions based on the analysis of trends in a number of studies. They considered the pattern of individual differences in romantic partner choices of university students using several psychological inventories and rating scales. Their data supported a more complex hypothesis than that proposed by Feingold and by Buss. In general, Simpson and Gangestad found that both men and women seemed to use either one of two strategies: The first is that some men will choose the strategy of preferring attractive partners who are likely to have high reproductive value, and some women will prefer males who possess adaptive attributes and resources; because all individuals will not be successful using these strategies, an alternative one should also exist whereby both men and women prefer a mate offering long-term investment commitment and loyalty to their partners. In this view, selection pressures could have produced alternative strategies, either of which could enhance the reproductive success of the partners.

Human Dispersal Patterns

A strong relationship has been observed between the nature and distribution of ecological resources and reproductive strategies used by a large number of mammal and bird species. The pattern is that males tend to control dispersal (the movement from natal to breeding area) more in polygynous species, while both sexes disperse at similar rates in monogamous species. It has also been found that, in most species, natal dispersal is related to the onset of sexual maturation and often is influenced by two causal factors, intrasexual competition and inbreeding avoidance. An analysis of the human ethnographic files indicates that, in those human societies for which data exists, 83% were polygynous, and that variability in reproductive success is greater for men than women.

To determine if the conclusions drawn from studies of other animal species that related dispersal and resource distribution could be found for humans, Clarke and Low (1992) analyzed data regarding human dispersal patterns in Sweden. Their analyses indicated that the relationships between resources and dispersal that have been found for other animals obtained for humans as well. In general, human men compete for resources and the possession of resources influences the strategies used (as well as the success) in acquiring women as mates. In Sweden, they found that richer men married younger women than did poorer men, and they had larger families; landowners were more likely to marry (and to marry younger women) than nonlandowners, and they also had more children.

Clarke and Low examined the population registers for 4,990 people born between 1795 and 1900 in four parishes. They considered dispersal rates from the natal parish related to several variables, among them occupational level, age at dispersal, age at marriage, age at birth of the first child, and legitimacy of the child. They found that women had a higher probability of dispersal than did men (as much as 60% greater in some parishes), and that the maximum dispersal for women took place at ages 20 to 24. This pattern of female age-related dispersal is consistent with the expectation that female dispersal is related to age of reproductive maturity, and probably reflects a reproductive strategy found throughout the animal kingdom.

For both sexes, married adults were less likely to disperse than single persons, people born late to large families were more likely to disperse, and women with children were 48% less likely to disperse than were childless women. Examination of the records for the different parishes revealed a pattern consistent with expectations based on resource distribution: The parish with the highest population density was on the seacoast and had vast fishing resources. It had the lowest dispersal rate. Another parish, although it too had a dense population, was the poorest in terms of resource availability. This parish had the highest level of illegitimacy and the highest dispersal rate. In all parishes, children of land-owning farmers were least likely to disperse: 80% of dispersers had no children and were not married. Mothers of illegitimate children, if they moved at all, tended to move when their children were young, an action that may have served to mask the illegitimacy of the child in the new community and, hence, enhance the likelihood that the child could find a suitable partner when adult.

In general, the probability of dispersal was significantly influenced by an individual's sex, parish of birth, and socioeconomic class. Clarke and Low concluded that the mating patterns found in Sweden were based on resource defense, with the likelihood of male dispersal related to local availability of resources, as well as to the individual's ability to gain access to them. They argued that these data provide support for the hypothesis that men in monogamous resource defense systems were less likely to disperse than were women because the males were more likely to be able to compete for those resources.

Clarke and Low acknowledged that, lacking statistics concerning lifetime reproductive success, strong conclusions regarding mechanisms are premature, but they indicated that such statistics are available for other regions in Sweden and are now being examined to investigate the specific factors involved in dispersal behavior in order to establish the generality of the findings across a broader range of societies. The results obtained to this point are, however, compatible with those reported earlier using quite different methods, subject populations, and sources of data.

Additional Anthropological Data

Smith (1987), reviewed data bearing on evolutionary–ecological models of foraging strategies and optimal group size. His analyses indicated that whenever the expected returns from solitary foraging are low relative to the per capita returns from group foraging, individuals will attempt to join the groups, even though their addition increases the group size above the optimum.

He observed that the reciprocal exchange of resources is a striking characteristic of many human social groups. The available data for hunter–gatherer societies indicated that they share meat resources (which have great variability over time) far more frequently than they share the less variable plant food resources. In times of abundance following a successful hunt, sharing of meat would not be costly to the provider, will benefit the recipient, and when the recipient makes a kill, will increase the likelihood of reciprocity. Not sharing plant food permits the development of a stable and constant supply of food for the immediate family and leads to increased socioeconomic independence of individual households.

When Smith considered the interbirth interval (IBI) of the !Kung San foragers in the Kalahari region of southern Africa he found that nomadic !Kung women had an average IBI of about 4 years (the age at which the children are weaned), while those who were sedentary (living at cattle posts) had much shorter IBI's. These data conform to expectations based on the assumption that reproductive behavior is adjusted to enhance reproductive success. If the IBI is shorter than 4 years, then infant mortality is high. While the death of an unweaned infant is followed by a shortened IBI to effect replacement of the lost infant, the death of older children has no effect on IBI. Smith concluded that such fitness-correlated evaluation of consequences arose through natural selection acting on either cultural or genetic variation. Once again, these anthropological data are consistent with expectations based on an ecologically regulated evolutionary system.

Some interesting aspects of parental sex preference were reported by Cronk (1993) who studied the Mukogodo people of central Kenya. Most societies that have been studied display a preference for male offspring because of their greater economic value to the parents, as well as the ability of the sons to support the parents when they become old. The pattern of parental favoritism in the Mukogodo favors girls very strongly, however. Cronk found that the Mukogodo are the poorest people in the area and tend to be firmly at the bottom of the tribal hierarchy in terms of wealth and prestige. As a result they also lack marital and reproductive opportunities. It is harder for Mukogodo men to find wives than it is for men from other tribes because the Mukogodos do not have the bridewealth needed to pay for a wife. Therefore, due to social stigma, they are not favored by women from other tribes. Women in the Mukogodo area are always in short supply because the few well-to-do men in the area can have as many wives as they can afford. As a result the women all find husbands among the wealthier, higher status locals or neighbors, or, failing all else they can marry one of the poorer, but numerous, Mukogodo men. Because of these factors the average Mukogodo woman has more children then the average Mukogodo man.

Cronk noted that this scenario fits the preconditions for sex-based parental investment in favor of girls. The sex ratio at birth is found to be just about normal, but the sex ratio comes to favor females later: In 1986 there were 98 girls and only 66 boys less than 5 years old. No evidence could be found that would suggest that the imbalance was the result of infanticide. The evidence indicated that the sons died at a higher rate because the mothers nursed female babies longer, and they took daughters to the mission dispensary more often than they did sons, even though the sons might be in great need of medical attention. Cronk noted that the parents claimed they preferred sons rather than daughters (an attitude that is prevalent for the other tribes of the region), but that their behavior, of which they might not have been aware, led to higher mortality of sons. Cronk found this unusual pattern of sex based prenatal investment to exist in a few other societies in which the sex ratio favored girls, and in all of them the girls either had better reproductive prospects or they provided greater economic benefit to their families than did boys. He interpreted these data in terms of the evolutionary parental hypothesis of Trivers and Willard (1973).

HUMAN NATURE

A Bit of History

It is accepted widely that to understand environmental influences on the developing and functioning organism it is necessary to take into account what appear to be universal relationships between the environment and behavioral and psychological traits. These sets of universal traits and developmental programs constitute what we mean by human nature. Although there is a great deal of flexibility, and many complex interactions that must be considered when seeking to understand human nature, impressive progress has been made in the attempt to develop such an understanding. It is clear that there are both species-typical monomorphisms and sex-specific dimorphisms that can be understood within an evolutionary framework.

Ernst Mayr (1982) noted that farmers and animal breeders have understood for many centuries a number of the principles on which evolutionary theory is based: They were aware of the immense variability within species and knew that there was a tendency for characteristics of parents to be transmitted to their offspring. Although Gregor Mendel published his studies of the distinct variations observed in peas, published in 1866, the work was ignored by biologists until about 1900, when DeVries rediscovered Mendel's rule that each parent contributed only one genetic unit to each segregating character. The universal law was that the Mendelian ratio would be 3:1 in phenotypic appearance obtained when crossbreeding simple genotypes. This universality, Mendel argued, was due to the segregation of dominant and recessive "particles" which existed in sets—in other words, genes and their alleles. Mayr considered this contribution to provide the conceptual breakthrough resulting in a unified evolutionary theory, referred to as the modern evolutionary synthesis, whereby naturalistic based evolutionary biology and molecular genetic theory are synthesized, which Mayr noted is the paradigm theory of evolutionary biology today.

Mayr considered the reasons why Mendel was ignored and concluded that it was partly due to the fact that he published very little, and what he did publish was not in the prestigious botanical journals that would have attracted the attention of biological theorists. Mayr (1980) also argued that the conceptual differences between naturalists and geneticists led to a failure to appreciate Mendel's contribution. The dominant geneticists around 1900 tended to confuse proximate and ultimate causation, and to espouse what Mayr called "soft" inheritance. This view of inheritance allows for the inheritance of acquired characteristics in the belief that there is a gradual change of the genetic material, either through use or disuse, or through the direct effect of the environment.

Evolutionary theory developed quickly when the naturalistic based, populational views of Darwin were synthesized with the rediscovered and newly developed science of molecular genetics during the middle of the twentieth century. The next major development was to invest the synthetic theory of evolution with an ecological perspective and to view the development of traits at the level of population genetics. The insights provided by this amalgamation led to the recognition that it is necessary to consider individuals as members of groups.

Cultural Evolution

Attempts have been to extend this thinking to understand the relationships between evolutionary processes and cultural evolution that involves, but is separate from, individual learning processes, being based more on culturally transmitted cognitive strategies. Robert Boyd and Peter Richerson (1985) developed ideas regarding cultural evolution using qualitative analyses and formal mathematical models to organize existing data and to suggest the kinds of data that should be gathered to understand human nature within the evolutionary and cultural spheres. The innovative aspect of their work is that they have used the formal principles of Mendelian and population genetic models and extended them to cultural transmission.

The unification they suggested has promise in providing a set of functional principles applicable to molar human cultures and complex animal societies, as well as to molecular genetics.

These developments have led to a realization that evolutionary principles can be used to understand existing legal (M. Wilson, 1987), and moral principles (Alexander, 1987; Petrinovich, O'Neill, & Jorgensen, 1992, 1993). It is important to understand the biases in behavioral traits that have been built into human nature (to paraphrase the song line, what *is* human nature all about, Alfie?). It is essential to know what it's all about in order to understand the kinds of moral principles and laws that represent what *ought* to be the structure of society. Degler (1991) pointed out that social institutions and practices need not follow biology. Rather, a society could devote its cognitive efforts toward achieving such things as sexual equality by encouraging male nurturance while moderating any biologically based tendencies for male violence that might exist, as well as encouraging and developing mechanisms to enable females to stand against such violence. It is my belief that such social engineering can be better accomplished in the light of an understanding of basic human nature, by designing interventions to take advantage of desirable biases, and to counteract undesirable ones. Finally, I believe that the research programs in evolutionary psychology that will be discussed next support the development of a rational understanding of human nature.

THE EVOLUTION OF MORALITY

I will speculate about what it might mean to consider morality as an evolved process, and thereby decide if there is any deep meaning and conceptual advantage to speak of moral *oughts* in evolutionary terms. This discussion will also set the stage for some of the arguments to follow in this book. First of all, one should remember that evolutionary mechanisms can be considered at two levels: One is the underlying level of ultimate factors where the outcomes are expressed in terms of relative reproductive success; the other is at the level of proximate factors where the concern is with the inherited physiological and behavioral mechanisms and biases that have been selected to further the ultimate payoffs.

When questions are posed at the level of what *is* the nature of morality this concerns events at the proximate level and the enterprise is primarily a descriptive one. Within the confines of that enterprise questions are asked about the norms describing what individuals do and the rules that are imposed to regulate individuals and groups. It is important to inquire into the degree of tolerance for individual differences permitted by society, and ask under what circumstances these differences can be expressed. I have suggested that the tolerance of variability in traits could well be critically important to maintain a biological system and that the behavioral manifestation of this variability enables the system to adapt to changes and differences in environmental demands in different places and at different times.

I noted some characteristics that could be part of the proximate moral ethogram. These behaviors were developed over the period of time when early humans were coping with the demands of the environment of evolutionary adaptation—when they were facing the pressures that were to shape the human gene pool, resulting in the uniqueness that obtains for the human animal. It is agreed generally that early human societies consisted of small breeding populations composed of the primary family group and more distantly related kin. There was probably a fair amount of dispersal of individuals from their natal community as population density came to exceed the carrying capacity of the environment. This dispersal occurred either when individuals dispersed to join other communities that were not as large or well established, or when groups of kin set out as pioneers to colonize yet another habitat. It is also agreed that these early social groups were relatively monogamous and that paternal investment increased the reproductive success of the family by assisting the mother during pregnancy and provisioning and protecting the highly vulnerable progeny during the extensive period when a young human is not capable of caring for itself.

What kinds of traits would be expected to develop in order to enhance survival and reproductive success under these circumstances? Some degree of physical dimorphism would be expected in such things as pelvic structure in order to enable women to bear larger children and to accommodate the development of the large cerebral cortex of the fetus, which makes it possible for the members of the human species to excel in the survival game. Larger size and greater physical strength would be a specialization useful to men in inter- and intraspecific competition, in coping with a hostile environment, and in having the strength to assist mothers through the period of child rearing. Given these conditions it would be expected that the reproductive success for men would be more variable than that for women, as it is.

If we move to the level of the community it would be expected that there would be practices, codes, and rules developed to regulate the pair bond and to legitimize offspring. The earliest surviving codes of behavior deal extensively with human social and sexual relations. Darlington (1969), noted that one of the earliest codes of law that has been discovered was that established during the reign of the Babylonian King, Hammurabi, during the First Babylonian Empire. His reign was from 1792 to 1750 B.C., and the black diorite column on which the 282 articles of the code were inscribed was erected in the last year of his reign. Darlington noted that, of the 282 articles, 68 dealt with family and sexual relations, condemned incest, protected children, punished injury on the principle of an eye for an eye, established rules for marriage, divorce, inheritance, adultery, concubinage, desertion by mates, and adoption. Among the most elaborate sets of rules and regulations found in most primitive societies are those pertaining to reproduction, regulation of families, and inheritance of goods. Given the primacy of the nuclear family unit in such societies it would be a paramount necessity, from an evolutionary perspective, to ensure the stability of the family, which is the basic reproductive unit.

Other aspects of reproduction and kinship would be expected to follow patterns that increase the fitness of the reproducing individuals, and indeed they do. In this chapter I have reviewed data bearing on homicide, and these data are consistent with expectations based on evolutionary principles. The data pertaining to mate preference patterns, dispersal from natal to breeding areas, foraging strategies, and the evidence regarding reciprocity in food sharing all are consistent with the expectations based on evolutionary theory. These data are not consistent with expectations using any single cultural hypothesis that I am aware of. I conclude that, at the descriptive level, the behaviors considered to be ethical for the individuals of the breeding community support the idea that these proximate mechanisms have developed in order to further the ultimate interest of increased reproductive success, and in the process, to enhance inclusive fitness. Indeed, the demographic data regarding reproductive success support the view that the ultimate functions are well served by the proximate mechanisms that have been developed.

Summary

I am arguing that the rules defining the morality of humans are based on experience-expectant systems that have evolved to make it possible to achieve the ultimate goal of transmitting genes to succeeding generations. There are a number of different proximate behaviors and beliefs that have been developed to further this ultimate goal, and they depend on historical accidents, the nature of the ecology during evolutionary time, and the structure of the gene pool of the initial breeding communities. In order to establish the reasonableness of arguments regarding early human evolution it is necessary to study the *is*: Facts are available regarding the nature of such things as courtship customs, breeding patterns, and family structure. It is these proximate factors that inform the moral *ought*. I have reviewed a number of "social facts" that are relevant, and they support the possibility of an evolved morality. I will, in Chapter 7, explore the structure of people's moral intuitions, and reach the conclusion that the results of those studies support the idea that there is a universal structure compatible with the expectations based on an evolved morality. It could well be that morality itself, in the broad ultimate sense, has evolved, and that individuals rediscover the cognitive principles that support the proximate behaviors making it possible to realize these ultimate functional goals.

Although it is argued that natural selection has shaped morality, it does not mean that the evolved tendencies will always result in a moral society. As mentioned several times, the very tendencies, biases, and predispositions that serve people and societies well in the pursuit of their ultimate reproductive success can lead to a rejection and persecution of those who are defined as being outside the reference group. The cognitive principles involved in the codification of social ideologies are of paramount importance, and the task of policy makers and those who monitor social institutions is to see that these ideologies are not used to pervert the desirable goals of evolutionary adaptation or to exploit those who are at a less-favored status.

EVOLUTIONARY PSYCHOLOGY

Evolutionary psychology attempts to use the basic principles of evolutionary theory to enhance the understanding of human behavior. Many social scientists still reject the idea that biological factors are important influences on social systems. This rejection stems from at least three sources: (1) The introduction of biological factors is held to entail an implicit or explicit acceptance of "genetic determinism" at some level; (2) because of the variability in social structures across cultures it is thought unlikely that there are strong biological universals; (3) some liberal political ideologues consider the use of biological factors to be a renascent version of Social Darwinism.

Genetic Determinism

Genetic determinism is taken to mean that traits are unchangeable, that such determinism denies free will, and that appeals to genetic factors require a reductionistic view unacceptable to many social scientists and humanists. There have been repeated forays into the sociobiological literature to find statements by one or more sociobiologists that exemplify these concerns. An astute critic of sociobiology, the philosopher Philip

Kitcher (1985), acknowledged that one cannot fairly represent the field of sociobiology by reference to the works of only one or a few individuals (even though he does not restrain himself always from such representations). Kitcher noted that behavioral dispositions are produced by processes involving both genes and the environments in which they are expressed. He argued that if the understanding of the nature of this gene–environment interaction leads to an appreciation of what is valuable, as well as to a modification of desires in accordance with such an appreciation, then the behavioral dispositions that result can lead us to free action.

Masters (1982), wrote that the newer generation of sociobiologists denies explicitly that inclusive-fitness models (which consider fitness in terms of an individual's success in transmitting genes directly to the next generations plus the genetic contribution of those related to that individual who share some common genes) necessarily invoke narrow genetic determinism. The argument can be made that invoking inclusive-fitness does not require an assumption that even remotely resembles genetic determinism.

Many concerns regarding genetic determinism are based on simple ignorance and misunderstanding. Even the brief discussion of genetics and behavior presented here should make it clear that contemporary evolutionists and sociobiologists understand and agree that genes do not code for any behavior, and that there are many steps between the proteins that genes do code and whatever behaviors are under consideration (see Plomin [1981, pp. 252–276] for a clear discussion of these issues). It is recognized that not only must all of the aforementioned intrinsic factors be considered but that the extrinsic factors, such as ecological and cultural influences, be considered as well.

If a trait is heritable, that heritability is important, and if individuals possessing that trait leave more offspring than those who don't possess it, then there will be a larger number of individuals with that trait in the next generation than there will be individuals without it. Sober (1984) used the example of the transmission of a propensity to be a cowboy from generation to generation. Because such generational transmission has been observed does not mean that the trait has to be genetically encoded. Heritability simply insures that the right sort of physical resemblance exists and this resemblance can then be genetically transmitted from parents to offspring. A greater birthrate among cowboys in one generation might increase the frequency of cowboys in the next if there is a resemblance between the physical traits and occupations of parent and offspring. This transmission of occupation may be due to the cultural fact that parents teach their children, and to the biological fact that the children inherit physical and behavioral traits that make it possible for them to be cowboys.

Heritability does not require a gene for cowboyhood, only a set of genes that make it possible, and enhance the likelihood, that an individual can become a cowboy, given the opportunity and tutelage.

A crucial distinction between genetic determinism and an evolutionary determinism that is more remote in time was made by Alexander (1979). Evolutionary determinism includes all the events involved in the process of natural selection that fixed certain genes during the period when the initial members of the species were in the environment of evolutionary adaptation, and this view does not involve genetic determinism by any stretch of the imagination. Remember, genetic determinism implies that the genes transmitted to an organism absolutely determine some aspect of that organism's structure, physiology, or behavior, no matter what circumstances the organism encounters. We know this type of determinism does not exist, even for such relatively simple things as height, which certainly has a genetic basis, but which just as certainly is influenced by such things as the nutritional state of the developing organism.

As spelled out in this and the preceding two chapters the proper way to consider evolutionary determinism is to include both genes and the environment. Natural selection occurs in the context of the environment and varies as a function of the gene frequencies that exist in the population at any given time. The environmentally influenced gene frequencies affect the likelihood that genes will be transmitted to the next generation. Thus, evolutionarily determined traits can be altered by modifying the environment in which individuals develop. This environment determines the range of reaction that can be expressed given the genetic material present, and will influence the likelihood that specific genes are transmitted to future generations. A broad interactionist view is at the heart of modern sociobiology and evolutionary psychology.

Because there is a degree of evolutionary determinism it is possible to predict sex ratios under different circumstances, to understand relationships between sexual dimorphisms and breeding systems, and between ecological characteristics and family structure. It is this evolutionary determinism (which is multiply determined and probabilistic in nature) that will enable us to understand and change human behavior more effectively.

In spite of the fact that the above arguments have been clearly and painstakingly developed over the years by people who argue that evolutionary mechanisms have important influences on physiological and behavioral development, the specter of genetic determinism is raised over and again. This specter is invoked not only by humanists and social scientists (as discussed above), but also by some geneticists and by the developing concerns of medical ethicists.

Lewontin has been one of the most consistent and articulate critics of sociobiology. Lewontin (1994) claimed that such things as the theory of innate criminality (proposed by Lombroso in the late nineteenth century) has been "modernized and, indeed, is taught at Harvard." He continues that there has been created a "vast literature [he identifies the individuals contributing to this literature to include Richard Dawkins and E. O. Wilson] and, in reaction, a smaller group of debunking critics of biological determinism has emerged [he mentions S. J. Gould, R. C. Lewontin, S. J. Rose, and Leo Kamin]." Lewontin remarks that many journalists and scientists adopt a "genomania," invoking a genetic basis for "every perturbation of the body corporeal or politic": genes for schizophrenia, for sensitivity to industrial pollutants and dangerous workplace conditions, for criminality, violence, divorce, and homelessness [he did not include cowboyhood]. He concluded with a reminder that every human being is the "nexus" of a large number of weakly acting causes, none of which determines the life of the organism because there are multiple causal pathways that influence human potential.

In this and the preceding two chapters I discussed a large number of studies that support the argument that genes do have some influence on aspects of human traits ranging from those involved in sensory processes to social systems, and, as I review these arguments, I do not find suggestions that there are genes for this and for that behavior as implied by these arguments. Most theorists arguing for an evolutionary psychology take pains to avoid such error (usually with success), and they very clearly emphasize the crucial importance of both genetic and environmental influences.

The argument that great care has been exercised to avoid simpleminded genetic determinism is further strengthened when one examines several of the recent books discussed: Barkow, Cosmides, and Tooby (1992); Buss (1994); Daly and Wilson (1988); Locke (1992); and Pinker (1994). One might not agree with the various arguments or conclusions, but I fail to find evidence of genetic determinism or any tendency to revert to two-valued heredity versus environment arguments. I think the message that such critics as Gould and Lewontin have been delivering through the years has been understood and accepted, and that those arguing an evolutionary psychology have been careful to avoid the pitfalls of simple determinism, molecular reductionism, or "just-so" adaptationist stories. I believe Lewontin (1994) is attacking a straw man.

Medical ethicists have worried about the heredity versus environment question when considering the ethical issues involved in gene mapping. For example, Annas and Elias (1992) caution us lest genes are "inaccurately seen" as more influential than environments, because this could lead us to view our actions as "genetically determined rather than resulting from free will." Proctor (1992) worries that the most all-encompassing potential danger of "genomics" is a growing trend toward a "biological determinism" that views human talents and disabilities to be "anchored in our biology." These worries led him to a further concern that the root cause for the onset of disease will be shifted from environment (toxic exposures) to the individual (genetic defects), and that industry may try to screen out the most vulnerable individuals rather than clean up the work environment. He argues this point of view, although he acknowledges later that it is not always easy to separate nature and nurture.

In the same collection of essays, Shuster (1992) states that a "conceit" exists to the effect that once the structures and functions of the genome are understood it may seem possible to have a gene-based explanation of all phenotypic characteristics, "including all aspects of human health, disease, and even behavior." She characterizes "modern biologists" as holding the belief that the description of biological phenomena is far less meaningful than the elucidation of the molecular mechanisms underlying them, and that these prototypic biologists want to understand biological systems in terms of molecular mechanisms rather than in terms of organisms, organ systems, or organs. She concludes that the leaders of the Human Genome Project have provided a reductionistic and deterministic argument presupposing that an identical genotype invariably produces an identical genotype, "just as identically programmed computers always perform the same functions." [I am led to wonder, as did Butch Cassidy and the Sundance Kid, "Who are those guys?"] I recommend a careful consideration of Pinker's (1994) views regarding the essential difference between humans and computers that will make it clear why Shuster's views are neither meaningful nor useful. The aims of evolutionary biologists require that attention be devoted to the ultimate, functional attainments as well as to proximate mediation. Shuster seems not to appreciate the fact that there are two different disciplines of biology, molecular and organic, and that the two profitably coexist.

I recommend that those in the medical profession, as well as bioethicists, study the article by Williams and Nesse (1991), in which they make a strong plea for a Darwinian view of medicine. Williams and Nesse discuss the advantages that obtain when biomedical science is viewed from an adaptationist perspective. They provide examples of several areas where new insights have been provided through a consideration of evolutionary principles, all of which argue that a better caliber of medicine will be practiced if the role of infections, injuries, response to toxins, genetic diseases, and aging are viewed with an understanding of the difference between the modern environment and that in which humans evolved. Their point is that an evolutionary perspective involving the level of ultimate explanation will add another dimension to the commonly invoked level of proximate explanation. They recommend that Darwinian medicine should be taught in medical schools by specialists in evolutionary biology in order to enable the science and practice of medicine to realize the benefits of recent advances in evolutionary biology. I add that medical ethicists would also be well-advised to learn some modern evolutionary biology in order to break the mold of thinking in terms of nature versus nurture when considering issues regarding the utilization of genetic information to improve the quality of health care.

Cultural Variability

It is often stated that cultures vary so much in their customs, rules, rituals, and laws that it is unlikely there are any biological universals that influence human nature. While it is true there are a variety of specific rules and structures that characterize different cultures, there also seem to be some general features that characterize the rules of all societies, and many of these relate to reproduction and inheritance.

For example, it has been suggested that traits such as cooperation and communication provide the cohesive elements for society. Cooperation and communication are most evident in those aspects of behavior that affect the reproductive success of individuals in society. In their classic book, *Patterns of Sexual Behavior*, Ford and Beach (1951) documented the argument that the most important sexual partnership is the relatively permanent union based on economic and sexual cooperation and point out that the most important forms of sexual activity in all human and most animal cultures are heterosexual in nature. Even though other types of sexual activities occur, with varying degrees of societal approval or disapproval, the heterosexual ones are of paramount importance for the society. This heterosexual reproductive unit is the basic emotional and economic unit of society. One of the primary functions of marriage forms is to regulate the economics of the culture and to structure the transmission of goods from one generation to the next. The argument can be turned around and questions could be phrased in terms of how there could be any cultural universals given the wide variety of customs found in different societies. It is no easier to account for universals using the concept of a set of cultural biases as it is using biological biases.

Ideological Objections

I would like to examine the charge that the acceptance of socio-biological explanations must inevitably lead to repugnant ideological positions. Kitcher (1985) worried that contemporary thought in the biology of behavior runs the risk of being used to support social injustice, but does remind us later (p. 9) that, "Everybody ought to agree that, given sufficient evidence for some hypothesis about humans, we should accept that hypothesis whatever its political implications." In the postscript to his book, Kitcher (1985, p. 435) once again sounded the alarm:

> Cataloging . . . errors [made by sociobiologists] . . . [are] important because the effects of accepting the pop sociobiological view of human nature are grave. That view fosters the idea that class structures are socially inevitable, that aggressive impulses toward strangers are part of our evolutionary heritage, that there are ineradicable differences between the sexes that doom women's hopes for genuine equality. None of these ideas should be adopted lightly . . . the true political problem with socially relevant science is that the grave consequences of error enforce the need for higher standards of evidence. In the case of pop sociobiology, commonly accepted standards are ignored. The mistakes merely threaten to stifle the aspirations of millions."

Before this characterization can take on any meaning it must be specified who are these "pop" sociobiologists, and who are the "serious" sociobiologists, and why they are so characterized. I argue that this interpretation is based on a selective presentation of the older and semipopular literature and evidence, a needlessly negative imputation regarding the intentions of the original sociobiologists, and a pessimistic prediction concerning the outcomes that could result if sociobiological arguments are correct. A prevalent argument that should be rejected, is that one should not seek knowledge and understanding about the human condition because the information could be put to bad use by bad people. The fact that evil people could use knowledge to attain disreputable goals should not override the consideration of the many good effects that can result from a basic understanding of human nature.

It can be argued, as Masters (1982) did, that many of the concerns and apprehensions that people have are based on misconceptions regarding the implications of the inclusive-fitness theory on which sociobiology is based. The proximate mechanisms that would support cooperation among the close kin of long-lived species favor the likelihood that behavioral plasticity will develop. Inclusive-fitness theory formally treats actors as having equal opportunities and makes an attempt to account for observed inequalities of outcome on the basis of general principles likely to influence behavioral outcomes. Inclusive-fitness theorists who have considered the nature of the biology of moral systems, such as Alexander, (1987) are careful not to argue that there is but one natural way of life and this way ought to be pursued: Such an argument would, indeed, be committing the naturalistic fallacy.

Caporael and Brewer (1991) agreed that introducing evolutionary perspectives to the study of human psychology does not lead to an image of human nature in which rape, warfare, and competition for dominance are more important than nurturance, cooperation, and concern for collective welfare. It would seem that the negative political and ideological concerns regarding a hopeless pessimism inherent in the use of inclusive-fitness constructs should be laid to rest once and for all. We should concentrate, instead, on gathering evidence that would be sufficient to extend inclusive-fitness theory beyond the realm of non-human behavior and to weigh its usefulness to understand aspects of human behavior and culture.

Selective Use of Evidence

Other criticisms are based on the charge that the use of evolutionary principles to understand human behavior has been selective, does not lead to clear predictions, and does not adequately consider and explore alternative explanations. This has occurred because, as Kitcher (1985) documented, some of the early and most prominent sociobiologists presented their work with an almost missionary zeal and attempted to herd all of the phenomena they could into the evolutionary corral. Their efforts often could be characterized by an overreaching optimism and overgeneralization. That such zeal existed in the past is understandable, and, I would argue, forgivable at the outset. The point is that such overgeneralization should not be allowed to persist. I believe that generalizations are now being made with careful consideration of reasonable alternatives, at least by the new generation of theorists, such as Buss, Daly, Gigerenzer, Kenrick, Pinker, and M. Wilson—all of whom are developing evolutionary perspectives in a manner that make them applicable to human sexual and social behavior, and with careful consideration for the power of alternative explanations.

WHAT HAS EVOLVED?

It seems likely that many human behavioral traits can be considered to be adaptive, evolved traits. Pinker (1994) provided a careful analysis of the proximate mechanisms that have evolved in the case of language. By the time children are 3 years old they display the correct qualities of grammar, with the morphology of their grammar organized into layers of roots, stems, and inflections. They can swiftly acquire free word order, subject-object-verb word order, or verb-subject-object word orders, show evidence of rich systems of case and agreement, use strings of connected (agglutinated) suffixes, gender marking, and whatever else the language community displays, all with equal ease before the age of 4. An interesting thing is that, as Pinker noted, these young children display "grammatical genius", but are notably incompetent at most other intellectual activities (reminiscent of the case of the wasps, which can achieve remarkable intellectual achievements, but in one aspect of behavior, provisioning nests, only). Young children cannot perform tasks that require them to sort beads in order of size, or reason about the conservation of the volume of liquid in containers of different shapes. Yet, they display most of the complex regularities of the basic organization of grammar, a task that a foreign adult would have incredible difficulty mastering. Pinker argues that this basic organization must be wired into the child's brain and be activated by the speech (if hearing) or the signing (if deaf) of other human beings with whom they interact.

Having said this, what are the preadaptations that would make the development of the linguistic machinery possible? One must have a brain that organizes the world into discrete, bounded, and cohesive objects. Second, there must be a tendency to organize objects into categories of the same kind. Pinker argues that babies are designed to expect a language to contain words for kinds of objects (nounlike), and kinds of actions (verblike). An extensive body of research literature (much of which is summarized in Pinker's book) strongly supports these suppositions. Infants do tend to organize the world by categorizing kinds of objects and actions when their mentalese is evaluated using eye fixation (if they are so young as to be completely preverbal), or asking them questions about pictures (if they are old enough to comprehend instructions). Not only do infants and young children parse the world using these particular categories of objects, actions, and kinds, but they display the basic elements of Universal Grammar, and reflect the prosodic elements of their language community, well before they have had any extensive exposure to a wide range of language exemplars. Pinker is correct when he argues that the development of language provides the tool to enable us to understand the human mind and to inquire into the essence of human nature.

One of Pinker's most valuable contributions is to break language down into a small enough number of units to make it possible to realize how the complexity of language could have evolved from a few basics. I believe his analysis suggests some of the steps that need to be taken to develop a more adequate general evolutionary psychology. The first step requires an understanding of the characteristics of the environment of evolutionary adaptation that existed for humans in order to identify those behavioral tendencies that would have enhanced the reproductive success of those members of the society who possessed them. It is easy to understand how the development of a complex language system that frees the organism from this time and that place would be of great advantage to cooperating and competing organisms. As Pinker (1994, p. 368) so aptly phrased it:

> After all, it doesn't take that much brain power to master the ins and outs of a rock or to get the better of a berry. But outwitting and second-guessing an organism of approximately equal mental abilities with non-overlapping interests, at best, and malevolent intentions, at worst, makes formidable and ever-escalating demands on cognition. And a cognitive arms race clearly could propel a linguistic one.

It is necessary to understand the characteristics of the environment in which the organism is presumed to have operated during the period of evolutionary adaptation if these preadaptations are to be understood. That environment permitted certain tendencies and selected out others for extinction. A good approach is to study the functioning of organisms acting in their contemporary environment, and a great deal of progress has been made to achieve an understanding of the influence of ecological factors by Egon Brunswik (1952, 1956) and by those of us who have studied the ecological and functional reliabilities and validities involving organisms behaving in representative environments (Hammond, 1966; Petrinovich, 1979, 1989).

Given that the strategies used to conceptualize language development within an evolutionary context have provided strong insights into human nature, it can be argued that it will be useful to develop a descriptive base of actions people engage in consistently enough that they might be considered to be universals. Pinker (1994, pp. 413–415) presented an extensive list of things that Brown (1991) thought might constitute the Universal People, a list that includes categories of actions involving language, intentions, reproduction, emotions, activities, fears and phobias, child-rearing practices, inheritance systems, and social customs. As Pinker noted, this is not a list of instincts but a list of complex interactions between a universal human nature and the conditions of living as a human on Earth.

Tooby and Cosmides (1992) also constructed an extensive list of functions that an organism requires to adapt to the demands made by a community of organisms. They suggested that one way in which organisms could cope with the imperative demands placed on them is to develop specialized content-specific modules, such as a face-recognition module, a sexual-attraction module, a semantic-inference module, a social-exchange module, and so on. As I see it the task is not so much to enumerate specialized adaptations, but to reduce them to a minimal number that have as little descriptive overlap as possible. When adaptive mechanisms are reduced to what can be considered a core number, then it will be possible to extend the conceptions in two directions. One is to identify the ultimate functions of those adaptations, and another is to decide how the actions serving the interest of those functions are accomplished. When this analysis has been done it will be possible to understand the physiological elements that could have evolved to support those adaptive functions. Using such strategies, events at each level can inform those at the other levels, and the universals that appear, upon first glance, to be so complex should reveal some of the secrets of their basic organization.

I have described the development of human speech and language at some length because they represent a behavioral complex that is programmed into the developing human organism and appear if the organism is exposed to the communicative acts of adults or peers. Given that such communication almost always occurs in the environment in which the young organism finds itself, a language displaying universal features will be developed. I consider the unfolding of these biological processes in response to environmental stimuli to provide a powerful analogy to approach the development of morality. It is reasonable to suppose that young organisms are imbued with biological tendencies that make them likely to develop emotional attachments to, and to communicate with, their primary caregivers, and that the young are empowered to cooperate and communicate with the members of their immediate community. Such tendencies would be expected to enhance the ultimate reproductive success of those developing organisms who display them and lessen the success of those who don't. In this way, biological tendencies might well come to be organized and recognized as the moral codes adopted by the members of a society. It is clear that all known societies do develop some kind of moral code and, while the specifics of the moral codes might vary, these specifics must not reduce the reproductive success of the individuals if the society is to survive and succeed.

Just as with language development, there occurs a process of moral development that only depends on the exposure to those environmental stimuli that would occur during the course of normal development. Because the moral code deals with a much broader and complex range of issues the specific codes will vary much more than is the case for languages. However, the moral codes will all be directed toward the same set of basic issues that all humans face in the struggle for existence with cooperating and competing neighbors, all of whom have to adapt to the characteristics of the environment in which they find themselves. The findings regarding the increased efficiency of communication that involves social contracts provides an opening wedge to understand at least one such moral adaptation. The existence of this cognitive module and the suggestion that there might be an anatomical basis for it suggests the direction that the search for an evolved morality might take.

I have outlined some basic ideas in evolutionary biology which I will emphasize when considering moral issues pertaining to human life. They are not often brought into play in that context but I believe the lack of application is due to a mistaken idea of the nature of evolutionary biology, rather than to a considered and informed decision to disregard such ideas.

6

Basic Concepts
Moral Philosophy

To place the issues regarding the nature of life in a broader perspective it will be helpful to consider some of the basic ideas moral philosophers have developed and to identify some basic philosophical distinctions that are relevant to consider in the present discussion. Moral philosophers have discussed at length the underlying dimensions that might regulate people's moral beliefs. Any detailed and comprehensive discussion of these complicated issues would serve no purpose. However, I will highlight a few that I consider to be relevant to later discussions regarding moral intuitions, and whose consideration will be valuable when I attempt to discuss moral principles in order to arrive at a system appropriate to deal with bioethical concerns.

ISSUES IN MORAL PHILOSOPHY

The concept of morality involves a determination of what is the correct, good, or proper thing one should do when confronted with decisions that concern other organisms. Are there basic principles that drive human actions and can these be used to derive appropriate standards of conduct? Can we identify a system of laws or precepts that are binding upon rational creatures and can we discover rationally the structure of that network? It has been assumed that much of human morality can be based on principles of what Snell (1988) referred to as an enlightened self-interest that should be based on reason, and which is adequately informed and illuminated by factual bases. It is hoped that such a set of values honors the pluralism that exists in modern societies, and allows a pluralism in moral principles as well.

Types of Moral Theories

There are two major classes of moral theories that have been developed to account for human behavior: consequentialist and deontological. I will discuss consequentialism at length because it can be cast in such a way that it is compatible with the cost–benefit analyses that are basic to evolutionary theories. Consequentialist theories define what is good in nonmoral terms. For example, "good" could be defined hedonically in terms of the relative amount of personal happiness or pleasure that results from an action, in terms of the satisfaction of people's preferences, or in terms of achieving an intellectual pleasure through the exercise of complex mental capacities (Brink, 1992). The right thing to do is decided in terms of the good of the outcome, however defined. It is important to recognize that consequentialist theories are concerned with the relative value of the outcomes of acts or the use of certain rules. Objects with moral standing, such as human beings, are assigned an absolute value and are not to be considered merely as a means to some further end.

One problem that consequentialism encounters concerns the way in which the values of different outcomes are to be calculated. Sosa (1993) identified two major alternatives that can be used to evaluate overall value: (1) Any act associated with a positive value can be considered "right"; (2) acting "rightly" means performing an act that maximizes positive consequences. Alternative 1 only requires that the value of the consequences of an act, on balance, be positive. The demand is that a person should act to increase the consequential balance and not that one should act as well as one could. Alternative 2 demands that a person act in a way that no other act is better, which seems to impose an impossible demand because of the difficulty of knowing or considering all possible options.

Another problem concerning consequentialist views is that there is little agreement over the way intrinsic value should be estimated. Unless the algorhythm used to drive the calculations is clear, the basic definition of good is difficult to establish, and I will return to this problem frequently throughout this book. There are several difficulties involved when assigning weights to different moral values after the operative ones have been identified. It is apparent that all values should not be assigned an equal weight, which raises the question of how one assigns an ordinal weight to the different values in order to decide that one value is stronger or weaker than the others. Once this is done, then the problem is how to combine the weights of the different values. The American moral philosopher Richard Brandt (1987) phrased the question in terms of how to decide that the value of speaking freely on political matters may be stronger than the value of owning capital goods, and that both are weaker than the value of not being tortured.

Once the operative values have been arranged in some ordinal scale the problem is to arrive at an estimate to decide on the best course of action. One suggestion has been to give each element a unit weighting (positive or negative), to take the sum, and act in such a way that the positive summated weight is maximized. Another is to use a multiplicative scheme instead of the above additive one. With this algebraic formulation each of the values is assigned a value, but if any of the values are zero the product will be zero, and that action would be undesirable. A variant on this weighting system is to decide that some one or more values are so important that only they can be assigned zero weights, and any action that results in a zero product would be considered undesirable.

When this latter scheme is used one is letting some values "trump" all others in the sense that if they are involved they must have a positive value or the action proposed is not permissible. An example of such a trump is to disallow any action whereby the relative welfare of many people is increased considerably which would provide a large number of positive value "points," but would cause the death of one or a few people. Many would argue that a situation such as this is morally repugnant, and the zero value assigned to causing the death of innocents allows that event to trump all of the other factors involved, making that action morally impermissible.

Smart (1973) attributes what he refers to as a "quasi-ideal" utilitarian view to represent the view of John Stuart Mill, although Smart believes that it is only necessary to establish an ordinal, and not an interval, scale. I suggest that this very critical issue in basic moral choices is one that could be approached by devising scaling methods that are similar to those used in the studies reported in the next chapter.

Because we lack definite and agreed upon rules to compare the overall values of consequences we are left with only a framework for a moral theory. Sosa (1993) argued that this state of affairs is satisfactory because the purpose of philosophy is to clarify theoretical issues, to identify problems, and to tease contradictions. To move to a less theoretical level is the task of empirical inquiry, and I will make such an inquiry in Chapter 7 where I describe research attempts to characterize people's moral intuitions.

Arguments continue over such niceties as whether an additive or a multiplicative rule should be applied to combine the different dimensions involved given the situation (Kagan, 1988). When two or more moral dimensions clash there is no easy way to decide which of the conflicting duties is stronger, and there is the question of whether some things "trump" others when they are present. As discussed above, these trump utilities would not just enter into the calculus of values, but would demand (or prohibit) certain actions when present, no matter what alternatives exist.

I suggest that a multiplicative rule, with a trump given to some principles, provides an appropriate way to develop consequentialist calculations. These philosophical issues will not be considered at any greater depth at this time. They are introduced to place some of the later discussions in a broader philosophical context and because such concerns arise when substantive issues are considered throughout this book.

BASIC AND DERIVED PRINCIPLES

One distinction that should be considered is the difference between basic and derived principles. A basic principle is an assumption that must be argued and established, all other premises must be related to it, and these others stand or fall in relation to the basic premise. For example, one might start with a basic premise that all morality stems from the will of God. This premise can be argued on the basis of theology, and evidence must be adduced regarding its reasonableness in the light of our knowledge of the universe. Then, one might state that adultery is wrong because God forbids it, and this decision, in turn, must be argued in terms of the evidence concerning the nature of God's will, on the basis of the interpretation of accepted scripture, etc. Considered in this way adultery is a derived wrong, derived from the basic principles regarding God's will.

One might proceed from a different basic premise: that the driving force of biological existence is the perpetuation of one's genes, and this premise can be argued on the basis of evidence regarding the evolution of organic systems. Then, one might state that adultery is wrong because it weakens the nuclear family, and that the presence of some form of the nuclear family enhances the likelihood of genetic replication. The appropriate evidence would require the establishment of the fact that adultery does weaken the nuclear family and that this state of affairs leads to a lowered reproductive success of the members of those families so weakened. Again, adultery is a derived wrong, only now based on an evolutionary principle.

It is possible to hold that adultery is wrong, per se, and that no further justification is necessary; adultery is an essential and basic evil. In this view the evil of adultery is a basic principle. The weakness of the procedure of using such specific actions as adultery, murder, incest, capital punishment, and the like as basic premises is that we run the risk of calling every action we dislike a basic evil, without considering what underlying general principles might support an overall pattern of likes and dislikes. In this way we truly run the risk of running aground on the shoals of racism, sexism, and other varieties of totalitarian thinking because we decide by arbitrary decision and assertion, rather than by rational argumentation. We should seek basic principles that can be argued coherently, can be stated with clarity, and that are applicable universally. Only if we take care to establish the reasoning that grounds basic premises can we arrive at satisfactory moral positions. It is possible to argue that morality is based on the wishes of little green men from outer space, and that all moral codes issue from their wishes. However, such a premise is unlikely to withstand the scrutiny of logic or to find evidential support, and (one would hope) is unlikely to gain widespread acceptance beyond the supermarket tabloid display. In the rational world there are logical safeguards against allowing arbitrary basic principles to guide moral actions, and I will argue a consequentialist position that I find compatible with evolutionary premises.

The question is how to ground the basic premises on which moral decisions can be based. The grounding problem is that of putting a non-arbitrary stop to the process of providing reasons to justify moral judgments. Becker (1973) listed some philosophical controversies (what he calls "quagmires") that make such grounding difficult. These controversies concern problems that arise when distinctions are made between value and fact, involve a consideration of whether different values are commensurable and additive, and whether it is possible to derive an *ought* from an *is*. The same problems arise when lists of rights are constructed delineating things people must do, or avoid doing, in the interest of not harming, threatening, or depriving others. Brandt (1980) remarked that developing a list of rights does not provide much of a manifesto in terms that are adequate to define a moral system to evaluate the relative merits of possible social changes.

MORAL AGENTS AND MORAL PATIENTS

As I will argue at length in Chapter 8, it is crucial to distinguish between what are referred to as *moral agents* and *moral patients*. It has been argued that the moral community consists only of moral agents, that it includes *all* moral agents, and consists *only* of moral agents, who are considered to have direct moral duties to one another. These agents must be able to understand the concepts of right and wrong, do right and wrong, and bear the load of all moral responsibilities and duties. Becker (1973) argued that a moral agent is expected to make mistakes, but is not expected to do what is known to be wrong, and must make every effort to discover what is right morally. This decision process is an active one and no moral judgment is any more substantial than the basic principles on which it is based.

    It might be useful to consider the concepts of right and wrong in terms of what can be called "good" and "bad" actions, and to use Smart's (1973) concept of "optimific." This concept defines a good agent as one who acts better (in a more optimific way) than the average, and a bad agent as one who acts in a less optimific way than the average. Similarly, a good motive is one that generally results in beneficent action while a bad one generally ends in maleficent action. In this way it is possible to conceive of a good agent in a particular situation performing a wrong action, while a bad agent performs a right action, or that a right action is done with a bad motive, while a wrong action is done with a good motive.

    If basic principles are viewed in this way it might be that a deeper level of analysis will help to decide the nature of moral rights and wrongs. For example, an analysis could be made in terms of some fundamental level, such as one that involved biological considerations. Becker suggested that matters of moral concern are involved any time there is a need to do something, especially if this need has significant life consequences. Concerns regarding morality will insist that people are responsible for their actions, and the decisions they reach will be taken to reflect on the agent's character.

    Moral patients, on the other hand, lack the prerequisites that would enable them to control their own behavior in ways that make them accountable for the moral outcome of their actions. Because they lack these essential prerequisites they cannot be considered to do right or wrong nor should moral principles be brought to bear in assessing their actions. The class of moral patients includes such individuals as human mental defectives, the senile, very young children, fetuses, and most, if not all, nonhuman animals. For example, one cannot consider an animal predator to be morally wrong when it captures and kills its prey. These actions are the result of evolved relationships produced in the context of the biological system within which the animals have evolved, and right and wrong are not operative principles within this context. The killing that takes place reflects the way the animals have developed in order to make a living, and goodness and badness are not reasonable principles. Similarly, a human who is incapable of reasoning or understanding abstract concepts (such as a very young child or a mentally defective adult) cannot be held responsible for an act that injures another, because such human patients are unable to understand the concept of right or wrong, or sometimes even the causal relationship between their action and the resulting injury.

    A distinction must be made between moral standing and moral relevance. Schonfeld (1992) considered this issue and arrived at the conclusion that moral standing is possessed by any entity whose continued existence and well-being is desirable and who has an interest in maintaining such a state of well-being. He argued that anthropocentrism is the starting point for ethics, and adopted the position that only human beings can have moral interests that impose duties on others.

These others (animals, plants, and ecosystems) do not have moral standing, but they do have moral relevance. Those with moral standing have duties and responsibilities toward entities that have moral relevance, be they ecosystems or organisms that qualify as moral patients. It is critical to note that moral standing is granted on the grounds of freedom and rationality. I will argue that this anthropocentric position can be grounded on evolutionary and cognitive bases to support the argument that only human moral agents have moral standing and that human moral patients have a higher moral relevance than do nonhuman entities.

Schonfeld (1992) reached the conclusion that it is justifiable to allow hierarchical gradation in moral standing (I prefer the term "relevance") of different entities as long as the hierarchy is based on facts such as uniquely human capacities. I would add that these facts involve rationality and sufficient cognitive capacity to conceptualize rule-bound behavioral systems.

It is essential not to include and exclude classes of organisms arbitrarily in their qualification for the moral standing due to moral agents, and the only way to avoid such arbitrariness is to establish explicit criteria that place an individual in the category of agent or patient. One such attempt has been made by Regan (1983) who used what he calls "the subject-of-a-life criterion." An individual is a subject-of-a-life if it has beliefs and desires, perception, memory, and a sense of the future; an emotional life together with feelings of pleasure and pain; preference and welfare interests; the ability to initiate action in pursuit of desires and goals; and a self-identity over time. Regan argued that these characteristics establish a moral value for such individuals, thereby qualifying them as moral agents, and every moral agent must be given the same egalitarian, respectful treatment due any other.

WHAT IS A PERSON?

Another problem concerns which organisms should be considered to be persons and when the status of personhood begins. Much of the debate regarding permissible procedures that can be used to intervene in the course of life involves questions regarding personhood. For example, questions in the realm of abortion often hinge on determining when a fetus should be considered to be a person. Questions in the realm of euthanasia hinge on a decision regarding when personhood ceases. It is clear what is meant when the term "human being" is used; it refers to the members of the biological species *Homo sapiens*. But when does a human organism become, and when does it stop being, a person? Some argue that even the fertilized, unimplanted egg should be accorded the status of personhood because of its potential to become a person. This view leads them to bestow a right to life at this early stage, and to argue that it is intrinsically wrong to destroy the potential person represented by the zygote. The potentiality argument will be considered and rejected in Chapter 10.

Other philosophers, such as Tooley (1983), argue that one should consider at what point in development a human being *is* a person, and not merely a potential person. A zygote should not be treated as a potential president of the United States because one cannot know if that zygote will develop into the president until it has become the president. According to this argument, one zygote should be treated in a manner equal to every other zygote at the point of conception. Parenthetically, it should be noted that Diamond (1992a) estimated that 50% of implanted embryos are miscarried, and when an estimate of the number of embryos lost before implantation is included, it is reasonable to estimate the total loss of fertilized zygotes to be as high as 80%. Given the small likelihood that any fertilized cell will become even a viable fetus, the potentiality of the cell becoming president is almost a vanishing probability. It would seem more reasonable to confer the right to life by virtue of some present properties of the organism rather than by virtue of potentiality. The term "person" should be understood in such a way that it applies to all entities with a specific set of properties, rather than rest on some problematic sequence of presumed developmental eventualities (see Chapters 8 through 11).

Rights

Because only moral agents can be held to have moral duties, and the concept of rights is a social, legal, and philosophical construct which can only be comprehended by human agents, the question arises whether moral patients can be considered to have rights, or whether their rights are so indirect that the problem should be considered in some other light. It is arguable that the concept of rights should be applied only to organisms that have the cognitive capacity to comprehend the terms in order to stake out a rights claim. The acceptance of this argument leads to a charge of speciesism that must be considered. An undesirable aspect of speciesism involves the declaration that no nonhuman animal or plant belongs to the moral community of the "right species"—*Homo sapiens*. Such a declaration denies all animals, as well as human moral patients, any moral rights.

Singer (1975) argued that by assuming that moral rules apply only to rational human beings (us!), and that this application is appropriate only by reason of being human, we are led to a position no different from those characteristic of racism and sexism. This argument must be addressed carefully and, in Chapter 9, I will maintain that the concept of rights only applies to those humans who are able to claim them, and that animals should not be considered to have rights (as Regan [1983], argued they should). Brandt (1987) adds that it is difficult to ascribe rights to organisms that cannot make a protest or feel resentment. Perhaps, he suggested, it is only essential to say that they would be justified in protesting if they could, and that agents have a moral obligation to treat infants, fetuses, and animals in certain ways, irrespective of whether they have rights. It seems reasonable to argue in terms of interests (as Singer [1975] argued), value, welfare, and duties. To establish any basic moral premise and argue it consistently, the question of whether rights, duties, interests, value, and welfare should be accorded to different classes of individuals must be carefully considered.

If we inquire further into the question of rights, then we must decide what are the basic rights that all people have. Most would agree that the positive rights must include those that ensure biological survival, as well as the negative rights not to suffer pain, hunger, thirst, and the like. As Paul Goodman (1972, p. 75) expressed it, "I want only that the children have bright eyes, the river be clean, food and sex be available, and nobody be pushed around." Do we have a right (basic or derived) to express our views freely and on all subjects (what if they are considered treasonous to the idea of rights itself)? Do we have the right always to receive respectful treatment? How does one establish the balance between rights and duties: Does the existence of rights entail a system of duties that might constrain or limit rights of an individual in relation to the rights of others?

There has been discussion regarding whether one should bring the question of equality to bear, especially when considering animal welfare. The question is whether organisms possess moral standing (or at least relevance) that invests them with value. It is arguable that all who are considered moral agents should be given their due with complete equality. The question still remains whether or not all moral agents have the same inherent value, and, if not, is it necessary to treat all individuals (including moral patients) in a manner that will recognize their relative value? The problem still remains how relative moral value should be calculated: Does a miniscule amount of value constitute enough to pass the threshold that justifies equal treatment, or is some greater value required to justify preferential treatment?

Value

Regan (1983) argued that an individual ought not to be evaluated as a receptacle containing more or less value in comparison to others. However, a careful reading of the literature bearing on moral decision making convinces me that, at some point, relative value almost always does enter into the decision process. For example, Regan used what is known as the lifeboat dilemma to develop his arguments. In this lifeboat dilemma one is asked to imagine that a ship has sunk and that there are five survivors in a lifeboat. The lifeboat will only accommodate four individuals, however, making it necessary to throw one individual overboard, and that individual will drown. In one scenario the five individuals include four humans and one dog. Regan concluded that it is morally correct to throw overboard the one dog in preference to any one of the humans. He argued that this decision is not based on any aggregate value, but on the fact that the dog has fewer opportunities for satisfaction than does any one of the humans. Thus, each individual human would suffer a greater harm than would the dog and would, thereby, be "worse off" because each would not realize a greater potential satisfaction. The dog suffers less harm than would any single human; therefore, the dog should be sacrificed. I believe that a relative value has been calculated, surreptitiously in this instance, and that this lesser value assigned to the dog is being used to justify a moral decision.

I will argue, as I did when discussing consequentialism, that when decisions must be made between the legitimate interests of different organisms some formal or informal value calculation is required and usually occurs, even if it is an "under-the-counter" calculation, and that the calculation should be based on explicit guidelines, such as sentience, interest, desire, or preference. I want to make it clear that all entities, whether moral agents or moral patients, can have value, that these values can take different magnitudes, but that some values might trump in certain circumstances. I believe that these calculations do take place, usually implicitly, and agree with Donagan (1977) that one problem with such consequentialist calculations is that they do not have any scientific basis (scientific in the sense of being done on the basis of a rational, explicit, and public calculus). Such calculations must be based on acceptable standards, as Donagan (1977) suggests, or there is nothing to consequentialism but advocacy.

Grave problems arise when comparing the relative merits of different values. Becker (1973) argued that it is possible to value a person or object in different ways, and that the meaning of the entity could be considered from different perspectives, the single entity taking a large number of different legitimate values. Most entities are likely to be valued affectively in more than one way, being liked by some and disliked by others. Because each entity can be bad for as many purposes as it is good, it can take many values. Consequently it is hard to imagine how one could specify *the* value of an entity; there are several values, and they are distributed in specified ways given different circumstances.

If the above argument regarding the conceptual impossibility of setting a single moral value for a given object is cogent, then there is a problem when making a decision regarding the proper course of conduct given that there can be several different values for the members of a set of interacting individuals. The need is for some nonarbitrary way to establish the different values and to quantify or rank them in terms of the relative weight they should have to arrive at moral decisions, given specified conditions.

A schema to ground the estimates of objective value was developed by Paul Grice (1991). He characterized living creatures in terms of what they *do*, and suggested that a standard to evaluate the goodness of creatures might be in terms of how adequately the behavior or creature does what it is supposed to do. He considered the complex attributes of rationality to be an accidental property of humans that provide a necessity for people to ground their concerns in logically consistent ways. This accidental property becomes the essential property of persons (what I have called moral agents), and people can be characterized in terms of the adequacy of their cognitive functioning. In Grice's view this moves rationality from an accidental property of moral agents to an essential one. He suggested that such a conception might provide the basis on which to derive some absolute moral values. He might be correct that this conception will move us in the right direction, but I suspect the amount of specification remaining is of staggering proportions.

Justice

Attention should be directed to the concept of justice. One basic element of this concept is that all similar individuals should be treated the same. Kant argued that one should act in such a way that those principles used to regulate specific actions could be accepted as a universal law. Rawls (1971) has examined the ideas regarding justice extensively and points out that happiness presupposes the enjoyment of primary human goods, such as health, a certain amount of wealth, and a respected place in a free society. He considered the principles of justice in the light of fairness within the structure of society, and argued that these principles should be considered to be agreements that free and rational persons have accepted from an initial position of equality. It is within the bounds of agreements regarding such principles that basic rights and duties are assigned and social benefits are divided.

Rawls believes that the idea of a social contract is of primary importance to establish justice. Feinberg (1989), construes Rawls' theory to fall within a social contract tradition, noting that Rawls emphasizes that one has an obligation to do one's part if benefits and opportunities, in terms of goods provided by the institution, are accepted. It is also important to Rawls, as Feinberg noted, that the rules should not be changed in the middle of the game because that would disappoint the honest expectations of those whose prior commitments and life plans were made with the assumption that the rules would be continued. Rawls argues, as noted in Chapter 1, that the terms of the contract should be established behind a veil of ignorance regarding which social position one will be in as a participant in the structure of the agreement. This veil of ignorance is intended to produce a fair symmetry between individuals as moral persons, because the participants would be inclined to achieve a fair balance for all concerned, and should develop agreements as if they did not know their role in the agreement.

To establish the basic principles we should, according to Rawls, invoke a difference principle: The position of the better-off is to be improved only if it is necessary to improve the position of the worst-off. This argues that persons who are equals should not agree to a principle which would require lesser life prospects for some, simply for the sake of a greater sum of advantages enjoyed by others.

Rawls (1971) based his argument on two principles: The first principle requires equality in the assignment of basic rights and duties, while the second holds that social and economic inequalities can be considered to be just only if they result in compensating benefits for everyone; in particular for the least advantaged members of society. There is no injustice in choices that produce greater benefits for the few provided that the situation of less fortunate persons is improved as well. Rawls points out that he refers primarily to our relations with other persons, and leaves out of the account how we are to conduct ourselves toward animals and the rest of nature. I will argue that a contract theory such as he has developed is compatible with the principles that characterize evolutionary theory and that this line of thinking can be extended more broadly with little difficulty.

In order for Rawls' theory to be applicable there must be a way to settle what he refers to as questions of priority of the plurality of principles that are involved. He considers the assignment of these weights to be an essential part of a conception of justice and that rational discussion depends on an explanation of how these weights are to be determined. The basic principle of justice is that all primary goods, which he identifies as liberty and opportunity, income and wealth, and the bases of self respect, must be distributed equally unless an unequal distribution of them is to the advantage of the least favored. Feinberg (1989) noted that the duty to uphold justice, as defined by the rules of established just practices and institutions, provides principles for design of these practices and institutions rather than principles to determine individual actions. As discussed above, the assignment of weights to a set of incommensurate values is a serious problem when attempting to use a set of moral principles to decide on appropriate courses of action.

The aim of this brief discussion of moral philosophy is to introduce ideas and concepts, which should be considered if we are to arrive at positions that are tenable philosophically. I have sketched some of the issues that philosophers invoke when they develop ideas of morality, and later, will bring these ideas to bear on the resolution of specific moral issues. I believe these philosophical concerns can clarify arguments regarding some of the issues related to reproduction and life that will be of concern in the second part of this book.

COGNITIVE SCIENCE

I will now consider ideas developed by those academics lumped under the title cognitive scientists. The field of cognitive science is a hybrid discipline of rather recent designation, but from a long and important tradition. The very first academics to be called psychologists were interested in problems of sensation and perception, learning and memory, thinking, emotion, and motivation, and pursued these interests through experimentation and the analysis of human introspections. The initial enterprise was supplanted by the aggressive onslaught of American Behaviorism, which incorporated a strong influence of Pavlovian reflexology. These Behaviorists argued that psychology should be interested in objective analyses of the lawful and universal relationships between stimuli and responses, and they endorsed a strong version of positivism. Evidence from animal experiments was considered admissible to provide understanding of human behavior because the assumption was accepted that the basic processes underlying behavior were the same for all species—a bastardization of Darwinian evolutionary principles.

An enthusiastic and exclusive emphasis on laboratory experimentation gradually gave way to an emphasis on problems that interested a large number of scientists in a variety of disciplines, as well as on issues discussed by philosophers concerned with mental events. These issues concerned such things as feeling (sentience), awareness, consciousness, desires and wants, interests, intentionality, imagery, representation, and the nature of language and communication. Not long ago the field known as experimental psychology designated itself as cognitive psychology, and the most recent development has been to expand the area further, and it has redesignated itself as cognitive science. This latter change was not a trivial exercise in labeling, but reflected the true hybrid nature of the emerging enterprise. The field of cognitive science involves a wide range of specialists including experimental psychologists, animal behaviorists (within biology they tend to be from the field of ethology, and within psychology from the field of comparative psychology), linguists, anthropologists, philosophers, computer scientists, and engineers. The hybrid vigor of this field is still expanding our understanding of the basic processes that interested the first psychologists, and that are of enduring interest to people in general. Some of the general principles developed by cognitive scientists will be discussed in Chapters 8 and 9 when the characteristics of moral agents are considered. These cognitive principles are important to consider because I will propose a cognitive test for moral standing in Chapter 9.

RATIONAL LIBERALISM

I will characterize the philosophical position that will inform some of the argumentation in this book as a rational liberalism, and believe that its principles should be applied in those instances when evolutionary and utilitarian considerations are not involved directly. The use of this liberalism will provide the operative principles when there is no direct concern with reproduction or when utilitarian calculations are not possible.

The type of liberalism that I will argue is based on John Stuart Mill's consequentialist ideas. Brink (1992) construed Mill's views to be those of act utilitarianism by which an act is right if its consequences for human welfare are at least as good as any alternative act available to the agent. Mill reduced hedonistic pleasures to a lesser role than the intellectual pleasures that are realized by actions, activities, and pursuits that exercise our intellectual capacities. It is intellectual activity rather than attaining in a certain sort of mental state that has the greatest value, and this activity is intrinsically more valuable than the lower hedonic pleasures. Brink noted that, according to Mill, this most important deliberative activity is involved in the reflective choice and implementation of structural plans in a manner that allows one to form, revise, assess, choose, and implement one's own plans and projects, and not simply that these plans and projects have certain kinds of contents. Mill argued that the most debilitating aspects involved in the treatment of women is their subjugation by sexist institutions and the exercise of attitudes that prevent women from developing their rational and deliberative powers.

Feinberg (1986) developed a liberalism based on two basic principles derived from Mill's classic essay "On Liberty" (1859/1962): Harm and offense. In that essay Mill argued for one very simple principle (which Feinberg split into two) to govern absolutely the dealings of society with the individual. Mill argued (p. 135), "That the only purpose for which power can be rightfully exercised over any member of a civilized community, against his will, is to prevent harm to others" and (p. 138), "The only freedom which deserves the name, is that of pursuing our own good in our own way, so long as we do not attempt to deprive others of theirs, or impede their efforts to obtain it." Mill believed that this freedom was absolute (p. 135); "Over himself, over his own body and mind, the individual is sovereign."

A subsidiary point that Mill mentioned, concerned the importance of recognizing that the doctrine applied only to mature human beings (what I referred to as moral agents) and not to those who are immature, defenseless, or unable to function at a mature level (moral patients). This emphasis led Feinberg (1986) to stress the necessity of determining that a behavioral decision is a voluntary one, performed by a competent, rational person in order to establish the moral permissibility of the action.

One problem introduced by adding the caveat that moral permissibility is determined by the voluntariness of a decision is that someone must evaluate the behavior, either to permit it as moral or sanction it as immoral. The problem is to avoid paternalism whereby the evaluator (e.g., the state) must stand to individuals as a parent (of course, a male parent) stands to his children. Feinberg considers paternalism to mean that the state stands to its citizens as a parent (a male parent) stands to his children. He distinguished between a hard and a soft paternalism. The former is one in which society forbids people to perform certain actions, either "for their own good" or "for the good of society," whatever their own wishes might be. Mill argued that an agent is a more reliable judge of what is good on its behalf and that even well-intentioned rulers will promote the good of citizens less well than the citizens would themselves. Hard paternalism is usually backed by coercive legislation and has been called legal paternalism.

Soft paternalism exists whenever it is decided that individuals are not capable of making a truly voluntary decision, because of temporary or permanent incapacitation or vulnerability, and must be protected for their own good, as parents protect their children. Soft paternalism allows respect for the voluntary and free choice of individuals. Legislation enacted in the interest of soft paternalism is to prevent harmful self-directed actions which are not voluntary or to intervene until the voluntary nature of the actions can be determined. With soft paternalism the law is concerned with the voluntary and rational nature of the choice and not with its wisdom or correctness.

Feinberg (1986, p. 36) accepted Mill's harm principle basic, defining it as "wrongs that are a setback to interests." He defined interests as those components of a person's well-being, with the test for harm being whether an action by another leaves the person's interests in worse condition than if the action had not taken place. A wrong is defined as an unjustifiable and inexcusable action that violates the person's rights. Feinberg supplemented the harm principle with an offense principle, which he defined as hurt produced by deep revulsion to the act of another, such as indecent exposure, open lewdness, solicitation for lewd purposes, or making ethnic slurs.

A subsidiary principal to the harm and offense principles was added by Feinberg (1986) which, although he reluctantly referred to it as "soft paternalism," he questioned that is really was any kind of paternalism. He decided to retain the term "soft paternalism" to continue standard terminology but did so (p. 16), "while muttering, from time to time, in *sotto voce*, that soft paternalism is really no kind of paternalism at all." I agree that it is not paternalism and suggest that it would be better to avoid completely the sexist and pejorative implications of the term "paternalism," and to identify it in terms of reason. The concept is meant to refer to a reasonable constraint on any complete and unbridled freedom, a qualification that is central to liberalism. Because the restrictions are being introduced for the purpose of ensuring that choices are the free, voluntary, and rational decision of an individual, I believe that the term "rational liberalism" catches the essence of the reasons why restrictions are placed on free choice.

An important distinction between paternalism and liberalism was emphasized by Feinberg (1986). Paternalism is based on the assumption that the state has a right to prevent people from engaging in behaviors that would be harmful to themselves. Liberalism is based on the assumption that the state has the right to prevent harmful conduct only when it is nonvoluntary or when temporary intervention is necessary to establish that the person is able to make a rational judgment.

A useful distinction can be made between paternalism and paternalistic. Paternalism uses a theory which imposes values and judgments, while paternalistic refers to behavioral actions. Thus, an action by society might be a paternalistic one because it interferes with the activities of an individual. However, this action by society does not necessarily imply a paternalism in the sense of being an attempt to enforce a set of values on the person. When imposing rational constraints one is not questioning the prudence of the choice but is attempting to determine that the choice is a free and voluntary one made by a moral agent.

There are several concerns that make it reasonable to place some restrictions on the free choices of persons, even though these choices might not violate either the harm or offense principles. One concern is that some acts are serious and irrevocable, such as self-mutilation and suicide. Before these acts are considered to be morally permissible it is reasonable to provide nonpunitive confinement when appropriate, and make available counseling, guidance, and therapy to enhance the probability that the choice made is a rational, informed, and voluntary one. I emphasize the question of paternalism because it will appear quite often when the permissibility of abortion is argued and when there are discussions of whether the new reproductive technologies should be used widely.

Mill argued that certain sorts of cooperative social capacities are among the higher intellectual capacities and that by exercising these cooperative capacities, interests are extended by engaging in new and more complex forms of practical deliberation than those available to individuals acting alone. Brandt (1987) argued a position regarding morality that is close to what I am espousing here. His argument (p. 354) was that, "a policy is justified from a moral point of view if and only if it is one that factually informed, rational, and otherwise normal persons would *want* for a society in which they expected to live a lifetime." He expressed the optimistic belief that the policies that would prevail in such a society would be most beneficial for society in the long run.

SUMMARY

This brief discussion of some of the basic concerns involved when considering questions of morality is intended to lay the groundwork for the substantive discussions to follow. Other philosophical questions were considered in Chapter 1 where concerns about the methodology of argumentation were discussed, and in Chapter 2, where I examined the issue of naturalism and discussed the naturalistic fallacy. The latter problem has been considered troublesome whenever attempts are made to ground a moral system on biological principles, but I argued that naturalism does not necessarily imply any fallacy. I also discussed one further issue in philosophical argumentation in Chapter 2: The slippery slope fallacy. I argue that it is a fallacy unless one specifies the processes involved and identifies the causal mechanisms producing an inevitable progression from a first step to an inevitable conclusion.

7

The Study of Moral Intuitions

Before discussing the outcomes of the studies we have done of the way in which people resolve fantasy dilemmas, some recent approaches toward a biological understanding of morality will be considered. Then, some basic moral issues will be developed that were selected because of their centrality to the arguments concerning evolutionary biology and moral philosophy that have been raised in Chapters 2 through 6. It is argued that understanding the dimensions of belief involved in the resolution of the fantasy dilemmas can provide an indication of the basic nature of moral beliefs, and that this understanding might be a step toward establishing the *is*. The intent of the empirical studies of moral intuitions is to identify the basic moral dimensions people use to resolve fantasy moral dilemmas. I will argue that the ways people choose to resolve these dilemmas reveal the coherence of moral belief systems.

BIOLOGY OF MORALITY

E. O. Wilson (1975) started the current interest and active debate concerning the biology of morality. He suggested that standards of good and evil might have evolved through natural selection of nervous system structures, such as those of the hypothalamus and limbic system. Such statements, as well as suggestions that ethics should be removed from the hands of the philosophers and "biologicized," were greeted with howls of outrage from many quarters. He did, however, stimulate serious consideration by philosophers, psychologists, and biologists regarding the possibility of developing a biologically based ethics, and, by framing the issues in an informed and provocative manner, he induced humanists, as well as social and biological scientists, to clarify the issues, to focus the discussions on the relevant factual matters, and to debate the merits and limitations of his philosophical and social positions.

For example, Ruse (1979) was one of the leading philosophers who took up the cause and suggested that although the most enthusiastic sociobiologists would not argue that the whole task of explaining the evolution of morality had been completed at that time, it could be claimed that the essential outline had been sketched, utilizing such mechanisms as kin selection and reciprocal altruism. Although Ruse emphasized the importance of evolutionary changes, he issued a strong caveat to the effect that if we wish to do something about human social behavior, then the most obvious place to start is with an evaluation of the structure of the environment, not the genes. He concluded, however, that a knowledge of sociobiology could improve human social relations, and that is the point that I am arguing here.

Ruse and Wilson coauthored a paper in which they considered the proposition that a biologically based moral philosophy could be developed as an applied science. Their basic assumption was (Ruse & Wilson, 1986, p. 173), "That everything human, including mind and culture, has a material base and originated during the evolution of the human genetic constitution and its interaction with the environment." They suggested that internal, biologically grounded moral premises do exist and can be defined precisely. They based these premises on the concepts of kin selection and reciprocal altruism, and emphasized that human thinking might be under the influence of what they referred to as "epigenetic rules" whenever these biological tendencies are involved. These epigenetic rules are genetically based processes of development that predispose individuals to adopt one or a few forms of behavior as opposed to others. I believe that it is better to consider this epigenesis in terms of biases rather than to invoke the idea of definite rules. They continue (Ruse & E. O. Wilson, 1986, pp. 180–181), "These [epigenetic rules] predispose us to think that certain courses of action are right and certain courses of action are wrong. The rules certainly do not lock people blindly into certain behaviour . . . but the choices are narrowed and hardened through contractual agreements and sanctification."

Ruse and Wilson point to developmental biases in cognition and behavior, such as an optimal degree of redundancy in geometric design, universal facial expressions to denote basic emotions, universal taste preferences, and various fears (including children's fear of strangers, snakes, and spiders). Certain phobias that seem to be acquired easily and generally are appropriate to survival needs, given the probable perils of life in the environment of evolutionary adaptation. They suggest that such phobias evolved through natural selection. Kellert and E. O. Wilson (1993) develop these arguments more fully and extend them to the understanding of problems people face when embedded in an urban setting.

While Ruse and Wilson have presented an enterprising and ambitious set of proclamations, the most careful development of the problems and principles involved in establishing a biology of moral systems has been done by Alexander in two books. Alexander (1979) reviewed principles in evolutionary biology that might shed light on human behavior (see Chapters 3, 4, and 5). Alexander emphasized the point that organisms have evolved to be altruists whose beneficence is directed, initially, toward relatives. He suggested that such organisms have evolved to be "maximally effective nepotists," and believes that the first priority for those investigating social behavior is to discover how such behaviors relate to reproductive success in current environments, as well as to puzzle over how these behavioral tendencies developed from activities that occurred in the environment of evolutionary adaptation. I agree with his strong conclusion to the effect that (Alexander, 1979, p. 143), "in the 120 years since Darwin, the burden of proof has shifted unequivocally to those who would defend any other argument."

Alexander carefully avoided committing the naturalistic fallacy by emphasizing the plasticity of human cognitive and social behavior that occurred in the unpredictable environments that humans faced throughout the geological history during which they evolved. Alexander follows a cautious line which defeats the kinds of criticisms that the original positions taken by E. O. Wilson evoked.

Alexander (1987) once again adopted a cautious tone, but one that approaches the central questions of ethics directly. He wrote, (p. 40) "Evolution is surely most deterministic for those still unaware of it. If this argument is correct, it may be the first to carry us from *is* to *ought*, i.e., if we desire to be the conscious masters of our own fates, and if conscious effort in that direction is the most likely vehicle of survival and happiness, then we *ought* to study evolution." He adopts a contractarian view of morality in which individuals act in ways that enhance their own ultimate reproductive interests. The interests of individuals can be furthered by cooperation with others (both relatives and nonrelatives) through direct and indirect reciprocity, and moral rules will consist of restraints on the methods people might use to fulfill self-interests that are deleterious to the self-interests of others.

Alexander found no evidence for an absolute core of morality He argued that there are cost–benefit decisions that individuals must make to deal with the structure of society in order to gain their ends. Actions are taken to balance costs and benefits in a manner that will produce harmonious associations, enabling everyone to pursue his or her own self-interest to some degree. It could be argued that this conception of biological determinism is sufficient as a weak absolute for a strong biologically based moral system.

Throughout his 1987 work, Alexander cautioned that no solutions are produced through an evolutionary understanding because morality is a matter that concerns whose interests one should serve and how much each individual's interests should be allowed to prevail over the legitimate interests of others. He emphasized that evolutionary knowledge can provide information about the reasons current conditions might exist, and that such knowledge can even lead to some predictions regarding the likely outcome of alternative courses of action that can be taken, given prevailing conditions. He cautioned that we should "watch out" when we decide to pursue any kind of biological approach to moral issues, but concluded (p. 225), "on the whole, we had better *proceed*." I am pursuing the optimism Alexander adopted when he argued that, to get people beyond the perils of error and unrecognized biases, one should teach evolutionary biology to the citizens of society. An understanding of evolutionary processes, added to those of philosophy, psychology, history, the social sciences, and the humanities could prove to be of tremendous value if we are to attain a just and moral human condition.

SOME BASIC MORAL ISSUES

There are several moral issues that will be investigated by building them into a study of moral intuitions. These issues were drawn from the many possible ones and selected because they seemed to be the most appropriate when considering problems in bioethics. Philosophers and evolutionists have developed most of these principles with enough clarity that evidence and logic can be brought to bear to estimate their relative importance. Each will be introduced in turn to set the stage for the presentation of the empirical research program into the nature of moral intuitions.

Should Numbers Count?

In Chapter 6 concern was expressed regarding the lack of success in developing an adequate method to either quantitatively or qualitatively establish the relative weights that should be assigned to different moral considerations. The problem becomes especially acute when one considers instances in which two principles, different but each applicable, lead to contradictory recommendations. The question is, which should prevail and why?

One seemingly simple issue involves the extent to which the number of individuals affected by a decision should influence the nature of the recommended action. At first glance it might seem obvious that, if a choice must be made either to harm or to benefit certain individuals, the number of individuals affected by the different choices should be a major factor determining what should be done. However, upon careful analysis the solution of the problem is not obvious at all.

An interesting argument that the numbers should not count was presented by Taurek (1977). He outlined a fantasy dilemma in which there is a lifesaving drug available and a choice must be made between saving one person who requires all of the drug, or saving five people, each of whom requires only one-fifth of the drug. The simple consequentialist solution would be to save the five because they constitute the greater number. Taurek argued, however, that this choice could be inconsistent with other moral convictions, given certain considerations. Assume that the one person owns the drug: Should that individual be compelled morally to save the five and, thereby, forfeit life? Because there are more of them are the five justified in forcibly taking the drug for themselves? Does the one person have a moral obligation to give the drug to save the five, or would that merely be a nice, unselfish thing to do, with it not being morally wrong to save your own life in preference to the lives of five strangers?

What if I, a third party, have the drug? What is the morally right thing for me to do: Should I give it to the five, thereby saving the greater number at the expense of the one, or is it permissible to save the one? Should I flip a coin to determine whether the one gets the drug or the five—a decision that gives each individual an equal chance of being saved. What should I do if the one is my sister, and the five are strangers: Should numbers prevail now that the special consideration of kin has been introduced? What if the one is a friend and the five are strangers: Does that make a difference in my moral obligation as compared to when all six individuals are strangers? What if, previously, I had promised the drug to the one, who needs it all, and then the five appeared, each needing only one-fifth of the drug to be saved: Does the social contract I have with the one regulate my moral responsibility? Finally, what if the one is a famous scientist engaged in promising pharmaceutical research, and the five are factory workers: Does the consideration of the probable beneficial contribution of the scientist influence my moral responsibility? As with most questions regarding morality, what seemed to be a simple matter on the surface becomes incredibly complicated as soon as the kinds of special considerations that always exist in reality are introduced.

I will not pursue his arguments in detail, but Taurek came to the conclusion that the numbers should not count when opposed to several special considerations of the kinds introduced above. In some circumstances he found it to be morally permissible to save the one in preference to the five. Part of his reasoning was that giving the drug to the one violates no one's rights because, in several of the basic situations he developed, none of the five had any legitimate claim to the drug. Taurek argued that it makes no difference whether the one person is saved when set against the 5 or against 50. If he were making the decision between two sets of strangers he would flip a coin to decide fairly: Heads the one wins, tails the 5 (or 50) do. This process gives each individual a 50% chance of being the winner. (Dickey [1992] offered a thoughtful objection to Taurek's strategy, which complicates the matter even more. He argued that if one assumes there is a distribution of the relative amount of loss for different people, then statistically there is a higher probability that a member of the larger group will exist who will suffer a greater loss than that expected for any one stranger.)

Taurek argued that, if the choice to be made is between one physical object or five *objects* (with each of the six being of equal value), he would save the five *objects* because of their greater value. However, he chooses not to think of human beings as containing a finite amount of objective value. This choice prevents him from using the combined value of people to reach a decision in a manner that would be permissible if objects were involved. Taurek's view assumes that, with humans, there are social obligations and rights that must be considered and that these social obligations take priority over (*trump*) any objective quantitative value other considerations might introduce. Individual human beings must not be considered as receptacles containing more or less value. (Regan [1983] adopted a similar position when arguing for the rights of animals.)

There have been several responses to Taurek's analysis, and those interested can find the Taurek paper, and three responses in Fischer and Ravizza (1992). The purpose of introducing the numbers issue at such length was to glimpse some of the complexities that enter discussions of even such a simple moral problem as the influence of different numbers of individuals on one's moral responsibilities. Empirical data concerning the importance of the numbers of individuals to moral intuitions will be presented below.

The Additivity Argument

An issue that is related to the basic numbers problem has been raised by Kagan (1988) who discusses what he called the "additive fallacy." This fallacy concerns the rules that should apply when different moral factors must be combined to decide what should be done in situations where there is more than one applicable moral factor that can be brought to bear. The problem becomes even more serious when different moral factors would lead one to incompatible conclusions regarding what should be done.

One obvious consequentialist solution could be to add the values together, and to recommend that course of action that has the highest value. While such a solution is attractive, due to its simplicity, it is just not adequate to the task. There is the obvious problem of properly assigning relative values to the different factors, and it is also clear that some factors trump others. As discussed in Chapter 6, one might consider it appropriate to use a multiplicative rule rather than an additive one. For example, if a given course of action involves killing a human in preference to an animal of another species, then it could be argued that the human trumps. The way to represent this trump is to express it as a multiplicative function, which assigns some positive "species" value to the human, but assigns a zero "species" value to animals of any other species. No matter what other values are assigned to the different types of people, if a nonhuman animal is involved it is of zero value, and anything multiplied by zero is zero. With this scheme the human alternative will prevail as long as the humans involved are assigned any positive value whatever.

Even this simple solution is not adequate because moral dimensions might be composed of individual factors that cluster together to determine the moral permissibility of a choice, and such "cluster values" might have to be considered as a complexly interacting set before being entered into any formulaic expression to arrive at a recommendation for action. A factor considered in isolation might lead one to recommend a specific action but, when considered in a context with other factors, would lead one to recommend a totally different action. For example, murdering a human being is not morally permissible under usual circumstances. However, if the murder is committed in self-defense, then the killing of the attacker could be morally permissible. How does one compare the relative value of one harm, or the imposition of a given action, as compared to other harms or actions? How does one place a relative value on helping to a certain degree as compared to harming to a certain degree? One could add more complexity to such examples, but I take the point to be obvious.

A simple additive principle will not provide an adequate rule by which to combine different moral factors. As Kagan (1988) argued, clusters of features must be identified that combine to justify certain actions, and the cluster identification must be based on sound fundamental moral theory. I believe that such fundamental theory could lead to recommendations regarding the moral thing to do that does not violate moral intuitions.

Consequentialist calculations could be attempted but, as with any measurement scheme, the assignment of qualitative or quantitative values must be done publicly, the rules must be explicit for the assignment, the rules for the combination of individual values will have to be grounded on a sound fundamental moral theory, and this enterprise might well turn out to be extremely difficult.

Action and Omission

This issue involves the relative moral permissibility of acting to cause an outcome as compared to failing to act, thereby letting the outcome occur by omission. Is it more permissible to let someone die than to kill the person? Is it more permissible to fail to benefit people than to harm them? The question has also been considered within the context of what is called the Doctrine of Double Effect, which distinguishes between ends that are intended and means that are used. Thus, some ends are intended, but others happen only as side-effects when the major intended end is attained.

I do not believe that concerns related to action and omission reflect a basic moral dimension. People do make decisions in cases where acts or omissions are involved, but it appears that it is difficult to arrive at any general rules that are adequate to regulate all cases. When specific cases are examined, the difference between the moral status of killing as compared to letting die is difficult to apply in any simple, consistent way to yield conclusions about issues such as abortion, organ transplants, euthanasia, or the distribution of scarce medical resources (Thomson, 1976).

Social Contracts

The important considerations that drive moral decisions involve a number of concerns related to social contracts. These concerns include such things as whether a promise has been made, whether ownership of resources was established, whether any of the participants caused the existing state of affairs, what were the intentions of the different agents, what is the relative ease and cost of the different possible actions, what is the relative certainty of the different outcomes, and what is the cost to society, as well as to the individuals involved? The conclusion that the existence of social obligations is important to determine the morality of decisions has been developed and supported by a number of philosophers, among them Boorse and Sorensen, 1988; Quinn, 1989; Russell, 1977; Thomson, 1976; Tooley, 1980; and Trammel, 1975.

All of the examples above involve arguments regarding social contracts and can be analyzed in terms of the cost and benefit of the various options. Quinn (1989, p. 158) pointed out that a, "basic and urgent moral task is to define our proper powers and immunities with respect to one another, to specify the mutual authority and respect that are the basic terms of voluntary human association." He concluded that, "we should recognize that, in giving each person substantial authority over what can rightly be done to him, the doctrine conveys an important and attractive idea of what it is to be a citizen rather than a subject in the moral world."

The idea of a social contract is centrally involved in many characterizations of morality. As discussed above, there are several dimensions involved, rather than a single factor. Some of the suggested dimensions involve concerns regarding personal rights as a result of ownership, as well as those social contracts entered into through agreements that establish obligations and promises. Some contracts are created because an individual is responsible for causing the situation, or because one has accepted and is fulfilling a role, with the understanding that risks might be involved. Many such contracts are the result of voluntary human associations and are occasioned by participation in society. All such social contracts depend on the ability of the moral agents involved to understand the sociolegal concepts on which all obligations and contracts are based, and it must be possible for participants to attain such understanding if the terms of a contract are to be enforced.

The costs to society should be considered as well. If societal cost is an important consideration, then some greater moral value might be assigned to individuals because they are able to contribute extensively to the technological, medical, or cultural welfare of society. Such special considerations are referred to as elitism. Conversely, individuals might have forfeited some of their moral claims and have lesser moral value because they subscribe to an abhorrent political ideology that directs hurtful actions toward others in society.

Another class of social contract that is important is one conditioned by biological associations. These contracts relate to obligations to kin, and to the members of one's own species. It might seem strange to think of these biological factors in terms of social contracts, but it can be argued that these biological factors result in societal structures that regulate social behavior as much as do the usually considered culturally centered ones. An additional consideration is that it is not morally permissible to use persons as a means because that constitutes an affront to their worth and dignity (Russell, 1977).

EMPIRICAL STUDIES OF MORAL INTUITIONS

In the field of psychology there has been renewed interest in questions regarding the nature and development of moral beliefs (Gilligan, 1982), as well as a more general interest in evolutionary psychology (Caporael & Brewer, 1991). The psychologists Jean Piaget (1932) and Lawrence Kohlberg (1971; see Modgil & Modgil [1985] for an overview and evaluation of Kohlberg's ideas) stimulated a great deal of discussion and research regarding the development of different stages of moral development. Piaget mainly concentrated on the stages of development of cognitive structures, while Kohlberg focused on the development of moral rules. Piaget's methods were to conduct intensive interviews with a few children and to pose problems to understand how they thought. He argued for a set of hierarchical stages in moral development that he believed all children move through in order.

Kohlberg conceived of six stages of moral development based on the comprehension by children of different ages of behavior representative of each of the stages. There has been considerable criticism of Kohlberg's basic positions, questioning the adequacy of the philosophical and theological assumptions he makes, and the limited scope of the empirical support and methodology on which his theory is based. One major problem is that the presumed developmental stages are derived from a unidimensional perspective based on principles of justice. Kohlberg assumed that moral development proceeds in a series of linearly increasing and invariant steps, with no reversions to more preliminary stages.

Carol Gilligan (1982) deplored Kohlberg's schema as representing a male orientation, and she argued that women's moral reasoning is organized around a core of attachment and affection rather than around Kohlberg's ideas of justice or Piaget's emphasis on the elaboration of legal rules. One problem is that Kohlberg, Piaget, and Gilligan have all relied on theory driven, unidimensional conceptual models to develop their empirical testing and have relied basically on limited subject samples to develop their models of morality. Although Gilligan and others have alleged that there is a gender bias in Kohlberg's theory, a critical review of the literature by Walker (1984) indicated that gender differences in moral development were found in only 8 of the 108 samples summarized, and that some of these differences occurred because of methodological flaws. An extensive study using the Kohlberg scheme was done by Walker, de Vries, and Trevarthen (1987), and they failed to detect an overall gender bias against women. They found that individuals at a high level of moral development tended to be split in their orientation between an emphasis on the type of response (attachment and affection) and a conception based on rights (justice). The fact that there could be at least two dimensions that cut across gender suggests that male versus female might represent an unfortunate typology, and that the reality is more that of at least two highly overlapping distributions of moral values.

The cross-cultural research literature bearing on social–moral development was reviewed by Snarey (1985) who concluded that Kohlberg's proposition that there was an invariant sequence in moral development was well supported, but that the theoretical model and the procedures by which the interviews are scored do not permit certain moral values to emerge. The values that were suppressed were those that were typical in some traditional folk cultures, working-class communities, and cultures that emphasized reasoning using collective or communalistic principles.

OUR INITIAL EMPIRICAL STUDY

The research program is intended to provide an empirical understanding of the nature of people's beliefs regarding moral issues pertaining to life. The goal is to identify and understand the attitudes people hold, taking as a guideline ideas that different evolutionary biologists and moral philosophers have considered to be important in the moral sphere. I have discussed some of those ideas in Chapters 2 through 6, arguing that it is important to understand the structure of the moral intuitions people use to make decisions. Moral reasoning can be studied empirically as long as it is informed by reasonable philosophical and biological principles, and I hope such is the case here. Whereas much of moral philosophy is based on concepts derived from cultural and societal based models, this research program is based on evolutionary principles, as well as a consideration of those suggested by moral philosophers.

When conceptualizing our research on moral intuitions it was decided, at the outset, to identify the important dimensions involved in the resolution of moral dilemmas by focusing on a range of concerns, rather than only a small number. This procedural choice was made to avoid overemphasizing the importance of a few arbitrarily chosen moral dimensions to the exclusion of others that could be considered to be important by those who have investigated the organization of moral principles.

To obtain some understanding of the coherence of the moral intuitions that people have, we constructed a questionnaire that contained two dilemmas used by moral philosophers to probe the structure of moral attitudes. One of these dilemmas is called the "trolley problem" (Thomson, 1976). In this dilemma a participant is told to imagine that a trolley is hurtling down a track out of control. If it continues on the track it will kill the beings on the track straight ahead. However, there is a switch that can be thrown to shunt the trolley to a side track, but the beings on the side track will be killed. The composition of the beings on the main and side tracks can be varied and the participant is asked to make a life or death choice by deciding to allow the train to continue, or to throw the switch directing the trolley to the side track.

For half of the participants in the first study to be described all trolley problems were phrased in a Kill wording. With the Kill wording all questions were phrased, "Throw the switch, which will result in the death of the one innocent person on the side track," versus "Do nothing, which will result in the death of the five innocent people on the main track." The participants were required to indicate the strength of their agreement or disagreement with each alternative.

For the other half of the participants the questions were phrased in a Save wording. With the Save wording all questions were phrased, "Throw the switch, which will result in the five innocent people on the main track being saved," versus "Do nothing, which will result in the one innocent person on the side track being saved." It should be emphasized that the outcomes of the Kill and Save forms are identical; only the wording of the questions differs.

The second fantasy dilemma was the "lifeboat problem" (Regan, 1983). In this dilemma it is proposed that a ship has sunk, there is a lifeboat with survivors, but some individuals have to be thrown over because of the limited capacity of the lifeboat. The composition of the lifeboat occupants can be varied and the participant is asked to choose who is to drown.

We included eight dimensions in these studies. The dimensions were chosen because they have been identified by philosophers and biologists to be important in determining the choices people seem to use to arrive at moral decisions. We asked participants to state their beliefs concerning some basic moral issues in order to determine whether the beliefs of the participants were coherent and consistent with those of the general U.S. population. In addition, we obtained some demographic information about the participants.

Participants

The participants in the first study were all University of California undergraduate students. While this is a highly selected population, it is an appropriate one to use to evaluate the adequacy of the testing method and to determine if the dimensions we chose are involved to any sizable degree in the resolution of the dilemmas. We obtained estimates of the relative importance of each of the dimensions and determined whether the items chosen as indicators of each basic dimension formed a coherent pattern.

In the first study (Petrinovich, O'Neill, and Jorgensen, 1993) the questionnaire was administered to two psychology classes at the University of California, Riverside, in 1990. The first was a general introductory psychology class with 387 students, and the second was an introductory psychology class with 60 students, all of whom were sophomore premedical students (identified as the biomedical class).

Methods

The participants were told that the questionnaire involved two hypothetical dilemmas that moral philosophers have used to understand the nature of morality. They were told that, although they might not want to perform any of the alternative actions outlined in the questions, they were to decide on the strength of their agreement or disagreement to perform each alternative (on a six-point scale ranging from Strongly Disagree, Moderately Disagree, Slightly Disagree to Slightly Agree, Moderately Agree, Strongly Agree). They were asked to use only the information given and not to introduce additional assumptions that go beyond the problem as stated. We emphasized that, although some of the questions would appear artificial, there were sound philosophical reasons for including all of them. Complete anonymity was guaranteed and that guarantee was honored by retaining only the coded identity of the respondents.

Trolley Problems

There were 21 trolley problems, each with a choice to switch the trolley (Action) or to do nothing (Inaction). The basic statement of these problems was as follows:

> A trolley is hurtling down the tracks. There are five innocent people on the track ahead of the trolley and they will be killed if the trolley continues going straight ahead. There is a spur of track leading off to the side. There is one innocent person on that side track. The brakes of the trolley have failed and there is a switch which can be activated to cause the trolley to go to the side track.
>
> You are an innocent bystander (that is, not an employee of the railroad, etc.). You can throw the switch saving the five innocent people, which will result in the death of the one innocent person on the side track. What would you do?

Lifeboat Problems

There were five lifeboat problems. An example of a lifeboat problem is the following: "A ship has sunk and there are six survivors on a lifeboat. Because of limits of size, the lifeboat can only support five individuals and you must decide what to do. Five of the six are normal adult human beings and the sixth is a collie dog."

"One individual must be thrown over to drown. What would you do?"

1. "Throw the dog over."
2. "Draw lots among the humans and throw the losing human over."
3. "Draw equal lots and throw the loser among all six over."

Again, participants responded on a six point, agree-disagree scale and the composition of the beings on the lifeboat was varied for each of the five lifeboat dilemma problems.

Personal Beliefs

The participants were asked to give a yes or no response to nine questions regarding their attitudes toward abortion, stated in the form, "Do you believe abortion should be legal if . . . " and to the same nine questions stated in the form, "Would you personally have (or encourage your spouse or girl friend to have) an abortion if. . . . " The questions were, in order: to save the mother's life; for any reason before the third month of pregnancy; the pregnancy was the result of incest; the pregnancy was accidental and unwanted; the fetus is defective; the fetus is not of the desired sex; for any reason before normal birth; the woman was raped; for any reason before the sixth month of pregnancy.

They were asked whether they approved of contraception, if they approved of a pill which, if taken shortly after conception will prevent the fertilized egg from being implanted in the uterus, and of a pill which, if taken 7 weeks after conception, will cause a spontaneous abortion of the embryo.

A yes or no response was requested to eight questions asking "Under what conditions do you approve of capital punishment?" The order of the questions was: for rapists; when the murder was done while the perpetrator was temporarily insane; for killing someone while carelessly cleaning a gun; under no condition; for premeditated murder; for killing a police officer; for killing a child by accidentally discharging a hunting rifle into a crowd; for child molesters.

They were asked to approve or disapprove (using the six-point scale) of seven questions related to the use of animals: for medical research that benefits humans but harms animals in the process; for medical research that benefits animals but harms animals of the same species; the use of dissection of anesthetized living members of nonhuman mammalian species to train human surgeons; to teach college undergraduates; and to teach high school students. Then they were asked to approve or disapprove of the removal of the life support system of a terminally ill patient who requests that it be done, and of a terminally ill patient who is not able to give or withhold consent because of medical condition.

Personal Data

Finally, they were asked to provide some information regarding their age, gender, ethnicity, religious affiliation, and family structure.

Basic Dimensions

Each of the trolley and lifeboat questions was coded a priori in relationship to each of eight different dimensions that were chosen because of their potential importance to ethics and morality. Examples of each dimension are as follows:

1. Action-Inaction: Almost all of the question were constructed to allow the participant to act (throw the switch) or to avoid doing anything (let the trolley continue on its path). Thus, it could be determined whether or not the action–inaction dimension was important in and of itself. The questions were constructed so that the importance of this dimension could be evaluated relative to the importance of all of the others that were included. (In this first study it was not an important dimension, but became important when the masking effects of the kill–save wording were removed, as discussed below.)

2. Numbers: Questions were included in which the number of individuals on the main or side track differed. Again, the other dimensions were embedded with this one in a manner that would allow us to determine whether or not this was an important dimension relative to the others when people make moral decisions. Sample item: Five innocent people on the main track versus one innocent person on the side track. Another item: Five innocent people on the main track versus your brother on the side track. (Numbers had a moderate effect, but other considerations often overrode its effect, especially when cross-cultural data were examined.)

3. Social Contract: Here the concern is with one limited aspect of the issue that relates to social contract (see Chapters 4, 5, and 6). Were the individuals in the situation through no fault of their own or by agreement with anyone (what we refer to as "innocent"), or was

there some responsibility or agreement that should be taken into consideration? Sample item: The one on the side track is an employee of the railroad company repairing track while the ones on the main track are innocent persons. (This effect was of moderate importance.)

4. Nazi: This dimension was included to introduce the effect of an abhorrent political philosophy. Sample item: The one on the main track is a uniformed member of the American Nazi Party whereas the one on the side track is an innocent person. (This effect was very strong and it was found, in all instances, that any other humans were strongly favored over the Nazis.)

5. Inclusive Fitness: Inclusive fitness is reflected by the degree the individuals are related to you, either genetically or socially. A major expectation based on evolutionary theory is that one should favor those most closely related, or members of an immediate social group (who might have some degree of relatedness and who might be expected to help you or your immediate kin, or to reciprocate at a later time the help you give them). The items involved outcomes beneficial to responder, kin, or friend. Sample item: A male friend from high school on the main track who is the same age as an innocent male on the side track. Another item that involves this dimension is the one used as an example of the numbers effect, which involved your brother and five innocent people. (This effect was a very important one, as expected.)

6. Elite: This dimension favors individuals who have attained high status in society. It could enhance inclusive fitness of the individual through benefits to the members of the community by enhancing the quality of life, as well as reflect a reverence for high achievement. Sample item: The one on the side track is the world's foremost violinist and the five are innocent people. Another item: The one on the side track is an innocent person, and the one on the main track is an eminent scientist who has just developed an innovative theory of perceptual processing. (This effect was not large.)

7. Species: This dimension matches humans against members of some other species. Sample item: The one on the side track is a young, adult human and the five are the remaining members of an endangered Highland Gorilla species. (This was consistently the largest effect.)

8. Endangered: To enhance the value of an alien species some of the animals were identified as members of an endangered species and matched against humans or members of a nonendangered species. Sample item: see sample for dimension 7 above, which pitted a

human against endangered gorillas. This question illustrates the fact that many of the questions contain more than one dimension: This question was coded for dimensions 1 (Action-Inaction), 2 (Numbers), 7 (Species), and 8 (Endangered). (The Endangered effect was very small).

Results

The results will not be discussed in analytic depth. Those interested in the methodological and statistical details can find that information in the technical publication of these data (Petrinovich, O'Neill, & Jorgensen, 1993). In general, the results supported the following arguments:

1. The stated personal beliefs of the participants were comparable to those that have been reported by the Gallup Poll for the U.S. population at large. For example, the proportion approving of abortion to save the mother's life was 95% for our sample (compared with 94% for the 1988 Gallup sample); 86% if the pregnancy occurs as the result of incest or rape (85% for Gallup); and 70% if the fetus is defective (60% for Gallup). The proportion approving of abortion for any reason before birth was 19% for our sample and 24% for the Gallup sample. There was little difference in the attitudes regarding what should be legal and whether the participants would have (or their "significant other" should have) an abortion.

Capital punishment was approved of by 84% of the sample in the case of premeditated murder (compared with 79% in the 1989 Gallup Poll). Capital punishment of rapists was approved of by 59% of this sample, and 51% of the Gallup sample. It appears that the expressed attitudes of our respondents concerning abortion and capital punishment resembled those of the general population in the United States. It is important to establish this resemblance, because it demonstrates that the beliefs of this sample of university students were similar to those of the general U.S. population, thereby supporting the argument that the participants can be considered to be a reasonable cross-section of the general U.S. population in regards to their stated beliefs. The importance of this issue will be discussed at greater length below.

There were no gender differences for any questions pertaining to the legality of abortion and only one significant difference on the questions regarding personal choice: women were less likely to personally choose an abortion for any reason prior to the third month of pregnancy (41%) than men were to encourage it (53%). Women approved significantly less of capital punishment when a police officer was killed (64%) than did men (75%). Women had a significantly lower rate of approval of medical research to benefit humans (51%) compared to that of men (72%), to benefit animals (47% vs. 65%), or of dissection of animals to train surgeons (51% vs. 67%).

2. The stated personal beliefs of the participants were related to their expressed religious preference. About one-third of this sample were Catholics, one-fifth Protestants, a few Jews (4%), with 21% indicating they had no religion (identified hereafter as the "None" group). In addition, 11% were Christian Fundamentalists, and 10% were classified as "other" (Muslims, Hindus, Buddhists, and Mormons, mainly). As might be expected, the questions most influenced by religious preference were those pertaining to abortion and contraception, undoubtedly because abortion and related reproductive issues are highly topical, with many organized religions taking strong stands on these issues. As mentioned above, there were nine questions concerning the legality of abortion under particular circumstances, the same nine questions involving personal choice, as well as two questions concerning antipregnancy pills. For the questions pertaining to abortion and the antipregnancy pills the religions tended to form two clusters, each with similar attitudes: Catholics, Protestants, and Fundamentalist tended to have similar attitudes, whereas the opinions of Jews and None clustered together. The members of the latter cluster agreed significantly more that abortion should be legally permissible in all of the circumstances our questions involved than did those in the Catholic, Protestant, and Fundámentalist cluster. There was an increasing level of agreement in the direction of a more permissive view toward abortion, ranging from "undesired sex" to which the overall approval was low (9%), and "for any reason" (19% approval), to approving strongly in cases of rape (86%), incest (87%), and to save the mother's life (95%). Both the pattern and level of agreement for whether the respondents would personally choose the option of abortion were similar.

The proportion approving of the use of two types of contraceptive pills was determined. One type of pill prevents the fertilized egg from being implanted in the uterus (80% approval), and the other causes a spontaneous abortion if taken 7 weeks after conception (51% approval). This latter figure is almost the same proportion that approved of abortion for any reason before the third month (55%). Women approved significantly less of the abortion pill than did men (43% vs. 63% for men), even though there was no significant difference in approval of the pill preventing implantation (78% vs. 83%). The same two religious clusters appeared regarding the contraception pills as for the abortion issue. There were no significant ethnic differences when differences in the religious preferences of the different ethnic groups were removed computationally.

3. The analyses of the dilemmas indicated that the responses formed

a statistically coherent pattern for 90% of the individuals. Most individuals were consistent in their responses, most seemed to take the problems seriously, as indicated by analyses of internal consistency, as well as by written comments to the effect that some of them were disturbed at having to make some of the choices requested. As mentioned when describing the dimensions, the Species dimension was extremely strong. It is clear that most individuals chose outcomes that benefit the human species, regardless of the alternative. In all problems, when a human (even a 75-year-old) was pitted against an animal (even the last remaining members of an endangered species of gorilla), the human prevailed. This result suggests that speciesism is a strong and deep-seated tendency for our respondents, which leads us to suggest that speciesism could well be a strong universal human tendency. The Inclusive Fitness effect was also very strong, as expected on the basis of evolutionary theory. A third sizable effect was obtained for the Nazi dimension. The Social Contract dimension, which involved individuals in the situation because that was their job, they were fulfilling an obligation, or had a responsibility, was of moderate importance, as was the Numbers dimension in this study.

Analyses indicated that two of the dimensions that have been suggested by biologists or philosophers to be important had a minor to no effect: The fact that the species is endangered had little effect, and elite had an even smaller effect. The Nazi dimension was included to investigate the effect of an abhorrent social doctrine, and it probably was an unfortunate choice. Nazis are perceived to be such social monsters that almost all agreed they should not be spared. Not expecting such a strong effect we did not pit the Nazis against animals, in which case one might have found a limit to the effect of speciesism.

4. The pattern of results was the same for the introductory psychology students and for the biomedical students, although the two classes differed considerably in terms of ethnicity and gender. The major differences were that the introductory psychology class contained 63% women, as compared to 48% for the biomedical class, and the majority of the introductory psychology class were white (53%), whereas 29% were Asian, 8% Latin, and 3% black. For the biomedical class 59% were Asian, and only 36% were white, with 3% black, and no Latins.

5. Although all of the participants were university students, their personal beliefs varied in ways that were similar to available norms for the general U.S. population, as discussed above, yet their resolution of the dilemmas did not vary in relationship to any of the demographic characteristics, except for some gender differences.

6. The importance of the action/inaction dimension will be considered when the results of the kill/save wording are discussed below.

The fantasy moral dilemmas were useful to identify the pattern of moral intuitions that people have, and the resolutions of these dilemmas provided compelling evidence regarding the organization of the different value dimensions. The use of fantasy dimensions provided a useful way to investigate moral intuitions, as others have found (Gilligan, 1982; Kohlberg, 1971), and it seems that several of the dimensions we included are important in the resolution of such dilemmas.

I suggest that this study of moral intuitions provides a "moral ethogram." We have succeeded (just as the ethologists succeeded with nonhuman animals) in providing a strong descriptive base of the intuitions of the individuals included in these two samples. Classical ethologists have been able to accomplish a great deal through the development of strong descriptive bases as a starting point to understand alien species. I argue that we have provided a strong descriptive base for the structure of moral intuitions and that this base could provide the needed basis to understand any biological and cultural universals in morality. In the present context we have a great advantage because we are members of the species we wish to understand. Even though the issues with which we are concerned may be more complicated than those involved in animal behavior, and may be subject to many more influences, our procedures provide a legitimate beginning to understand some of the considerations that regulate the belief systems of humans.

Limitations

What are some of the limitations that could cast doubt on the validity of using the empirical methods described here?

Limited Participant Sample

Some have argued that it is not permissible to base (or even to suggest) general conclusions regarding universal laws on such a restricted sample of participants as that used here. The participants were mostly young university students, and it has been argued that no generalizable conclusions can be drawn on the basis of such a limited sample. It was noted above that there was a consistent pattern for most subjects in the resolution of the fantasy dilemmas. However, no systematic differences were detected in the way the dilemmas were resolved when the respondents were categorized in regards to major demographic variables, such as religion or ethnicity, and only slight gender differences were detected for some problems. Given the fact that there were robust differences in attitudes, especially related to religion, the lack of association between demographic characteristics and dilemma outcomes supports the view that the outcomes of this study may reflect stable, underlying human value systems. Unger, Draper, and Pendergrass (1986) developed an Attitudes About Reality Scale and they, too, found a significant difference in attitudes based on religion. Their scale was designed to measure a philosophical dimension ranging between a belief in social constructionism and a belief in logical positivism. They found that Catholics tended toward logical positivism significantly more than did those indicating no religious affiliation.

The findings of our study supported the idea that the resolution of the dilemmas did not depend on differences among the participants in obvious demographic characteristics, within the range of differences that existed in the limited sample discussed up to this point. The large differences between expressed attitudes that were related systematically to religious affiliation suggested that the fantasy dilemmas might be assessing a deeper level of intuitions that might be considered to reflect an underlying human nature. I will argue that the dilemmas provide a useful tool to search for moral similarities and that these similarities might not be variable across human cultures because they represent both biological and cultural universals.

To determine whether there are limits to the generalizability of the pattern of results for different samples of humans, a study was done to investigate the pattern of outcomes with a quite different sample of people. This study, discussed below, used Taiwanese university students, over half of whom were affiliated with an Eastern religion, and very few affiliated with a Western Judeo-Christian religion.

Limitation of the Questionnaire Method

We chose to use a questionnaire to survey the importance of a broad range of issues and to investigate a broad range of attitudes. This strategy was chosen to obtain enough items to decide whether or not there was internal consistency in the way individuals used the value dimensions, as well as to evaluate the degree of conformity with the instructions. It is important to note that the strength of the effects found justifies the reasonableness of our coding scheme.

Intuition vs. Action

The objection might be made that this research concerns only intuitions, and that it is not possible to determine whether the intuitions revealed would be translated into action. Of course, this objection is justified. However, the intent of the research was not to understand or predict what people would do, but to probe the structure and coherence of their systems of moral intuitions. The impetus for the research was provided by the views of moral philosophers and evolutionary biologists regarding how people construct the world of morality. I believe that these dilemmas reveal some aspects of moral intuitions. It would seem that understanding how people resolve these fantasy dilemmas might be a good basis on which to begin to understand the actions people do take, but such a translation is not part of the present undertaking, although it remains a fascinating question.

The Value of Using Fantasy Dilemmas

Some philosophers and psychologists have argued that it is not reasonable to examine the moral beliefs of people using such an artificial method as that involved in the resolution of fantasy dilemmas. A reading of the philosophy literature reveals that many of the dilemmas that moral philosophers use in argumentation are based on the resolution of fantasy dilemmas removed from the ordinary constraints that people encounter in their everyday lives. Kamm (1992) employed "some farfetched hypothetical cases" to avoid preconceived commitments and emotional responses that could pertain to questions regarding abortion. She considered such fantasy dilemmas useful in discovering the relative weight of factors. The advantage is that a few factors of particular interest can be considered in relative isolation, rather than being embedded in a web of other considerations that would be present in the natural ecology.

Pascal (1980) devised a fantasy situation to understand individual standards of right and wrong. He picked what he referred as "a situation which seems perhaps a little silly" because it was so improbable and disconnected from any existing world situations that individual prejudices and preconceived notions would play no part in the decisions. There seem to be numerous precedents and good reasons to use fantasy dilemmas in the attempt to understand the structure of moral intuitions.

It should be pointed out that psychologists understand that there are factors that cloud any clear interpretation of responses to direct questions regarding attitudes and beliefs. Among such problems are tendencies to make socially desirable responses, to provide answers that the respondent believes the questioner wants to obtain (sometimes, even to be contrary to them), or to respond to demand characteristics of the situation in which the questioning is done.

To counteract such tendencies, and to obtain more valid estimates of the belief systems involved, at least two strategies have been employed. Instead of relying on the face validity of the questions asked, some tests use an empirical scoring method. With this method a large set of questions is administered to groups of individuals who have been classified by some relevant group of experts to represent clear instances of the categories of interest: for example, introverts and extroverts. Then, a set of questions is developed, and those questions are retained that introverts answer one way and extroverts another. Such items are keyed to be "'plus" or "minus" on the Introversion–Extroversion scale, and a scale score is developed that is based on the number of plus and minus responses. It matters not at all what the content of a question is; what is important is that one type of person tends to agree and the other type to disagree, and respondents are compared to the scores of the criterion reference groups.

One problem with this method is that it takes a large amount of time and energy to develop and validate questions. A more serious problem is that the value of the scale depends on the adequacy of the basic categorization of individuals in the criterion sample as being introverts or extroverts. If the psychiatric or behavioral theories on which the diagnosis of the criterion group is based are inadequate, then the empirical scale will be inadequate as well. Such empirical scaling methods always run the risk of chasing their tails; you only find out what your theoretical biases allowed you to include as items in the study. This risk could be especially damaging in the study of morality because it would be difficult to establish any meaningful criterion groups.

Another method (and the one involved in the case of the fantasy dilemmas used here) is to remove many of the obvious elements of reality from the items and to let the various factors come into play using scenarios that are unlikely to be encountered in everyday reality. It is hoped that this level of irreality will make people less inclined to decide on the basis of social desirability or to become enmeshed in guessing the intentions of the investigator. Consider the trolley problems; seldom do people face the decision of performing or not performing an action to choose between the life and death of different individuals. The very level of irreality could remove some of the barriers to expressing an underlying tendency, and this expression might well be free from the constraints of experiences that vary for different individuals. Because the dimensions involved in the various dilemmas are not explicitly identified, the influence of specific teaching regarding the particular moral decisions to be made might also be minimized.

Many of the respondents in the studies of dilemmas did not find the resolution of the dilemmas to have been a pleasant experience, because so many of the dilemmas involved two unpalatable choices. Yet, they did take the questionnaire seriously, and consistency analyses indicated that the individuals resolved the dilemmas according to consistent and stable strategies. Incidentally, in the class period following the administration of the fantasy dilemmas, the classes were very interested and active in the discussion of both the research methods and the moral issues. This observation further attests to the fact that the task was taken seriously, and suggests that such a procedure also has considerable pedagogical merit.

The greatest drawback to the use of the dilemmas is the choice of the dimensions to be included. If only one dimension is used (for example, a dimension of justice, as used by Kohlberg), then one is likely to find that, if anything, individuals resolve dilemmas using the dimension of justice—hardly any other positive outcome is possible. To avoid difficulties due to the choice of a narrow set of dimensions we chose to include a number of dimensions (eight, at the outset) that have been emphasized by philosophers and biologists to represent important factors people use to make moral decisions.

The use of fantasy dilemmas involves what Fischer and Ravizza (1992) refer to as "a controlled-ethical thought experiment." Using this method one could isolate one factor (say, action and inaction) and evaluate its effect with everything else held constant, as Kamm suggested. The ideal is the Newtonian one of the true experiment in science: Hold all variables constant but one and vary it systematically; then hold that variable constant, and vary yet another one systematically, and continue this process until all variables have been subjected to systematic variation. It would not be possible to use such a procedure in the everyday world, but it is possible to investigate a wide range of dimensions under the controlled conditions of thought experiments, as is done with the fantasy dilemmas.

In our use of the thought experiment we have chosen not to adopt the Newtonian ideal of controlling one single variable at a time but have pitted one variable against the others in a manner that allows us to assess the action of each against a different assembly of alternatives in each question. In some questions respondents were permitted to act (or not to act) to save a larger number of individuals who were not related to them versus a smaller number of individuals who were related to them. In this example we have action (or inaction) considered in the context of both the number of individuals and the degree of relatedness. The advantage of this systematic procedure is that it permits the evaluation of a larger number of alternative dimensions with relatively small numbers of choices. The use of multivariate statistical procedures enables us to untangle, computationally, the relative importance of each of the individual dimensions included.

Another important point is that these fantasy dilemmas are not removed totally from the kinds of decisions policy-makers do have to make. Fischer and Ravizza (1992) documented several ethical decisions that have had to be made in recent history, and pointed out that these decisions embody the characteristics of the fantasy dilemmas we used here. Amongthe historical incidents they discussed was the decision by the

British government in World War II not to divert German bombs from highly populated London to less densely populated Kent, Surrey, or Sussex. The policymakers chose not to favor the greater number of Londoners who would be killed by the bombs because they decided that it was morally impermissible to sacrifice a lesser number of innocent people to save an even greater number. Another instance was the decision by the British government to engage in the terror bombing of such nonstrategic cities as Dresden rather than to continue the strategic bombing of targets that were of direct military importance. They justified the choice using the doctrine of double effect: that the death of the civilians in Dresden was a foreseen, but not the primarily intended, side-effect of air raids which were themselves permitted because the end was to win a just war. The consideration of such issues as abortion, infanticide, use of reproductive technologies, euthanasia, and suicide involve making serious moral decisions regarding the course of life that are not all that different from the choices required in the fantasy trolley and lifeboat problems.

The moral systems constructed on the basis of the resolution of the fantasy dilemmas need not, and should not, remain isolated in a conceptual vacuum. Examples can be found of actual moral decisions which involve the various dimensions that were used in the construction of the fantasy dilemmas. One can then examine whether the resolutions of those real dilemmas were done in the manner expected on the basis of the relative importance of the moral dimensions revealed by the fantasy dilemmas.

Problems Related to the Wording of Questions

The possible importance of effects produced by the way in which specific questions are phrased poses a problem if the interest is to apply these results to basic issues in moral philosophy. One mode of exposition in moral philosophy involves the process of wide reflective equilibrium discussed in Chapter 1. With this method an individual's moral judgments are gathered and analyzed to develop an understanding of the individual's moral intuitions, as was done in the study reported here. When the set of arguments has been constructed, then one can work back and forth from premises to observations, and make adjustments between judgments, moral principles, and background principles. The intent is to probe the logic and consistency of the basic premises to arrive at rules and guidelines adequate to understand the consequences that result from the use of basic moral premises. The weight of evidence in such an endeavor relies on the clarity, universality, compelling nature, and intuitive acceptability of the manner in which people resolve the moral dilemmas, and in establishing the logic of how the pattern of results flows from the premises. The goal is to understand the structure of moral intuitions in order to develop adequate guidelines for action that meet the test of sensible ethical standards by which one ought to live.

However, if the manner in which the questions are worded influences the conclusions that are arrived at by philosophical observers, then one is dealing with extramoral, methodological considerations, and such considerations must be understood in order to arrive at conclusions that have merit as universals. There is a problem if one is led through a certain chain of reasoning to a given conclusion when the initial question is one that elicits a high degree of agreement, and to yet another conclusion when the initial question elicits a low degree of agreement. If the interest is to understand the logical conclusions that certain basic philosophical premises necessitate, then influences that are produced by the way a question is phrased are distressing. Fischer and Ravizza (1991) argued that in order to generate a set of moral judgments based on a corresponding set of moral principles it is desirable to screen out effects due to variations in phrasing.

Data have been obtained on the effect of the wording, as well as the context in which questions are embedded, on the resolution of the fantasy dilemmas (see Petrinovich & O'Neill, 1995). The results of that study indicated that there was a strong effect due to whether the dilemmas were phrased in Kill or Save wording: There was a greater likelihood that people would agree and the level of agreement was stronger with the Save wording, even though the outcomes were identical with the two wordings. The manner in which questions were worded, therefore, had a considerable systematic influence on the decisions of many individuals in the sample. However, the coherence of the pattern of answers and the size of the different effects was not influenced, indicating that the basic dimensions are robust.

When different sets of dilemma questions were developed by manipulating the strength of initial agreement or disagreement an effect was found only if the same type of dilemma (e.g., trolley problems) was used for all questions, but not if different kinds of dilemmas were involved for each question. These results indicated that the concerns expressed by Fischer and Ravizza (1991) were important in some regards but that the most important universal moral tendencies were revealed no matter what the wording or context. It can be concluded that it simply will not do to rely on data generated from a limited set of problems phrased in a limited way if one wants to probe the deep structure of moral intuitions.

CROSS-CULTURAL STUDY

To speak more adequately to the criticism that the results of the first study, using only U.S. university students, cannot be generalized because the sample of people was too limited, a study was conducted in Taiwan. The participants in this Taiwan study were university students; without exception, Chinese was their first language. As mentioned above, one important aspect of the Taiwan sample is that over half of the individuals were affiliated with an Eastern religion, and very few were affiliated with a Western Judeo-Christian religion. There were a number of individuals who indicated no religious affiliation, and none of them were affiliated with a Christian Fundamentalist religion. The Taiwan sample was chosen because it would be expected that, if religious upbringing is an important factor influencing the resolution of the dilemmas, then those raised in households emphasizing the beliefs of an Eastern religion might resolve the dilemmas quite differently. If such a result occurred, then it would limit the generality of our first study across peoples; if it did not occur, then the argument for generality would be supported, as would the position that the moral dimensions found to be important reflect underlying universals.

We obtained data on 173 Taiwanese university students, and another sample of 120 University of California students, from yet another introductory psychology class. As mentioned above, these two samples differed in one major characteristic: For the Taiwanese sample 52% were affiliated with an Eastern religion (as compared to only 8% for the U.S. sample); only 10% with a traditional Western religion (compared to 71% for the United States); and 38% had no religious affiliation (compared to 21% for the U.S.). This high proportion of Eastern religious affiliation is what we had hoped for with the Taiwan sample.

A revised questionnaire was developed and translated into Chinese: Then the Chinese version was translated back into English to eliminate slippage in meaning due to translation, and the new U.S. sample was tested with that translated version. Some revisions were made that incorporated suggestions by our Taiwanese advisors to eliminate items that could be politically sensitive in Taiwan. This decision was made to avoid jeopardizing the willingness of the Taiwanese authorities to allow us to conduct the study. On these grounds the Nazi and Endangered species dimensions were eliminated and some new items were added to examine the remaining dimensions in more depth. All questions were phrased only in the Kill wording.

The stated beliefs of the Taiwanese were almost the same as for the U.S. samples, there being only two large and statistically significant differences. One of the differences was a greater approval of abortion by the Taiwanese if the fetus is defective (88%), as compared to only 70% approval for all of the U.S. samples; the other was a lower level of approval of capital punishment for child molesters—Taiwan, 28% and U.S. samples, 57%. There were no significant differences between the U.S. and Taiwanese samples in attitudes toward medical research.

Once again, the analyses of the dilemmas indicated that the responses formed a coherent pattern for most of the individuals (for 82% of the individuals, as compared to 87% for the U.S. control sample, and 90% for the U.S. sample in the first study). Species and Inclusive Fitness were, once again, the two most important dimensions. One difference that appeared is that the Action–Inaction effect was large for both of the samples using this new questionnaire, but not for the first U.S. study. This difference indicates that the Action–Inaction dimension was influenced by the manner in which the questions were posed, and additional statistical analyses indicated that the difference was produced by the Kill–Save wording effect. The effect for Social Contract, again, was moderate, and the Elite dimension, again, was very small. The Numbers effect was very small for the Taiwanese, but not for the U.S. control sample.

Another consistent effect was that the Taiwanese were less likely to use the strongly agree or disagree categories than were those in the U.S. sample. It appears that the relative importance of the dimensions with this new questionnaire for the Taiwanese sample was similar to that found for the United States, which leads to the conclusion that there are no obvious differences between those affiliated with Western or Eastern religions in the resolution of the dilemmas.

Reynolds (1991), examined religions from a sociobiological perspective. He began with a belief that religious doctrines all take an interest in the processes of reproduction and, after examining the data bearing on the socioecology of reproduction, concluded that religions were more than just interested. His analyses supported the conclusion that religions mapped a complete set of permissible attitudes and beliefs about sex and reproduction, beginning at adolescence and extending through parenthood. He noted that this strong interest in the reproductive process existed for religions in all parts of the world and that all of them established the right and wrong conditions for contraception, abortion, and infanticide. In addition, all religions control adolescent sexuality, regulate marriage, divorce, remarriage, and widowhood. These results were quite consistent with the earlier observations made by Darlington (1969). Reynolds observed that, although the specific theological justifications differed among the various religions, Buddhists and Hindus tended to oppose the use of contraception, contrary to the beliefs of Western Protestants, and that almost all organized religions oppose unrestricted abortion.

In our study the Taiwan sample was composed of a sizable percentage (29%) affiliated with the traditional Taiwanese religion, which is a mix of Buddhist, Taoist, and Confucian dieties, along with other folk heroes that local worshippers have come to revere, such as Kuan Yin (the Goddess of Mercy), Kuan Kung (a General honored for bravery), and Koxinga (a revered 17th century warrior). The other Eastern religions represented in our Taiwan sample were Buddhists (19%) and Taoists (4%).

Some teachings of these eastern religions have a bearing on the moral issues with which we are concerned. *Lao Tzu* is considered to be a classic in the thought of Taoism (Lau, 1963). One of the prominent themes regards the virtue of submission as a value in itself, which leads to the admonition to follow behind and not take the lead. In Book Two, Chapter 43 (p. 104) it is written, "That is why I know the benefit of resorting to no action. The teaching that uses no words, the benefit of resorting to no action, these are beyond the understanding of all but a very few in the world." It is argued that survival is the supreme goal, and the means to this goal is to hold fast to the submissive; never act, yet nothing is left undone. Again (Chapter 57, p. 118), "Hence the sage says, I take no action and the people are transformed of themselves," and (Chapter 63, p. 124), "Do that which consists in taking no action. . . . "

This emphasis to not take action is also found in Buddhist theology (Zimmer, 1975). A monk of the fundamentalist Jaina sect, if thrown overboard from a ferryboat by wicked people, must not struggle by swimming, but must drift and permit the currents to take him to land: He must not upset or injure the water atoms. When one considers the issue of causing the death of animals, the Buddhist monk is only guilty if he longs for meat, or if an animal has been killed for him and he knows it. Should he happen to receive scraps of meat along with rice that is offered he can swallow the meat without becoming polluted. Thus, it is not what is done that carries moral weight as much as the intentionality.

Chan (1963) characterized the views of the neo-Confucianism of K'ang Yu-Wei, noting that he argued that all creatures in the world aim to seek happiness and avoid suffering. K'ang considered the sufferings of mankind to be so innumerable as to be unimaginable, and among the major sufferings he enumerated were premature death, being a slave, being a woman, and being childless.

The fact that we found few differences in the moral intuitions of the United States and Taiwan samples attests further to the generality of our findings across humans. The only difference between the two sets of studies was the large Action–Inaction effect found with the new questionnaire, but this difference was obtained for both the U.S. control sample and the Taiwan sample that were tested with the new questionnaire, and this difference was due, therefore, to the particular survey and not to a cultural difference.

Reanalysis of the First Study

Because there were indications that the different survey forms produced different results we reanalyzed the earlier U.S. data, removing the

Nazi and Endangered dimensions (which were not included for the Taiwan or U.S. control sample). When this was done the Action–Inaction dimension was found to have a similar, and large, effect for all samples, with the other dimensions remaining almost the same size as before.

We then compared all four groups (U.S. introductory psychology, U.S. biomedical psychology, Taiwan, and U.S. control) on those questions that were common across all groups and surveys. The rank order and magnitude of the effects were almost identical for all groups, with the one exception of the Numbers effect, which was of moderate size for all of the U.S. samples but very small for the Taiwan sample. This variation in the Numbers effect is the only large difference found between the two cultures; the Taiwanese seemed not to use Numbers as a dimension to resolve the dilemmas, while all of the U.S. groups did. Although there were some small differences in the absolute magnitude of the effects detected by the two different surveys, there was no change in the relative rank of the dimensions across the different samples. The general order was Species, Inclusive Fitness, Action–Inaction, Numbers, Social Contract, and Elitism. It appears that the relative importance of the dimensions with the Taiwanese sample is similar to that found for the United States. There were no obvious differences between the different types of individuals tested. Those affiliated with Western or Eastern religions, born, raised, and educated in Taiwan or the United States, with Chinese or English as a first language, all tended to resolve the dilemmas in similar ways, attesting further to the generality of our findings across humans. It is interesting to note that, despite the emphasis to not take action in the teaching of Buddhism and Confucianism, the Action–Inaction dimension was emphasized similarly for those affiliated with Western and Eastern religions.

Huebner and Garrod (1993) studied moral reasoning among Tibetan Buddhist monks in Nepal using culturally adapted Kohlberg dilemmas. Their results supported Kohlberg's claims that his system of characterizing moral reasoning is universal. These results were obtained even though the Buddhist theology is quite different from most Western religions, given the emphasis on rebirth whereby one can return as an animal, a hell-being, or a beggar. Life in and of itself is not sacred to the Buddhists because all beings are caught in a cycle of existence such that everyone and everything is guaranteed endless life. Despite the fact that 51% of our sample were affiliated with a religion that accepted aspects of Buddhist theology, we found that the basic moral dimensions were remarkably stable across the cultures, as Huebner and Garrod reported.

Snarey (1985) noted that, for traditional folk cultures, the use of the Kohlberg schema did not allow some of the specific characteristics of those cultures to emerge, and Huebner and Garrod also suggested that the Kohlberg model of moral reasoning may be of limited use to understand aspects of the moral reasoning of monks in a Buddhist culture. Yet, there was a degree of universality found using the Kohlberg model. We also found a high degree of universality using our dilemmas to study the structure of moral intuitions. It is interesting to note that the species effect is as strong for those raised in the Buddhist tradition as it was for the Western samples, even though it is possible that one might be reborn as an animal, and there is an admonition to avoid eating meat.

Gender Differences

As mentioned above there were some gender differences in the resolution of the dilemmas. In general, women favored a more egalitarian approach. For example, women were more likely to prefer a lottery, with each individual having an equal chance of surviving, rather than to make the life and death decision directly, and this preference was evident on both questions where it was a possible alternative. Women were also less likely to act to kill their brother or to actively push someone in front of the trolley (although they were just as likely to throw a switch, which would kill the person, as were the men). Women also chose more often (although not the majority of them) than did men to open a barrier killing a human to save five dogs, and a majority of women, but not of men, would do so to save 1000 dogs. These patterns resemble those reported by Gilligan and Attanucci (1988) to characterize the moral system of women.

Women also tended to agree more than did men when questions were worded in a Save manner than when they were worded in a Kill manner. These findings suggest that there may be some interesting differences in moral intuitions that are related to gender, and this possibility will bear more detailed examination, given the conflicting interpretations that can be made of the existing data (Gilligan, 1982; Walker, 1984).

The Chinese religions, from the time of Confucius to the present, consider women to be inferior (Chan, 1963). An illustration of the Chinese view is provided by Lin Yutang (1938, p. 179), who quoted one of the Aphorisms of Confucius: "Women and the uneducated people are most difficult to deal with. When you are familiar with them, they become cheeky, and when you ignore them, they resent it." Despite the differences in the teachings of the Western and Eastern religions, and the different social norms that exist in the cultures, there were few differences related to gender between the cultures.

Prediction of Stated Beliefs from Scale Strength

The question here concerns whether people who differ in the way they resolve the moral dilemmas also differ in their answers regarding personal beliefs. In the main study the Species, Inclusive Fitness, and Action–Inaction dimensions resulted in significant and substantial primary correlations with questions regarding approval of medical research. For all samples, individuals who were highly favorable to humans on the Species dimension tended to favor medical research to benefit humans and animals, and favored dissection of animals to train surgeons. The Action and Inclusive Fitness dimensions also correlated for the Taiwan and U.S. control samples for these items. These correlations support the belief that the fantasy dimensions are related to the structure of expressed beliefs and suggest that they might be meaningfully involved in belief systems that could be related to behavior.

CONCLUSIONS

No purpose would be served by going into any further detail regarding these empirical studies, or of later ones that have been completed. The cross-cultural study is reported by Petrinovich and O'Neill (1994b), and the wording and framing results, which were treated in only a cursory fashion above, by Petrinovich and O'Neill (1995). At this juncture, it is clear that the a priori dimensions identified through our reading of the literature in evolutionary biology and moral philosophy are related to the way in which human moral intuitions are organized. I believe that this understanding provides some indication of the biases that exist due to both universal biological and cultural factors, and believe that this kind of information could make it possible to advocate moral positions that can capitalize on the fact there are human moral biases, and to recognize that, sometimes, there are underlying predispositions that must be counteracted.

The results of these studies supported several expectations. It was expected that people would choose alternatives that enhance inclusive fitness, and they did: Members of our own species are favored over those of any other species; relatives, and even friends, are favored over strangers; individuals who espouse a destructive political ideology are strongly condemned. A study of fantasy dilemmas by Burnstein, Crandall, and Kitayama (In Press) supported the conclusions we reached regarding the importance of Darwinian heuristics involving kinship and altruism. They found results indicating that when decisions involve life or death they are made to benefit close kin ahead of distant kin, young over old, healthy over sick, wealthy over poor, and premenopausal over postmenopausal females. However, under everyday conditions where there are no life-threatening circumstances, the young and old are helped rather than those of intermediate age, the sick rather than the healthy, poor rather than wealthy, and females rather than males. The pattern of these results suggests that the biological inclusive fitness dimension is given great weight when decisions involve life and death while, under more benign circumstances, cultural biases regarding politeness and conscience are of more consequence. Burnstein, Crandall, and Kitayama (in press) examined the ethnographic research in non-Western cultures and concluded that the results of that research support the conclusion that people behave to enhance their inclusive fitness.

In our study we found that, other things being equal, Numbers are important, as is Social Contract (in our study it was narrowly defined in terms of the individuals being employed by the trolley or lifeboat companies, and thereby assuming some liability). Elitism was of no importance, nor was having the status of an Endangered species.

We found that the Action–Inaction dimension was one of the three largest effects when only the results for the Kill forms were considered. This finding supports the arguments of those moral philosophers who argue that there is a moral significance between killing and letting die. This Action–Inaction outcome is not one that was expected on a biological basis, and it seems to represent a different kind of imperative than the other, more biologically tinted ones.

I would also like to emphasize that the existence of an evolutionary adaptation does not signal that a trait is one that involves the moral thing to do. Fetzer (1992) pointed out that evolved traits are not necessarily moral—nature is, as they say, often red in tooth and claw. If an evolutionary ethics is based on kin selection and altruism, then it will require supplementation to be complete because rationality must be added to biology and evolution. As Fetzer phrased it, biology is a necessary but not sufficient condition for morality. I would suggest that the Action–Inaction dimension might constitute one of those strictly rational (cultural?) conditions that should be given attention when constructing a rational, evolutionary ethics, and that a different set of principles may be found to be applicable depending on whether situations are benign or life threatening.

There was some evidence that gender differences were important: Women seemed to have been somewhat more egalitarian than men, and tended to agree more strongly when the dilemmas were worded in a Save rather than a Kill form. These outcomes generally are what would be expected within an evolutionary framework, and they were found for all of the subject samples we have examined. From the evolutionary perspective, major differences in behavioral tendencies would be expected to appear between men and women in view of the different reproductive strategies that are appropriate to each. Because we are stuck with sexual reproduction it will be impossible to attain a society that is sex blind—one's sexual identity is bound to be of central importance for the other members of any human society that continues to reproduce itself.

I conclude that the data that have been presented and discussed in this chapter support the idea that people's patterns of moral intuitions are coherent and are consistent with what one might expect on the basis of expectations based on the Darwinian hypothesis of inclusive fitness. When people are asked to make choices based on life or death intuitions, humans are favored over members of any other species, kin over other humans, close kin over distant kin, and social contracts (although rather narrowly defined in our empirical studies) are of considerable importance. In addition to these evolutionarily viable expectations it was found that when the alternatives were phrased in terms of killing, the Action–Inaction effect was large, which suggests that there is a socially influenced effect that makes it less permissible to kill than to let die. The fact that the Numbers effect was small in Taiwan as compared to the U.S. control sample suggests that this might be an important culturally influenced effect. Some effects that might have been expected to be important were not: Elitism and the status of endangered species did not seem to influence choices.

The fact that personal beliefs differed for different religions, but that the resolution of the moral dilemmas was not affected, suggests to me that the structure of moral intuitions that we are investigating are at a deeper level than stated personal beliefs. We have only scratched the surface in terms of looking at gender differences and such differences deserve further studies in which an attempt is made to separate behavioral events involving sexual reproduction from those that involve more socially mediated gender influences.

The groundwork has now been laid for the specific arguments to be developed in Part II, where a series of issues will be considered regarding the beginning of life. The ideas developed up to this point will be applied to each issue considered in the hope of developing a rational and consistent, as well as biologically and philosophically sound, analysis of these crucial issues in human morality. I believe that the social and biological sciences have an obligation to consider the possible relevance of basic theory and data to social issues and to bring them to bear on problems regarding policy formation.

II

Issues in Reproduction

8

Contraception, Abortion, and Infanticide

Issues and Arguments

For many years there has been worldwide discussion, action, conflict, legislation, and adjudication regarding whether, when, and how it is permissible to use contraception, to permit abortion, and to allow infanticide. The abortion question has received a great deal of discussion of late, and it is to that question that I will direct most of my attention. A comprehensive set of principles will be developed that are adequate to include all issues pertaining to the beginning of life. There have been strong and strident arguments regarding these issues, and almost every conceivable position has been espoused by people identified with a wide variety of political and religious ideologies, occupations, and academic specialities.

GUIDELINES FOR ARGUMENT

I argued, in Chapter 1, that it is important to develop a rational moral philosophy that is derived logically from a set of basic premises which do not ignore empirical facts. Various arguments that have been proposed will be submitted to a critical analysis, bringing relevant factual information to bear, in the hopes that a system can be developed with the desired quality of conceptual clarity. The requirement of universality is of paramount importance if we are to arrive at a system that is free from special bias or partiality to those things we value because of our own privileged status in society, be they related to race, creed, sex, nationality, endowments, or whatever. The arguments developed here will lead to a series of positions and recommendations that do not violate my intuitive sense of right and wrong. Even though everyone might not agree with these moral positions it is important that the reasons why they are being argued, as well as the bases for why one might disagree, be clear.

PHILOSOPHICAL CONCEPTS

One of the major philosophical issues to consider regarding the problem of abortion involves the determination of personhood. Many of the philosophical arguments regarding abortion revolve around when personhood begins, and the legal arguments concerning the permissibility of abortion seem to be based on the agreement that it is persons who are entitled to constitutional protections. I will argue that personhood begins at birth, and that the concept of moral agency raises a separate issue that involves moral standing as well as a consideration of the concepts of the responsibilities and duties of individuals in society. The empirical findings discussed in Chapter 7 support the position that there are several important dimensions involved in human choices regarding morality: Species, Inclusive Fitness, Action-Inaction (the difference between killing and letting die), and Social Contract. These principles will be brought to bear to develop the moral arguments regarding abortion.

BIOLOGICAL CONCEPTS

To encourage and sustain a just society it should be recognized that human beings are embedded in the fabric of organic nature. The position taken here is that justice depends on recognizing that kinship is a deep-seated, biologically crucial aspect of human nature, and that a just society must permit a positive expression of human loyalties based on principles of consanguinity, in the senses both of ancestry and close association. Human needs must always be considered in the broad framework of the human condition related to the ecological realities within which human needs and choices are expressed.

To provide an adequate framework to understand behavior in the context of contemporary society the ideas of kinship and reciprocity must be augmented by a recognition that certain social contracts are important. It will be argued below that these social contracts have strong biological bases that must be recognized. Sociolegal rules are the embodiment of a moral system. It is important to develop and understand the systems of morality that people respect intuitively in order to enable society to apply rules and laws in ways that might lead to a just and stable society.

Attention was given, in Chapter 3, to some facts regarding phylogeny, which is often misconstrued by those not familiar with evolutionary mechanisms to range from "lower" to "higher" animals, along the great chain of being, similar to Aristotle's Scala Naturae. This conception is just plain biological and conceptual nonsense, and its use results in a set of presumptions that muddy discussions of the development of organisms. For example, some of the conclusions arrived at by Sumner (1981), while they are argued admirably in most respects, will not stand because of his faulty conception of phylogeny. Such inadequate conceptions often lead philosophers to a faulty interpretation of the neurophysiological facts that they believe should be used to ground moral principles. The facts I refer to involve the changing characteristics of the nervous system of various organisms at different stages of development, and these characteristics are used to define the beginning of moral relevancy and, sometimes, person-hood.

COGNITIVE CONCEPTS

Some of the cognitive concepts brought to bear concern the intellectual and affectional characteristics that confer a privileged status (and responsibility) to an organism. The questions involve such things as how can it be known whether an organism is expressing pleasure or pain, and how can it be decided whether an organism has the interests, wishes, and desires that indicate intentionality and reveal the essence of consciousness? When is an individual capable of understanding complex abstract principles at a level sufficient to arrive at decisions regarding right and wrong?

DEFINITIONS

To avoid terminological problems I will define some of the terms that are important regarding the beginning of life. The basic elements involved in sexual recombination are the male germ cell (the sperm), and the female germ cell (the ovum). The act of copulation results in a male orgasm, a crucial aspect of which is the ejaculation of a variable, but extremely large, number of sperm. It is estimated that, on average for humans, 35% of these sperm are ejected by the female within 30 minutes of insemination.

The fertilized single-cell is called a zygote and, as mentioned in Chapter 3, Diamond (1992a) estimated that the total loss of fertilized zygotes could be as high as 80%. Within 24 hours the zygote divides into 2 cells and by the third day there are 16 cells, called the blastocyst. The blastocyst moves through the fallopian tube into the uterus, and by the end of the second week following fertilization it is firmly embedded in the uterine wall. It is also during these first 14 days that events occur that lead to multiple births. Some have suggested that, prior to the first 14 days (the time at which the cells are embedded) we should refer to the collection of cells as a preembryo because, at this stage, the embryo is not an individual—it could be two or more individuals. Singer (1993) noted that the laws and guidelines in Britain use this distinction to allow experimentation on the embryo up to 14 days after fertilization.

Until the eighth week the embedded cells are referred to as an embryo and after that time as a fetus, although the convention is not strictly followed. By week 8 some brain waves can be detected (but no functional significance can be attached to them) and most organs can be identified in a rudimentary form. Fetal movement, called quickening, can be detected by the mother between the 12th and 16th weeks, and the fetus is considered to be viable between 20 to 28 weeks after conception. Some refer to an infant as a neonate up to about one week after birth, and as an infant after that age.

Viability refers to that time when the fetus is potentially able to live outside the mother's womb with artificial aid. In *Roe v. Wade* the Supreme Court considered the time of viability to be between 24 and 28 weeks (King, 1980). As will be discussed below, a precise time when viability begins is problematic because the likelihood of survival at different ages varies a great deal given specific conditions. Hack and Fanaroff (1989) reported that the survival rate is almost zero for fetuses with birth weights less than 600 gm or whose gestational age is less than 24 weeks. A fetus that weights 700 gm or more, or is beyond 25 weeks of gestation, has more than a 50% chance of survival.

King (1980) noted that there is no general agreement regarding the point at which viability occurs, because the condition of the mother, of the fetus, and the quality of medical care available all are variables influencing the probability of survival. Another set of facts that could be relevant concerns when pregnancy can be detected after fertilization. The occurrence of fertilization can only be detected after implantation of the blastocyst in the uterine wall. The detection is done using chemical tests based on hormonal analyses, and these tests are only able to indicate that pregnancy may have occurred. The tests are not a reliable indicator that a pregnancy will be likely to continue. Diamond (1992a) estimated that as many as 50% of implanted embryos are miscarried spontaneously, and these miscarriages are usually unrecognized by the mother, being attributed to unusual events in the menstrual cycle. The uncontroversial positive signs of pregnancy occur much later, when fetal heartbeat and movements can be detected by an examiner, and radiological or sonographic detection of the presence of the fetus can be made.

MORAL AGENTS HAVE PERSONHOOD BUT ALL
PERSONS DO NOT HAVE AGENCY

A distinction was made earlier between basic and derived principles (see Chapter 6). The interest, now, is to establish some basic principles that can guide decisions regarding abortion and the other issues pertaining to the beginning of life. It was proposed that there are individuals, called moral agents, who all agree are members of the moral community. It was argued that moral agents have automatic moral duties to one another and to moral patients, and that, being moral agents, they possess rights. On the other hand, there are moral patients—individuals who lack the qualities that confer agency—who are not held accountable, in terms of morality, for the outcomes of their actions. I will argue that these moral patients cannot be considered to have either moral responsibilities or duties, and that only those who have the status of persons can qualify for moral agency. However, all those who have the status of personhood are not moral agents; more is required.

To decide whether an organism has personhood the necessary and sufficient qualities that signify that status must be defined independently in order that they can be factually grounded on a scientific basis. I am using the term "scientific" in the broadest sense, meaning that the relevant facts must be established on the basis of public observations that any qualified observer can make. To establish objectivity it is necessary that, given the same event, an observer will classify it the same on each succeeding occurrence (called intraobserver reliability) and different independent observers will classify it the same on each succeeding occurrence (interobserver reliability). The scientific facts that will be referred to are behavioral and biological, including physiological and neurophysiological factors. I want to emphasize that the qualities that constitute the necessary and sufficient conditions on which to base personhood or moral agency should not be based on a mere definitional gambit. There must be a specification of the crucial properties that serve to qualify an individual as a member of a class that is to be accorded personhood, as well as those that establish moral agency.

Macklin (1984) questioned the relevance of scientific data to ground moral philosophical issues. She considered the fact that different writers allude to different bits of scientific evidence, such as presence of the full genetic code, the onset of electroencephalographic activity, or the myelination of nerve tracts to mean that the scientific data taken as relevant depends on antecedently held views about morality. Because the interpretation of scientific observations is done within some conceptual framework does not make those observations irrelevant, however. This inherent subjectivity only means that the basic conceptual framework that is being used to organize and interpret observations has to be justified carefully, and that the relationship of the observations to the framework has been specified clearly and unambiguously.

The first question to ask is whether membership in the human species satisfies the necessary and sufficient conditions to support the status of personhood. Everyone agrees that all normal, adult human beings are qualified to be both persons and moral agents. This means that they should have all the rights that are accorded agents, and should be held to all the duties and responsibilities that are prescribed by custom, law, and morality. However, not all human beings are accorded the full rights of moral agents and not all humans are considered to have a right to life. An individual who commits premeditated murder may forfeit the right to life that belongs to moral agents: most people approve of capital punishment for premeditated murder (85% in the study reported in Chapter 7), and the laws of most countries either mandate capital punishment under many circumstances, or ensure that the perpetrator loses the freedom to which all normal adult humans are considered to have a right. Given special circumstances, actions that might be considered murder are approved; these include such things as killing in self-defense, while temporarily insane, killing in war, or protecting against evil (however the society defines it).

Under some circumstances it is agreed that a person has the right to have a life-support system disconnected if the person requests that it be done while in a sound mental state, is incurably and fatally ill, and is suffering great pain. This approval of euthanasia suggests that, while it might not be permissible to kill, it is permissible to let die, given special circumstances. These exceptions to the rule that all humans have a right to life suggest that being a member of the species *Homo sapiens* is not a sufficient condition to confer continuing moral agency, and that mere species membership cannot be the basic principle on which agency should be based.

Using species membership to justify agency, without spelling out what the exact properties are that confer it, is arbitrary, and such arbitrary classifications of different kinds of humans have been used to justify the cruel and immoral use of individuals throughout history. Such arbitrary classifications have been used to support endless social inequalities, such as racism or sexism, and to justify genocide. Singer (1975) has extended the argument to apply to animals other than humans. He points out that animals are classified arbitrarily as nonagents and that this classification is an instance of speciesism, which he places on the same level as racism and sexism. He is correct, unless it is possible to develop a clear set of relevant properties that remove arbitrariness from the basic moral principles.

The species test cannot be applied consistently to serve as a basic principle. Many animals have mental abilities that are superior to those of some humans, and some would argue that it is morally more permissible to kill a human infant who lacks a cortex (anencephalic) than it is to kill a free-ranging, healthy adult chimpanzee, for example. All humans are not seen as being of equal value. As was found in the study described in Chapter 7, almost everyone agrees that it is wrong to kill human beings (unless some special circumstances is invoked, such as being godless or not of our god-belief, being an aggressor, or being the embodiment of some other designated class of evil). Remember, in the empirical study reported in Chapter 7, it was found that people tended not to kill kin or members of their social community, choosing instead to kill a human being with whom they would not be acquainted. There is something running through all of these instances that indicates membership in the human species will not be the sufficient basic principle on which moral standing can be based.

If membership in a typological category, or taxonomic class, is not adequate to qualify for the status of a person, then the proper test must be one that relates to the qualities of individuals. Moral status should not be assigned automatically because of membership in any arbitrarily selected category. Tooley (1983) illustrated this point nicely. He asked us to assume that there are two individuals, John and Mary. John is the member of a species, 99% of whom are moral agents, while Mary is a member of another species, only 1% of whom are moral agents. Assume that the two individuals possess the same qualities and these qualities would entitle them both to be moral agents. In this case he suggests (correctly) that we cannot give John preference because of his species membership. I suggest that the case can be argued just as strongly even if we know nothing of the personal moral characteristics of either John or Mary. We cannot, and should not (other things being equal), favor one or the other without evaluating them individually. Both Tooley and I come to the conclusion that any test of personhood must be applied at the level of the individual and should not rest on membership in some typological category. (It should be emphasized that all evolutionary principles must operate, basically, at the level of the individual.) Because it is not possible to test all individuals in the universe we should at least have tested representatively enough to permit the establishment of estimates of the values of central tendencies and variances, as well as the range of possible values of those characteristics that will be used to assign moral agency.

Suggested Characteristics for Personhood

Many writers have discussed the characteristics that would confer personhood on an individual. The importance of establishing the status of personhood is tied to what has been called "recognition respect" (Kleinig, 1991) which means that such individuals are entitled to have other persons take seriously, and weigh appropriately, the fact that they are autonomous entities. This state of respect requires other persons to constrain their behavior and decisions in a way that will respect the autonomy of the person affected.

Often the argument is based on the assumption that the status of personhood is when moral standing is attained as well. I believe that personhood and moral agency are separate categories with different defining characteristics. Some of the listings of characteristics that have been suggested to confer the status of personhood (and moral agency) on individuals certainly include the appropriate qualities, but a close examination of them leads one to believe that they have been constructed in such a way that only humans, especially philosophers, will meet them all with ease.

Tooley (1983, pp 90–91) has listed 15 characteristics that, at one time or another, have been suggested to be the requirements that one must have to be given the status of personhood.

1. The capacity to experience pleasure and/or pain.
2. The capacity to have desires.
3. The capacity to remember past events.
4. The capacity to have expectations with respect to future events.
5. An awareness of the passage of time.
6. The property of being a continuing, conscious self, or subject of mental states.
7. The property of being conscious of being a distinct entity.
8. The capacity for self-consciousness.
9. The property of having mental states that involve propositional attitudes, such as beliefs and desires.
10. The capacity to have thought episodes, involving intentionality.
11. The capacity to reason.

12. The ability to solve problems.
13. The property of being autonomous.
14. The capacity to use language.
15. The ability to interact socially with others.

Tooley, you, and I meet all of these requirements, so we can nod in satisfied consensual agreement. Warren (1973) considered five traits to be most central to personhood in the moral sense, and they explicitly include, at the least, characteristics 1, 3, 6, 7, 8, 11, 12, 13, and 14 of the above list. She suggested that 1, 2, 6, 11, and 12 might be good candidates to be the minimal necessary conditions, with perhaps 13 included as well. An individual satisfying none of these characteristics undoubtedly would not be considered to be a person. She arrived at the conclusion that some human beings are not people, and there may well be people who do not possess the qualities that define human beings.

Tooley (1983) suggested that the three necessary and sufficient criteria that an individual must have to be a person are: (1) Rationality, meaning the capacity to reason, think, solve problems, and make decisions by weighing alternatives; (2) consciousness, including self-consciousness, and requiring thoughts that generalize; (3) desires, meaning the capacity to envisage future states and being a subject of momentary interests.

Later Tooley (1983, p. 349) adopted an even more restrictive set of criteria, which involved almost all of the 15 listed above when he suggested:

> (i) Nothing can be a person unless it has at least one of the properties on the list;
> (ii) Anything that has all of the properties is a person. Most people . . . would agree that anything that has . . . all of the following capacities is a person, and that anything that has never had any of them is not a person: the capacity for self-consciousness; the capacity to think; the capacity for rational thought; the capacity to arrive at decisions by deliberation; the capacity to envisage a future for oneself; the capacity to remember a past involving oneself; the capacity for being a subject of non-momentary interests; the capacity to use language. Given such a list the information provided by a scientific study of human development will enable one to conclude that humans up to a certain point in their development are not persons, since they possess none of the properties on the list, and that humans beyond some other stage are definitely persons, since they possess all of the properties on the list.

It is clear that an individual possessing all of the qualities enumerated by Tooley should be considered to be a person, as well as a moral agent. One problem is that the defining qualities enumerated are those that define full moral standing and the task at hand has not really been accomplished, especially when one wishes to consider the possibility of assigning moral standing to non-humans, or to nonadult humans. There are humans who possess none of the listed qualities, as well as other people who possess all of them: the question that is not addressed satisfactorily is where one can draw the line for moral standing when an individual possesses some, but not all, of the characteristics suggested. This inability to draw a definite line is troublesome because it is the status of these individuals that is at issue.

The exhaustive listing of all of the qualities that define personhood reminds me of arguments regarding whether animals have true language. One approach taken by some has been to list all the particular features of human language that linguists have identified and then to ask whether or not any animal has all of these characteristics. If not, some have suggested that no animal could be considered to possess true language. The outcome of this procedure seems obvious; no animal other than humans can ever be considered to have true language. If the taxon, true language, is keyed on the basis of all of the qualities of an arbitrarily chosen reference group, such as humans, it is unlikely that any other group will qualify for membership in the class. What really has taken place is a decision by definition, not one based on the essentials that should qualify an individual to possess true language. The chore of distilling the characteristics of human language is an interesting and useful descriptive enterprise, but the outcome regarding the essence of "true" language is predetermined by the strategy chosen. Such a strategy will not move us toward the goal of arriving at a satisfactory decision regarding the characteristics a communication system must possess to qualify as a true language.

The weakness of the strategy of listing all the peculiarities of a selected system, and then declaring it to be the epitome of the class in question, can be illustrated in another way. I could define true language by listing every formal characteristic of the English language to constitute the criteria that any language is to be keyed against (it might horrify some that the English language should serve as the exemplar of rational language systems). No other language will possess all of the peculiar characteristics of English. Therefore, no other language would be classified as a true language. The procedure is nothing but a definitional gambit masquerading as a serious enterprise in classification. Listing all of the characteristics of different languages can be a useful exercise if one wants to compare languages one to another. Such an exercise can lead to a meaningful understanding of language types, as well as to an understanding of such things as the influence of ecological conditions on the structure of language, but the exercise, as described, will not take us beyond the definitional level.

Louis Herman has devoted many years to the study of the cognitive capacities of dolphins. In particular, he has studied their capacities to communicate with humans and with one another. He proposed the following scenario (1988, p. 349) which illustrates the point I am developing from the dolphin's perspectives:

First dolphin: I saw a human swimming!
Second dolphin: Did he leap out of the water? Did his speed reach 15 or more knots? Did he hold his breath for five or more minutes? Did he dive to 300 ft or more? Did he have hard-wired tail flukes?
First dolphin: No, no, no, to all of that.
Second dolphin: Well, then, you shouldn't call if "swimming." Nothing about it even remotely resembles swimming."

If the dolphin's extraordinary ability to swim is used in a definitional gambit to characterize the essence of swimming, then no human is ever going to qualify as a swimmer. Herman has argued that dolphins have been taught a true language and he objects to proscriptions against the use of linguistic terms "reserved" for humans. I do not intend to discuss animal language any further here, but it is a concern of great importance whenever the moral standing of animals becomes an issue of concern.

The point of the argument is that care must be taken to avoid arbitrary classification schemes that only adult humans can satisfy if the real interest is to set the criteria for personhood or moral agency. If an arbitrary scheme is used, then we are guilty of indulging in reasoning that does involve speciesism and most schemes that have been developed, even by animal welfare advocates such as Singer and Regan, have difficulty avoiding the specter of speciesism.

Summary

I have discussed problems involved in establishing the criteria for personhood because it is a necessary step to qualify an individual as a moral agent. It is important to avoid assigning personhood in such a way that species membership is the sole defining characteristic; if this is done then one has fallen into the trap of speciesism, which decrees that personhood is synonymous with being a member of the class *Homo sapiens*. Some persons qualify to be classed as moral agents, and this classification invests them with both responsibilities and duties. I have outlined some of the qualities that philosophers have suggested to constitute the necessary and sufficient conditions an individual must meet in order to be considered a person (and, thereby, a moral agent in the view of many), and have expressed doubt regarding the usefulness of all of these listings. Before discussing the qualities I consider necessary and sufficient to characterize moral agency, I will discuss some arguments that have been raised to question the use of personhood as a relevant concept, especially when considering the morality of abortion.

Arguments Regarding Personhood

One reason that personhood has been the subject of strong concern is that the United States Constitution protects "persons" by granting them rights that the state must respect. Tribe (1990/1992) argues that the Constitution contains broad provisions whose meaning requires judicial interpretation and judgment. One of the most important of these broad provisions he considers to be the Fourteenth Amendment which reads that no state shall deprive any person of life, liberty, or property without due process of law; Dworkin noted that the word "liberty" is not self-defining. Dworkin (1993) agreed that it is a precondition of legitimate democracy that individual citizens be considered to be equals, and that their fundamental liberties and dignity be respected. In his view, unless those conditions are met there can be no genuine democracy.

The Supreme Court consistently has held that the liberty protection of the Fourteenth Amendment's due process clause prevents the states from enacting laws that, if enacted by Congress, would be invalid under the protection of individual rights contained in the Bill of Rights. In regards to abortion, the *Roe v. Wade* decision made any state law that would absolutely forbid abortion within the first trimester unconstitutional, decided that abortion may be regulated in the second trimester to preserve and protect the health of the mother, and could be outlawed altogether (unless the woman's life is threatened) when the fetus has become a viable being (which is defined as being in the third trimester) in order to protect the fetal life. Only a miniscule number of abortions are performed in the third trimester and many of these are done legally to save the woman's life.

The Court has traditionally, when considering cases involving abortion, asked first about the rights of the person (the woman) to determine whether a fundamental liberty is involved, and then considered reasons (such as protection of the fetus's right to life) that might justify that liberty's abridgment. As Tribe construed it, the asserted liberty is the right of the woman not to be forced to remain pregnant. After this liberty has been considered, then constitutional concerns regarding the fetus are in order.

The Fourteenth Amendment is explicit regarding the fact that it refers to all persons which I will argue clearly does not include the unborn in the class of citizens of the United States Justice Blackmun wrote, in the majority opinion in *Roe v. Wade*, that the Constitution does not define "person" in so many words, but that the word "person," as used in the Fourteenth Amendment, does not include the unborn. Throughout its history, the Court has rejected the argument that the fetus is a person from the moment of conception, and has ruled that a state or local government could not adopt any single theory of life, such as the theory that life begins at conception. Any law that absolutely prohibits abortion is unconstitutional because it embodies a controversial interpretation regarding the sanctity of life that is enforcing one religious view regarding life over others, which is forbidden by the First Amendment. Dworkin (1993, p. 166) concluded that, "the right to procreative autonomy, from which a right of choice about abortion flows, is well grounded in the First Amendment." The Court also held that the right to decide about abortion belonged to the pregnant woman.

A less legalistic statement of the difficulties involved in the use of a particular set of values to determine public policy was expressed by Kamm (1992). She argued that, in a pluralistic society, it is common for different people's values not to coincide and, in a free society, such differences should be respected. Although the values of different people do not coincide, it is possible to express the concerns involved in higher-order language so that people who do not share one another's beliefs can communicate with and understand one another. The attempt should not be to convince others of the correctness of a value system, but to convince them that the belief system is coherent and reasonable in terms of an overall set of moral principles, be they philosophical or theological. The intent is to reach an understanding that all need not abide by any particular set of values, but, as long as the value set is reasonable, does not violate explicit legal principles, and does not infringe on the basic freedoms of others, it should be respected by all.

Tribe also developed an important point, when discussing the line between abortifacients and contraceptives. He considered fertilization to be a process and not a moment, noting that once a sperm has penetrated the outside of an ovum, the process of fertilization takes about 24 hours, at the end of which the chromosomes of the egg and sperm are intermingled and the complement of 46 chromosomes is in existence. The American Medical Association (AMA) defines conception as the point at which the fertilized ovum is implanted in the uterine wall (which rules out the two-thirds of fertilized ova that naturally fail to implant). Tribe (1990/1992, pp. 123–124) finds it peculiar to think that two-thirds of the people who have ever come into existence have been lost through this normal feature of human reproduction.

There is compelling evidence that the potentiality of the organism is never completely resolved throughout the entire process of development. The question of exactly up to what point developmental influences are primarily genetic, beyond which they are the product of experiential influences, has been shown to be a meaningless one. Similarly meaningless is the question regarding the moment of conception at which the "blueprint" of the potential organism is available for development. For the reasons enumerated above, Tribe finds it impossible to maintain that the Constitution protects a fetus just as if it had already been born.

King (1980) would like to eliminate consideration of personhood in light of the *Roe v. Wade* decision by the U.S. Supreme Court. In this decision the Court held that, although the fetus is not a person for the purposes of the Fourteenth Amendment to the Constitution, it is entitled to protection at viability. King rejects arguments that the point of birth is a significant enough event to mark the point at which personhood begins, and I will disagree strongly with that point.

The concept of personhood was also considered to be unhelpful to resolve the fundamentals of the abortion controversy by Macklin (1984), who spoke of the almost total absence of attempts to demonstrate a strictly "scientific basis" for determining when personhood begins. A reading of the bioethics literature led her to conclude that not a single proponent who argued that personhood was an important benchmark considered the determination of personhood to be a straightforward *scientific* question.

It has been suggested, and I will argue, that the point of birth should be considered to signal the start of personhood. Tooley (1983) rejected this suggestion on the grounds that, although birth is "certainly a dramatic event," there is not enough of a difference to mark a significant boundary between the characteristics of the full-term fetus and the neonate that would justify a change in the conception of moral status. Although there is a major difference given the fact that, at birth, the newborn is not dependent on the mother's life-support system, this single difference does not seem enough, to him, to justify the status of personhood.

Sumner (1981) argued that while birth is the point at which the specific relationship between mother and fetus is terminated and when the neonate, for the first time, is enabled to rely on its own body systems for survival, this change does not alter the nature of the neonate. He accepted the position that pregnancy can be construed as a relationship between host and parasite (a view resembling those of Haig and Profet, discussed in Chapter 4), and that after birth there are two independent beings. Sumner (1981) considered birth to be a shallow and arbitrary criterion of moral standing and concluded that there appears to be no way of connecting it to a deeper account. Sumner also pointed out that choosing viability as the crucial threshold to recognize moral standing is fraught with the same problems as those attendant upon birth. He concluded that it is arbitrary, and not useful, to pick any point during gestation as the one at which moral standing is acquired. I will agree with the latter statement and will argue that there is a "deeper account" to justify using birth as the point for moral standing to begin.

Dworkin (1993) also wants to set aside the question of whether a fetus is a person on the grounds that the determination of personhood remains too ambiguous to be helpful. He considers a fetus to be a person only in the sense that it has a right to be treated in ways that creatures that are undeniably persons (you and me) should be treated. However, Dworkin does mention several aspects of socialization occurring at the point of birth that he believes are strongly involved in establishing what he calls "the sanctity of life." He mentions the importance of emotional involvement and commitments, and the personal investments people make in themselves and others—what I have called a social contract. Once a human life starts Dworkin states that a process has begun, and interrupting that process frustrates an "adventure under way." He also appeals to the importance of social and individual training and choice that culminates in satisfying relationships and achievements, arguing that individual rights must be considered and balanced against the rights of the moral community. I will argue that the point of birth should be used to signal the start of personhood, and that this solution can be grounded in terms of biology, rather than being based on the concept of the sanctity of life that Dworkin favors.

Problems with Viability as a Criterion

Some of the major problems with the viability criterion are apparent in the arguments King (1980) advanced to justify the use of this criterion. She considered the major problem to be the one I alluded to earlier; it is difficult to argue that viability occurs at an absolute, specific point during gestation. The likelihood of viability is distributed as a function of the age of the fetus and has many different distributions depending on a multitude of background variables, including the weight and general physiological condition of the fetus, the physiological condition of the mother, age of the mother, her prenatal behavior, nutrition, and substance use, availability of prenatal care, competence of available physicians, quality of the medical staff and facility available, the facility's access to modern equipment and technology, awareness of the medical staff concerning technological advances, and on and on.

King's recommendation in light of these problems is that the point of viability should be updated regularly to keep pace with recent medical advances. She decided that one should take a conservative stand and consider every fetus to be entitled to legal protection at the earliest possible age that there has been a verified survival, and that is at 24 weeks within the language of *Roe v. Wade*. King (1980) went one step further, and argued that, given the magnitude of error in estimating gestational age, there is a compelling state interest in any potential human estimated to be within 2 weeks of the age of the youngest fetus known to have survived. She argues that 22 weeks of age should be considered the age at which viability begins, given the current status of medical technology. I wonder why the error should be considered to be in one direction only. It would seem just as credible to assume that the 24-week figure really is a value from a distribution with a true value of 26, as much as that it is a value of 22.

The problems I see in all of this are at three levels: One relates to the nature of the statistical arguments she has chosen to estimate the point of viability; a second is her discomfort in attaching moral standing to unknown developments in medical technology; and a third is the arbitrary and exclusive focus on the fetus. I will argue that, although the point of viability does not provide an adequate criterion, the point at which personhood begins does provide an objective and adequate criterion, and that point occurs at birth.

The statistical decision advocated by King is to take the most extreme value (the youngest fetus that attained verifiable viability under any circumstance) and then move the viability cut-off point back 2 weeks from that point given a lack of certainty regarding gestational age. It is well known that any statistics based on the range of observed values are among the most unreliable, because the range will vary greatly from sample to sample drawn from the same population, and the range will increase as the number of cases increases. This increase as a function of the number of cases considered occurs because when one adds cases the range can only stay the same as it was or increase (the range is defined by the two most extreme values—but there is no interest, in the present context, with the maximum value because the time of birth provides an absolute cut-off at the high end of the distribution). If one keeps adding cases the lowest value can only become lower (or not change). If there is a statistical distribution of values, and if there is a bizarre one in a billion case, then by adding enough cases that one in a billion that does exist sooner or later will be encountered, and it will be that bizarre value that is used to determine the norm.

One traditional statistical decision is, rather than moving to an even more extreme value, to disregard the most extreme value at each end of the distribution and to use the second most extreme scores as the best range estimator, or to disregard some small percentage of cases at the extremes. These decisions are made, not because the most extreme values are beyond regard, but in the realization that their values are just as likely to be the result of such things as measurement, computational, or sampling error and do not provide more valid estimates of the true extremes. King's solution is to err in the conservative direction by decreasing the lowest observed value by 2 weeks. I argue that one should accept the assumption that it is possible to commit an error, that the direction of that error is unknown, and that it is more acceptable to assume that the error is random in direction, rather than assuming the error deviation is always in one direction. It can be argued that the one in a billion value that we could use as our criterion value might not even belong to the distribution of values contained in the population of concern, but is a member of a distribution with completely different parameter values, which means that it is a member of a different population from the one we are concerned about.

I find it difficult to argue that the law, which is to be applied to all members of society, should be based on a value that is lower than the most atypical value observed in the population. If we are to make just decisions, then we should come down on the side that is likely to yield the most valid estimate of the true value of the parameter in question. If a general law regarding morality is to be developed, then it seems strange to base the law on a single atypical point when, in fact, all of the other fetuses at that age that have been identified in the population did not survive.

I also question the wisdom of grounding the critical point regulating the basic philosophical principle governing moral decisions on yet-to-be-found advances in medical technology. If one is going to accept a specific time as the point at which viability appears, and that time is to be signaled by some specific physiological qualities that depend on advances in medical technology, then that point must be set in reference to the distribution of values expected using the specific medical technologies available to the particular fetus and mother in question. That distribution is the one that relates to the probability of survival of individuals with the set of specific characteristics in the circumstances with which we are dealing, and that distribution of values is the reference distribution on which secular law should be based. If medical facilities are inadequate, doctors are inexperienced, or the mother's prenatal condition is poor, then the distribution of values should reflect these facts when establishing the age of viability if it is to be a truly valid estimator.

Murray (1987) reached a conclusion quite similar to the one I am arguing. He regarded viability, at best, to be a "slippery concept" that has a "moving front." The age of viability must be a statistical concept that is based on the age at which some specified percentage of newborns will survive, and the resulting distribution of values must be used to refer to specific infants, under specified conditions, and in particular settings. As I discussed, when evaluating King's criteria for setting the age of viability, the issue must be considered to be a probabilistic function of, at least, such things as birth weight (BW) and gestational age (GA). Murray suggested that one such index could be cast as a BW/GA=10; meaning the BW and GA combination at which 10% of infants survive. A BW/GA=50 would be the BW and GA combination at which 50% survive, and so forth. The calculation of this family of values is similar to the process population ecologists use to construct what is called a life table for a given species under particular circumstances and specified environmental conditions. Once this family of statistics regarding survival rates are available the proper criterion value can be argued on the basis of rational principles. The interpretation of these numbers could change as the particular circumstances change in light of the adequacy of the available medical facility and other aspects of the situation, such as the state of existing medical technology, that reflect our ability to promote an infants' survival.

King (1980, p. 76) deplored the Court's extraordinary deference to the medical profession regarding the reasonable likelihood of survival on which the point of viability depends. She considered this deference to be unwarranted, especially given the importance of that decision to all of society. I join her in this uneasy feeling, and I find her arguments regarding the fact that the medical profession neither wants, nor is especially competent, to deal with the question of the justice of decisions regarding viability to be compelling.

Because the point of viability is not "forever fixed in time" King worried that there can be criticisms regarding the use of viability as a criterion on which to base legal decisions. However, she still argued its usefulness as a biological concept that can be applied universally. I agree that we need, and want, a universal biological concept to ground our basic moral principles, but cannot agree that viability is sufficient. I will continue in the next chapter, to argue that personhood is one concept that can be grounded biologically and behaviorally, and that moral agency is a second basic concept, that can be grounded cognitively.

Dworkin (1993) is not entirely consistent in his arguments regarding the moral status of the fetus. As mentioned above, he stated that the fetus should be treated "as if" it was a person (p. 23), while at the same time maintaining that this does not in any way presume that the fetus has rights or interests of its own (p. 12). He characterizes the latter position as one that very few people actually believe (p. 13). Although he initially suggests (p. 11) that life has an "intrinsic, innate value" that begins when its biological life begins, he also suggests that sentience could be used as a provisional boundary to set the point at which interests begin—at about 26 weeks, a time coincident with the present time for the onset of viability (p. 17). Dworkin also noted that 30 weeks might be argued as the point when sentience begins if that time is accepted to mark the point of cortical maturation, and he seems to suggest (p. 18) that the point of cortical maturation is preferable because it is the more complex capacities, rather than the capacity to feel pain, that "ground a creature's interests in continuing to live" (p. 18). He seems to be awash in a sea of indecision. I will argue, when I consider Tooley's neurophysiological criteria for personhood, that arguments that depend on the level of cortical maturation are not tenable in view of the data concerning the development of the complex neural structures of the kind Dworkin is considering.

Yet another problem is that relying on establishing the age of viability, as suggested by all of the writers discussed above, focuses totally on the fetus, with a complete disregard for the mother, or for the characteristics of the social context in which the fetus will be introduced, including the medical support that will be available. Kleinig (1991) argued that the claims of the mother, father, and wider social factors must be taken into account when considering the significance of abortion. The view of viability usually advocated is too narrowly focused on only one component of a complex system, the fetus, and that makes it an unreasonable one to use to set the point of viability that will apply to all participants in the decisions involved regarding the beginning of life.

9

The Critical Importance
of Personhood

I argue that the onset of personhood marks a critical stage in the development of life and that it signals the start of a contract between the neonate and society. The point at which personhood begins is birth, and a series of critical events occur at that point which confer the public status of personhood on the neonate. These events signal an obligation that society should honor the needs, interests, and welfare of the neonate. This critical developmental stage is not unique to humans, but is general in the ontogeny of most birds and mammals, and the period immediately following birth is a period that is crucial to normal psychological and social development.

BIRTH AS A CRITICAL POINT IN
HUMAN DEVELOPMENT

Although several of the writers I discussed in the preceding chapter denied explicitly that enough changes occur at the point of birth to justify a differential treatment of the viable fetus, as compared to the neonate, a careful reading of most of these writers convinces me that they recognize that something quite critical does occur at birth, but they choose not to emphasize it. I believe that this reluctance to emphasize the significance of the point of birth is due to an almost total focus on the characteristics of the fetus rather than on the total matrix involving the mother and society. It will be useful to consider the view of those writers because, even though they deny the critical moral nature of the point of birth, each suggests that it does signal a crucial developmental stage.

For example, King (1980), while arguing that birth only signals the fetal capacity to survive independently of the mother, acknowledged that the neonate possesses the ability to interact with humans other than the mother, while the fetus is unable to do so. Later, King acknowledged that birth is the point at which other humans, for the first time, can see, touch, and communicate with the developing infant, but she denied that this point, the one at which the characteristics of human interaction explode, should have any relevance in terms of the establishment of legal protection. It seems to me that the capacity to interact with other humans is critical enough to establish an interest on which legal protection can be justified.

Tooley (1983), who also dismissed birth events as significant enough to establish moral standing, acknowledged that these events involve, not only independence from the mother, but that, at this time, the neonate begins to enjoy complex visual experiences. He argued that the events that make "something" a person are psychological in nature because a person is defined by the sort of mental life he or she enjoys. The problem is that his arguments are still all focused on the "something" and not on its interaction with the world that constitutes society. Once again, I find an admission on his part that something critical has taken place.

Although rejecting birth as an adequate point to use to establish moral standing, Sumner (1981) emphasized the importance of the unique prenatal relationship between the fetus and the mother, which broadens into a bond between the infant and mother at birth. He identified this developing bond as the basis for a personal relationship that creates personal history. Sumner also mentioned that the mother and fetus should perhaps be considered as only one person, thereby making it impossible to consider that any interpersonal conflict between mother and fetus can occur at all prior to the point of birth, although the aforementioned ideas of Haig (1983) and Profet (1992) raise some questions regarding the biological soundness of this point.

The point of birth as a critical stage was also rejected by Wertheimer (1971, p. 51), who wrote, "a newborn infant is only a fetus that has suffered a change of address and some physiological changes like respiration." Earlier, however, he acknowledged that, at birth, the child leaves its own private space and enters the public world, making it able to be looked at, acted upon, and interacted with.

In Kamm's (1992) view, the fetus is in the mother's private territory, and at birth it can reside both in its own private (phenomenological) territory, as well as in public territory. She also made the interesting observation that a fetus growing in a laboratory (say, as a result of an in vitro fertilization) could be construed to have the status of a person because it is a public entity, while that growing in the body of the mother is not a public person. This interesting observation suggests that society could have an obligation toward a public person whether or not the publicity is a function of normal childbirth or a technological advance.

Benn (1973) pointed out that people have an "instinctual tenderness and protectiveness toward babies." One of my strong concerns was expressed by English (1975), who noted that many approaches that characterize human development consider only the fetus, rather than the relationship between the fetus and the woman. English considered birth to be a crucial point, not because of changes in the characteristics of the fetus, but because of the changed responsibilities of the mother when the fetus becomes a neonate.

The importance of relationships between individuals to determine moral status was emphasized by Lomasky (1982) who complained that it is inadequate to think of individuals as self-contained entities who possess rights only by virtue of their intellectual attainments. He made the sound evolutionary argument (Lomasky, 1982, p. 170) that, "Parent and child, friend and friend, citizen and compatriot, are related to each other by ties that do not similarly bind them to all other individuals." He continued that, while the fetus is a human organism, it lacks the public and interpersonal contacts that enable the crucial identification to take place. He proposed a thought experiment whereby a fetus was magically annihilated and replaced by a different one. In this case its demise would be neither known nor lamented by anyone. However, at birth, the status of the fetus changes from a private to a public one, and postnatally such an annihilation would constitute homicide, even though the neonate could magically be replaced (or is replaceable) by another, with no one being the wiser.

For Lomasky, birth is a "quantum leap forward" in the process of establishing the social bonds that support the identity of the infant as a unique individual. He considered the moral significance of birth not to be what the newborn baby can do but what it now is, an identifiable individual that can elicit responses as a unique object of concern to the members of society. Once again, these are the aspects that provide the basis for the individual's entry into the social community as a person, and which create the responsibility that moral agents have to care for and protect that new person.

A concurring view was expressed by Regan (1983) who suggested that moral bonds between family members and friends qualify as special considerations that justifiably can override other moral principles. He pointed out that these relationships function as social contracts between loved ones. When such a contract exists they are built on mutual trust, interdependence, and the performance of mutually beneficial acts—what I have been identifying as actions that increase inclusive fitness.

A position similar to that of Lomasky, and that I am arguing, was adopted by Harris (1992), who dated the start of *a* life (as opposed to life) being at birth, the first point at which one can identify an individual whose life can be saved. This statement highlights an important distinction that should be made between the onset of biological life (which begins when the zygote is formed), and a life, which begins when that individual is a recognizable, public, biographical being.

The recitation of statements by prominent philosophers argues that even those who would deny that birth is one of the critical points in moral development agree that enough profound changes take place at birth to support my conviction that one should conceive the point of birth as a critical point in the development of the characteristics that command social respect. The neonate can live detached naturally from the mother, it directly experiences the external milieu for the first time, and it is a social object with a public identity that society can recognize and interact with for the first time. The tendency to disregard the importance of birth is due to an almost total focus on the *physiological* characteristics of the fetus, and that is a mistake. I will emphasize, below, that moral status does not involve only the characteristics of the "something," but of the "something" in relation to the "somewhere"—the complex matrix that constitutes human society.

Early Emotional Interactions

I emphasized the importance of cognitive events due to my interest in developing a biologically based and cognitively oriented system that is adequate to ground a rational model of morality. There are a large number of emotional factors that have been discussed at great length for many years, and which should be acknowledged. Freud, and succeeding psycho-analytically oriented theorists, emphasized the existence of different stages of human psychological development and centered attention on the importance of social interactions that begin at birth and continue into adolescence. Freud considered these early experiences to be critical determinants of the adult personality, which he considered to be well formed by the end of the fifth year. These experiences, especially psychosexual ones, were considered to be especially involved in the development of personality disorders later in life.

In his superb intellectual biography of Freud, Frank Sulloway (1979) documented that Freud was well acquainted with the writings of Darwin, which had a strong influence on him, especially *The Descent of Man* (1871).

However, Freud's biological views tended to be proximate and reduction-istic, rather than having the functionalistic characteristics of Darwinian evolutionary theory. Sulloway developed the argument that Freud was seeking to create a biologically based theory of human thought and be-havior, and that this theory employed many biological constructs, such as the existence of what we now refer to as imprinting and critical periods in development.

Many of the Freudian constructs concerning development were cast in a framework that was compatible directly with the principles of evolu-tionary biology and ethology that were extant at that time. Bowlby empha-sized the importance of the early interactions that are always present between a mother and her children. He wrote (1969, p. 61), "the basic social unit of man is a mother, her children, and perhaps her daughter's children, and . . . the way societies differ is in whether, and in the extent to which, fathers become attached to this unit. . . . " This view is compatible with those I have developed here based on evolutionary considerations.

The general point of view advocated by Bowlby receives strong sup-port when one considers some of the behavioral characteristics that have been shown to be important in the development of later social interactions: Such things as smiling by the infant of a few weeks of age, a tendency to attempt to fixate visual stimuli that have two black dots on a pale back-ground (which resembles a face), a propensity to touch and to cling, and a responsiveness to being picked up. The psychologists Emde and Gaens-bauer (1981) spoke of an early period of endogenous smiling by neonates that is irregular, and appears in response to a wide variety of stimuli in several modalities. While this smiling behavior is not a dependable re-sponse that signifies anything in particular on the part of the infant, it does elicit a social response, particularly from the mother, and could well be important in the development of a social bond. The face of the mother, while feeding her baby, is ideally positioned to be fixated on and tracked by a neonate who, while being breast-fed, often will have open eyes that are focused on the mother's face.

Collis (1981) identified patterned movements by the neonate that are similar in form to those that will play a subsequent role in interactions with objects and persons, and noted that these movements can be observed just after birth. Again, these nonintentional movements by the neonate could serve to develop a social bond by eliciting responses from the members of human society.

The importance of social interactions that occur during the first days of life was emphasized by Bowlby (1969). These interactions involve such things as the infant being picked up, talked to, and caressed. These actions lead to an interest on the part of the neonate in watching people move about; this in turn leads to an interest on the part of members of society in socially interacting with the infant. It will be recalled that Locke (1993) stressed the importance of experience- and activity-dependent systems to regulate the cognitive development of the infant, and that the role of motherese is to forge emotional bonds between the infant and the social community. Research indicates that the adult figures to whom children become attached are those who respond quickly, and with a high intensity, to the infant's activities. Bowlby believed that social attachment occurs between 6 and 9 months of age, and interpreted all of this evidence to indicate that babies behave to maximize the kinds of stimuli that emanate from humans. These actions by the neonate bias the mother to behave in special ways toward babies, and a social bond is thereby established very early in life.

When the infant is separated from the mother it "protests" by becoming agitated, frantic, and emitting distress vocalizations. The evolutionary explanation of the functional significance of such behaviors would be that the protest increases the probability that the mother will locate the infant—as was discussed for elephant seal pups and mothers in Chapter 3. It is plausible to assume that, in the environment of evolutionary adaptation, this vocal response of the infant to separation could have adaptive value and would have been selected for in the course of evolution.

An innate interest in faces could enhance the process of attachment to the caregiver and be reciprocated by the caregiver. For example, in a brief commentary Ellis (1992) discussed evidence that newborn infants (at an average age of 30 minutes) displayed greater tracking with head and eye movements to a schematic face as compared to a face containing either scrambled features or a blank head shape. Two-day-old infants can reliably discriminate their mother's face from that of a stranger. Jacobs and Raleigh (1992) presented research results that were similar to those discussed in Chapter 4. They noted that neonates prefer the human voice over other acoustically complex stimuli, the maternal voice over that of other females, a female voice over male voices, and that a neonate younger than 3 days old will work to produce the mother's voice in preference to the voice of another female. These facts all indicate an important role for the experience-expectant systems outlined in Chapter 4 for the development of social behaviors.

The responsiveness of the human fetus to its acoustic environment, as well as the fact that infant auditory preferences can be influenced by what is heard prenatally, were demonstrated by De Caspar and Spence (1986). Several studies discussed by Jacobs and Raleigh (1992) indicate that even the effects of prenatal influences can be detected in the newborn. The fetus has experience-expectant systems that lead it to be receptive to certain classes of stimuli, and all of the developing systems are influenced by metabolic, chemical, and nutritional states of the uterine environment. In addition, the fetus is differentially affected by auditory stimuli, especially those important in language. I suggest that the only thing lacking for the fetus to be a person is a public appearance. Once again, I am stressing the importance of the characteristics of the social milieu, and arguing that it is not sufficient to focus only on the characteristics of the fetus to establish personhood.

All of these data (as well as those discussed in Chapter 4 when the views of Locke, 1993, and Pinker, 1994, were considered) argue that the first emotional attachments seem to have a cognitive characteristic from the outset. Trevarthen (1992) emphasized the fact that human mothers, fathers, and siblings are uniquely and instructively playful with neonates. He notes that the baby songs and rhythmic body games used by mothers seem to solicit intense attention, cooperative movements, and vocalizations from her infant. While the infant may not yet be consciously participating in the interactions, the infant has become a part of the social network and is entitled to be regarded as a person. Social attachment can be viewed, then, to have a biologically adaptive function (Lamb, Thompson, Gardner, Chornov, & Estes, 1984). Kraemer (1992) reviewed the extensive research that supports the argument that social attachment is not an optional overlay of more basic functions, but is an organizing feature of those functions. The first priority of the infant seems to be attachment to objects with particular stimulus characteristics. All of the interactions between the infant and society, especially those with the mother, support the argument being developed here—at birth the infant enters the society as an interacting social citizen.

Birth as a Critical Biological Point

The signal importance of the event of birth for the development of factors important in social behavior has been emphasized for most species of birds and mammals. In Chapter 3, under the heading "Ethological Mechanisms," events were described that take place at birth, or shortly after, in the life history of many species of birds and mammals. These events mark the beginning of evolved adaptations to the environment and set the bases on which later social behaviors will be established. These very early experiences regulate the development of many of the crucial interactions that are involved in later courtship, mating, and parental behaviors. One such important mechanism is that of both parental and sexual imprinting by young organisms which occur shortly after birth or hatching.

In humans there has been extensive study of the bases on which such complex characteristics as human language are developed, and it is clear that the development of the abilities to perceive, to understand, and to articulate the sounds used in language appear spontaneously in response to the language to which the very young infant is exposed. It was concluded that, upon exposure to the sounds of the local speech community, babies develop a tendency to make sounds that will be important in producing the speech of that language, and that the young quickly acquire an ability to distinguish the speech sounds of their own language community. It has been noted that, among the primates, only human infants engage in the spontaneous vocal play, called babbling, early in life. A similar pattern is involved in the development of manual babbling for those children who grow up using American Sign Language (ASL), which indicates that these developmental patterns are not peculiar to the speech system, but are involved in communication by whatever means.

Many of the events involved in the development of social behavior have been identified at the point of birth, and in humans, to continue for many months and even years. It is at the point of birth that the fetus becomes a recognizable, public entity that responds to members of the society, and it is here that social interactions begin. The almost immediate salience of events that are important to social development strengthens my conviction that the point of birth, does signal the point at which the developing human organism should be recognized as a person. The start of personhood is marked by the point of birth, and it is at this point that both the mother and society acquire duties and responsibilities toward the neonate. When the stage of personhood is reached, a biological and cognitively based social contract has been struck, and the needs, interests, and welfare of the neonate must be respected from that point onward.

Even a cursory examination of human behavior and beliefs makes it apparent that human infants are accorded a special status by society and that this status is not accorded to young organisms of other species. This special status is the result of an anthropocentrism that is based on the principles I have referred to as inclusive fitness, as well as a deep-seated and pervasive tendency toward speciesism. The strength of these tendencies, as well as of the importance of a social contract, were empirically demonstrated in the studies discussed in Chapter 7.

It is neither unnatural nor immoral for humans to favor their own species, their own kin, and members of their community when moral decisions must be made. Let me emphasize that this does not mean that the welfare and interests of other living beings should not be considered among the duties and responsibilities that human moral agents must assume. It only means that the social contract involves a special entailment for humans and, especially, for certain kinds of humans to whom we are either biologically or socially related.

Dworkin and the Sanctity of Life

Ronald Dworkin (1993), a moral philosopher who also has a degree in law, argues a position based on the sanctity of life. He offers arguments to resolve some of the differences between the restrictive and permissive positions regarding abortion. As I will discuss further in Chapter 10, he defends abortion rights primarily on the basis of the First Amendment, arguing that freedom of choice about abortion is a necessary implication of the religious freedoms guaranteed by that Amendment (as well as on the grounds of the Fourth, Fifth, and Fourteenth Amendments).

The central conception that Dworkin invokes concerns the sanctity of life, and he argues that it is applicable in either a theological or a secular sense. He suggests that the word "sacred" could be replaced by "inviolable." In any event he means the term to apply to beliefs about human life which influence our opinions regarding how and why our own lives have intrinsic value, and he is concerned with how these beliefs influence the way we live. Sanctity, in his view, can be based on any number of theological systems of belief, can exist for people who are not religious but who have general convictions about the intrinsic value of human life, and for atheists who have convictions about the meaning of human life that are, for them, foundational to personal morality. All of these systems hold that the value of human life transcends its value for the creature whose life it is, which he argues is a religious belief, even when it is held by people who do not believe in a God.

Procreative decisions are considered to be fundamental because they touch the "ultimate purpose and value of life itself." He appeals, as do many theologians, to the "miracle" of the creation of life which, I must admit, I find to be no miracle at all. The reproduction of life is one of the most basic biological processes common to all living things. All species are programmed in ways that almost assure reproduction will occur under normal circumstances. With humans the acts leading to reproduction are simple, easy to perform, fun, within the physical and mental abilities of almost everyone, and can be done almost anywhere, and in a wide variety of ways. Rather than a miracle it seems that sex is a common, if somewhat risky, biological pleasure.

Dworkin argues for the existence and paramount importance of what I have called deep moral intuitions, and I believe it clarifies matters to consider this class of intuitions in the light of the ideas I have developed to understand all aspects of reproduction; those of evolutionary biology.

The advantage gained by considering matters in this way is that the evolutionary level could well represent the foundational mechanisms, biological and cognitive, that produced all of the variants of belief expressed by the theological, irreligious, and atheistic belief systems. I find such an approach preferable because it suggests an underlying set of universal principles and mechanisms instead of dealing with the different functional outputs that reflect a universal evolutionary basis.

Whenever Dworkin has to consider the relative value of different organisms he engages in cost–benefit analysis of the kind I have used to characterize evolutionary mechanisms. For example, he writes (1993, p. 60), "Abortion . . . is therefore a moral wrong unless the intrinsic value of other human lives would be wasted in a decision *against* abortion." He wonders how we should measure and compare the waste of life, which he considers an insult to the sanctity of life, on different occasions and for organisms of different qualities and ages. In his view the waste of life is greater if a teenage single mother's life is wrecked than is the case when an early-stage fetus ceases to live, and in general, uses a chronological gauge of value, such that the death of an adolescent girl is worse than the death of an infant girl because the adolescent's death frustrates the investments she and others have already made in life. He emphasizes (p. 87) the importance of "the ambitions and expectations she constructed, the plans and projects she made, the love and interest and emotional involvements she formed for and with others, and they for and with her."

In this view something is "instrumentally" important if its later value depends on its usefulness, and on its capacity to help people to get something else they want (which I translate into a general tendency to maximize reproductive success). I argue that it is more parsimonious to employ the unifying set of principles involved in the concepts of reproductive success, reproductive value, and social contract (as I have defined them). These terms can be considered to provide the basis of all of the different events that Dworkin has identified to be of paramount concern.

These concerns and issues which must be considered have been explicitly identified by Dworkin. My disagreement is based on the belief that the concept of sanctity of life does no more than identify that there is a strong and universal set of moral intuitions, and I believe it is possible to ground these intuitions by using an explanatory biological system. I agree that we all take seriously the values that unite us as human beings at every stage of every human life, but do not think that sanctity is the helpful way to consider the agreement. Dworkin agrees that the meaning of life is universal, but believes that this meaning is interpreted differently across different cultures, groups, and peoples. I believe it possible to establish principles at the basic biological level rather than at the level of behavioral manifestations mapped onto these foundational systems, and will argue that Dworkin might be better served if he sought to unpack the properties of personhood rather than appealing to the concept of sanctity of life.

MORAL AGENCY

At this point I will once again discuss the concept of moral agency to strengthen the argument that the status of personhood is a special step in developing the social contract which holds society together. A basic distinction was drawn between moral agents and patients in Chapter 6. Only moral agents are members of the moral community, and all moral agents must be considered to be equal members of that community, with equal rights, responsibilities, and duties. Rawls insisted that the justice due moral agents involves a guarantee of the equal opportunity to attain an adequate life, and he invoked the presumption of a veil of ignorance that one should assume when setting moral standards in order to further insure equality. The clear intention is to include all innocent, normal, adult humans as universally qualified for membership in the agency club. On the other hand, there are moral patients from whom one cannot expect a realization or understanding of the concepts of duties and responsibilities. Such patients are animals, young children, and adult humans unable to function at a sufficient cognitive level. Some of these organisms, such as young children and mentally defective humans qualify for personhood but not agency; they clearly are persons whom we publicly recognize, but they should not be held to the accepted standards of right and wrong that moral agents are obliged to respect. Animals do not qualify for personhood under my biological and social contract conceptions of personhood. They cannot be held to our moral standards of right or wrong, but they are due respect for their welfare.

The test for life is a purely biological one, and includes plants, all nonhuman animals, and humans at all stages of development. However, the defining characteristics for life are not germane to the discussion regarding abortion. The test for personhood that has been proposed applies to all the members of a given species and, for the abortion argument as I have framed it, is met by human organisms at birth. It is at the point of birth that human moral agents are charged with duties and responsibilities regarding the welfare of the neonate, a moral patient. The test for moral agency is a cognitive one based on the ability to understand the obligations that are involved in all rational moral considerations. To act in ways that can be considered to be right or wrong one must be able to recognize abstract principles, to manipulate them, and to understand the basic rules of logic that ground rationality. The neonate is a person but not yet an agent, and as Kamm (1992) reminds us, moral agency is a special right granted to members of the particular society within which special social contracts are enforced.

Kleinig (1991) cast the issue in the light of human values, arguing that we are considering issues that involve standards that are valued by (and for) human beings, and it is only for such humans that judgments of value can have significance. Kleinig suggested that this "choice-relevant, choice-constraining, or choice-determining activity" is a uniquely person-centered enterprise, and is the most human of all activities. He suggests that the valuing component of human experience is an "anthropogenetic" attribute; while other animals can display the rudiments of valuational activity, only humans can consider propositional moral concepts on which such valuations depend.

If we accept the fact that moral agency depends on the ability to understand and manipulate logical structures, and that rights come only with agency, then the fetus can have no basic rights. The fetus cannot have desires because, as Benn (1973) indicated, desiring something entails having the concept of the thing desired; a fetus, being unable to conceive of things (not having been exposed to them), cannot desire.

Tooley's Neurophysiological Criteria for Personhood and Moral Agency

It is difficult to decide exactly when a developing person should be accorded agency and, thereby, be assigned the rights and duties that are attached to that status. Tooley (1983) adopted a set of neurophysiological criteria to signify moral standing and I will argue that these are inadequate to serve that purpose. He is correct in his belief that any serious philosopher attempting to decide the point in development when moral standing begins must have a sound and thorough understanding of the relevant scientific information bearing on the issue. He correctly pointed out that agency cannot be equated with such things as sentience, perception, learning, or awareness because all animals, including most invertebrates, will meet these criteria. All such organisms would qualify, then, to be "persons" and have moral standing he argued, if we accept those characteristics to satisfy the necessary and sufficient conditions for moral standing. He rejected the use of simple functional criteria, such as the ability to be conditioned or to demonstrate habituation as adequate to satisfy the conditions for moral agency because it is more difficult to condition infants than it is to condition many invertebrates. Therefore, using conditioning as a criterion would give moral standing to invertebrates but deny it to human infants. This he considered to be an intuitively unacceptable conclusion, and I agree.

Because of the problems involved in invoking simple behavioral processes to ground moral standing he seized on characteristics of neurophysiological development as the criteria to be used. Tooley chose properties related to the development of the nervous system, and pointed out that such development continues for a considerable time after birth. He referred to such things as the development of the myelin sheath (which insulates nerves; the development of which has been taken to indicate that the nerves have become functional—or, at least, that they can be); the formation of new synapses (the functional connections between neurons); and the differentiation of neurons (especially in the phylogenetically late appearing cortical structures such as the frontal lobes). He argued that it is unlikely that the structure and connectivity of the nervous system found in the brain of a newborn, or even a 3-month-old, provide the adequate physiological basis to support higher mental function. The primitive Moro reflex disappears at about 10 to 12 weeks of age, and he took this as yet another indicator that reorganization of neural functioning is still taking place at that age.

Tooley attached critical significance to the development of Stage II sleep spindles in the electroencephalogram (EEG) that occurs at about 3 months of age, and on the basis of these observations suggested that the age of 3 months is a period of critical development. He accepted the conclusion that EEG and neurophysiological patterns become more clearly organized and integrated at this time, and that this organization signifies the beginning of such behavioral functions as drowsiness, sleep behavior, and sleep cycles. These changes, he argued, qualify the infant for personhood at the age of 3 months. The matter is even more strongly settled, in his mind, because study of the deoxyribonucleic acid (DNA) content of brains of children who died before 6 months of age indicated that there was a rapid increase that reached a stable adult level at about 3 to 4 months of age. Tooley (1983, p. 40) concluded, "This cluster of changes occurring at around three months is certainly striking, and the suggestion that it reflects a significant underlying cerebral development is surely plausible."

Tooley summarized all of his arguments by reminding us that an individual should be considered to be a person if he or she is a subject of nonmomentary interests, which implies the existence of a unified consciousness over time involving the ability to have thoughts. His examination of the evidence led him to conclude that there are excellent reasons for holding that newborn humans do not possess any capacity for thought, but that a limited capacity for thought may exist at 3 months of age, and that this capacity endows the 3-month-old infant with the necessary and sufficient properties to qualify for moral standing. He concluded (p. 411), "If forced to speculate, the age of three months might be as reasonable a guess as any." I find this to be a startling statement because he is using it to establish the foundation for the attainment of moral standing, the most important decision in his entire argument. If the intent is to establish the point at which moral standing begins, then I would hate to see such a critical decision grounded on a "reasonable" guess driven by the force of "speculation." One must worry about the concern of Macklin (1984) who raised the caution that we must beware that the scientific data chosen to ground moral beliefs are those that are convenient to support antecedently held views.

Can Tooley's neurophysiological arguments bear the extreme weight they must support to sustain his argument? The relationships on which he depends are not strong. For example, myelination is a crude index of the maturity of the functional status of neural circuits, and in adults, many types of nerve fibers are only thinly myelinated or are completely un-myelinated, such as certain fibers involved in the pain system (Anand & Hickey, 1992). The relationship between the onset of EEG patterns and the start and complexity of thought is problematic. Anand and Hickey re-ported EEG data suggesting that the distinction between wakefulness and sleep exist at 30 weeks of gestational age, and that well-defined periods of quiet sleep, active sleep, and wakefulness occur in utero at 28 weeks. There are now data indicating that the course of the development of synaptic branching and connectivity, includes a considerable amount of cell death for a considerable period in early postnatal development. All of these data suggest a much more complicated picture than Tooley presents.

A functional orientation regarding the development of the neural structures that would mediate pain was adopted by Anand and Hickey (1992). They were interested in the question of whether neonates can experience pain, in order to decide whether one should take the risks associated with the use of anesthetics when surgery is performed on neonates. They also addressed the question of when in development a fetus might have the neural structures that are involved in signaling pain sensations. Their review of the evidence led them to conclude that the neonate has the structures required to signal pain and that the physiolog-ical changes associated with pain in adults are present for the neonate as well. They concluded that humane considerations indicate that neonates and young infants should be assumed to experience pain and stress, and that analgesic and anesthetic procedures should be employed if they are subjected to any traumatic medical procedures.

The evidence regarding the human fetus led them to conclude that the pain pathways, subcortical structures, and cortical areas necessary for pain perception are developed by about 28 to 30 weeks of gestation. These data suggest that at about 28 weeks the fetus might well be given the status of a moral patient and be accorded the treatment appropriate to organisms that can sense pain. The significance of this suggestion will be considered in the next chapter.

It is known (Shatz, 1992) that humans are born with almost the entire number of neurons they will ever have, but that the mass of the brain at birth is only about 25% that of the adult brain, reaching 45% at 6 to 7 months, 65% at one year, and 93 to 95% by the end of the fourth year, about the time of weaning in many hunter–gatherer societies (Lancaster, 1986). For the rhesus monkey the mass at birth is 68% and for the chimpanzee 45% of the adult brain weight. The increase in the mass of the brain is due to the growth in size of the neurons and the elements of connection (dendrites, on the input side of the neuron, and axons, on the output side), with an increase in both the number and the extent of connections. The growth of the brain and change in density of connections seem to take place regardless of the overall quality of environmental stimulation, suggesting that the system is well-buffered from environmental variation and that normal social experience is sufficient to provide the requisite minimal experience necessary for neural development. Brain development consumes 87% of the basal metabolic rate of human neonates, a value that drops to 64% at two years, and declines to 23% for adults. These figures suggest that a great deal of neurological change is occurring for a considerable period of time following birth.

Rakic, Bourgeois, Eckenoff, Zecevic, & Goldman-Rakic (1986) studied the density of the cortical synapses of monkeys and found a steady increase in density that almost reached adult levels at birth, but continued to develop to a peak at 2 to 4 months of age. Beginning at this age the density levels declined, at first rapidly and then slowly, to the adult level by 2 to 4 years of age. In these monkeys there was an overproduction of synapses, followed by their elimination, and there are good reasons to believe that similar changes occur in the human nervous system, although at different development ages.

The findings regarding the development of the neural substrate for language in humans was reviewed by Greenfield (1991) who concluded, that there is neuroanatomical evidence for profound neural changes occurring up to 12 to 15 months of age, with some cortical circuits continuing to develop until the child is 2 to 4 years of age. These circuits involve connections between the motor cortex and Broca's area, the latter being involved in complex language processing. She also offered functional and developmental evidence that Broca's area, at age 2, begins to receive functional input from the anterior prefrontal cortical area, and she reminded us that the period between 2 to 4 years of age is when morphologically complex grammar emerges in language.

The evidence regarding neural specializations involved in the development of emotional and cognitive behavior was reviewed by Locke (1993). The identification of spoken and written words typically is conducted in the left cerebral hemisphere, while the interpretation of linguistic prosody is carried out in both hemispheres. The human infant has structural mechanisms on both sides of the brain that participate in affective communication, and these structures begin to develop quickly at birth. The left hemisphere assumes control of the cognitive activities associated with language. Locke interpreted this pattern of development to mean that the neural machinery needed for spoken language is active early in development, and that only later does the neural substrate for linguistic processing become available.

Studies indicate that the thickness of the temporal cortex increases throughout the first year of life, with a distinct peak at approximately 6 months, and that intra- and interhemispheric cortical association bundles begin to myelinate at about 5 to 6 months of age. At about these same ages several motoric developments occur: Among them are babbling, one-handed reaching, and rhythmic hand activity. These correlated neural and behavioral developments seem to represent important milestones in the development of speech and language.

My point in reviewing these findings is not that there is neurophysiological evidence which indicates that the developmental age for moral standing should be changed from that adopted by Tooley, but that it is possible to produce a coherent set of findings that would support the acceptance of a variety of ages at which some profound organization or reorganization of the neural substrate for complex cognitive function takes place. I do not believe that neurophysiological data can provide an adequate grounding for moral standing. The proper basis will be provided by indicators of complex mental functions because they are the stuff of thinking and rationality. Therefore, the criteria for moral agency—for deciding whether an organism is capable of reasoning and understanding right and wrong—should be cognitive rather than one based on neurophysiological developments, which have only a loose and inferential relationship to mental function.

A review of the evidence bearing on the phenomenon of infantile amnesia, by Howe and Courage (1993), developed the argument that infantile amnesia occurs because early in life the infant does not have a cognitive sense of self. Infants have been shown to have the ability to learn and to remember, as can most animals of most species, but these experiences are not recognized by the infant as specific events coded as to time and place, and happening to a "me." When discussing the characteristics of the visual system of the human neonate they pointed out that the system continues to develop anatomically and functionally for a considerable period of time after birth. Initially, the central foveal region of the retina is poorly defined and the cortical receptive fields are organized quite primitively. During the first three postnatal months there is a period of rapid development of the retinal cortical fields.

The evidence indicated to Howe and Courage (1993) that the neonate has poor visual acuity, contrast sensitivity, and color vision. Beginning at 3 months of age infants have been shown to perceive forms, their perception of patterns shows sensitivity to the Gestalt principles of proximity, symmetry, good continuation, and common fate. Infants demonstrate object constancy and can use binocular and monocular cues to determine the location of objects in the environment. Human infants, then, are capable of feats of learning, perception, and memory (as are animals of many species), but there is still a great deal of development that must take place in order to achieve a high level of cognitive functioning.

I have been arguing that personhood commences at birth, and based the argument on the dramatic biological and social changes that take place at the time. Utilizing the point of birth to signal personhood moves the focus of the scientific basis from a single focus on the characteristics of the fetus-neonate to a broader one that incorporates the functional context in which behavior occurs. That context includes the fetus, the mother, and the rest of society, and is justified in reference to general ethological principles. Here, I am once again moving from a focus on the individual organism, and the structure and function of the nervous system of the developing organism, to one that emphasizes the cognitive functions involved in the ability to understand right and wrong. The criteria that should be employed to evaluate the level of rationality of organisms must be grounded on the principles of cognitive science.

Characteristics of Cognitive Systems

To identify the precise nature of the criteria that would indicate that an organism is a rational, cognitively competent individual (thereby qualified as a moral agent) is a task that would require a discussion at least as extensive as that given to any single issue that will be considered in this book. At this juncture I will be content to outline some of the general characteristics that an organism must possess to qualify as a moral agent. I believe that such a cursory analysis is sufficient because, as I have construed the issues of contraception, abortion, and infanticide with which we are here concerned, none of these issues involves any consideration of the moral agency that is dependent on the possession of rationality. The criteria must be examined more carefully when considering the moral standing of animals, and will be done in another forum.

One manner of deciding moral agency is to use the legal criteria that prescribe agency as a function of age. By age 21 one is considered to be an adult almost everywhere; at the age of 18 one can consume alcohol in some states; at the age of 16 one can be licensed to drive a car in some states; at a certain age a young woman can have an abortion without parental consent, and so on. On the other hand, it might be more reasonable to insist that agency be based on qualities that are assessed for the particular individual in question. Is this individual able to arrive at rational, logical conclusions at this time? Does this individual possess the required abilities to make decisions and successfully execute them while operating a vehicle? One standard of legal intoxication that is widely used is an assay of blood alcohol level. The test is not arbitrarily based on the number of drinks consumed in a given period of time (which comes down to an investigative nightmare), but on a measured value that (one hopes) is a valid indicator of intoxication, which (one hopes) is a valid indicator of the ability to do such things as operate a vehicle in a satisfactory manner.

There is little reason to believe that the cognitive abilities that signal moral agency will be age-determined. They will be age-related, but the critical question concerns at what age, for example, do we stop saying that an individual is too young to be held responsible and should now be considered to have all of the duties and responsibilities (as well as the rights) of an individual with moral standing? The law is far from consistent in decisions regarding when to prosecute a person as a child or as an adult. There seems to be little consistency in decisions to determine when the desires of a child should override those of an adult in such things as custody disputes, whether the child should receive medical treatment, or who should administer any wealth that has been accumulated or inherited by the minor. Some individuals never attain moral standing due to mental characteristics that make them unable to reason or to understand the nature of causality, no matter what age they might attain. There seem to be insurmountable difficulties involved in attempts to determine the presence of moral agency using only an age criterion.

The proper cognitive criteria for moral agency should rely on cognitive function, not on chronological age, or the structure of the nervous system, or the route by which a decision is reached. The appropriate criteria should not concern what is inside the head but the quality of the decisions reached. The qualifications should concern the question of whether a decision that is arrived at is an adequate one.

John R. Anderson (1990) has approached the problem of cognition from a valuable perspective. He considered cognition to be an aspect of the human species that exists to allow the individual to reach goals that provide a satisfactory adaptation to environmental pressures. This emphasis on adaptations places the problem in a framework that is compatible with the type of evolutionary perspective espoused here. Anderson (1990, Table 6-1, p. 245) identified three common aspects of what he refers to as rational analysis: The first concerns the goal of human cognition; the second concerns the structure of the environment relevant to attaining these goals; and the third concerns the cost involved in applying the cognitive process.

He identified four major aspects of cognition that are involved in rational analysis. The first is memory and the goal is to get access to needed experiences from the past. The relevant structure of the environment is based on observations of how the need for information tends to repeat itself when certain tasks appear. The cost is the effort and time required to retrieve the memory.

The second aspect is categorization and the goal is to predict features of new objects, which depends on some understanding of how the structural features of the environment cluster together, with the cost being the time required to formulate hypotheses. People form categories in at least three ways: Linguistic labels are attached that provide the idea that a category exists; there is feature overlap where it is natural that a number of objects overlap substantially and these features are used to establish a category; it is noticed that a number of objects serve similar functions and a category is formed to include them on the basis of similar function. Categorization is important to human decision making because when an object has been recognized to be a member of a large category a great deal can be predicted about that object from general knowledge regarding the nature of the category itself. Such a process can have great adaptive significance, freeing the individual from having to solve every problem anew. Categorization provides the individual with the ability to utilize heuristics that allow decisions to be reached more quickly, and sometimes speed of response is the key to survival.

The third aspect is causal analysis and the goal is to predict future events, using statistical models of causal structure as they have been encountered in the environment, with the cost being the time involved in the formation of hypotheses. There is no question that the ability to understand causation is an important quality for moral considerations because one must be able to understand the probable and possible effects of actions on the future course of events as they influence oneself, the environment, and other organisms. Anderson suggested that it should be assumed that individuals will obey the same causal relations over situations as well as over time, which assumption is part of the concept of an enduring individual. The concept of an enduring subject of nonmomentary interests, it will be remembered, was one of the major requirements that Tooley settled on to qualify individuals for moral standing.

The fourth aspect of rational analysis is problem solving and the goal is to achieve certain structures and states in the external world, the achievement of which are influenced by how the problems vary in difficulty, and how the similarity of each step in the solution is related to the final goal, with the cost being the amount of external effort and the time required to try alternative plans, as well as the amount of internal effort and time required to generate the alternative plans. Problem solving involves decisions regarding what actions to take, the evaluation of alternatives, and could involve some actual trial and error. An important aspect of problem solving involves the probabilistic nature of reality that must be considered when evaluating the varying costs and benefits of different possible plans.

A more detailed and complete theoretical delineation of the probabilistic nature of reality was developed by Brunswik (1952, 1956), and extended by Petrinovich (1979, 1989) and Gigerenzer and Murray (1987). The Brunswikian analyses consider the structure of the ecology, the organisms construal of that ecological structure, and the resulting actions the organisms performs to achieve a satisfactory functional adaptation to the perceived demands of the ecology. The probabilistic texture of this causal network has been described in considerable analytic detail and bears careful examination. Figueredo (1992) extended the Brunswikian model in a way that is adequate to gain a general understanding of the processes and mechanisms involved when development is considered within three different time frames: that involved in individual development; that required for ecological changes to occur; and that extensive time typically required for evolutionary change to occur.

Anderson's view of cognition seems an appropriate way in which to consider problems involved when making moral decisions in a complex world. The four aspects of cognition he outlined are clearly crucial ones. He suggested that the only aspect that might bear further consideration, and added to his system, is that of the development and use of language. The kinds of sociolegal concerns that constitute the moral rules and regulations of society are phrased linguistically, and some kind of language ability is required to comprehend and understand problems in order to manipulate concepts and decide on actions. On the other hand, there might be good reasons for not considering any special linguistic abilities in order to avoid some of the restrictive aspects of anthropocentrism. It is conceivable that a robot, a chimpanzee, dolphin, or a space being could show evidence of all of the aspects of cognition, if the communication channels were available to achieve a satisfactory level of communication. If so, these beings could share the same rights, problems, and obligations that burden the rest of us moral agents.

The aforementioned views of Howe and Courage (1993) add some important considerations to the general cognitive concepts proposed by Anderson. They marshaled the argument that a sense of self is basic to the development of autobiographical memory, and that by 18 to 24 months of age the infant has a concept of self that is sufficiently viable to serve as a referent around which personally experienced events can be organized in memory. They argued that the development of this cognitive sense of self emerges logically prior to critical aspects of language development, such as the correct utilization of pronouns (e.g., I and you), and the ability to talk, at first about immediate events and later to recollect distant past events. These cognitive abilities are all characteristics that have been identified as essential to attaining the status of full personhood and that are necessary in order to meet the cognitive criteria for moral agency.

Implications

Tooley's philosophical positions are rational and well-reasoned and I regard them to be the most persuasive that I have encountered. I have questioned his decision to equate personhood with moral standing and believe that this decision involved him in a hopeless tangle in the rights thicket. Parenthetically, moral standing should be considered to be a continuum beginning with the late gestational fetus (who may be sentient), through the neonate (who has personhood), to the cognitive moral agent (who has duties, obligations, and rights). Tooley's reliance on neurophysiological evidence to establish moral standing was unfortunate because the evidence he used will not provide the critical support required for the most crucial aspect of his argument. Neurophysiological evidence is destined to fall short, in my view, because it focuses entirely on the characteristics of the fetus or infant, ignoring the mother and the social context in which morality should be established as a meaningful concept.

The argument I have developed establishes birth as the point at which the neonate acquires personhood, and it is that point at which the mother and society are invested with duties and responsibilities for the welfare of the neonate. It is also at that point that the mother's exclusive custody of the fetus ceases. The argument I have made avoids sanctioning infanticide, whereas that of Tooley must permit it, at least up to 3 months of age, if one follows his argument strictly. I argue that infanticide is not permissible, unless there are extreme special conditions (see Chapter 10) because it violates the biological and social contracts by which moral agents are bound. Benn (1973) worried that the rights language used by Tooley violates our moral intuition that it is immoral to kill babies, and Benn was led to a conclusion similar to the one I am arguing.

Tooley attempted to soften the impact of his conclusion regarding the permissibility of infanticide by invoking three considerations: first, even though animals are nonpersons, people still believe that it is morally wrong to treat them cruelly; second, most people are deeply attached to their children simply because they are their children; third, the anthropological evidence based on societies that practice infanticide does not indicate that the people showed less concern for the well-being of those children who were allowed to live. These things, he suggested, will lessen the likelihood that infanticide will take place at all and, if it does, it will not spill over to produce a cruel society. I believe that separating the status of personhood and the status of moral agency acknowledges the first point, is built on the second point, and does not raise the specter of infanticide at all.

The criteria for moral agency are not germane to the issues of contraception, abortion, or infanticide as I have construed them. I have used Anderson's organizational schema to outline the operative cognitive criteria because they do bear on the issue of when people not only attain rights, by my argument, but when they can be held culpable for failing to perform duties or assume responsibilities for the welfare of moral patients. These cognitive criteria for moral agency will be discussed elsewhere when questions of whether animals can have rights are considered.

SUMMARY

Some of the biological and philosophical concepts developed in the first seven chapters were brought to bear, in these last two chapters, to deal with three related issues pertaining to the beginning of life: Contraception, abortion, and infanticide. In Chapter 10, the possibility of giving special status to a fetus because it is a potential person will be considered and this possibility will be rejected on philosophical and logical grounds.

The test of moral standing that is based on the ability of the fetus to survive if disconnected from the mother and attached to other life support systems (viability) was examined, and was rejected as an adequate criterion for personhood. This rejection was based on two considerations: rejection of using the state of medical technology to define the point at which personhood begins; and an acceptance of the argument that, prior to birth, the mother has complete (and private) custody of the fetus.

One crucial point that must be established is when personhood begins, and it was argued, on biological and psychological grounds, that the birth episode provides that point. When the fetus attains the status of a person its welfare and interests must be guaranteed because it now is protected by the social contracts that define society, and that must be assumed by all moral agents, including the mother and the rest of society. Infanticide is not permissible because the infant, at birth, acquires personhood, a state which those with moral standing must honor and, in a just society, moral agents must guarantee the infant's welfare in order for the child to attain at least a minimally satisfactory quality of life.

10

Contraception, Abortion, and Infanticide
Polar Positions

This discussion is organized around two polar positions regarding the permissibility of abortion: restrictive and permissive. As I proceed I will develop the position I consider to be the most defensible one in view of the biological, philosophical, and psychological principles discussed previously. By adopting this format I can speak to several important issues that should be developed further: problems regarding the potentiality of the developing organism; the nature of the relationship of ontogenetic and phylogenetic developmental processes; and the relevance of rationality and consciousness to the abortion question. After these arguments have been pursued I will consider some policy issues in the next chapter. These issues concern matters of public policy, political considerations, implications regarding sexual equality, and society's obligations to provide a minimally acceptable life for its incoming members.

POSITIONS CONCERNING ABORTION

Restrictive Abortion Arguments

The most restrictive view is based on the assumption that all fetuses have an absolute right to life from conception onward, and in the most extreme form, no exception is permitted in respect to special circumstances. For Catholic theologians the moral status of the fetus begins at the point during gestation when it gains a soul—a quality which is hardly verifiable by any empirical test. The time at which ensoulment occurs has been the subject of considerable argumentation and disagreement by different theologians throughout the years. Catholic dogma now insists that ensoulment occurs at the point of conception (the theory of immediate animation), and forbids all abortion under all circumstances, with one possible exception under the doctrine of double effect—abortion could be permissible if the operation is an innocent act whose effect is to save the life of the mother (e.g., the removal of a malignant uterine tumor), the pregnancy is terminated as a result of the procedure, but there was no direct intention to abort the fetus.

The National Right to Life Committee also adopts the position that life begins at fertilization and argues this position based on their interpretation of the facts regarding fetal development and biological science. For example, John Willke, who is president of the Committee argued, (1990), for the restriction of abortion beginning at conception. He avowed that his position was based on a biological view, not a theological one, and argued that a theological argument did not provide a permissible yardstick when developing policy in a secular state, a point I endorse heartily (although I will reject his biological view).

Some philosophers and medical authorities advocate a less restrictive position and argue that abortion should be permissible until the fetus begins to show a human shape or outline, and possesses the basic human organs (this would occur at about 6 to 8 weeks). In many European counties, the law permitted abortion until quickening (at 12 to 16 weeks). More moderate positions held that abortion is permissible until the point of viability is reached, at about 22 weeks (as argued by King, 1980) or between 24 and 28 weeks, as the U.S. Supreme Court held in *Roe v. Wade*.

Pioneer abortion rights advocate, Lader (1966) sketched the concepts that various religions have adopted regarding the time at which abortion is no longer permissible: Muslims date personhood from 14 days after conception; early Christian dogma followed Aristotle and adopted the principle that the ensoulment of males occurred at 40 days and of females at 80 days (as Lader pointed out, no one ever explained how fetal sex was to be determined at that time to make it possible to implement this policy); the Shinto faith holds that the child becomes a human being only when it has "seen the light of day" (the position I argue here); the Islamic belief is that life begins for the fetus after 150 days; Buddhist and Hindu theology treat abortion as a social rather than religious issue; Judaism, in general, places the life and health of the mother above that of the fetus and raises no religious obstacles to the destruction of the fetus for medical necessity; traditional Protestants, in general, approve of abortion to save the mother's life or preserve her health, and in cases of rape and incest, on the basis of the argument that the latter cases constitute an affront to human life and dignity; and Fundamentalist Christians (as well as the 1992 Republican party platform) adopt a position similar to that of Catholic theologians, disapproving of abortion for any reason from the point of conception, with the possible exception of rape or incest.

There seems to be no clear theological guideline that is accepted generally, although most Western religions do advocate the acceptance of some more or less severe restrictions. It is difficult to insist on theologically based conceptions because such conceptions are based on a set of un-falsifiable supernatural beliefs, and such varying religious commitments will not stand the empirical tests required to establish the sufficient conditions for moral values, or secular law. One might have a deep religious conviction and strongly believe in a set of theological principles. If so, one would be well advised to act (as far as legally possible) in accordance with those beliefs. Those who do not believe in abortion should not have one, but should allow others the freedom to behave in accordance with their own belief systems. Moral principles based on theology should not be the basis of secular law that will apply to those of us who do not accept that particular set of religious beliefs. I agree with Willke that it is inadmissible to apply a theological test to develop secular law, especially in a country such as the United States, where Constitutional law is firmly and explicitly based on the separation of the powers of Church and State.

Potential Persons

An argument that should be examined is one that bases moral standing on the potential an organism has to develop into a person at some stage of development. The argument is that abortion should not be permitted because there is a potential for the zygote, embryo, and fetus to develop into a person; persons have moral standing and this status provides them with protection against being killed. One argument is that, because the fertilized egg has the full genetic complement that will characterize the adult organism, it should be protected.

Sumner (1981) reasoned that if this logic is accepted, then it should be extended to apply to the ovum and to the sperm as well, because they each possess the potential to be joined with the other, and thus to be considered as potential persons. Sumner pointed out that, if this argument is pursued to its logical conclusion, then it is clear that contraception should not be morally acceptable, and this conclusion leads to the logical extension that copulation should be approved only with the intention to procreate, as Catholic dogma does expound (Ratzinger and Bovone, 1987). Both contraception and abortion would be equally wrong by the logic involved in using potentiality as a basis. If the argument against abortion is to be based on potentiality, then conception is an event of the same significance as viability or birth; it is just another step in the actualization of the potential for creating a person that is contained in the female ovum and the male sperm. It can be argued that, if intentionally refraining from procreation is not seriously wrong, then neither is the destruction of potential persons. If the potentiality argument is accepted it is not possible to maintain a rationally based moral distinction between abortion and contraception (or even copulation without the intent to reproduce). Hardly anyone but the most restrictive Catholic theologians find these to be intuitively acceptable positions, however.

Considerations regarding the potential organism were rejected by Harris (1992) on the basis that it is just as reasonable to argue that, at conception, we are all potentially dead; but no one would accept this potentiality as a sufficient reason to treat us as if we are already dead. The woman who has an abortion wrongs no one because in ending the life of the fetus she deprives the fetus of nothing that it can value; as I noted in Chapter 9, the fetus cannot value or desire things. The outside world of experience, to which all desire is directed, does not yet exist for the fetus. By not having the abortion, the mother does not benefit a person because there is no one she brings into existence. This seems to imply that costs and benefits do not exist when considering potentiality, making it impossible to apply the type of arguments I have been developing to evaluate the adequacy of moral decisions; the operative terms are not in existence.

It has often been suggested that the consequences of having an abortion should take into consideration the possibility that the aborted fetus was Ludwig van Beethoven. The argument continues that not to have had Beethoven would have deprived the world of the positive joy and beauty that Beethoven's music has produced for untold numbers of listeners. This loss of positive value is used to oppose abortion of all fetuses under any normal circumstances. The problem with this argument is that, as Harris noted, when a fetus is aborted it is not a Beethoven, and the rights and wrongs of that abortion have to be settled by a consideration of the moral status of the fetus at the time. Harris (1992, p. 180) wrote, "The fetus we abort will never become anything, and it is nothing but a fetus at the time it is aborted. It is as senseless to bemoan its loss as the loss of a Beethoven as it is to celebrate its loss as the pre-empting of a Hitler." This argument is important and will be discussed in another forum where I will consider the question of the genetic screening of embryos.

It has also been argued that one should not abort a defective fetus because, although the individual that develops will endure terrible suffering, something good might come from the existence of the person that develops. I agree with Harris (1992, p. 182) who hoped that "no sane, let alone moral, being would think it worth preserving disability and disease on the off chance that some good might come of it at some unspecified and unpredictable point in the future."

Feinberg (1980, p. 183) raised what he called "the paradoxes of potentiality," and proposed an interesting scenario worth quoting at length:

> Dehydrated orange powder is potentially orange juice, since if we add water to it, it will be orange juice. More remotely, however, it is also potentially lemonade, since it will become lemonade if we add a large quantity of lemon juice, sugar, and water. It is also a potentially poisonous brew (add water and arsenic), a potential orange cake (add flour, etc., and bake), a potential orange-colored building block (add cement and harden), and so on ad infinitum.

Kleinig (1991) agreed that there is a paradox if anything at all can be potentially anything else at all, and that the existence of this paradox makes it absurd to use an appeal to potentiality as a basis for moral assertions.

A scenario was developed by English (1975) who used the parallel between abortion and the self-defense model. Her argument asks you to assume that you know there is some finite possibility of being attacked and raped at night, but you go out in spite of this small, but real, possibility. One view is that you could stay home at night, and that by going out you have no right to defend yourself by killing the attacker because you willfully placed yourself in jeopardy. As English pointed out, this argument parallels the view that abstinence is the only acceptable way to avoid pregnancy. By taking the risk of engaging in intercourse you must accept the consequences, and even if you do use a contraceptive procedure and it fails, you must accept the consequences of pregnancy and not have an abortion. You were taking a calculated risk, are obliged to suffer the consequences, and required to protect the potential person that has resulted. By the way, the inherent sexism in this argument resides in the fact that only women, and not men, can be pregnant and suffer the consequences of this logic. I will examine the implicit sexual inequality involved in several of the arguments regarding abortion in the next chapter.

The potentiality argument against abortion not only makes it difficult to justify contraception but also leads to another conceptual difficulty. As Warren (1973) reminded us (and, as I have been arguing throughout), everything that is genetically human is not necessarily morally human (in the sense of agency), and every entity with human genetic potential does not have the potential to become human in the moral sense. An extreme example would be the anencephalic human fetus that will become a genetically human infant (at least for the short time it will live) but will never attain moral agency.

A normal fetus does not have the attained status of personhood at any stage of its development; it can only be accorded the potentiality of personhood. I argue that, whatever our duties to potential people may be, they always can be, and should be, overridden in any conflict with the obligations to actual people who are moral agents. As Singer (1992) argued, there is no rule that a potential being has the same value as an actual being, and he offers two illustrations to support this argument: Pulling out a sprouting oak is not the same as cutting down a venerable oak; dropping a live chicken into boiling water is worse than doing the same thing to an egg.

Tooley argued that the obligations that moral agents have are to individual persons, and if these persons do not exist there can be no obligation. While failures to benefit a potential person are harms done to that potential person, Harris (1992) suggested that this does not mean that there is any harm done to the person it might have become—the person does not exist at the time the harm is done. In fact, no person will ever exist. Using this argument it would seem that causing the death of a potential person is morally on a par with failing to bring a person into existence.

Although I find it to be conceptually and logically clearer if the language involved in discussions of rights is avoided, I agree with Warren's argument (1973, p. 115) regarding the permissibility of abortion: "But even if a potential person does have some prima facie right to life, such a right could not possibly outweigh the right of a woman to obtain an abortion, since the rights of any actual person invariably outweigh those of any potential person, whenever the two conflict." Elsewhere, Warren (1977) concluded that any responsibility one might have toward a potential person is at least "billions of times" weaker than that toward an actual person.

If potentiality is going to be given any consideration, then there must be a high probability that the potential will be realized. Otherwise, blocking that potential is of little concern. As mentioned above, the potential of a zygote to become a person is so slight it can be argued to be of little moral import. Devine (1978) has suggested that the point at which twinning is no longer possible (about 14 days) should be taken as the point at which potentiality begins. He suggested this point because it is not possible to consider that there are two persons that could exist prior to this time because the two do not yet exist, nor do we know that the second one even will exist. Donceel, (1970/1984) adopted a similar position, considering the metaphysical impossibility of conferring moral status on two beings, which may or may not eventuate, and used this impossibility to argue against immediate animation.

Singer (1992) also rejected the claim that an early embryo is a human being on the grounds that human beings are individuals, and the early embryo is not even an individual, given the possibility that it may split into more than one. Singer emphasized the importance of the continuity of existence by an amusing scenario: Suppose there is an embryo in a dish on a laboratory bench, and we call it Mary. However, the embryo splits into two identical embryos. Is one still Mary, and the other Jane, or is Mary no longer with us and we now have Jane and Helen? If the latter conclusion is accepted what happened to Mary? Did she die and should we grieve for her? The moral of this story is that the embryo should not be considered to be a human being, nor is a fetus a human being in any morally significant sense.

Even with the late term fetus the concept of potential seems to lack power, and I believe (as does Singer) that specific considerations favoring the existing person, the mother, should override those of the potential person, the fetus. I want to emphasize that this conclusion does not depend on any utilitarian calculation of relative value, but on the qualitative distinction between an actual person (who is a moral agent as well) and a potential person (who, I argue, is not yet a moral patient).

Additional logical considerations concern why protection should always be considered at the level of the individual mother or the individual fetus. Rather than considering only individuals with some requisite potential, why not argue in favor of protection of *pairs* of individuals with a requisite potential; that is, the mother and fetus as a unit? Harris (1992, p. 64) raised this issue regarding twins. He asks, "Why this mystical infatuation with the individual? Why not accept the truth, that some individuals share part of their history with other individuals . . . ?" When considering the factors relevant to the status of personhood I argued that one should not confine oneself to an exclusive focus on the fetus, but should expand beyond the fetus to include the mother, and even further, the other members of society. From this perspective, persons are social before they are individuals. All of these problems involved in defining the unit of concern should be considered when making moral decisions regarding reproduction.

Although the fetus does not have the status of personhood it might be argued that the interests of the members of society other than the mother should carry some moral weight. The question is, should the wishes of other family members to not abort prevail over those of the mother? I doubt that the wishes of the community should be allowed to prevail over those of the pregnant woman, who is the person at risk. The major concern I have is how does one draw a line to determine when and under what circumstances the community should be allowed to force the woman to continue a pregnancy, and who are the relevant members of the community who should be allowed to determine the issue. I can think of scenarios that involve the wishes of a benevolent family despot who wants heirs and insists that any pregnancy be brought to fruition; a husband who wants a large number of children, even though it might ruin the wife's health; a society that wants soldiers and breeders. In most benevolent and rational families there are social bonds that lead to common agreements that all want to honor. Thus, in most situations there will be no conflict, and a pregnancy will be brought to a happy conclusion. However, in those instances where the woman is adamant that the fetus should be aborted her wish should trump that of all others in the community.

The case that people have a prima facie obligation to produce additional people because being glad to be born makes one glad that one was not aborted was argued by Hare (1975). One should be glad one's parents copulated in the first place and did not use effective contraception. He concluded that, according to the Golden Rule, one has a duty neither to abort nor to abstain from procreation. Tooley (1983) considered this argument and agreed that one should be glad to be alive, but not that this gladness results in a duty to procreate (or not to abort), because the actions of the parents, while they led to the child's existence, were not done to the child but to parts of the physical world. As Tooley (p. 246) phrased it, "A pleasant rearrangement of biological entities resulted in an organism that subsequently gave rise to the person. . . ."

The Natural Fate Argument

The importance of having sex because it is an expression of love that is crucial to sociability, with a positive accrual to both the man and woman, was emphasized by Kamm (1992). I add that the act of sex, leading to and resulting in an infant, is an important event in the development of a meaningful social contract between the parents and between them and the infant. Abstaining from sex, then, could involve a great social (and, of course, biological) loss; sex represents both the biological input and the social glue on which human freedom depends.

Tribe (1990/1992) characterized the arguments of "pro-life" supporters to advocate a principle of natural fate. This theme embodies the view that one should respect and preserve "natural" sex roles and that the rules for sexual morality should reflect and respect that nature. The natural fate of a fetus inside a woman is to come to term, and abortion is wrong because it does not allow the natural course of things to prevail. Tribe noted that pro-life supporters do not approve of government intervention in the private relationships of individuals, nor do they approve of government involvement in child rearing, even though some of these practices might verge on the abusive. He suggests that special restrictive treatment of the pregnant woman is, in reality, an attempt to exert power over women who happen to be pregnant, and this power is not exercised over parents in general.

Another aspect of Tribe's argument concerns the pro-life supporters' endorsement of parental and spousal consent. This consent requires that parents or spouses be notified in order for abortion to be permissible, and the enforcement of waiting periods between abortion consultation and the procedure. Attempts to gain the information necessary to apply such laws, Tribe argued, involve encroachments of privacy that would be considered violations of the Constitutional right to privacy. For this reason, he objects to such notification and enforced waiting period requirements.

A Moderate Position

Davis (1993) presented arguments that might move the restrictive and permissive camps toward a common ground that will not be totally acceptable to either camp, but which might satisfy most of them to some extent. She characterizes the critical issues for what she calls principled and pragmatic pro-choice supporters as being those that address the question of what sort of restrictions of a woman's liberty would be least unconscionable, while recognizing the importance of the woman's ability to decide whether to continue a pregnancy for herself without paternalistic interference, state-mandated scrutiny, or obnoxious intrusion on her privacy. She rejects viability as a satisfactory criterion because it depends on the state of existing medical technology and relies on expensive and invasive techniques.

Davis suggests that the pro-life supporters should accept the position that abortion should be unrestricted before 16 weeks of gestational age on the grounds that this point is justified by acknowledged facts of fetal development, facts about human psychology (both sets of which are unspecified), the degree of parental investment on the part of the mother, and the public awareness of the woman's state of pregnancy. She maintains that this solution "splits the difference" between denying some fetuses life and some women liberty, and that such a solution will be the most satisfactory possible. Each side gets some of the things it most values, although it gives neither side all of what it wants. In her view this is the most satisfactory solution until we remove current inequalities in society, make contraception readily available to all (especially indigent girls) and develop a working understanding of how to deal with fetal deformities. She concludes (and I agree) that it is unlikely that such a moderate view will be accepted given the fact that there is no clear agreement regarding what goals justify these attempts at moderation.

Summary

The restrictive position regarding abortion cannot be sustained on a rational basis. The theological basis on which the position depends does not provide the adequate ground required of a universal basic principle on which secular law should be based. If a nontheological argument is made, based on the fact that the zygote contains the full genetic complement of the potential person, one is driven to a logical position that forbids contraception, and such a position is intuitively unacceptable in moral terms. If one states the argument in terms of potentiality, then further quandaries arise that will not sustain the status of a potential person over that of an actual one.

Permissive Abortion Arguments

Sumner (1981) summarized important aspects of the permissive position quite clearly. The permissive position is based on both a positive and a negative "rhetoric of rights." The positive ones are the right of women to control their own bodies and reproductive life, and the negative ones are a denial of the fetal right to life. Whenever the concept of rights is adopted there are interpersonal duties imposed. These rights are not necessarily basic rights, but some must be natural rights that belong to an individual because of intrinsic qualities of that individual, and such qualities must be independent of mere agreements or conventions. Although all rights entail duties, there may be duties that are not based on correlated rights. In other words, I might have a moral duty toward a neonate because of the fact that I am a moral agent, but this duty is not because the neonate possesses a right.

It is possible to advocate a libertarianism that argues for a graded rights theory and allows different kinds of rights. One such theory holds that a normal human adult has liberty rights, a child has welfare rights, and a fetus has no rights. The problem with this approach is that it is difficult to justify the assignment of the differing qualities of rights in other than an arbitrary manner, and the approach becomes difficult to defend, or to implement, in terms of policy recommendations.

Sumner argued that too often rights theories appear to be devised for a world populated entirely by competent adults, in which there are no mad or retarded individuals, or any young people. This construal makes it difficult to apply rights theory to the abortion problem, because the fetus cannot be considered to be a competent being in any sense. I believe that rights theory cannot be applied to the abortion problem but can be applied to the problem of determining moral agency. Sumner wants to avoid using the concept of personhood as a moral standard because it invites confusion between the conditions for being a *natural* person with those for being a *moral* person. I believe that the gain in conceptual clarity is the precise strength of considering personhood separate from that of moral agency.

In Sumner's view the problem for the permissive position is to define an abrupt natural threshold that can be used to justify the denial of moral standing to the fetus, but not to the neonate. Just as the problem for the restrictive position is to avoid having to disapprove of contraception when taking an antiabortion stance, the problem for the permissive position is to avoid sanctioning infanticide when advocating a total approval of fetal abortion, and Tooley does run afoul of this problem. The permissive position is "utterly and unalterably" dependent on denying moral status to the fetus, in Sumner's view. He concluded that it would be foolhardy to believe that those arguing the permissive position cannot provide a credible defense, but that the task is a daunting one. I agree, and believe that when we separate the duties a moral agent has toward a person from the rights inherent in moral agency, we will have moved toward the accomplishment of that daunting task.

One of the most permissive abortion arguments was presented by Tooley (1983). The philosophical position underlying his position is clearly and forcefully argued, and will bear careful study by all interested in the philosophical issues involved in the abortion debate. However, there are two major problems that I believe undermine the acceptability of his conclusions. One is his failure to distinguish between personhood and moral agency (see Chapters 6 and 8) when setting the conditions for moral standing. The second (see Chapter 9) is his interpretation of, and complete reliance on, the neurophysiological evidence to establish moral standing. A minor disagreement concerns his incorrect view of phylogenesis (see Chapter 3)—a problem for many moral philosophers who discuss the abortion and animal rights issues. I will outline Tooley's arguments, and present my disagreements below.

Tooley (1983) based his concept of rights on the definition of a person, and attached the right to continue to exist to the status of personhood. He argued that to have the right to exist, an individual must be able to conceptually understand that it is a subject of experiences, as well as to have the concept of temporal order, which includes the identity of things over time. By this argument an individual has a right to continued existence when there is the capacity of being aware of the self as a subject of experiences. The question becomes one of determining when in development a human organism becomes such a person, and this requires the specification of the relevant natural properties that mark a person.

The basic argument can be summarized to involve seven critical steps (see Tooley [1983, Chap. 9, pp. 303–305] for a more extended statement of these steps).

1. The permissiveness of abortion depends on the moral status of the fetus.
2. Biological species membership is not in itself of moral significance.
3. A person exists when the organism is an enduring subject of non-momentary interests.
4. Destruction of potential persons is not intrinsically wrong.
5. Refraining from producing additional persons is not intrinsically wrong.
6. The property that makes an organism a person is the property that determines wrongness, and it does so independently of the organism's value.
7. There may be degrees of wrongness as a function of the amount of the critical property the organism possesses. The wrongness of destruction of an individual relates to the level of consciousness that the individual is capable of enjoying.

Except for the suggestion of the concept of relative value in point 7, Tooley's arguments are strong and convincing. To reach a satisfactory conclusion, he must specify the property that imbues the organism with personhood (which he considers to confer moral standing) and, as I argued in Chapter 9, he fails to achieve that specification, which he based on neurophysiological criteria. I also believe that his failure to make the distinction between the concept of a person, and that of a moral agent, has clouded the issue so that the position, as he has developed it, is not salvageable.

My argument is that the fetus does not have the status of personhood because it is a private entity known directly only to the mother, and it is dependent, under normal circumstances, on the life support the mother provides. At the point of birth the mother surrenders this privacy and the fetus becomes a public neonate. At this point the fetus (now neonate) becomes a citizen in our society—a person. The neonate begins direct interactions that lead to the development of social behaviors of a cognitive concept of the self, and moral agents have an obligation to honor the now existing social contracts that protect the interests and welfare of this new citizen.

I will develop my argument regarding the crucial nature of person-hood in yet another way. First of all, the Supreme Court's construal of the equal protection clause of the Fourteenth Amendment considers the entity of a person to be a crucial one, stating that it is persons that have a constitutional right to be treated as equal, and that the constitutionality of abortion, according to the due process clause of that Amendment, depends on a woman's right to privacy.[1] Justice Harry Blackmun, in the majority opinion of *Roe v. Wade*, pointed out that American law had never treated fetuses as constitutional persons. The question arises whether or not each state is free to decide that a fetus has the legal status of a person within its borders. Dworkin concluded that they do not because states do not have the power to override provisions of the U.S. Constitution. If a fetus is not part of the constitutional population then states cannot make it one, adhering to the supremacy clause of the Constitution, which declares it to be the highest law of the land. Thus, as Dworkin noted, those who argue that the Supreme Court should leave the question of abortion to the states have in effect conceded that a fetus is not a constitutional person. I believe that it is preferable, in the light of the above, to attempt to disambiguate the concept of personhood in a way that makes constitutional law comprehensible in terms of a consistent set of moral principles.

A fundamental and inconsistent challenge to the current views of the status of the fetus was made by the California Supreme Court which held that a person can be convicted of murder for causing the death of a fetus, even though the fetus has not reached the stage of viability. In the case in question a 21-year-old woman was shot during a robbery attempt. She survived but her male fetus, 22 to 25 weeks old, died as result of the shooting. Generally, the courts have ruled that the fetus must be viable before it can be given the legal status of personhood. In her report of this case Lewin (1994) noted that preceding rulings have been used to deny claims that a fetus should be entitled to a tax deduction, that a pregnant prisoner should be freed because her fetus could not be jailed without a trial, that a pregnant driver was entitled to use the car-pool lane because she was carrying a passenger, and that pregnant women who took drugs should be prosecuted under laws that prohibit giving drugs to a minor. In this ruling the Court ruled that "as long as the state can show that the fetus has progressed beyond the embryonic state of seven or eight weeks" it can be protected from homicide. Thus, for criminal purposes fetal death can be considered murder, but fetal death due to abortion is not prosecutable. This, then, establishes one set of principles in criminal cases and another in abortion cases, hardly a consistent or rational approach. The decision seems to be motivated by current anticrime sentiment than by an antiabor-

---

[1]This discussion of Constitutional issues is indebted to Dworkin's (1993) presentation in three chapters in his book.

tion one. In fact, the court clearly excepted abortions from their ruling. This ruling has profound implications for the abortion issue, because it seems inconsistent with all other rulings in this area and contradicts the current judicial interpretations. I expect that any convictions under the ruling will be appealed to the U.S. Supreme Court.

Another case, that will be discussed in Chapter 12, involves the use of a frozen embryo. In this case the mother's ovum was fertilized by the father's sperm and frozen because it was not needed for immediate use. The couple divorced and the woman wanted to donate the embryo to be implanted in a woman who could not conceive, but the woman's ex-husband (the source of the sperm) did not want the embryo to be used in that manner. The court ruled that the ex-husband's wishes should prevail and that the frozen embryo should be destroyed. In this instance, the point of fertilization did not signal personhood, because the embryo could be killed if the father so chooses.

Assume a fantasy situation in which a woman is implanted with an embryo through the process of in vitro fertilization. It is possible to argue that the characteristic that establishes the value of the fetus is that it is human, and its humanity should protect its right to life. Assume, further, that this particular embryo was mistakenly drawn from a pool of embryos and that, mistakenly, the embryo is not that of a human, but that of a dog, and that it is possible for the woman to carry it to term. Upon birth a human fetus would be accorded the respect and dignity due a person. However, the neonate puppy would not be accorded personhood, but would be accorded the status of doghood. The critical event that determines the status of personhood is the public appearance of a human at birth. This person is predisposed to be socialized as a member of the human social community and is accorded the fledgling status of a person.

Consider an intermediate situation. What if the technique, called embryofetoscopy (a procedure that enables one to view the embryo in the uterus as early as the age of 6 weeks) is used. This examination reveals that the embryo is indeed that of a human. Does this preclude the possibility of an early abortion if the mother so chooses? I believe that it does not because the embryo (or fetus) is still only a potential person, and if the potential person's interests conflict with those of an actual person (who is a moral agent as well), then the moral agent's interest must prevail. Only at the point of birth does the mother surrender her private moral custody of the fetus, and the law should respect that state of affairs.

Yet another interesting problem is discussed by Singer (1992). He constructs a fantasy incident in which a woman plans to go on a mountain climbing expedition in June, but in January she discovers she is two months pregnant. She plans to have a family in the future, but also enjoys mountain climbing. Singer argues that it is not wrong to have an abortion in this case because it only delays the entry of a person (although not this particular potential person) into the world. He extends the incident to suppose that the woman decides to abort the embryo, but takes a cell from the aborted embryo and is able to reimplant that cell so that an exact genetic replica of the aborted fetus would develop—the only difference being that the neonate would appear six months later than would otherwise have been the case. He doubts that this arrangement would satisfy opponents of abortion. The point is that it is the procedure of abortion, coupled with an idea about the sanctity of life, that foes of abortion find objectionable, and not the outcome. It should be mentioned that the sanctity of life idea does not extend beyond humans, or foes of abortion would have to adopt vegetarianism and forego eating anything that destroys life from the moment of its conception.

According to the view I am arguing, abortion is morally permissible, and should be legal, at any time before birth, and this should be permitted at the mother's considered discretion. Although abortion involves the active killing of an organism, it should not be considered to be murder under the laws that regulate our society. As Fleischman argued in an Op-Ed article in *The Los Angeles Times* (1990), abortion is not murder any more than using the death penalty is murder, nor any more than sending soldiers to die in war is murder. Society sets conditions under which killing is permitted and there are many such conditions when we do permit killing.

We do not spend millions of dollars to cure rare diseases, although by not doing so we are passively killing suffering human beings. Such difficult choices are justified on the grounds that the resources spent will benefit very few, and could be better used to cure the many who suffer from, and could die as a result of having more common diseases. Yet, such decisions as the above are not considered to be acts of murder under our system of laws. If a fetus is conceived because of rape or incest, then abortion is approved and the fetus can be killed, but that is not considered to be murder under the law. It is permissible to kill in self-defense, but the perpetrator of the killing is not charged with murder. It is clear that there are many circumstances in which killing and letting die are permissible, and I argue that abortion is another such circumstance.

A variant on the abortion scenario was reported by Terry (1993) in which a pregnant woman did not want a surgical delivery, but insisted on a natural childbirth. The woman, a Pentecostal Christian, was advised by her physician to deliver her 37-week-old fetus by a Caesarian section because the fetus was not receiving enough nutrients or oxygen from her placenta, which would cause the death of the fetus and possibly result in severe brain damage. The parental couple refused, citing personal and religious beliefs that led them to insist on a natural birth in the belief that God and a miracle would protect the unborn baby.

The State of Illinois appointed a public guardian as lawyer for the fetus and he argued that it was necessary to do everything possible to maximize the chances of the fetus to attain a satisfactory life. Hospital officials acknowledged that it had an obligation to the mother but also argued that they had an obligation to the fetus. It was noted that a Caesarian birth is two to five times more likely to result in the mother's death than natural birth. One bioethicist was quoted as saying that the advocacy of a forced operation illustrated how pregnant women are treated in the courts, and that one would never be required to donate a kidney to your own child. Yet, the State of Illinois wanted to compel this woman to risk her life and violate her religious beliefs. The public guardian went so far as to argue that when she went into labor it would be justified to give her an anesthetic and perform the operation, and concluded that if the mother refused to have the operation she should be fined after giving birth.

The Illinois Appellate Court confirmed a lower court ruling that the state could not force the woman to have the surgery, and before the public guardian could appeal the decision to the Illinois Supreme Court, the baby was delivered through natural childbirth. Whether or not the child suffered brain damage that will impair its function is not known at the time of writing. In this instance, the mother's decision to avoid medical intervention prevailed over the physician's decision that surgery was required in the interest of the fetus.

At birth infanticide is not permissible in a just society, and certainly should not be permissible at the mother's discretion. I will discuss this issue at greater length in the next chapter where I consider the problems occasioned by the existence of fetuses, infants, and children who must suffer unjust conditions and will not receive the minimal requirements to sustain a satisfactory life.

In Chapters 8 and 9, I argued that personhood is a quality that has a strong anthropocentric component: Those individuals qualifying for personhood will all be members of our species. Although this is the case, the conclusion is not the result of a definitional gambit but depends on the specification of biological characteristics. I should add that members of other species can also have personhood within their own species and kinship networks, and they would not be expected to respect our personhood. Because animals of other species have the status of personhood within their own social network, this suggests that beings from another planet would have moral agency, providing they possessed the requisite characteristics that qualify for agency. I argued for the universality of the importance of species and kin identity to provide general principles that are among the basic laws of evolutionary biology. These principles regulate the interactions of the members of all species that are socially involved with one another, at least to the extent of having sex.

SUMMARY

I have developed an argument for a permissive abortion policy which avoids the major problem of the one advocated by Tooley. By separating the status of personhood from that of moral standing, and considering all participants in the game of life, it is possible to advocate abortion until the point of natural birth, without permitting infanticide. The neonate is protected by a social contract that must be assumed by society at the point of birth. The attainment of moral agency confers rights, duties, and responsibilities on the agent, and guarantees the freedom and welfare of moral patients.

11

Abortion
Policy Considerations

I will conclude the discussion of abortion by examining some policy considerations based on the positions argued. It is important to understand that there are different levels of public policy and that some levels require stronger justifications than do others. The most stringent requirements concern those actions that are morally required (or forbidden) for all moral agents. These actions are so compelling that they usually are enacted into secular law and if these laws are violated the miscreant will be punished. Here, we are dealing with strict moral values that must be clearly spelled out and justified. An example of such an action would be a theft from a needy person who, as a result of losing the goods you have forcefully taken, dies. You have violated the needy individual's rights by taking his or her possessions, you caused the death, and are liable for prosecution as a murderer.

Less strict levels involve actions that can be disapproved of strongly but not be prosecutable. Such actions would be considered to be in bad taste, and engaging in them would be considered to be instances of insensitivity. Here, public disapproval and criticism are the appropriate sanctions to be applied. An example can be provided using a lifeboat example. Assume there are two people in a lifeboat, and only one has brought food and drink and refuses to share them with the other passenger, who dies as a result. The person who brought the supplies has no absolute duty to help the other person, nor does that other person have a right to the provisions. The failure to act to save the life would be considered to be in bad taste and one could well receive strong public criticism by responsible members of society, especially if there was little doubt that there might eventually have been a successful rescue. The offense, however, would not result in legal prosecution, but could well be criticized as immoral.

Bringing these arguments to bear on the issue at hand, abortion, it would be considered to be morally wrong and legally punishable to take the life of a neonate. Although, by my argument, you have not violated the rights of the neonate, you have violated a social contract between the person who is born and the community. This social contract regulates society and all moral agents are bound to honor it. When an infant is killed there should be prosecution for homicide. If a pregnant woman, after deciding to become pregnant, and having decided not to have an early abortion that was available for the asking, decides at the eighth month of the pregnancy to have an abortion, because the opportunity has arisen to take an all-expense-paid trip to Paris, it should not be illegal to have the abortion, but it could be considered reprehensible, and the individual making such a choice could be subjected to social derision, censure, and ostracism. As far as public policy is concerned it could be argued that the woman making a decision to have a late abortion has an obligation to consider the facts regarding such things as the possibility of pain perception by the fetus during the late-third trimester in order that her decision is informed fully. However, the choice should be hers based on the argument that an existing person's interests always trump those of a potential person. Incidentally, the above scenarios should not be taken to imply that women frivolously have abortions in order to enjoy holidays in Paris or experience the thrill of mountain climbing. The point of these examples is to argue that it should be permissible for women to do so in terms of the legality of the choice. Most women do make the responsible and moral decision, as emphasized by the fact that, in 1987, 51% of abortions were done at less than 9 weeks gestation, and only 10% at 13 weeks or later, with an infinitesimal number occurring during the third trimester, usually because of medical complications.

Thomson (1971) emphasized that if prospective parents do nothing to prevent a pregnancy, do not choose to have an abortion, take the neonate home instead of putting it up for adoption, then they have assumed responsibility for it. She argued that these actions give the infant rights but, for reasons I have outlined before, I believe it is conceptually clearer to argue that the parents (moral agents) have assumed duties and responsibilities for the welfare of the infant (a moral patient), and that they cannot withdraw this contracted support without suffering the legal sanctions of society. They have an obligation to provide for the infant, or to arrange that it will be placed somewhere in order that such support can be provided. These obligations depend on the assumption that such choices can be made by parents; that we live in a just society where the developing infant will not be condemned to starve or die from lack of medical care.

A lengthy quotation from Sumner (1981, p. 70) frames some of the issues that should be kept in mind when one considers the permissibility of the decision to have and to justify abortion:

> To what extent must the pregnancy have been intended? Must a woman ensure that some reliable method of contraception is employed? What of the failure rates associated with even relatively reliable methods? To what extent does ignorance of the mechanics of conception (or contraception) constitute lack of intent? How can we be certain whether a woman wished to become pregnant? How can *she* be certain about her own aims? What if she changes her mind after intercourse? What sort of burden must pregnancy impose on a woman? How probable must a threat to her life be? Is it sufficient that childbirth has a known mortality rate, and that abortion is less risky? What counts as a threat to health? To what extent would we include anxiety, distress, or depression as such a threat? What if the burden is mild discomfort or some restriction on activities? What if it is economic, as it might be if a model had to forego income until she regained her formerly svelte figure? How low must the quality of life available to the fetus be in order to justify abortion? Which congenital defects are severe enough? What role is played by socioeconomic conditions affecting the child's future? How long must a pregnancy have endured before the woman will be deemed to have accepted a commitment to continue it? What considerations will override that commitment? What if the woman did not realize she was pregnant? What if she avoided finding out? And so on and on.

Most of the above concerns are private ones that the conscientious pregnant woman must face. I question whether any of these concerns are proper ones for societal regulation, prescription, or proscription. The woman should have the best available information concerning the implications inherent in such concerns, then should be allowed to choose according to her own conscience and best interests, on the basis of her informed opinion, but not with coercion under the guise of counseling, nor with the threat of legal sanctions as a result of her informed choice.

If a policy more restrictive than the one I have advocated is adopted, then the society must, at least, meet the requirement that the woman has had complete access to adequate sex education, information regarding the consequences that result from sexual activity, and she should receive information about, and assistance in, family planning. There must be information and instruction regarding available contraceptive methods, the medical risks, and the failure rates of each, or such restrictions become punitive and paternalistic.

SOME SALIENT CONCERNS

Maternal Mortality and Morbidity of Abortion

The American Medical Association (AMA) Council on Scientific Affairs implemented a resolution made at the 1991 annual meeting of the

AMA that there should be a study of available data regarding the mortality and morbidity associated with illegally induced abortions prior to *Roe v. Wade*, and to compare those statistics with the data incurred through legal abortion today. In their report (1992), the Council noted that until the mid-nineteenth century the induced termination of pregnancy was legal in the United States through the first trimester. By 1900 abortion was prohibited by law throughout the United States unless two or more physicians agreed that the procedure was necessary to preserve the life of the pregnant woman. This change was justified on the grounds that it discouraged illicit sexual conduct, a growing concern about the hazards of abortion procedures on women's health, and effective lobbying by physicians. In 1973, in its *Roe v. Wade* decision, the Supreme Court ruled that states could not interfere with physician–patient decisions about abortion during the first trimester, and could intervene during the second trimester only to ensure safe medical practices reasonably related to maternal health. In 1977, the Hyde Amendment restricted the use of federal funds for abortion, a restriction the Clinton administration has tried to remove. The U.S. Senate, however, voted on September 28, 1993 to continue the ban on federally funded abortions for most poor women, adding the exceptions of pregnancy due to rape or incest to those pregnancies that threaten a woman's life.

The AMA Council reported that the number of legal abortions increased from about 745,000 in 1973 to almost 1.6 million in 1985, and the number of maternal deaths from legal abortion dropped from 25 (33 per 100,000 procedures) in 1973 to 6 (0.4/100,000) in 1985. This dramatic drop in maternal deaths was attributed to the enhanced skills of physicians performing abortions, their ability to handle complications, and to a shift from sharp curretage to suction curretage, particularly during the first trimester. Improved access to legal abortion reduced abortion-related mortality by enabling women to undergo the procedure earlier in pregnancy when it is safest: the proportion of abortions performed at less than 9 weeks of gestation increased from 38% in 1973 to 51% in 1987, and the percentage of second trimester abortions declined from 14 to 10%. Between 1979 and 1985 the death rate from legal abortion was 0.5 per 100,000 procedures in the first trimester, 1.2/100,000 in the second, and 5.8/100,000 during the third.

The rate of maternal death is much lower as a result of abortion (0.6/100,00 between 1979 and 1986) than it is to live birth during that period (9.1/100,000). The Council's conclusion was that the risk of dying from pregnancy and childbirth has decreased substantially over the past 50 years, but remains substantially greater than the risk of dying from a legal abortion.

They also noted that death from legal abortion is more common for minority women than white women. They attributed part of this higher death rate to mandatory waiting periods, parental consent laws, notification laws, a reduction in the number and geographic availability of abortion providers, and a reduction in the number of physicians trained and willing to perform legal abortions. These factors all add to the risk by increasing the gestational age at which the abortion will take place, especially for adolescent mothers, those living in rural areas, and those who are poor and will, therefore, have difficulty with financial arrangements for travel and medical costs.

They concluded that increasingly restrictive abortion laws are likely to disproportionately affect young, poor, and minority women. The restrictive legislation advocated by antiabortion groups promote the killing of those poor and minority women who choose to have a legal abortion. This killing of a person is done in the name of protecting the life of the unborn child, who has not yet attained viability, and certainly not personhood during the first trimester.

Barringer (1992) reported that the rates of abortion to live births in the United States has been declining slowly since 1980, from 359/1,000 births in 1980 to 344/1,000 in 1990, with a total of 1.4 million legal abortions in 1990. Sandra Waldman, representative of the Population Council, was reported to have estimated that about 1.6 million abortions are now performed annually in the U.S. (Seelye, 1994). Unwed women had 79% of the abortions, and 35.5% of the abortions were performed on women of color.

Cook (1991), noted that the Netherlands has publicly funded and widely available abortion services, and the abortion rate is the lowest in the industrial world. She attributed this low rate to widespread access to sex education and information as well as programs providing contraceptive advice and voluntary sterilizations. Her conclusion was that the Dutch approach is a more ethically beneficent way to reduce the rate of abortion and she questions the motivations behind arguments to deny access to new methods such as RU 486, the "abortion pill." It would seem that there might be a message in all of this to the right to lifers who sincerely want to decrease the number of abortions.

The Case of RU 486

It can be argued that complete information should be provided along with ready access to such resources as the relatively risk-free drug, RU 486. The controversy that has surrounded the introduction of this drug provides a useful case history regarding the complexity of the issues and the political machinations that occur when the issue of abortion is involved.

The use of this pill to induce abortion removes much of the risk involved in physical abortion procedures, such as suction or curretage, and it can be used at the onset of pregnancy, which decreases the cost to the mother both in terms of risk and level of parental investment. The concern of antiabortion advocates who are committed to the view that life begins at conception is that the pill can be dispensed in clinics and offices of any physician trained to detect pregnancy and to cope with its complications. This is an important development given the estimate reported by Philip Hilts (1994) that 31% of all women and 83% of women outside urban areas have no abortion provider in their county. The widespread availability of RU 486 would make it more difficult for antiabortion groups to target abortion providers because any medical facility could provide the service.

It has been reported that RU 486 pill is not only effective when used to cause an early abortion, but also highly effective when used as a morning-after pill. Glasier, Thong, Dewar, Mackie, & Baird (1992) studied 800 women in Edinburgh, Scotland who took the pill under controlled conditions within 72 hours of unprotected intercourse. They found the pill was relatively free of undesirable side effects, and none of the women or adolescents using it became pregnant. The normal expected rate of pregnancy, based on the stage of the reproductive cycle when it was used, was 17%. Fewer side effects were found than with standard birth control pills. RU 486 not only terminates or prevents a pregnancy, but has been used to treat Cushing's disease, a rare adrenal gland disease, and might have promise as a treatment for autoimmune deficiency syndrome (AIDS), breast cancer, menstrual pain, and a form of brain cancer (Regelson, 1992). Initial test results were promising enough to justify an extensive clinical trial to study the effectiveness of RU 486 to inhibit intracranial tumors that develop in nonmalignant meningiomas, which account for 15 to 18% of all tumors of the central nervous system. Positive results would be important because many of these meningiomas cannot be treated with surgery.

In terms of reproduction, the pill prevents the implantation of the fertilized egg in the uterus, an event that occurs 13 to 14 days after conception. Antiabortion groups oppose the use of the pill on the grounds that its use "stops a beating heart." Wanda Frantz (1991), president of the National Right to Life Committee, stated this position, and, erroneously, argued that the earliest possible point at which it is possible to use RU 486 is 2 weeks after implantation. She wrote that after implantation one cannot use the term "fertilized egg" because at this time there is an embryo, and maintained that the pill used at that time "kills unborn children" who are between 5 and 7 weeks of age. Her claim regarding the time at which RU 486 can be effectively used is not correct in light of the Scottish study.

Susan Carpenter-McMillan was quoted in *The Oregonian* (October 8,

1992) to the effect that anything that interferes with implantation is in effect aborting a life. Dr. Richard Glasow, education director of the National Right to Life Committee, has been quoted to the effect that the morning after pill was, in fact, the moral equivalent of abortion, and that saying otherwise was "more of the verbal gymnastics that pro-abortion advocates use so routinely." Here, we see a pattern of misleading statements regarding the medical evidence, which seem to be based on a firm reaffirmation of the principle of immediate animation at fertilization which they insist all must accept.

The terms used by those on both sides of the issue have been chosen to arouse emotions rather than to lead to a debate regarding factual matters or to explore the philosophical bases of differences. Opponents of abortion insist that their advocates refer to the fetus as a child, because it evokes a stronger image supporting family values. Rather than speaking of abortion as the termination of a pregnancy or as prochoice, the opponents instruct their followers to address the issue as one involving right to life, and abortion is characterized as murder of the unborn child—they are not antiabortion, but are prolife. RU 486 has been called "a human pesticide" by those opposing its use. Those on the other side of the issue insist on couching their argument in terms of a woman's right to her own body, and they refer to RU 486 as a contraceptive, rather than an abortion pill, arguing that it prevents pregnancy rather than interrupting it. It seems safe to expect that reasoned discussion and cool argumentation is not the intention of either side, but that the rhetoric is phrased in a manner that will arouse passion, and lead to a series of good "sound bites" for the media to exploit.

The regrettable consequence of the antiabortion activities is that the European manufacturer has been unwilling to distribute the pill or to conduct research in countries which have "wide hostility to abortion" or where there is "a hostile political climate," as prevailed in the United States during the Reagan and Bush administrations. The company fears boycotts, wants to avoid risks of liability, and worries about the financial repercussions that could occur due to boycotts of their products by antiabortionists. The U.S. Food and Drug Administration (FDA) prohibited the import of the drug for personal use, beginning June 1989, and only a limited number of studies were permitted, none on abortion, in the United States. Once again, ignorance prevails at the expense of individual liberty, and at a cost of human suffering because society has been intimidated by the moral views of a self-righteous minority.

The Clinton administration expressed interest in testing RU 486, and Leary (1993) reported that the European company has agreed to license the drug and its technology to the Population Council, a non-profit research organization based in New York City. It was reported by Seelye

(1994) that the French manufacturer (Roussel Uclaf) has agreed to let the Council select a U.S. manufacturer and to sponsor an application to the FDA for approval to market the drug, a process that could take a couple of years. The delay in moving the process along was due to the continuing fear that antiabortion groups will boycott pharmaceuticals sold by the American subsidiary of the European company. Indeed, it was reported in *The New York Times* (June 2, 1994, Sec. A, p. 21) that abortion foes plan to boycott products produced by Roussel Uclaf and its German parent, Hoechst A.G.

More complexity has been introduced because Uclaf's parent company is Hoechst A.G. of Germany, and its leading officers are Roman Catholic. There has been speculation that the company stalled negotiations in the hope that President Clinton would not be reelected in 1996. However, the political pressure from the United States has become too strong, what with threats by Oregon representative Ron Wyden that action might be taken to seize the patent if no action was taken to begin clinical trials. The company officials, therefore, are under threat of economic pressure from abortion-rights groups, threats of economic boycotts from antiabortion groups, threats of political action with economic implications by pro-abortion politicians, pressure from Pope John Paul II to halt the use of the drug, which has led to fears that the decision to release the drug would force the company to deal with the Pope's opposition and to have problems in countries that are much more Catholic than is the United States. It is small wonder that it is difficult to sort things out in any rational fashion given the currents of controversy and threat that have been introduced.

RU486 is now available in France, Britain, and Sweden (where it is estimated that more than 150,000 women have taken the drug with a rate of 96% effectiveness), and a Chinese version is used widely in China. In France the pill is available to women who have been pregnant for no more than 49 days, in Britain to those who are no more that 63 days pregnant, and the U.S. trials may use the 63-day period.

Another advance that was reported was the development, in India, of a birth control vaccine which effectively prevents pregnancy for a full year (Joshi, 1992). Preliminary tests indicated that it stimulates the normal activity of the woman's immune system to prevent the fertilized egg from sticking to the wall of the uterus. The vaccine does not seem to have undesirable side effects, is safe, and is reversible. There is a possibility that the vaccine might prevent fertilization of the egg, and, if that is the case, antiabortion activists should not be concerned. However, if the vaccine does act to prevent implantation, then the same opposition will stand as with RU 486.

A review of the RU 486 scenario indicates that there are many potential or proven applications of the compound, yet basic research and clinical testing has been blocked effectively for several years. One would hope that the 400,000 women estimated to have breast cancer in the U.S. (Regelson, 1992) would act, with the help of their families, to nullify the action of the antiabortion lobby through direct political action and a preferential purchase of any products produced by a manufacturer that is boycotted by antiabortion groups. The mind boggles at the fact that a vocal group of activists with peculiar views regarding the beginning of life could impose their biological views, religious beliefs, and moral strictures on all of us.

Psychological Effects of Abortion

Concern is often expressed that women who have an abortion suffer deep psychological stress, either immediate or delayed, as a result of the choice. Under the auspices of the American Psychological Association, Adler, David, et al. (1992) conducted a careful review of the existing scientific literature concerning the psychological effects of abortion on the women who have them. The studies they reviewed were those they considered to be the best available because they provided quantitative measures of psychological responses following legal abortion. None of these studies supported the conclusion that abortion was likely to be followed by severe psychological responses when compared to the responses following normal birth. The psychological responses to abortion (and to birth) can best be understood within a framework that considers factors that influence normal stress and coping. It was found that a woman's psychological response to abortion was influenced by factors such as degree of self-esteem, stability of the relationship to the father, perceived social support, and the degree of confidence in the correctness of the decision to abort. The research literature does not support the premise that guilt is a general phenomenon found among those who have elected to abort. However, there are individuals who, because of their own moral beliefs, live with regret for having had an abortion, and they should be counseled to consider the possibility of suffering emotional distress given their beliefs.

The Council on Scientific Affairs of the AMA (1992) reviewed the question of emotional problems that are seen following abortion, and they, too, concluded that the incidence of severe negative reactions was low, and that the predominant feelings were of relief and happiness, with sadness, regret, anxiety, and guilt being generally mild when they did occur. They also studied adolescents, and concluded that those who obtained an abortion were no more likely to experience emotional problems than those who gave birth or who were not pregnant.

I conclude that abortion should be readily available and economically feasible for all who desire it, and adequate information should be available regarding physical and psychological implications of abortion, to the extent that these implications are known. There should be a deeper commitment to obtain more adequate scientific understanding of the medical, biological, and psychological implications of abortion. It has been governmental policy in recent years to avoid considering issues involving sexual behavior because open discussion about such matters offends the "family values" of conservative fundamentalists of many stripes, although that phase seems to have less potency at the time of writing, being countered by the values of Clinton appointees, such as Dr. Joycelyn Elders as Surgeon General.

If a woman decides to forego an abortion and to have a child, then adequate prenatal care must be assured. If the mother is not able to care and provide for the infant, then there must be an assurance that a placement is available for the infant in adequate surroundings that will maximize the likelihood of its medical and psychological well-being. Unless society is willing to provide these kinds of support, it has no business considering any restrictive position regarding the permissibility of abortion for any reasons whatsoever. The current emphasis on the viability criterion leads to an immoral position, unless such proscriptions are accompanied by tangible emotional and economic support.

I can conceive of a gray area where a pregnant woman might be strongly urged to forego a late abortion if an adoptive parent is available. This could be urged because the mother has already invested a great deal in the development of the fetus, that little further investment is necessary, and that the probable pay-off in terms of the welfare of the potential neonate and the adoptive parents (who are citizens of human society) should be considered. Even here I believe the informed choice should be the mother's in terms of the *legality* of her having a late abortion. Otherwise, the society will be assuming an inadmissible paternalism toward the mother and is guilty of enforcing a clearly sexist policy. Although the pregnant woman's decision to have such a late abortion would not be an illegal act, it might well be considered an insensitive one, to be met with public disapproval.

Davis (1993) introduced a cautionary thought when considering the alternatives of abortion and adoption. She noted that it is common for people to consider adoption to be a more humane alternative than abortion. However, adoption is not always a humane solution to the problems involved in abortion: It is difficult for children with significant emotional or physical problems to find homes; difficult to place racially mixed children; if abortion were generally unavailable there likely would be many more children born than would be able to find adoptive homes; and the psychological consequences for a woman who surrenders a child she carried to term could well be more devastating than those that result from having an abortion. To this list can be added the concern that there is no assurance that the adoptive family will provide a suitable home. While all of these concerns are only problematic, they do indicate that adoption is not always a preferred solution and certainly indicate that a woman should not be forced to carry a fetus to term in order that it be put up for adoption.

Tribe (1990/1992) argued that a woman should not be forced to carry a fetus to term and to undergo a delivery. He noted that the Supreme Court has required extremely strong justification to compel criminal suspects to undergo procedures such as stomach pumping or surgical removal of a bullet in the suspect's shoulder. Clearly, these are far less invasive procedures than those involved in gestation and delivery. Laws that restrict access to abortion and insist that pregnant women carry their pregnancies to term can be considered to deny women equal protection of the law. A blanket requirement to carry to term not only results in inequality but it does not give any consideration to the characteristics, interests, and welfare of the child. Some have suggested that women could be compensated for being forced to undergo the hardships of pregnancy and motherhood. However, it is arguable that such forced and involuntary servitude is a severe violation of one's rights under the U.S. Constitution.

In her review of Tribe's book, Davis (1993) considered his constitutional arguments to force the acknowledgement of abortion rights. She noted that these rights must exist because it is not allowable to compel women (and women alone) to submit to constitutionally prohibited invasions of bodily integrity. She argued that women must be allowed the same sorts of sexual and reproductive autonomy that the Constitution accords men in order to guarantee equal protection under the law, and women should be able to enjoy those procreative rights and liberties that have been upheld as constitutionally protected (such as the use of contraception and the decision of whether to have children). Women should not be required to make sacrifices that the law does not impose on other members of society.

The role of physicians in the entire abortion debate raises ethical concerns. Most of the laws that exist, or are proposed, insist that the decision to abort must be made by a patient in consultation with a physician. While there is no doubt that the patient must be aware of medical risks to make a voluntary and informed decision, there is no reason that the physician should be allowed to have final say regarding the moral permissibility of abortion. The medical profession insists that physicians and medical staff have the right not to perform abortions if it contradicts their moral beliefs. However, the rest of society is not free to choose which rules and laws they will obey. We do not allow the police to enforce only those laws that are in accord with their particular moral beliefs. All must pay taxes to support what many consider immoral wars. Men must serve in the armed forces to fight wars they do not believe in, and if they refuse they are not free to go on with their normal lives.

Garrett Hardin (1972) suggested that what physicians want is power without responsibility; many physicians want the power to deny an abortion to a woman who wants one, but to bear neither personal nor financial responsibility for the consequences that result when the woman has to continue the pregnancy. Hardin suggested that physicians who believe they should interfere in the abortion decision should, at least, pay some of the costs of raising the unwanted child, change a few hundred diapers, take the child on weekend trips, etc. Hardin (1972, p. 107) concluded, "If he does not—and no physician ever does—all his fine talk about 'responsibility' is just a-blowing in the wind."

A serious problem exists regarding the availability of abortion services, as noted by Rimer (1993). Many doctors decline to perform abortions because of their deeply felt religious or ethical concerns, or fear instilled by death threats and harassment by antiabortion groups. Others object to the tedium and to the relatively low pay for performing the procedure. Rimer reported that a study done in 1991 found that only 12.4% of American medical schools and other training programs routinely teach residents how to perform abortions, down from 22.6% in 1986. 31.2% offer no training in abortion, a figure that has now risen to 38%).

Belkin (1993) reported in *The New York Times* that the number of medical residency programs that require abortion training in the United States has dropped by half, and that drop is one of the major reasons that most of the nation's counties (especially those in rural areas) do not have a single doctor who will perform the procedure. Given the fact that teaching hospitals are not training doctors to provide abortion Belkin reported that Planned Parenthood of New York is providing training in abortion procedures in the interest of giving physicians increased knowledge and competency in the technical matters of the medical procedure, as well as experience in conducting the counseling that should be done when abortion is considered. It seems that the medical profession has not provided adequate medical care to a significant segment of American society.

GUARANTEEING A MINIMAL LIFE

I alluded to the problem of assuring the welfare of infants born into a society and discussed the responsibilities that a just society must assume.

We are all aware of the incredible numbers of people dying of starvation and disease in many African and Asian nations in recent years. Hundreds of thousands of people have died and continue to do so. Yet, governments, such as that of the United States, have refused for several years to allocate federal funds to provide assistance for abortion or to assist in family planning through sex education. Under the Reagan and Bush Administrations the U.S. government has denied family planning aid to China because of that country's coercive population control programs that were alleged to involve the forced use of abortion. Republican conservatives influenced the U.S. government, in 1985, to halt its contributions to the United Nations Population Fund, which, according to *The New York Times* (September 16, 1992, Sec. A, p. 9), hobbled the fund's work in both Asia and Africa. The U.S. policy took shape in 1984, just before an international population conference in Mexico City, where the Reagan administration made a strong stand against abortion and population control in general. The U.S. policy entailed a refusal to support programs that distributed contraceptive devices or even provided instruction regarding contraception and family planning.

There clearly is a need for assistance in family planning in developing countries. For example, it was reported by Brooke (1994) that the abortion rate for Latin American women is higher than the rate for women in the United States, although abortion is illegal in every Latin American country but Cuba, and in spite of the fact that these countries are predominantly Roman Catholic. It has been estimated that there are probably 4 million induced abortions a year in Latin America. Available data indicate that 5.2% of women in Peru from 15 to 49 years old had an induced abortion each year, 4.5% in Chile, 4.4% in the Dominican Republic, 3.7% in Brazil, 3.4% in Columbia, and 2.3% in Mexico. Interestingly enough, the rate of abortion in the Netherlands among women 15 to 44 is only 0.5%, 1.2% in Canada, 1.4% in England and Wales, and 2.7% in the United States. Abortion is legal in all of these countries, yet the rates are lower. The increased rate of abortion is likely due to the fact that there are many more unplanned pregnancies due to a lack of family planning programs and little information or encouragement regarding the use of adequate contraception.

Holmes (1993), reported that the Clinton administration has changed the policy and worldwide population control is being supported, with the Administration resuming financing for the U.N. Population Fund. Timothy E. Wirth, State Department Counselor, was quoted to the effect that the Administration's position is to support reproductive choice, including access to safe abortion. Population experts cited figures that about 125,00 women die each year (about one-fourth of all maternal deaths) as a result of improperly performed abortions, with most of the deaths taking place in developing countries.

Robey, Rutstein, and Morris (1993) noted that there is a significant decline in fertility in developing countries (not considering China where there is concern regarding the degree of coercion involved). Birth rates have declined by one-third since the mid-1960s (from an average of six children per woman to a current level of four). This rapid decline seems not to be due to improvements in health care and education that occurred as the result of decades of economic change, as for the United States and Britain for instance. The drop in birth rates occurred quickly even though there has been no improvement in the quality of living conditions, and these demographers attribute the change to the growing influence and increased scope of family planning programs that involve the use of new contraceptive technologies and to the educational power of mass media, especially television. The changes in behavior that have produced the drop in fertility seem primarily to be due to the increased use of effective contraception (including voluntary sterilization after the desired family size is reached). The increased use of contraception has been accompanied by an increase in the age at which women first marry, an increased length of time after childbirth before the woman conceives again, and an increased use of abortion.

The authors believe that another potent factor diminishing the appeal of large families is the better education and the rising status of women in these societies. The single most important factor, however, seemed to be the increased use of contraception: If contraceptive use increases by 15% women bear, on average, one fewer child.

I consider it to be completely immoral to permit children to be born into a world where they will almost surely die, without any attempt being made to aid parents to avoid such births should they want to do so. In such extreme circumstances, one might even be driven to rationing assistance, which indirectly approves of infanticide, at least to the degree of letting a starving or diseased neonate die a natural death as quickly as possible when there is no possibility of providing needed medical assistance, or even enough food. Such passive infanticide can be argued to be permissible if the resources saved result in the sparing of other children who have a better chance to survive and attain a worthwhile life. I will discuss the issue of infanticide further in the next section.

It can be argued that it is morally acceptable to let the starving die under some circumstances, especially if they are neonates and young infants, if there is a strong certainty that these unfortunates will exist for but a short period, and with great suffering before they die. Kamm (1992) considered the problem of whether we should create persons at will when we have good reason to believe that they might not have a number of years of life with some satisfactory degree of health and welfare. In circumstances where the minimum required for a life is not available, an innocent organism should not be forced to endure great suffering that leads to painful death. This state of affairs should not be allowed, especially if it exists because of the failure of society to take actions that might have avoided the development of such desperate circumstances. At the very least the governments of civilized societies should provide all possible contraceptive aid and, if that fails, make abortions readily available if requested. It is curious that those who advocate restrictive contraception and abortion policies do not accept the responsibility for the death of incredible numbers of infants and children who are born and die as a result of a theologically driven moral righteousness.

John Stuart Mill (1859), in his essay "On Liberty," argued that an individual is not accountable to society if the actions under consideration concern the interests of no person other than the individual actor. Society can justifiably express a dislike and disapproval of an action, but the individual should not be subject to legal punishment under such circumstances. I have adopted this argument by urging that abortion should be legal until birth: Prior to the time of birth there is no other person than the mother in existence.

Mill (1859, p. 239) believed it to be a moral crime to bring a child into existence unless there is a fair prospect of "being able, not only to provide food for its body, but instruction and training for its mind." Harris (1992) endorsed Mill's argument and extended it to justify the position that it is wrong for a mother to bring needless suffering into the world when she could have avoided so doing. Harris (1992, p. 93) concluded that, "If life is so terrible for such a person that non-existence is clearly preferable, then she should be killed. No moral person could stand by and see another creature suffer so much." A child should not be brought into the world unless certain minimal conditions of life are assured, and if these minimal conditions cannot be secured the child born has been wronged.

THOUGHTS REGARDING INFANTICIDE

I have argued that if a child is brought into existence there should be some reason to expect it will survive and enjoy at least the minimal existence that constitutes a satisfactory life. What should be the moral concern when it is not possible to provide anything approaching a minimal life, due to the prevalence of disease, inadequate food, shelter, or other means of support?

Hrdy and Hausfater (1984, p. xiv) offered a general definition of infanticide as "any behavior that makes a direct and significant contribution to the immediate death of an embryo or newly hatched or born member of the perpetrator's own species." In the present context I will broaden this definition to include both infanticide and pedicide (the killing of children). Hrdy and Hausfater discussed several levels at which curtailment of reproduction occurs (contraception, abortion, infanticide, and pedicide), and these events can occur actively or can be allowed to occur passively, such as nutritionally neglecting a child, exposing it to the elements, or abandoning it to a setting in which it will receive inadequate care.

Infanticide is not an unusual occurrence in human societies. Scrimshaw (1984) noted that it was commonly practiced by ancient Greeks, who destroyed weak, deformed, or unwanted children; by the Chinese, who wanted more sons than daughters; in Japan, India, by Eskimos, in the Brazilian jungle, in London in the 1860s, in nineteenth-century Florence, and in France. Scrimshaw documented the fact that in many of these instances the infanticide occurred very early in life, before the organism had been accorded the status of a "real person in the society." As I have discussed at some length in Chapters 8 and 9, there have been a range of times at which the onset of personhood has been considered to begin, ranging from fertilization, to 40 to 80 days after fertilization, to quickening, to the point of viability, to the time of birth (as I have argued), to 3 months after birth (as Tooley has suggested).

Other points have been accepted in other cultures, and prior to reaching the point of personhood, infanticide is permitted. Among the Machigenga of South America a newborn is not a person until its mother has nursed it, often a day after birth; among Andean Indian groups the first year of life is the critical point; the Peruvean Amahuaca do not consider children fully human until they are 3 years old; in early Japanese society humanity commenced at the time of naming, which occurred on the seventh day after birth. An examination of historical and ethnographic records indicates that infanticide is not an unusual event and that active infanticide has been acceptable at a variety of ages in a number of different human societies.

Passive infanticide occurs even more widely and by a number of means, among them placing the child in a dangerous situation, abandonment, "accidental" death, excessive physical punishment, and inadequate biological support of various kinds. Scrimshaw (1984, p. 462) concluded, "Perhaps the greatest tragedy of all in today's world is that modern contraceptives and even induced abortion have not sufficiently replaced infanticide as a means of fertility control."

The most systematic studies of infanticide have been those of Daly and Wilson (1984, 1988) who organized their investigations around a set of evolutionary hypotheses suggested by Alexander (1979, p. 109). They phrased Alexander's suggestions regarding the parental inclination to care for a child in terms of three cost/benefit questions: (1) Is the infant the putative parent's own? (2) What is the infant's fitness potential? (3) What are the parent's alternatives? Daly and Wilson examined the ethnographic materials in the Human Relations Area Files (HRAF) and also considered the available data regarding children who were homicide victims in Canada. They found evidence for infanticide in 39 of the 60 societies contained in the HRAF files. There were 112 infanticidal circumstances noted in the files, and in 15 societies (20 circumstances) they involved adulterous conceptions, as per hypothesis 1. In 21 societies the killing or abandonment involved children who were deformed or very ill at birth, as per hypothesis 2. In 14 societies (56 circumstances) maternal overburdening was the cause (twins, second born child, a weaker child, a female, a birth spaced too soon after the preceding child, or too many children already present) as per hypothesis 3. The prediction that parental reproductive strategy would provide the reason for infanticide was supported for 97 of the 112 infanticidal circumstances. Of the remaining 15 only one seemed contrary to parental fitness interests. I agree with Daly and Wilson's conclusion (1988, p. 58) that, "the circumstances in which infanticide occurs and is legitimized correspond remarkably well with the circumstances in which such infanticide is likely to enhance the fitness of the actors."

The Canadian homicide statistics provided 8,032 cases of homicide, and of these cases 1,153 children were the victims, and 158 of these were infants. Without going into detail their analyses supported four predictions: (1) The probability of child homicide by parents will be maximal with very young infants, will rapidly decline with the child's age, and this pattern will be reversed if the homicide is committed by nonparents; (2) infanticidal mothers will be relatively often unmarried; (3) infanticidal mothers will be relatively young; (4) children will be at greater risk of homicide in stepparent households than in natural-parent households. These results support the general hypothesis that in contemporary Canadian society, where infanticide is condemned in all circumstances, infanticide does occur. Although the act of infanticide decreases the immediate fitness of the parents through the loss of an existing child, the pattern of its occurrence fits expectations based on lifetime fitness predictions.

If we are to be consistent in our moral decisions we, as members of contemporary human society, should do all that we can to see that circumstances are not allowed to arise in which children are born who cannot expect a minimal life. A dilemma occurs when the actions of our society are not just, and we permit infants to be born (in our own and other countries) under circumstances where the infant is almost certain to die or to exist in a miserable condition. It might well be that under such circumstances the moral thing to do is to allow such children to die quickly if there are not resources available to save them, and to use available resources to save individuals who have a higher probability of surviving, and in whom parental effort already has been invested more heavily. The best thing would be to live in a just society where one would not have to face such decisions, but our policymakers often take courses of action that lead to these almost inconceivable circumstances.

Some object that making life and death decisions of these kinds is "playing God," but such decisions still provide the only sane course of action given the informed consensus of medical personnel and demographers, who can screen the individuals that would be affected, and who can set reasoned standards based on accepted medical principles. At least, this is a position that should be examined, rather than falling back on an emotional appeal based on a lack of moral courage, or on a misguided theological appeal to the sanctity of life. This is especially the case where the choice of suffering that is being made for the victims (parents and offspring) in no way will be shared by the policymakers.

SEXUAL INEQUALITY

The issue of sexual inequality inevitably lurks in the wings when policies regarding abortion and reproduction are discussed. Kamm (1992) raised the issue directly in several ways. First of all, only women have to support a fetus physically during development, while men do not, which leads to the subordination of women from the point of conception, with an inevitable inequality of responsibility. The male partner suffers many fewer obligations when mutually consenting negligent sex takes place and pregnancy results. He can disappear and avoid any responsibility, while the woman must decide whether to abort or to bear a child, and if she bears the child she must take the responsibility to sustain it during gestation, endure the risks associated with childbirth, and accept an interdependence with the child for a substantial period of time after its birth.

A woman is required to provide life support to a fetus, and is even expected to do so at sacrifice of her own well-being, but a court will not require a voluntary father to give up part of his body or even provide a bone marrow transfusion to a child, should the father not want to do so. Some of the unequal burdens could be balanced if it was assured that the man would contribute financial and emotional support to the woman, and that he would assume some of the parental burdens, such as taking parental leave whenever that is feasible. Such steps would help to alleviate the unavoidable sexual inequality. However, in our society it is difficult even to assure that fathers contribute to the financial support of their born children if the parents separate.

While there seems to be strong concern that a woman should bear responsibility for pregnancy due to voluntary sex, there is no strong concern regarding the "rights" of frozen fertilized eggs that could develop if implanted into a womb. This leads to the interesting dilemma that, according to some arguments, eggs outside the womb can be disposed of but those inside a woman's body may not be aborted. Another interesting sexual inequality was identified by Harris (1992). Males who contribute gametes to be used for subsequent fertilization and implantation are customarily paid a small sum for their trouble. However, women who provide female gametes customarily are asked to donate eggs free of charge. Harris wondered if this economic differential should be interpreted as an instance of sexism or should it be considered a sign of greater respect for women because it demonstrates a disinclination to subject women to a form of prostitution. The readers will have to resolve this question for themselves.

The Tennessee Supreme Court ruled that a divorced man could prevent his former wife from using, or donating to someone else, embryos that had been fertilized in the laboratory with his sperm and then frozen for possible later implantation (Smothers, 1992). The court sidestepped the issue of whether the cells were "human beings" or "property" by concluding that they occupy an interim category with "potential" for human life. An interesting aspect of this case is that the court held that the man cannot be made to become a parent against his will. Ellen Goodman (1992) made the satirical suggestion that this might be the first man in America to win the right to an abortion. The woman appealed to the U.S. Supreme Court, which turned it down without comment (Greenhouse, 1993).

Kamm offered the opinion that it is only when the control of a woman's reproductive life is at stake is there concern about fetal rights. She attributed this imbalance to a general desire on the part of society to control women. The U.S. Supreme Court, in a decision with a bare 5 to 4 majority, struck down a provision in Pennsylvania law that required a married woman to tell her husband of her intent to have an abortion (Greenhouse, 1992). Clearly, the rights of men and women are not viewed equally when reproduction rights and obligations are involved.

There is current legal debate over whether a mother can be prosecuted for child abuse if she engages in substance abuse during pregnancy. It has been ruled that a pregnant woman who injected cocaine when she was about to go into labor had not abused the baby, although it was born demonstrably traumatized (Johnson, 1992). The Connecticut State Supreme Court held unanimously that state law gives no legal rights to the unborn. Although the Court considered the mother's conduct to be "egregious" the fetus was ruled not to be a child, and the woman not a parent, until the moment of birth. The ruling in this case can be considered a validation of the arguments that I have have made earlier regarding birth as the determining event for personhood. Every effort should be made to assure the continued welfare of the affected child, but what the mother did is not legally prosecutable. The State of Connecticut had not, at this writing, decided whether to appeal the case to the U.S. Supreme Court in order to make the argument that the law does have jurisdiction before birth.

The problem of drug usage in pregnancy is one that appears with increasing frequency. Johnson (1992) reported that, since the mid-1980's, at least 167 women in 24 states have been charged with abusing an unborn child. Appeals Courts have thrown out the charges in all cases that have reached them so far. It has been reported that black infants have a higher mortality rate than do white, and that the incidence of smoking, drinking, and abusing drugs is also higher for black women while pregnant. A study in California indicated that 14% of black mothers surveyed showed signs of drug use when they arrived at the hospital to give birth, a rate that was twice that of any other ethnic group. Although the prevalence of substance abuse was higher among blacks, substance abuse is prevalent in all segments of the U.S. population. The point I am making is that the existence of substance abuse among pregnant women is but another problem the courts are going to have to think through in a careful manner in order to arrive at just decisions, given the reality of the society we have created.

The views of the Connecticut Supreme Court were supported in a California case. It was reported in *The New York Times* (October 28, 1992, Sec. B, p. 9) that a Southern California court sentenced a woman to six years in prison because her breast milk, tainted with methamphetamine, had killed her baby daughter. The significant point in this case was that the ruling involved the transmission of drugs to the infant after birth, the argument being that once the baby is outside the mother's body the actions of the mother have a legal impact on the baby. The mother was considered liable on the grounds that she could have chosen bottled milk instead of breast milk.

One wonders whether this concern for neonates and infants would be extended to subjecting a baby to such insults as second-hand cigarette smoke after it has been born. It seems more logical to fight to protect from damage the born child that exists as a person, than to protect the unborn, in whom there is less parental and societal investment. A rhetorical question can be posed: Does this selective imbalance of factors exist because postnatal events, such as second-hand smoke, affect the rights of men as well as those of women?

Another sexual inequality exists in employment policies that differentially affect women. If a pregnant woman cannot have a legal abortion, then this woman assumes a burden that a man does not have; an employer might well have a lesser inclination to hire the woman for fear that she will be lost from the workplace due to a pregnancy that cannot be interrupted. The man who was co-responsible for the pregnancy could well benefit in the job market because he would be favored over a pregnant woman if employers have inclinations not to have pregnant women on the payroll. The implication is that, in the interests of equality, those who want women to carry all pregnancies to full term should work to reduce the burdens of pregnancy by requiring men who father children to assume the predominant responsibility (with paternal leave) for a postnatal child, at least for a few months (nine?). Such policies provide the Rawls veil of ignorance when the consequences of voluntary sex are to be assessed. There might well be more equitable treatment of pregnant women if men had to bear a more equal burden as a consequence of conception.

More evidence of the sexual inequality that prevails regarding reproduction is provided by arguments that women of reproductive age should not be hired to work in occupations in which there are potential toxic hazards. The argument is that these toxins could affect any fetus that might be conceived and develop in such hazardous circumstances. The Pulitzer Prize-winning journalist Susan Faludi, in her book *Backlash* (1991), provided extensive documentation of the erosion of women's reproductive rights since the 1973 *Roe v. Wade* decision. There have been extensive restrictions of the constitutionally guaranteed freedom to have an abortion, the imposition of fetal protection laws to subject women to criminal prosecution, and to selectively deny them employment opportunities in many male-dominated occupations. The denial of equal employment opportunities is done in the name of protecting any fetus that might be conceived from the hazards of industrial chemicals, and these restrictions are often applied only to women, even though the toxic substances (such as lead) pose a reproductive danger to both men and women. Restrictive employment practices have been taken so far that they have led to instances in which employers have insisted that women working in jobs which involve exposure to toxic substances must undergo sterilization or lose their jobs.

There seems to be no concern expressed when a father moves his family to take a job in an area where the environment contains high levels of toxic elements, such as high levels of lead or smog. The family is expected to endure such risks because of the need of the father to work and support his family, even though the health of the children is jeopardized. The logic seems to be that a man has to have employment to support his family, while a woman does not need to be employed because she can always find a good man to support her. There seems to be a deeply ingrained inequality in many attitudes and policies that are used to justify such societal arrangements.

The argument is not that anyone should suffer at all, but that men and women both should have the benefits of full moral standing, and that the differences in their reproductive biology should result in shared, but different, responsibilities. One can be treated as an equal, even if all are not treated identically.

The late Judge Lois G. Forer, in her book *Unequal Protection* (1991), drew on her experience as a practicing attorney and trial judge to identify and illustrate that women, children, and the elderly (what she refers as the "others") do not enjoy equality under the law. She pointed out that Anglo-American common law was developed by, is interpreted and administered by, and favors propertied adult males of sound mind. She examined some 4,500 cases which were assigned to her court over a 16 year period, and discussed about 60 cases that she considered to be miscarriages of justice, and all involved women, children, and the elderly. None of these cases of inequality involved rational adult males, corporations, or associations, and none of the inequalities she found seemed to show a pattern of inequality on the basis of race, to her astonishment.

Review of these cases led her to several general conclusions. Regarding the legal status of women, she developed the point that the Supreme Court has relied on the common law, accepting a "gender-neutral concept" based on the assumption that if women are treated the same as men, then equality is achieved. In 1974, the Court held that pregnancy is not a gender-related disability! Although she defended the legal system in terms of its attempt to maintain fairness and equality, the cases she presented indicate that in every phase of the prosecution, from arrest through imprisonment, the law impacted more harshly on women offenders than on men. Courts have ordered medical procedures to be done on pregnant women on the grounds of the state's interest in the fetus, with the woman's rights subordinated in the interests of protecting a concept of the family. When the rights of the "others" are involved the rights of the family are given precedence without any corresponding duties mandated on the part of men or of society.

The situation is even worse when children are involved. Forer documented that the Supreme Court has repeatedly denied children the constitutional rights of due process and equal protection of the law adults enjoy. Children often are left in homes in which they have been abused in order to keep the family together. The common law denied children rights, while contemporary law subsumes the rights of the child to those of the family. Forer concluded that neither affords children equal protection.

Elderly persons are deprived of their liberty and sometimes institutionalized for the convenience of their families, without proof that the individuals violated any law or were dangerous to themselves or to others. She argued, and documented, that the elderly suffer prejudice when they appear in court as witnesses or litigants because the law applies standards and procedures to them that are appropriate to a "reasonable man in the prime of life." Forer (1991, p. 43) argued that we cannot have a truly democratic society if we rely on the "anachronistic dogmas of the common law or legal fictions such as gender neutrality, the reasonable man standard, and the denial of differences between children and adults."

One other issue that bears on the question of sexual inequality concerns pregnancy due to rape (leaving incest aside). As reported in Chapter 7, almost 90% of the people we surveyed approved of abortion in cases of rape and incest. Such pregnancies pose a problem for many policymakers, even those generally opposed to abortion. Some of those who are in favor of restrictive abortion policies often explicitly approve of abortion to save the mother's life, as well as in cases of rape and incest. Approval of abortion in these instances is hard to accept if one wants to insist on an adherence to the rule of logical consistency. The fetus, which is being killed, should be entitled to the same "right to life" as argued by those favoring restrictive abortion policies for fetuses in general. I am at a loss to understand how one can approve of killing under such circumstances and decide not to approve in other circumstances. I believe that consistency requires restrictive abortion proponents to adopt a strict blanket policy against all abortions from the moment of conception. Dworkin (1993) considers it contradictory to argue that a fetus has a right to life that is of sufficient weight to justify prohibiting abortion, even when the birth would ruin the life of the mother or family, but that right ceases to exist if the pregnancy is the result of a sexual crime of which the fetus is wholly innocent. With the permissive policy I have argued, no problem arises, because a woman has no special obligation ever to permit her body to be used to support a fetus, and certainly none if the attachment of the fetus was forced upon her.

Ironically, not permitting free access to abortion could well result in dissuading people from starting a pregnancy for fear that it cannot be ended should circumstances warrant the termination. If risk-free contraception was available, and if forced sex was an infrequent event, then unwanted pregnancies could well be rare occurrences. If the restrictive reproduction and abortion policies insisted on by segments of society are abolished, then there might well be fewer abortions (as is the case in the Netherlands), fewer unwanted and neglected children, and more children produced as a result of rationally based desires and decisions. I think it an inescapable conclusion that allowing people to make such reproductive decisions would be to the benefit of the entire society.

DEFECTIVE FETUSES

There may be some gray areas where a case by case analysis should be made. For example, what should the policy be regarding the responsibilities and duties of a moral agent toward a defective infant? It can be argued that a woman should not continue to carry a defective fetus. The existence of the eventual defective infant has effects on other members of society because of the vast amounts of money and medical facilities that must be committed to permit the infant to pursue even a minimally satisfactory life. But, what should be the policy if the infant is now born and found to be defective? It can be argued that a life of suffering makes the being worse off than if it had never lived, and that there is no harm in letting an infant die under such circumstances. A question then arises regarding the degree of defectiveness that would support such a decision, or would permit the active termination of the life of a neonate or infant. There should be some appropriate panel of experts to determine the merits of such cases, taking into account the quality of the infant's existence, the effects of the infant's existence on the well-being of other members of society, and the expected course of life for the infant. The problem should be viewed not only with regard for the interests of the fetus, neonate, or infant, but with regard for the mother, and, when necessary, the most equitable use of society's limited resources on behalf of other needy individuals who might benefit more. Such a panel should certainly include those with legal knowledge, medical experts, and someone qualified to examine the issues from the standpoint of rational argumentation. It would also seem appropriate to have people who can examine the moral and philosophical implications as well as the deeper humanistic concerns, and who can explain such implications to policymakers.

Warren (1982) presented an argument that is congruent with the general position taken here. Once the infant is born the end of the mother's absolute right to determine its fate is marked. Warren considered the same kinds of concerns that Sumner outlined, and that I have raised, regarding the course of action that should be taken regarding infants born into societies so impoverished that the infant cannot be cared for adequately without endangering the survival of existing persons. If there is no other society willing and able to provide care, then is killing the infant, or allowing it to die, necessarily wrong? Similarly, if the infant is born with such severe medical anomalies that its life would be short and miserable, is it morally wrong to cease support, or to withhold treatment, rather than to prolong such a tragic life? These are all terribly difficult issues and require careful and thoughtful decisions by qualified expert ethicists, medical experts, and policymakers.

CONSEQUENTIALIST VALUE

There is always a temptation to adopt a consequentialist position that attempts to resolve problems of conflicting interests by assessing the relative value of each of the individuals involved. The intent is to determine what action results in the greatest net gain in value considering all of the participants involved, and to recommend that action. As discussed before, the problems with such a neat and simple solution is that it is not possible to assign a numerical quantity that corresponds to any absolute value, nor to know by what arithmetical rules the calculations would be done, even if an adequate assignment of value could be made. There is no clear-cut way to determine the weight of different factors that might be involved, and no formula to guide either the establishment of the weights or the rules for combining them.

Sumner (1981) argued that it will not be possible to devise a formula to weigh the various factors involved in many moral decisions because the relevant factors display too many variations and combine in too many novel and unexpected ways. Even if one could decide on the value of the individual factors, it is not possible to predict the pattern of their interactions. Some variables seem to intuitively "trump" others, in the sense that if they are present they cancel out all of the others, each of which would contribute some value if the trump was not present. I suggest that the value of species, and of actual versus potential persons, are two such trump factors. This suggestion is supported by the results of the empirical studies described in Chapter 7. I have tended to use these factors as trumps when they appear in the various problem that have been considered. As suggested in Chapter 6, unless the rules that guide consequentialist calculations are spelled out explicitly, there is nothing to consequentialism but an advocacy based on good intentions, with a fond hope that rationality will be the result. Caution must be exercised, and careful reasoning employed, when attempting to make estimates of relative value.

Informal consequentialist value assignments can be found in the thinking of many policymakers. For example, King (1980) argued that the fetus should not be entitled to the same degree of protection at every stage of development, which implicitly assigns relative values to the different stages. She pointed out that society protects most securely the interests of its most mature and responsible members and tends to favor the interests of parents over the interests of children when their interests collide. Later, however, she wrote that the interests of the mother and a viable fetus should be weighed equally in resolving conflicts between them. When considering whether to withdraw intensive care from a neonate or infant, King suggested that we might calculate the medical costs in dollars required to provide intensive care, and use these costs to develop guidelines concerning when it is permissible to withdraw such care. I suspect that it will be difficult to defend the use of such rules regarding relative value unless they are based on explicit rules and based on a coherent system of morality. In all moral dilemmas in which a choice must be made between the legitimate interests and welfare of different individuals, the problems involved in cost–benefit analyses are present.

Gillespie (1977) also runs into the problem of assigning relative value with his suggestion that, in situations involving a conflict of interest, the comparative strength of the competing beings should be determined by their state of development. He argued that an infertile ovum has no value, a zygote minimal value, an almost full-term fetus more, but less than its mother. Such a valuation scheme suggests at least an ordinal scale, which could lead to guidelines for action but, if any other factors other than the temporal scale of normal chronological development are introduced, then the system will require some rules for combining the values of the different factors, and these are not easily arrived at, as Kagan (1988) has pointed out so effectively.

Kamm (1992) discussed some hypothetical examples that merit consideration. One example involved a woman who decides to become pregnant in order to experience what it feels like, but will abort because she has no intention of carrying the fetus to term. Kamm considers this to be a frivolous reason for a pregnancy and abortion, and that it should be regarded as inappropriate. Suppose, however, that the woman is cancer-prone, but that the chance of her having cancer would be reduced if she became pregnant and then aborted. Kamm finds this to be inappropriate, even though the reason for the pregnancy is now a weighty one.

She takes the issue one step further, supposing that the woman is dying of cancer, but there is a drug that will make her pregnant and cure the cancer, but the fetus will have to be aborted. Kamm finds this to be permissible, using the doctrine of double effect; the pregnancy (and subsequent abortion) is only a foreseen side effect of the cure rather than the intended means to the cure. In all of these examples the cost is the same because the fetus is aborted in all cases. However, the benefits to the woman increase from thrill seeking, to enhancing the likelihood of the woman's health, to saving her life. I agree with Kamm that in the first instance the behavior is immoral and the woman should be viewed as reprehensible, yet the choice should be hers to make, and that choice should be condemned but legally permissible. Contrary to Kamm, I find the second case to be justified given a finite probability that the existing woman will benefit, even if at the expense of a potential person. In the third case I think it is not necessary to invoke the doctrine of double effect—saving the life of the existing woman should prevail over the cost to a potential person.

It would be argued, from an evolutionary standpoint, that the amount of parental investment (PI) is one factor that should be taken into account when assigning value. Early in development the mother has relatively little PI and the father almost none. However, this PI increases rapidly for the mother and, at birth, assumes an ever increasing value for both parents. Does this imply that older children should be protected more than younger ones or infants? The older children are more firmly a part of the social firmament than the younger ones and have had more physical and emotional resources invested in them. The likelihood of survival of infants and children increases with age, so that it is more likely that they will live to make their own genetic contribution to succeeding generations. When discussing the issues involved in guaranteeing a minimal life, I adopted just such a value argument based, essentially, on the relative PI and the likelihood of survival of those involved. Any rational consequentialist calculation of quantitative value, as well as any use of the concept of relative value, will have to cope with issues such as these, and they should be resolved in a manner that is convincing to the members of society who must accept and live by the decisions based on the outcomes of such calculations. However, facing these issue proactively is vastly to be preferred to reverting to slogans, emotional appeals, or historical precedents that do not fit current circumstances.

POLICY SUMMARY

I have argued the proposition that abortion should be permitted until the time of birth. One caveat that should be emphasized is that any such permissive policy must be accompanied by an assurance that information is available regarding medical risks involved, as well as the medical, economic, and psychological costs and benefits of the available courses of action. The possibilities of finding individuals willing to adopt a full-term neonate should be considered, and information concerning rational family planning should also be made available to prospective parents. One should be able to presuppose that information regarding contraception is available, and that contraceptive procedures are readily available to the couple.

Infanticide should be considered to be murder under normal circumstances. The only exceptions might be when the developing child would have a life so limited that it will not be able to attain the minimal qualities of a satisfactory life. Any such exceptions should require the approval of a panel composed of qualified experts who have adequate information regarding fetal and infant development, medical prognosis, moral issues, legal ramifications, and who can forecast the degree of available support that society is able and willing to provide such an infant.

The problem of the inherent nature of sexual inequality in reproduction should be kept in mind, and any policy decisions made should attempt to minimize the social and economic imbalance between the sexes. The problems involved in assessing relative value should be acknowledged, and care must be taken when attempting to assign absolute quantitative, or relative qualitative, values to different kinds of organisms. It must be recognized, however, that such value assignments will be required whenever the conflicting interests of different individuals must be taken into account to arrive at moral decisions.

MORAL DIMENSIONS

The studies described in Chapter 7 attempted to understand the nature of people's moral intuitions. When the outcomes of those studies are considered in relation to the policy recommendations made here they seem to be quite congruent. The argument that personhood begins at birth was made on the basis of results found generally, in the ethological literature, to hold for both birds and mammals. Processes that begin at the birth of the human infant were also considered, and it was argued that birth is a quantum leap in development. This point marks the time at which the fetus is now a public neonate, and the four moral dimensions that we found in our empirical study to regulate people's fantasy resolutions are the applicable ones: The strongest is the species dimension which, at the point of birth, assumes a public importance; the second is the social contract with the neonate, now a public person who must be honored by moral agents; the third includes those factors that regulate the process of inclusive fitness, which are biologically ingrained, can be recognized by the members of the community in terms of phenotypic similarities, and bring into play a system of tendencies to favor kin and community; the fourth is the tendency to approve more of passively letting organisms die rather than actively killing them, respect for this tendency is found throughout discussions regarding abortion and infanticide, and this action–inaction (kill–let die) dimension was found to be important in the study of dilemma resolutions.

SUMMARY

It was argued that restrictive views regarding the morality of abortion are flawed and cannot be argued logically, nor applied universally. The concept of moral rights was argued not to be applicable to a fetus. A highly permissive abortion policy was argued—abortion should be legal until the point of birth. The concept of rights was argued to apply only to moral agents, and the very definition of moral agency requires the recognition that there are rules, duties, and responsibilities that must be understood by anyone considered to be a moral agent. Because these abstract principles are used to guide moral decisions, the criterion for moral agency must be based on the attainment of the cognitive capacities sufficient to understand right and wrong. It is with the attainment of these cognitive capacities that the issue of rights can be introduced, along with the encumbrances of duties and responsibilities toward moral patients.

Policy recommendations were considered that could implement the arguments outlined in this chapter. The necessity to provide sex education, family planning assistance, and to ensure the universal availability of contraceptive measures was argued. Adequate prenatal care must be available readily, and society must guarantee that the minimal standards for a satisfactory life are available to children. The problems of sexual inequality inherent in reproduction, and how the defective fetus and infant should be treated were considered. The general point of view adopted here is that all issues must be evaluated with the interests of all parties considered: Those of the developing organism, the mother, the family, and the rules that should govern a just society.

The policies recommended have a strong biological, philosophical, and psychological basis. They are grounded on the factual foundation of biology, evolution, and cognition, and seem to represent a step toward the type of moral system idealized in Chapter 1. There, it was argued that an adequate system should be rational, logical, comprehensive, and impartial in its application. It was also suggested that the moral system should not violate standards of intuitive acceptability, and the positions arrived at do not violate my sense of intuitive correctness. Finally, there were a number of difficult questions raised and left unresolved (especially those of determining consequentialist value), but their existence is acknowledged and their solution can be considered at some other time and place.

12

Reproductive Technologies

Recent developments in biological science have raised a series of wonderfully complex issues related to reproduction. These developments include the ability to use artificial insemination (AI), a technically simple procedure to allow couples who cannot reproduce normally to conceive and produce young using their own egg and sperm. The more interesting techniques, from the standpoint of moral issues, involve the various kinds of in vitro fertilization (IVF) procedures which are used to fertilize the mother's egg with a donor sperm, or fertilize a donor egg with the father's sperm, the fertilized cells being implanted into the mother for gestation. If the mother is not able (or willing) to carry a fetus to parturition, then a surrogate mother can be implanted with fertilized cells, and this surrogate can carry the fetus to parturition. An interesting aspect of these procedures is that there are three separable kinds of parenting that must be distinguished: genetic, gestational, and social. The moral and legal issues involved in these procedures will be discussed after the procedures themselves are described. One additional issue to be considered is the possibility of cloning human embryos, a possibility that can easily be realized, and that has caused great concern among ethicists.

TECHNIQUES OF REPRODUCTIVE ASSISTANCE

Artificial Insemination (AI)

Artificial Insemination has been used with natural human parents for over 200 years (see Corea [1986] for a brief history of AI). Ironically, the possibility of AI was demonstrated by an Italian Catholic priest in 1779, who artificially inseminated frogs, fish, and dogs in his laboratory. The first woman was artificially inseminated with her husband's sperm in Scotland, in 1790, and the first recorded AI using donor sperm was done in Philadelphia, in 1884. By 1930 (and during World War II) donor sperm occasionally were implanted in British wives in cases in which a husband was infertile. About 15 cases of AI using the gametes of the parents and 15 using donor male sperm were reported in Great Britain in 1945. By 1960 it was estimated that only 20 physicians were regularly performing AI. Between 1949 and 1960 the birth of fewer than 20 AI children were reported in which the sperm of a donor male was used. Beginning in 1960 a great increase took place, with 5,000 to 7,000 AI children conceived with donor sperm born each year, reaching an estimated 6,000 to 10,000 by 1980.

The AI technique has been available to the medical profession for many years, and a considerable number of people want to use the technique if it is available. Hull (1990) cited an estimate that as many as 2.4 million married couples experienced fertility problems in 1982. It was estimated by Caplan (1986) that, in the 1980s, more than $200 million was spent each year in the United States on medical interventions to correct infertility. The Ethics Committee of the American Fertility Society (AFS) (Hull, 1990) estimated that one in fourteen couples in the United States might need assistance from a third party, whether through use of a donor, or with the assistance of a health professional, if they are to reproduce at all. Not only is there a heavy demand for AI, the procedure is not extremely expensive: in 1987 there were an estimated 172,000 AI's, at an average cost of $953 each.

Although the techniques used to gather and to freeze donor sperm have been available for a considerable time there has been a very slow development of sperm banks. Corea (1986) suggested that development was slow because such banks posed a threat to the patriarchal family, challenged male dominance, and provided women with a means of rebellion. In the United States the first test-tube baby conceived with frozen semen (IVF) was born in 1954. By 1965 there were only 24 babies born in the United States and Japan using thawed, frozen sperm, and by 1973 only 571 births had been recorded.

Steinbock (1992) reviewed the history and politics of fetal tissue research in America. She noted that, in 1985, Congress created a Biomedical Ethics Board empowered to create a Biomedical Ethics Advisory Committee that was to report on human genetic engineering, and to develop federal rules for human fetal research. The funds required to conduct such studies were never appropriated, however. In 1987 the National Institutes of Health created a Human Tissue Fetal Transplant Research Panel which submitted a report on December 5, 1988 recommending several guidelines for fetal tissue research, chief among them that donors cannot designate the recipient of fetal tissue or receive any payment. Steinbock's conclusion was that the debate over fetal tissue research has become "politicized" and officials generally have ignored the careful deliberations of their own appointed commissions.

Caplan (1986) stated that no research or clinical trials had received federal support in the United States, at the time he was writing, and that 23 states had prohibited fetal or embryo research. Mahowald, Silver, and Ratcheson (1987) noted that in 1974, the year after the *Roe v. Wade* decision, a congressional moratorium was imposed on federal funding for fetal research. The infrequent use of frozen sperm with humans is in stark contrast to such use by animal breeders. It was estimated that 60% of dairy cows and 2 to 4% of beef cattle were inseminated with frozen sperm, as were 136 million turkeys, 700,000 swine, 35,000 horses, and 3,000 goats.

There has been no comparable resistance to conceiving babies in laboratory dishes, although it is a far more complicated procedure than that involved in gathering, freezing, and implanting sperm in the uterus of a mother. It does seem that the IVF techniques have been available for many years, and that the use of IVF in humans has not developed at the rate that might have been expected, given the strong need for such procedures. But, more of the political ramifications later.

In Vitro Fertilization (IVF)

The major difference between IVF and AI is that, with IVF, the fertilization is done in a culture dish, and the fertilized ovum is implanted in the female. Caplan (1986) dated the first successful use of standard IVF in Britain to be 1978, and noted (Caplan, 1988) that nearly 2,000 births utilizing this technique occurred in Britain, alone, with many others in the United States, Australia, the Netherlands, and other countries. He estimated that there is about a 25% pregnancy success rate per attempt, with a live-born child being produced in only 10% of the attempts. These rates of pregnancy and birth do not differ much from those associated with sexual intercourse between fertile parents.

The standard IVF technique uses an optical surgical instrument (laparoscope) to inspect the internal abdominal and pelvic organs of the woman. Prior to the procedure the ovaries have been stimulated artificially by hormones administered to the donor (or the mother, if she is "donating" her own egg) to produce more than one egg. The eggs that are removed are inspected microscopically to determine which ones appear to be structurally the most sound. One or more of the eggs are then fertilized in a culture dish using the husband's or a donor's sperm. The eggs are then observed for about 72 hours, at which time they will have grown to the eight-cell stage (zygote) in the artificial medium. The developing zygotes are examined, and three to four of them are transferred into the prospective mother's uterus.

The IVF procedure can be similar to that used with AI, if the mother's egg is fertilized by the father's sperm. This procedure can only be used for women who have normal fallopian tubes.

The procedure of developing the fertilized cells in a culture dish makes it possible to examine them and to weed out those that are developing abnormally, to screen for genetic defects, or to establish the sex of the child. The female gametes are extracted from follicles stimulated through the use of fertilization drugs, and one or two of them are inserted, together with the father's sperm into a catheter and transferred to the end of a fallopian tube where they develop before lodging in the uterus, as is the case with normal conception. This procedure closely approximates natural fertilization, is safe, and can be used when the male sperm is not up to par. However, the procedure costs about $3,500 per attempt, and there are about the same percentage of pregnancies (25%) as obtained with fertilization through natural intercourse. There is no evidence that conception through IVF leads to any adverse effects on the mother or the child. Caplan (1988) suggested that there was no evidence that the use of the glass dish rather than the protein of the uterus as a medium has any medical significance, and he pointed out that the IVF technique should be considered in much the same light as is the use of entry into the world assisted by forceps or caesarean section.

The IVF technique, in which the embryos are implanted directly into the uterus is relatively expensive. Kolata (1992b) estimated that such an implant costs about $8,000. Hull (1990) estimated that approximately 11% of infertile couples will attempt IVF, and these will spend at least 4.5 years and $22,000 to achieve pregnancy in 20 to 25% of the cases. There is danger of a tubal pregnancy, which must be aborted, in about 2 to 17% of IVF procedures. The advantage of IVF is that the fertilized ovum, being in a glass container, can be examined to detect abnormalities and, if there is any sign of abnormality, those cells can be discarded. There is no evidence to indicate that babies conceived with IVF will be physically handicapped or damaged (Steinbock, 1992).

Steinbock (1992) cited a worldwide estimate that, by 1988, there had been as many as 12,000 IVF births (2,000 in the United States). Pear (1992) reported in *The New York Times* that Public Health Service data indicated that 2.3 million married couples, with the woman of childbearing age, were either infertile or unable to conceive after 12 months of intercourse without contraception. Pear reported an estimate that there were more than 3,100 babies born each year using IVF in 1990 and 1991, with the charge for each treatment between $3,000 and $8,000. However, a couple might have to go through more than one treatment, resulting in an average total cost of more than $20,000 to obtain a baby. Pear cited government estimates that Americans spend $1 billion a year to combat infertility.

Neumann, Gharib, and Weinstein (1994) made a detailed examination of the cost of IVF at a number of facilities. They reported that the average cost of an attempt is about $8,000, and that 10 to 15% of the attempts result in at least one live birth, ranging from 12% in the first attempt to 7% in the sixth. The average costs per delivery ranged between $66,667 for the first attempt to $114,286 for the sixth. The cost was greater for older couples: In cases in which the woman was 40 years or older and there was a factor of male infertility, the costs per delivery ranged from $160,000 in the first attempt to $800,000 in the sixth. Collins (1994) estimated that about one million people a year in the U.S. use infertility services, involving almost 27,000 attempts. He estimated the cost after tubal surgery in 1983 at $32,000 per live birth (which would be $85,000 in 1994 dollars). For normal delivery it costs an estimated $9,845 for a singleton birth, $37,947 for twins, and $109,765 for triplets.

In Caplan's (1988) view, the low success rate of IVF disqualifies it as a legitimate therapeutic procedure. The typical rule of thumb used by American insurance companies to qualify a procedure as therapeutic is a 50% success rate over a five year span. He worried that fiscal motivations may be leading the medical profession prematurely to shed the language of experimentation in favor of that of therapy. There is a clear desire by many people to use IVF, and I suggest that more energy and funds should be given to research to improve the techniques as well as for basic research on sperm, ova, and embryos to produce a higher proportion of babies per attempt, and at less cost. However, it is also clear that the procedure is expensive, is still in an experimental stage, and people who are considering using it should be provided with all available data and receive counseling regarding possible problems.

Many of the moral issues involved in AI, IVF, and surrogacy should be considered to be in the realm of commerce, and just such a concern occasioned Pear's 1992 article referred to above. There are now 270 clinics in the United States that offer IVF. Advertisements and brochures used by the clinics claim that they have success rates ranging from 25 to 50%, estimates that are much higher than those documented in medical journals, which estimate a figure between about 15 to 25%. Often, it is difficult to determine whether the estimates are based on the rate of fertilization, or the rate of live births. Because of the possible misrepresentation of success rates, the AFS plans to start an accreditation procedure for embryo laboratories, with the aim to provide a basis for the U.S. Government to use to evaluate medical claims.

With the IVF procedure the sperm, ovum, or both can be from the parents or from a donor, making a number of possible combinations, some of which affect the genetic relatedness of the embryo to the rearing parents (to be referred to as the contracting parents). If the mother's egg is externally fertilized, then the contracting woman is the gestational mother, and she and her husband are both the contracting couple and the social parents, but the husband has no genetic relatedness to the child. If the father's sperm is used with a donor egg, then the wife is the gestational and social mother, but has no genetic relatedness to the child, and the contracting couple only have one-half the genetic relatedness to the child, as compared to the degree of relatedness obtaining with natural fertilization (or with AI when the parental gametes are used). If the implanted sperm and egg are both from donors, then the contracting couple have no genetic relatedness to the child, but the contracting woman is the gestational mother, and the contracting couple are the social parents. The legal tangles that can result if the contracting couple separate, or if donors assert their "biological rights" could be awful to behold.

Surrogate Mothers

Andrews (1987) noted that many state legislatures have "reacted with horror" to the idea of surrogate motherhood, and especially, to the idea of payment for surrogacy. In those states that allow paid surrogacy one question concerns whether the payment is for a product (the child) or for services rendered. At the time she wrote, Andrews counted five states that had banned surrogate motherhood altogether, and seven others that banned only paid surrogacy, while three others banned paid surrogacy but allowed unpaid surrogacy with extensive regulations. Four other states made all surrogacy contracts void and unenforceable, and four others voided only contracts for paid surrogacy. One of these states, Nebraska, made the contract unenforceable, although the biological father was given enforceable parental rights and obligations. The California Supreme Court ruled that surrogacy contracts are enforceable in one case in which a surrogate was paid $10,000 to bear a child for a couple. After the contract was drawn relations between the couple and the surrogate broke down and both sides sought declaration of motherhood. The Court ruled in favor of the contracting couple.

Many other states have formed commissions to study the issues. Usually these commissions are made up of legislators, legal authorities, physicians, clergy, and "members of the public," with an occasional psychologist, psychiatrist, or social worker included.

When a surrogate mother has the fertilized ovum implanted in her uterus there is yet another level of complexity introduced. It is possible to implant the unrelated surrogate mother with the fertilized cells from the father's sperm using the mother's egg. When the surrogate mother is implanted with the egg and sperm of the contracting couple, this couple would be both the genetic and social parents, but the contracting mother would not be the gestational mother. If the father's sperm was used with a donor egg, then the contracting couple would have one-half the genetic degree of relatedness to the child (compared to the relatedness that obtains with natural reproduction), the contracting father would be the genetic father, the contracting mother would not be the gestational or genetic mother, and the contracting couple would, upon birth of the child, be the social parents. The same circumstances would prevail, in terms of genetic relatedness, if the IVF sperm from the father was used to impregnate the surrogate mother, whose own egg was used. In this case, the surrogate mother would have the same genetic relatedness to the child as would the contracting father, the contracting mother would have no genetic relatedness, and the surrogate mother would also be the gestational mother, with the contracting couple being the social parents.

If donor sperm cells were used to fertilize the contracting mother's egg, which was then implanted into the surrogate, then the contracting parents' genetic relatedness to the child would be one-half of normal, and the other aspects would be as in the immediately preceding case. Finally, if the surrogate mother is implanted with a donor sperm and a donor egg, then the contracting couple would not be genetically related to the child, the contracting mother would not be the gestational mother, but the contracting couple would be the social parents. This situation is the same as would prevail when a couple adopts another mother's natural child. With these varying degrees of genetic, gestational, and social relatedness the legal complexities that are possible regarding inheritance and custody in the event of death, divorce, or any dissolution are even more staggering.

A case reported in *The New York Times* (Gruson, 1993) involved the 35-year-old wife of a 31-year-old man. She was unable to carry a child, they were unable to make arrangements for a satisfactory adoption, and decided to use a surrogate mother. The search for a surrogate mother was expensive, and they failed in three attempts to make the arrangements. They finally asked the husband's 53 year old mother to be the surrogate and, after considerable hesitation, she agreed and was implanted with the couple's embryos. The third transplant was successful and a normal son was born. In this case the contracting couple are the genetic and social parents, the man's mother is the gestational mother as well as the genetic and social grandmother (shades of the song, "I'm My Own Grandpa," written by Moe Jaffe in 1947, and recorded by the Grand 'Ole Opry regulars Lonzo and Oscar, among others). Another interesting aspect to this case is that the transplantation was done (for this Roman Catholic family) by a Christian gynecologist who performed the technique in a Christian Fertility Institute for no charge. The gynecologist was quoted as saying, "This is the work, I believe, God called me to do."

MORAL ISSUES

The existence and availability of these fertilization procedures raises interesting moral as well as legal issues. As mentioned above, it can be argued that most of the issues involved in AI, IVF, and surrogacy do not involve questions of science, but are primarily in the realm of commerce. Although this is true, the biological issues should be kept in mind, because the legal and moral issues will yield to the evolutionary arguments I have developed to this point. The major problem is to cut through the emotionally charged aspects of the situations to arrive at some rational understanding of the essential questions involved. To that end I will develop some analogies with economic exchanges of services and products in other areas of commerce, and I will exploit these analyses when considering policy implications.

LeRoy Walters (1987), director of the Center for Bioethics, Kennedy Institute of Ethics, characterized four patterns of response regarding the morality of these reproductive technologies. The first is the restrictive Vatican position which completely disapproves of AI and IVF (as well as contraception) because any separation of lovemaking and the procreative reasons for sexual intercourse are unacceptable. The second position is represented by the Catholic Bishops of the United Kingdom, who approve of IVF if it uses the gametes of the married couple, but rejected the intrusion of any third party into the marital relationship. The third position is represented by the first report of the Australian committee formed to consider issues regarding IVF. In their first report they argued that gametic donation should be approved when the married couple are unable to produce their own gametes, or when there is a known and serious genetic defect that could be transmitted to offspring. The committee considered research with early human embryos to be unacceptable. The fourth position is the permissive position adopted in the final report of the aforementioned Australian committee (reported one year after the position described above), which is the same position as that of the Warnock Commission in the Britain and of the Ontario, Canada Law Reform Commission. These groups all accepted the legitimacy of AI, IVF, and laboratory research with early human embryos, even if there is no direct intention to transplant them. As with abortion, the major positions adopted on these issues will be represented by considering the two polar positions: restrictive and permissive.

Restrictive Position

The restrictive position is represented consistently by the Vatican, and is typified by the *Instruction on Respect for Human Life in Its Origin and on the Dignity of Procreation* (Ratzinger & Bovone, 1987). The *Instruction* is an affirmation of the *Discourse to Participants in the Twenty-third National Congress of Italian Catholic Jurists*, delivered in 1972 by Pope Paul VI. Ratzinger and Bovone refer to this *Discourse* as teaching that "has not been changed and is unchangeable." I discussed some points of the *Instruction* when considering the Restrictive position regarding abortion in Chapter 10, and will not repeat those points.

Among the Vatican's arguments that are pertinent to the present discussion are the following:

1. Prenatal diagnosis is morally illicit if the request for such a diagnosis is made with the intent to have an abortion should the results confirm the existence of a malformation or abnormality.
2. Research on human embryos and fetuses is illicit, whether the organism is viable or not, because these entities are the remains of human beings and must be respected in the interests of upholding human dignity.
3. In vitro fertilization is not permitted because it is immoral to produce human embryos as disposable "biological material," and because every person has a right to be conceived, and to be born, "within marriage and from marriage."
4. The freezing of embryos constitutes an offense against the respect due to human beings and is contrary to personal dignity.
5. Artificial insemination by married couples is immoral under any circumstances because it is not the fruit of the conjugal act, and AI using donors is contrary to the unity of marriage, the dignity of spouses, and the child's right to be conceived and brought into the world from marriage. If a woman is unmarried or a widow, then the use of AI is morally unjustified whoever the donor may be. The only possible conditions under which AI can be admitted is if the technical means is not a substitute for the conjugal act but facilitates it. (No sperm without copulation, and certainly not with masturbation!)

6. Surrogate motherhood is forbidden because it does not meet the obligations of maternal love, of conjugal fidelity, and the right of a child to be conceived, carried in the womb, and reared by its own parents.
7. Marriage does not confer upon spouses the right to have a child, but only the right to perform those natural acts that exist to further procreation. Physical sterility can provide the occasion for other important services in the life of the human person, such as adoption, various forms of educational work, and assistance to other families, to the poor, or to handicapped children.

In 1992 the Roman Catholic Church issued a new universal catechism, approved by Pope John Paul II, which was the result of six years work by a commission headed by the aforementioned Joseph Cardinal Ratzinger (Riding, 1992). The new catechism addressed directly several issues regarding the new reproductive techniques. The statement regarding genetic engineering was that it is immoral to produce human embryos destined to be exploited as though they were disposable biological matter. Attempts to engineer chromosomes or genes that are not for therapeutic ends, but are intended to produce selected human beings of the desired sex or to meet other preselected criteria were condemned. It was asserted that such engineering is not permitted because it goes against the personal dignity of the human being.

The Vatican position is clear, understandable, and consistent, but I find it difficult to accept for the same reasons I expressed when discussing the restrictive positions regarding abortion. It should not be mandatory morally for all members of society who are not of that faith, to accept the theology that informs the Vatican position. Secular law, as guaranteed by the Constitution of the United States (which is the basis of our society's legal system), should not be grounded on theological beliefs, and it should not be necessary to accept the theological beliefs on which the Vatican's position is based to the exclusion of all others that have been argued through the ages, and which constitute the beliefs of the majority of people on earth.

The National Right to Life Committee represents a different restrictive position. It argues that the union of the sperm and ovum marks the beginning of human life, rejects the possibility of abortion at any time, and bases these arguments on what they consider to be biological grounds. I disputed this immediate animation position in Chapter 10. The immediate animation argument, when not based on a theological commitment (such as that used by the Vatican), does not justify the firm opposition to AI, IVF, or surrogacy (as long as no fertilized ova are discarded) that the Right to Life people espouse.

Permissive Position

The 1984–1985 Ethics Committee of the AFS presented arguments that can be used to represent the permissive position (Hull, 1990), and some of the points they made can be summarized as follows:

1. Mandatory sterilization has been judged to be unconstitutional, and the rights to conceive and raise one's children is an essential basic civil right. Caplan (1986) argued that the desire to have children comes close to constituting a universal desire found among every human society (and an evolutionary perspective suggests that it is more than "coming close"). If it is assumed that there is a universal desire to have children, then it is reasonable to include the capacity to bear children among those abilities and skills (e.g., perception, emotion, and cognition) that constitute basic human nature, as I have argued throughout. Caplan considered the universality of these desires to provide a sufficient basis to consider infertility a disease. He contended that the disease of infertility should be assigned a relatively high priority for the care and treatment of those who desire to exercise this aspect of their human nature. At the very least, he argued, those afflicted with the "disease of infertility" should be made aware of all options available to them, including adoption and foster parenting, and public policy should facilitate the utilization of these options, as well as the use of the new reproductive technologies.

The medical bioethicist Zaner (1984) argued that the position assumed by the Vatican (to the effect that people who cannot have their own natural offspring should forego pregnancy and perform good works in the community instead) "is little short of plain arrogance." He rejected the notion that a physician, or any other authority figure, should be empowered to decide on the procedures an infertile couple should use to overcome their state of childlessness. Zaner pointed out that, if the disorder involved bad eyesight, poor teeth, diabetes, or cosmetic surgery, then there would be no question that it was the patient's right to choose whether or not to seek treatment, as well as to decide what kind of treatment to undertake. When the disorder in question is infertility many want the choice to be made by doctors, lawyers, and theological chiefs. It seems doubtful that anyone has the wisdom, nor should they have the ethical authority to decide what is an acceptable risk for a couple to take. Only the couple can balance the values involved to make a decision appropriate to their specific circumstances.

Nelson and Milliken (1988) developed arguments that are similar to those taken by Zaner. They considered a pregnant woman to be an autonomous adult, with the same prerogatives as other adults to control her life and to determine what will happen to her body. Their view is that physicians should not substitute their value judgments for those of the woman involved. They concluded that it is best to set the balance point between the interests of the mother and the fetus in favor of the mother in any conflict that might arise. This position is consistent with arguments that the interests of existing persons should take precedence over those of potential persons, a point that has been argued in several contexts throughout this book. The limits of the ethically permissible behavior appropriate for a physician is to attempt to persuade a pregnant woman who is refusing medically indicated treatment to change her mind, but the physician should be allowed to go no further toward coercive action.

2. Those not able (or not willing) to marry should have the right to reproduce, given the realities that unmarried people cannot be forced to use contraceptives, to have an abortion, or to relinquish their rights to rear an illegitimate child.

3. Because a couple is free (if fertile) to reproduce as often as wanted, couples should be free to procreate with the help of a donor's gametes or uterus.

4. No health professional or member of society who is conscientiously opposed to gamete donation or surrogacy has a moral obligation to provide these services to infertile couples. (I consider this to be an inconsistency given the fact that health professionals are not considered to have the freedom to refuse to treat a person of whom they disapprove morally, or who has a medical condition they find deplorable. Yet, they can impose their values on a couple's reproductive interests.)

The Ethics Committee of the AFS responded specifically to the Vatican *Instruction*, raising five major criticisms which I have paraphrased (Hull, 1990).

1. The Committee cannot understand why parental love must, in all circumstances, mean sexual intercourse.
2. The meaning of marriage should involve the relationship, not necessarily a specific reproductive act.
3. The *Instruction* commits a naturalistic fallacy when it too easily accepts natural procreation procedures as morally normative.
4. The proximity of the fetus to birth might be argued to confer a higher moral value upon developing life.
5. One should consider hazards to the mother as well as the rights of the developing fetus (Amen!).

Those advocating permissive policies, such as Harris (1992), recommend that people who are at risk to transmit a genetic disorder should be able use the IVF techniques to have their embryos screened at the preimplantation stage so that only healthy embryos will be implanted. It has also been pointed out that, in the indefinite future, it will be possible (and should be permissible) to correct genetic defects in the embryo, either at the in vitro preimplantation stage or in vivo during pregnancy.

Those opposed to abortion should realize that, by identifying embryos with genetic abnormalities, one would be able to avoid the abortion of a defective fetus that can now only be detected through amniocentesis. The ability to detect, and if defective, not to implant the embryo would be preferable to abortion after 20 weeks of age, as is the present practice: given that amniocentesis usually is not done until the second trimester of pregnancy. Of course, this solution will not be acceptable to those who accept the dogma of immediate animation upon insemination.

In vitro fertilization procedures are much less risky to the health of the mother who does not want to bear a defective fetus, and who has decided to abort if the amniocentesis test indicates there is an abnormality. Bayles (1984) cited a study indicating that prenatal diagnosis decreased rather than increased the number of abortions. This decrease reflected the decision made by women who were at risk, and for whom this risk would have led them to abort, to be reassured that the risk was minimal, and who therefore, chose to continue the pregnancy. The in vitro detection of a defective embryo does not halt the process of fertilization because, in most instances, several embryos are stored and available for implantation as a replacement for a defective one. Further discussion of these issues will take place when considering problems associated with embryo donors.

Summary

The two polar positions discussed reflect differences similar to those regarding abortion. A major difference between the two positions is that the restrictive position focuses exclusively on the embryo or fetus, it emphasizes the sanctity of life from insemination, with the Vatican position representing a preoccupation on the necessity of sexual intercourse occurring with intent to procreate. The permissive position focuses on the interests of the reproductive couple embedded in a societal context, emphasizes the relationship between all individuals involved, and does not involve theologically based arguments.

Cloning Human Embryos

One of the most recent developments involves the use of IVF procedures to clone human embryos. Kolberg (1993) reported that, at the 1993 meetings of the American Fertilization Society, Dr. Jerry Hall, director of the In Vitro Fertilization and Andrology Laboratory at the George Washington University School of Medicine, Washington DC, used a simple procedure to clone humans by separating individual embryonic cells and treating them in such a way that they would divide again. This technique has been used with mammals such as sheep and cattle for several years and should be a routine procedure to carry out with humans. Dr. Hall did not take the experiment to the point at which the embryonic cells would be capable of being implanted in the uterus. His intention was to ask a basic research question and to raise the ethical issues involved, and he attained both goals.

It has been noted that routine IVF procedures involve implanting multiple embryos in order to enhance the likelihood of success of the procedure, and few raise questions regarding the ethical acceptability of that practice. It is also an acceptable procedure to freeze some of the extra embryos extracted for later implantation in case the first IVF attempt is not successful. In both of these cases the eggs are individually fertilized by different individual sperm and there seems to be little ethical concern. However, the possibility of cloning has given rise to serious ethical concerns with the fear of Brave New World scenarios being invoked.

One possible use of the cloning procedure would be to create two identical individual embryos, test one for genetic defects and, if it is found to be free of defects, implant the other, intact one. This procedure has been questioned on the grounds that this would be sacrificing one identical twin for another. Caplan was quoted as finding the idea of creating embryos solely for the purpose of genetic diagnosis disturbing and morally suspect (Kolberg, 1993). In the same article another bioethicist, John Robertson, of the University of Texas, Austin, considered the idea of using clones for diagnosis to be not much different from taking any single embryonic cell for testing. I wonder why it is not permissible to take an identical twin, but is permissible to take what is essentially the fraternal twin produced by IVF. Another striking case in which there was little criticism of the morality involved occurred when two Siamese twins were separated. The separation was done with the full understanding that only one of them could survive, and it was decided that whichever one was in the best physiological condition would be allowed to survive and the other sacrificed. This decision seems to have been acceptable to most people, given the reality that the choice was between having one or neither of them survive.

The idea of cloning clearly strikes a discordant note for many people. *The New York Times* (November 6, 1993, Sec. A, p. 22), had an editorial comment entitled "My Brother the Clone," which began with a scenario in which a man and woman are in the office of a physician who specializes in IVF. The doctor shows slides of children who are prototypes for stored clones that can be implanted, and the physician delivers a commentary regarding the expected characteristics of each specimen—one with allergies, one with no health problems and tall, but recommends one who has "good health, long bones, and fantastic hair and skin." The editorial writer presented this as a "frightening though possibly farfetched scenario." The dangers suggested are that people could have "designer children," or they could have identical twins born years apart (having raised identical twins I am receptive to that possibility), or could save a duplicate embryo that could be implanted in the mother if the born child needs an organ transplant. The editorial concluded that the researchers should continue their research but that physicians and bioethicists should consider the ethical questions in advance of the development of the technique.

Postmenopausal Mothers

Yet another recent development causing concern among bioethicists is the use of IVF procedures to impregnate post-menopausal women. A 59-year-old Britishwoman was implanted with donor eggs which had been fertilized with her 45-year-old husband's sperm, and she gave birth to twins (Chira, 1994). Riding (1994) reported that a 62-year-old woman had been implanted and was 3 months pregnant at the time he wrote. An interesting debate has arisen, with politicians of at least three countries (France, Italy, and Britain) proposing legislation to ban, or at least to regulate closely, any implantation of postmenopausal women.

One explicit reason offered by those opposed to postmenopausal implants is a version of the natural fate argument discussed in Chapter 10. The argument runs that older women should not have babies because it disrupts the proper order of things and will be detrimental to the welfare of the child who, when 10 years old would have a mother who is 70 years or older. The natural fate argument is not applied to men, because men are able to procreate into ripe old ages without any artificial means being used. One observer noted that this procedure produces a major assault on what we think the timing of events ought to be regarding who is old and who is young.

A thread of sexism seems to run through many of the arguments. Linda Wolfe (1994), in an Op-Ed piece in *The New York Times*, noted that, when her brother of 62 impregnated his 30-year-old wife, no one debated the ethics of his fathering a child at that age, even though he would be 75 when the child finishes eighth grade and 85 when the child graduates from college. As Wolfe observed, when elderly men sire new children, their reproductive feat is celebrated rather than criticized, and the child is regarded as a crowning achievement in the man's life. This differential view prevails even though women are likely to live about 7 years longer than men, so the child is likely to enjoy both parents with an older mother than an older father. Wolfe claimed that the average age of women seeking babies through IVF is 51, while the average age of people entering nursing homes is 85—providing the child with the likelihood of about 34 years of having two parents, which would seem enough to get them to some level of maturity. One fertility expert was quoted by Riding (1994) to the effect that he had helped about 100 women between the ages of 45 and 55 to become pregnant and no one ever asked the age of the father.

Clearly, there are risks that the uterus of a 60-year-old woman might be deficient in supplying blood to the fetus, which could impair brain development. However, the fact is that fathers over 40 have an increased risk of producing a fetus with genetic defects—yet, this concern is not used to argue that older men should be prohibited from reproducing. A report in *The New York Times* by Angier (1994) indicates that the risk to the fetus is indeed greater with older fathers. She cited remarks by Dr. James F. Crow, the eminent University of Wisconsin geneticist, who discussed statistical evidence supporting the premise that an older father is more likely to sire a child with a birth defect than is a younger man.

Dr. Crow noted that the overall genetic mutation rate in sperm cells is six times greater that it is in eggs. He attributed the increased risk to this faster mutation rate: By age 20 the male sex cells have divided about 200 times, by age 30 about 430 times, and by age 45 about 770 times. He also noted that many of the large scale chromosomal defects associated with female mutations can be detected in prenatal tests, whereas the small genetic errors produced by point mutations in the male are likely to remain undiagnosed until birth. Dr. Crow recommended that one could eliminate a considerable proportion of mutations if males either reproduced at a young age, or stored their youthful sperm for use later in life. From an evolutionary perspective, however, it should be noted that older fathers have displayed high genetic quality in the sense that they are hardy enough to have survived to a ripe old age. It should be noted that this same argument would apply for older women as well. Angier remarked that good fathering skills "like cheese, wine and redwood trees very likely improve with age." In any event, there seems to be just as many reasons to suspect that the deleterious effects of aging on reproduction are not unique to the woman, and might even be more serious for men.

It seems reasonable that, as Chira (1994) suggested, postmenopausal women should be screened to assure they are healthy enough to bear the physical strain of pregnancy, and to check such afflictions of the elderly as high blood pressure, risk of gestational diabetes, and less flexibility of the pelvis. It seems just as reasonable to be concerned about genetic mutations when older men reproduce, although the factors involved are more difficult to detect.

The French Health Minister was reported by Riding (1994) to have stated that artificial late pregnancies were immoral as well as dangerous to the child and that it was "egoistic" for women to become pregnant after menopause. The French Social Affairs Minister was prompted to draft a bill requiring that a judge give approval in every case of AI where the embryo has no genetic link to both parents, and the Health Minister's bill will state that medically assisted procreation techniques, particularly IVF, will be reserved for women of childbearing age only. Although he favored banning the use of AI for lesbians, as well as widows who wish to be impregnated with the sperm of their dead husbands, he decided not to seek a formal ban in those cases.

Italy's Health Minister has also proposed a ban to limit artificial pregnancies. Beck (1994), reported that the British Health Secretary, Virginia Bottomley, is planning to confer with other countries to develop ethical controls that would prevent the use of infertility treatments for older women, even if they pay the costs themselves. Beck raised the question of why this great furor has occurred, given the fact that the postmenopausal fertilization involves very few women, who are relatively secure financially, and who have made a strong commitment to have a baby. It seems safe to presume that these women will be able to provide a suitable home for the desired child. Beck wondered why concerns aren't directed to problems involved with unmarried 15-year-old school dropouts whose unplanned, and often unwanted, baby will put her on welfare for many years, or one who is perhaps only 21 and having her fourth baby by four men, none of whom will father the child. Postmenopausal women most likely do not use illegal drugs, or pass along the AIDS virus, or force a fetal alcohol syndrome on the child by drinking to excess, and they are likely to seek adequate prenatal care.

There is an age bias that has been reflected in the policies of adoption agencies which refused, for many years, to place children with parents over the age of 40, a limit that has recently been increased to 45. The strong concerns expressed regarding postmenopausal pregnancy seem to reflect at least three underlying biases: One favoring natural fate, another reflecting sexism, and a third ageism. These problems are the result of the developing technologies as well as the incredibly rapid advances taking place at the molecular levels involving gene action, human genetic mapping, screening, and manipulation.

Moral Implications

At this point the issues regarding the use of the various reproductive techniques can be brought into perspective by considering the different levels of the intuitive moral acceptability of the various possibilities. It seems to be acceptable, to all but those holding the most restrictive position, to screen a fetus for a genetic defect if the risk of the screening to the mother and fetus is low and if there is a treatment (such as a dietary regimen) that can prevent the expression of the disease. It also is acceptable to many to screen for a defect if the parents are known carriers and it can be determined whether the fetus is a carrier or has the defect, whether or not there is a possibility of treatment. People justify such screening on the basis that it allows the parents to make an informed choice of whether to abort or not, thereby resulting in fewer abortions (given that a proportion of them will found to be unaffected) or, if abortion is not acceptable to the parents, to plan for the future knowing the status of the fetus. Screening is more acceptable if the disease is severe than if it is a more mild disorder. There are at least three important factors that seem to be involved so far: Risk, treatability, and severity of the defect, with the likelihood of phenotypic expression probably coming into play when relevant.

The use of IVF is approved by most when the couple is known to carry a genetic defect and wishes to have the fertilized embryo examined in order to decide whether to implant it or not. Most also approve of the use of IVF (in one or another of its manifestations) when the couple is infertile but wants to be the gestational parents of a child, whether it is theirs genetically or not. Many disapprove of using IVF in order to avoid having sex with a man, as is the case for some lesbian couples. The use of IVF is strongly disapproved if the couple want to control the gender of the child, and bear only a child of the desired sex.

Most seem to approve of genetic manipulation to insert a gene to correct a genetic defect, and many approve of gene therapy that would correct a genetic problem in an individual's reproductive cells so that the defect will not be passed on to the recipient embryo's offspring. Fewer approve of genetic engineering to enhance a specific characteristic, such as height, if that were possible. Most disapprove of any eugenic engineering that could be done by inserting genes to change or improve polygenic, complex traits such as personality or intelligence, in the unlikely event that became possible.

One principle that seems to be operative is that it is permissible to do things that alleviate or prevent human suffering and to make it possible to realize certain human potentials, such as reproduction. However, questions begin to be asked when there are attempts to "fool mother nature." These worries are expressed in a variety of forms ranging from theologically oriented attitudes that one should not attempt to play God or interfere with the natural fate of events, to evolutionary concerns that changes

in the structure of nature might result in unknown and unsuspected deleterious side-effects.

There is also a strong undercurrent that one should not engage in
manipulations merely in the interest of indulging a preference, such as
selecting for gender. Many consider it questionable for individuals to be
unwilling to take the luck of the draw, and believe people should accept
the burden of a defective child, whether they want to or not. We are willing
to place constraints on some of the most important decisions that affect a
person's well-being and dignity when it involves reproduction, but we do
not place these constraints on other aspects of life. People are free to pollute
and abuse their bodies, possess a gun that poses danger to others, and
engage in disastrous activities, even to the point of burdening others in the
society who have to care for them. All of these things are permissible, but
we are not free to make reproductive decisions that affect us, even though
we are the only existing persons influenced directly by the decision. The
problems occasioned by the postmenopausal fertilization are so recent that
few crystallized positions have been developed. The initial reactions, however, reveal what seem to be some strong basic tendencies toward letting
nature take its course, ageism, and sexism.

POLICY IMPLICATIONS

One problem relates to the identity of the parents who must assume
the legal duties and obligations toward a child produced through AI or
IVF. As mentioned above, there can be three parental claims depending on
the specific circumstances: one involves the biological or genetic claim
based on the sperm and egg used; the second involves the gestational
claim, which can be the implanted spouse, or a surrogate mother; the third
involves the social parents who have contracted for and will have the
responsibility to raise the child.

There are clear precedents that can be derived from rules regulating
the adoption of children born to natural parents. There are many "blended
families" in which a mother's children and those of a new husband are
reared together in a common household. The use of donors or surrogates
does not introduce any new considerations beyond those existing for such
blended families. The existence of genetically unrelated individuals
should not impose any insurmountable barriers for lawmakers, therefore.
The rearing parents should be assigned parental rights, duties, and obligations toward the children in all situations where that is possible.

Wilkerson (1993) reported on a case that reveals some of the complexities of the legal issues, even with straightforward adoption. The Michigan Court of Appeals ruled that a Michigan couple who raised a 2-year-old child from birth had to return the child to her biological parents in Iowa. The Michigan court avoided ruling on the biological questions but deferred to the ruling of the Iowa courts that the child should live with the biological parents.

The biological mother was unmarried at the time of the birth and surrendered the child when she was 2 days old. At birth the mother named a man as the father whom she knew was not, and it was this man who gave consent for the adoption. Three weeks after the adoptive parents had taken the baby home to Michigan, the mother, regretful over the decision, told the biological father about the baby, the couple agreed to fight for custody of the baby, and married. The Iowa courts ruled that the adoption proceedings were not binding and genetic tests were taken as proof of the biological father's parentage. Because he had never relinquished his parental rights, even though he had neither seen the child nor contributed to its support, the court nullified the adoption proceedings, and the Iowa Supreme Court ordered the child returned to the biological parents.

The case is interesting because it involves the definition of parenthood: The social parents argued they are the rightful parents because they are the ones who nurtured the child and are the only parents she knows; the biological parents argued that biology is the proof of parenthood. As Wilkerson noted, it seems that this is a case where no one can win: The child is losing the emotional bonds (and her personal identity) that were forged for years by supportive, well-off parents; the biological parents face an unsettled situation with a child who has lost the parents she has always known, and the child and parents face a difficult adjustment in a quite different social milieu. The biological claim of the father has been given primary consideration, the gestational claim of the mother seemed to be of lesser significance, and the claims of the social parents were discounted.

Usually, the gestational claim is weak, especially if a legal contract has been executed between contracting parents and a surrogate mother, or in the case discussed above, between a biological and contracting adopting parents. The only troublesome problem is that bonding can occur between the gestational mother and the fetus, and certainly to the neonate. Because such bonding is likely to occur it is essential that agreements be drawn carefully, that psychological factors be considered by all consenting participants in any adoption or surrogacy arrangement, and that the neonate be surrendered to the adoptive parents as soon as feasible.

Genetic parentage is of paramount importance from an evolutionary perspective. Most individuals prefer to have their own normally conceived, genetically related children, with AI, IVF, adoption, and surrogacy the last resorts of desperate parents who cannot conceive naturally, yet who want to raise children somewhat related to them biologically or, at the very least to raise them as soon as possible from the point of birth. Given that a couple has chosen an artificial avenue to reproduce it is unlikely that they will have difficulty accepting the neonate, given the biological, social, and psychological events (described in Chapters 3 and 9) that occur at birth.

Another question concerns the composition of the parental unit. Few problems arise when the couple is heterosexual, middle-class, and main-line. Although all states that have dealt with the issue of AI by donors have decreed that any child born to married parents is to be regarded as their issue, and the husband is held responsible for support (just as any genetic father would be), some problems have appeared. A Canadian woman who used AI with donor sperm, doing so without her husband's consent, was held to be guilty of adultery (Corea, 1986). The state of Georgia passed a law legitimizing donor AI children, but *only* if a physician had performed the insemination. These decisions reflect an excessive degree of paternal-ism, and often are accompanied by statements to the effect that restrictive rules are necessary to deter women who would become pregnant irre-sponsibly.

The question of paternity is a sensitive one for all human societies. With natural reproduction there is no question who the mother is, but paternity is always uncertain, even in the best regulated households. The male who agrees to AI with donor sperm is required by law to assume paternity, but he does not have that responsibility unless he has consented to the procedure. If there is no consent by the husband, then the child has been considered to be a bastard. If the child is defined to be illegitimate it was considered, until 1969, to have no claim on the father's estate. For the child to be legitimate the husband has to agree to the AI, and it has been argued that a widow should not be permitted to use the frozen semen of her dead husband. However, a Los Angeles District Court upheld the right of a man who killed himself to will his frozen sperm to his girl friend should she want to use them to become pregnant. The dead man's children objected to the ruling and have appealed the decision. Once again, the wishes of the man prevailed over all others.

There is a presumption by many professionals concerned with repro-ductive issues that AI should not be available to single women or to homosexual female couples. Hull (1990) reported that only 5.6% of women requesting AI did not have a relationship with a male partner, and that 61% of physicians surveyed indicated that they would reject an unmarried recipient without a partner. Corea (1986) cited an instance of a British fertility clinic director who wrote that he would refuse AI for a single woman, a couple of mixed race or mixed religious denomination. Given that most couples who request AI are married, the problems are not of major concern, but any laws and regulations that exist must take exceptions into account and, certainly, philosophical arguments regarding moral permissibility must resolve these possible exceptional cases.

Surrogate Mothers

Unique questions arise when a surrogate mother nurtures the fetus to birth. Andrews (1987, p. 191) outlined some of the issues concerning surrogacy that regulatory lawmakers should consider:

> [W]hether surrogates should be paid, what type of screening participants should undergo, what safeguards are necessary to assure that participants have given voluntary, informed consent, whether the couples who are the intended parents should be recognized as the legal parents, whether the surrogate should have a certain time period after the birth in which to assert her parental rights, and whether the resulting child should, later in life, be able to obtain medical information about the surrogate or learn her identity.

If it is decided that a surrogate can be paid, then it must be decided whether the payment is for a product or for services rendered. If the payment is for a product, then it seems reasonable that full payment should be contingent on the presentation of a live-born neonate, with up-front money paid at conception, and a partial payment at some definable stage such as quickening or viability. A problem still remains regarding the proper course of action if the neonate is born defective. Is a rebate appropriate because the product does not meet the specifications of the contract? I believe that questions of this kind pose considerations that are intuitively unacceptable, and this level of intuitive discomfort leads me to conclude that the analogy to the delivery of a commercial product should not be used to develop the operative principles.

The alternative view is that the surrogate is offering a service to the contracting couple: She is a paid incubator and compensation should be regulated from that perspective. Appropriate analogies can be drawn using instances in which other contracts for services exist, such as with professional athletes who are paid because of their physical abilities, with considerable risk to their well-being in several sports. The appropriate approach should be the same as that used when entering into any contractual arrangement. There should be a clear specification of the responsibilities of the surrogate mother in terms of her prenatal behavior, and an agreement that she is to surrender the infant at birth. If the contracting parents die during the pregnancy, then it would seem reasonable that the surrogate mother (who is the gestational mother) should have first right of refusal to keep the infant if she so chooses, and contractual arrangements should have been made in the eventuality that the surrogate mother does not wish to assume such responsibility for the child.

There is always the possibility that the surrogate mother will change her mind during the course of the pregnancy, and either decide she wants an abortion, or that she wants to keep the baby for herself. In the first instance I would argue that the abortion should be permitted, but that the surrogate mother should be held financially liable for expenses that the contracting parents have incurred, plus be liable for appropriate damages. Of course, given the financial realities involved in such situations this possibility just may be one of the risks contracting parents must take. It would not be humane, considering all of the parties directly and indirectly involved, to hold to contractual arrangements that would damage the interests of the contracting parties by forcing the gestation and birth of a child by a desperate, despairing, or uncooperative surrogate mother.

I do not find it reasonable that the surrogate mother should be allowed to retain the infant, any more than any commercial contractor should be able to appropriate a custom-made product that is designed and financed by a contracting party. If I design a custom sailboat, pay you to construct it, and you then refuse to give me possession of the boat upon launching because it exceeds your expectations and you have fallen in love with it, I should be able to take possession of the boat, and to sue you for any damages that I might have suffered. It seems to me that this analogy is the appropriate one to use in regard to surrogacy.

An analogy has been made between surrogacy and prostitution on the grounds that contracting the use of one's uterus for surrogacy is perilously close to contracting for the use of one's vagina for prostitution. Thus, surrogacy is considered to be "degrading to womanhood." I find these arguments unconvincing. We do not ban boxing, football, hockey, or wrestling because they involve what could be described as degrading acts of violence between freely consenting men. In fact, we reward them handsomely for abusing and injuring each other. It is interesting that when it is a woman who profits through a commercial arrangement involving any aspect of reproduction, that "protectionist" arguments are selectively raised. This seems to be another instance, as Brown and Gilligan (1992) have argued, in which women are objectified and idealized, while at the same time they are being trivialized and denigrated.

I do not know of any studies of the characteristics and motivations of those who volunteer to be surrogate mothers. I can think of at least four reasons for a woman's decision to become a surrogate mother. One highly laudatory motivation would be an impulse to give a "gift of life" to those parents who themselves are unable to reproduce. If the gift was blood or an organ given to someone who needed it, such an action would be considered exemplary. I think that, if the decision to be a surrogate mother springs from such a motivation, it should be viewed as a beneficial act. However, I suspect that decisions are seldom based on this motivation.

A second motivation might be purely an economic one: The surrogate mother considers it to be a commercial transaction. One problem is that women who become surrogate mothers for economic reasons are usually from a relatively poor stratum of society, and the contracting parents are financially well off. Again, if we take away the mystique of reproduction, I find this to be no different from contracts for services in any hazardous, typically male, occupations, such as police, soldier, or firefighter, or in typically female occupations, such as maid, cleaningwoman, or nurse. To close avenues that economically disadvantaged individuals freely choose to take strikes me as little more than yet another instance of paternalism.

A third motivation to become a surrogate could well be to expiate the guilt of having had an abortion. The research evidence, discussed in Chapter 11, indicates that the degree of guilt or other psychological trauma following abortion is no greater than that following normal birth. Even if guilt did motivate a few women, this would not argue against permitting a woman to become a surrogate in a "prolife" spirit, providing there has been careful psychological screening of the surrogate mother, as there should be in every case.

Finally, some might be motivated to become surrogate mothers because they like the experience of pregnancy and birth, but do not want the responsibility of raising a child. I find this a relatively unlikely scenario and would have serious concerns regarding the psychological status of such an individual. However, this is a conceivable motivation. When I review all of these possible motivations I consider none of them to be morally impermissible. Paid surrogacy seems to involve no moral concerns that would justify legally prohibiting it, given that proper contractual safeguards are established.

One major stipulation in any surrogacy arrangement should be that the surrogate mother agrees to surrender the infant upon birth and understands the importance of not interacting with it. I have emphasized the central importance of those events that occur at birth to the development of emotional bonds. I argued that personhood begins at the point of birth and a social contract between the neonate, the mother, and society is established at that point. It could be a disastrous mistake to allow social attachments to be formed between the surrogate mother and the neonate. Yet public policy does permit contact for a period of time between the surrogate and the neonate, and I suspect that those policies cause considerable psychological distress to the surrogate mother. Viewed from this perspective, the case of the Michigan couple who lost custody of their two year old adopted daughter is especially distressing.

Andrews (1985) reviewed some of the proposed and pending laws that would apply when a surrogate mother changes her mind after the birth of a child. Several states proposed that a surrogate mother should be given twenty days to change her mind after childbirth. A law proposed in Minnesota allowed a two week period for the surrogate mother to revoke her consent and for the father to be reimbursed for fees and expenses if she did so. All of these considerations are unwise and harmful, because they increase the likelihood of undue psychological stress for all of the parties involved. Surrogacy contracts should be regulated in the same manner as any other contract for services, especially in view of the psychological factors that come into play at the point of birth.

Policy Recommendations Regarding Surrogacy

The problem of surrogacy should be considered in the light of two biological realities: The psychological factors influencing the gestational mother during pregnancy (here the mother is a surrogate) and social events that take place at the time of birth, which involve the neonate and the social environment, and which could include the surrogate mother. Regarding the reality from the surrogate's perspective, there is an essential biological link between the surrogate mother and the fetus, and that reality must be given serious consideration. Because the progress of the pregnancy can have profound psychological effects on the surrogate mother, it is essential that there be strong and binding legal agreements between her and the contracting parents. All agreements must be entered into freely and the surrogate mother must receive intensive counseling regarding the experiences she is likely to have during pregnancy. There should also be a careful psychological evaluation of all parties concerned. If, in the view of a qualified psychological panel, the surrogate mother is not likely to honor the contract because she will not be able to regulate her prenatal behavior in a satisfactory manner, or she is unlikely to surrender the neonate, then the arrangement should not be initiated. If the contracting parents are likely to have problems accepting a child who was not the result of a natural birth to the contracting mother, or if the parents will not be able to provide a satisfactory environment within which the child can develop, then the agreement should not be initiated. These evaluations of the contracting parents are no different from those used when a couple wishes to adopt a child, and it would seem reasonable to follow such procedures when surrogacy is involved. It should be required (and several states do so) that psychological data be collected and that the participants review, with qualified personnel, the medical, genetic, and psychological information concerning the surrogate mother prior to entering a contract.

There should be no personal contact between the surrogate mother and the contracting parents after the contract has been struck, in order to avoid repercussions that might develop, such as guilt on the part of the contracting parents who would then take custody of the neonate from a surrogate mother they know personally. Doubt and guilt could easily be communicated by the contracting parents to the child. Given that the surrogate mother and the contracting parents have no contact, a monitor should be appointed to provide for unforeseen needs that might arise on the part of the surrogate mother, and to maintain continuing contact with her throughout the course of the pregnancy.

I believe it is essential that the surrogate mother have as little contact with the neonate as possible from the moment it is born. I have argued that the point of birth is the time at which personhood begins for the neonate, and it is the point at which social bonding begins, with the attendant moral obligations and duties for the parents. If contact does not occur between the surrogate mother and the neonate, this reduces the likelihood there will be psychosocial problems for the infant, and an immediate separation should lessen problems for both the surrogate mother and the contracting parents.

One problem is that many of the arrangements between surrogate mothers and contracting parents are done through an infertility center. If the infertility center is involved financially, whether it is a for-profit or nonprofit agency, then it is in the center's interest to drive the bargain to fruition. A financial involvement makes it essential that an impartial, state-regulated panel establish and certify all arrangements. Robertson (1983, p. 177) discussed a case in which a psychological evaluation was made, and the psychologist warned that the surrogate mother had traits that could make it difficult for her to surrender the child. The infertility center (whose fee would have been jeopardized) did not inform either the surrogate mother or the contracting parents of this evaluation, and serious legal problems occurred.

Once the biological and psychosocial factors have been considered, the surrogacy arrangement should be handled as a contract for services rendered and regulated as an act of commerce, subject to the laws regulating such commerce. Robertson argued that surrogacy can be viewed in the same light as many methods used to assist people to rear children, and that the surrogacy arrangement should be structured to strengthen the marital bond of the contracting couple. There are approved methods that have been used for many years to assist in child rearing, such as the use of wet-nurses, neonatal intensive care unit nurses for premature babies, day-

care workers, and baby-sitters. Sperm sales are permitted, as are the donation of eggs and adoption of a child. It is difficult to see how the planned
nature of surrogacy makes it an unacceptable method to satisfy the reproductive needs of contracting parents. I see no basis for denying couples
their fundamental reproductive rights, nor do I find properly pursued
surrogacy arrangements to be morally distasteful.

One final point, regarding both surrogacy and adoption, concerns
whether information should be provided to the surrogate child. Should the
child be told about the surrogacy arrangement at an appropriate time and
provided data regarding the genetic, ethnic, and psychological background of the surrogate mother? Some states have provided that, upon
reaching the age of eighteen, a child born as a result of a surrogacy contract
may obtain copies of any documents that have been filed and, in the event
that the surrogate mother retained the child, similar information would be
available regarding the biological father. The individual born as a result of
a surrogacy contract should have the right to disclosure of all available
information, both for medical reasons, and to fulfill the need that most
people have to be aware of their biological "roots." The time of such
disclosure need not be determined by age, but it would seem appropriate
that such disclosure be made at any time the individual is to enter into
marriage or to have children of their own.

RESEARCH USING EMBRYOS

Why Conduct Fetal Tissue Research?

The issue of using embryos for research has been the subject of active
discussion among ethicists, the medical profession, and lawmakers. Those
who advocate fetal tissue research, and whose goal is to implant fetal
tissue for therapeutic purposes, argue that this line of research should be
pursued because fetal cells, tissue, and organs can be used to repair defects
in existing humans. Among the possible uses for such transplants are
to repair inherited enzyme defects, to treat diabetes by transplanting pan-
creatic cells, to use myocardial tissue from embryos to repair major vessels
of the heart, and to treat Huntington's chorea, spinal cord injuries, leu-
kemia, aplastic anemia, and radiation sickness. Mahowald et al. (1987/
1990) described some especially promising advances in transplants of fetal
brain tissue to treat Parkinson's, Alzheimer's, hypogonadism, and certain
genetic and traumatic neural tube defects.

The initial optimism regarding the potential value of transplantation
procedures has been justified by several subsequent successes. The im-

plantation of fetal tissue into the brains of Parkinson patients has successfully ameliorated symptoms for several patients (Widner, et al., 1992; Freed, et al., 1992; Spencer, et al., 1992). These reports elicited strong interest because of the uniform success of different surgical approaches, and compelling biological justification for why the implants are be effective. It appears that the fetal dopaminergic cells effectively produce dopamine in those patients who have lost their endogenous dopaminergic neurons. The lack of dopamine is implicated in these disease processes, and the replacement therapy has been effective with patients displaying problems caused by the long term use of exogenous chemical treatments. The results are still preliminary because the patients were quite different in etiology and symptom patterns and the sources and amounts of fetal tissue differed as well. In spite of these differences, however, all three of the preceding studies reported positive outcomes.

The success of these studies indicates that intensive systematic research should be pursued. There are many questions that need to be addressed, as outlined in an editorial by Fahn (1992) in *The New England Journal of Medicine*.

> Thus, we are encouraged, but many questions remain unanswered. What is the optimal amount of fetal tissue? Is frozen tissue as good as fresh? What should be the target sites for implantation? How many sites would be ideal? How long will the benefit last? How long will the implants survive? Do the implants make synaptic connections? Will the release of dopamine produced by the implants be regulated by the host brain? Will the procedure protect against worsening of the disease? Will a transplant be effective in severely affected patients who no longer respond to levodopa therapy? Investigators studying Alzheimer's disease and Huntington's disease are also keeping an eye on the results of these studies; the possible usefulness of fetal-tissue implants has not escaped their attention. (p. 1590)

Studies using fetal tissue implants offer promise that the technology might be developed to the extent that it will be possible to reverse certain kinds of brain damage, especially in those instances where a biochemical malfunction is at the basis of the disorder. The strong interest in fetal tissue research is occasioned by the fact that fetal tissue tends not to be rejected by the host organism's immune system, and the tissues and organs obtained from fetuses are usually devoid of pathology and contaminating microorganisms. It is clear that continual and rapid progress has been made toward understanding and treating a number of disease processes through transplantation of fetal tissue.

Harris (1992) argued that if fetal tissue can be used to save the lives of existing humans, then strong moral arguments would be required to justify denying society those benefits. If these techniques are not perfected, then one must justify permitting the consequent loss of life. In Harris's view, not taking advantage of the potential benefits of fetal transplants and genetic engineering would not only be crazy, but would be "wicked" in the absence of compelling moral reasons against developing them. He argued that there are no such compelling reasons.

The Techniques

Mahowald, et al. (1987) described the process involved in the transplantation of brain tissue from an aborted fetus:

> Abortion is induced and performed through a method intended to preserve the desired fetal tissue. A specific segment of brain tissue is then removed from the fetus and placed in a strategic area of the recipient's brain. Within weeks, the healthy tissue begins to function as part of the organism into which it was transplanted, and symptoms of the disease decline. (p. 260)

There are several sources of fetal tissue. The one described above used tissue obtained from an abortion, and this source probably provides the healthiest tissue for transplant. It has been suggested that tissue might be taken from a dead, nonviable, or miscarried fetus. The problem with these tissues is that they are often not medically useful, either because they are not in a healthy condition, they have genetic defects, or the miscarriage occurs too early for the tissues to be usable.

The Department of Health and Human Services has decided that experimentation with an aborted fetus that is viable after delivery is not permitted. If the purpose of obtaining fetal tissue is for nontherapeutic research rather than for a direct therapeutic use, there are three major conditions that must be met: (1) vital functions of the fetus cannot be artificially maintained; (2) procedures that would terminate the heartbeat or respiration of the fetus cannot be employed; and (3) the purpose of the research must be the acquisition of important biomedical knowledge that cannot be obtained by other means.

The procedures required to successfully transplant fetal brain tissue cannot satisfy the second condition because all of the vital signs of the fetus are stopped by the procedures used to take the brain tissue. Fetuses born with such severe defects that they will not be viable in the long term, such as anencephalic babies (babies missing all or most of the brain), might live long enough to provide a useful source of tissue and organs within these guidelines. A report by the Medical Task Force on Anencephaly (1990) noted that only 41 anencephalic infants had been involved in transplant procedures: 37 provided kidneys, 2 provided livers, and 3 provided hearts. Only 11 kidney transplants, no liver transplants, and one heart transplant were successful. Part of the problem in the use of anencephalics as a source of organs is the requirement of total brain death, because it renders the organs unfit for transplantation. Under current restrictions, anencephalics do not provide a significant source of organs, especially given the high demand.

Another major source of embryonic tissue for research is the use of the spare embryos obtained with IVF, in which more embryos generally are cultured than used. It is possible to use these nonimplanted, spare embryos for research purposes rather than to discard them immediately. It is arguable that it should be permissible to use spare cells for therapy or research rather than to destroy them.

Steinbock (1992) pointed out that most American IVF programs do not fertilize more eggs than they plan to place in the uterus because they want to avoid adverse publicity and controversy with right-to-life groups. Adopting this procedure avoids any problem of what to do with spare embryos. Steinbock suggested that the sensible procedure would be to extract as many as twenty or thirty embryos and fertilize them all, select the embryos with the best chance of achieving a successful implant, and freeze the other healthy embryos if needed for later use by the couple. If pregnancy is achieved, or the couple decides not to continue with the IVF, then the spare embryos could be donated to others or used in research. Steinbock adopts a moral position based on interest theory, and considers it a moral wrong to refrain from using fetal tissue from aborted fetuses (and, I presume, to discard or not fertilize sufficient embryos) when there is the potential to save and improve the lives of thousands who do have compelling interests.

Policy Questions

There is a further question regarding the possibility of creating embryos specifically for research purposes with no intent to transplant. One source of this type of tissue is from women who have decided to be sterilized, and who can donate the eggs that are taken during the sterilization procedure. These eggs can be fertilized and the embryos used as research embryos. As Harris (1992) pointed out, the only difference between the usual spare embryos and these research embryos is the intention of those who culture them. He argued that if it is right to use spare embryos for research, then it is right to produce them directly for research, and he comes down solidly on the side that if fetal tissue research is morally right, it would be morally wrong not to do such research because it is done in the interest of alleviating the suffering of living humans.

It is interesting that a woman who is to be sterilized is accorded the right to donate the eggs she possesses at the time of the operation, and a woman who suffers a miscarriage can donate the fetus, but the woman who chooses to have a legal abortion does not have the right to dispose of the aborted fetus as she chooses. Steinbock (1992) noted that federal regulations impose a more restrictive risk standard on research using embryos and fetuses than it does on research using children. Harris (1992) questioned whether it is ethical to deny a woman who chooses a legal abortion the right to enhance the welfare of potential beneficiaries by donating her aborted fetus to be used for research or transplantation.

Some have argued that one should not use tissue from an aborted embryo because abortion is an act of questionable morality. Without quarreling with the dubious assumption regarding the immorality of abortion, this argument is another instance of special pleading, solely because the techniques involve reproduction, and we are once again faced with emotions based on the "sanctity of life." Steinbock (1992) adopted the sensible position that, as long as abortion is legal, it is not wrong to use fetal tissue for medical purposes. In fact, she concluded (as did Harris) that it would be morally wrong not to use it.

The arguments made to forbid research with properly obtained embryonic tissue are not applied to other areas of medical research or public policy. For example, many deplore the dropping of the atomic bombs on Nagasaki and Hiroshima, but few argue that we should not study the effects of radiation on those unfortunate humans who were exposed to it. This does not endorse a simple consequentialist position that people can be used as a means to obtain a laudatory end. If an unfortunate event occurs, then there is no evil involved in using whatever positive knowledge can result from the misfortune that occurred.

Even though the circumstances that prevailed when the data were gathered involve such unspeakable events as the "experiments" of Nazi doctors who froze concentration camp inmates to death, among other things, it dishonors the victims if any valid information that can be gleaned is not used to benefit existing people, some of whom could be their kin. The victims are dead, and if any good can result from the cruelty they suffered, then it stands as a monument to their suffering, no matter how atrocious the intentions of the perpetrators. Unfortunately, the experiments were seldom conducted adequately, so the information cannot be trusted and is not scientifically useful. The particular procedures were motivated not by questions with any scientific merit but by the dictates of genocide and sadism. The position argued here avoids the doctrine of double effect, because it avoids the undesirable quandaries introduced when the concept of intentionality is introduced. I do not justify or condone any practices based on the doctrine of double effect, but argue that whatever good can result from evil that has occurred in the past should be used.

Hilts (1991) quoted Dr. Janice Raymond, professor of women's studies at MIT, to the effect that the decision to abort is difficult enough, and women should not be burdened with yet another decision of whether or not to donate the fetal tissue. She maintained that using aborted fetuses for such purposes makes women into mere containers for the fetus. Steinbock (1992) commented that this no more makes women into fetal containers than the fact that retinas can be used for research makes donors mere eyeball containers. Once again, a different standard is being applied to issues regarding reproduction than is applied to other medical issues, only this time it is being argued by a feminist.

When the permissibility of using fetal tissue for transplantation is considered, the only person who should be considered is the pregnant woman. This woman is the patient of the physician treating her, and the physician's responsibility is to that existing person—the woman—not to the potential person—the fetus. At this stage the fetus is the private concern of the woman, not the patient of the physician. If the fetus is aborted, the woman should be asked to consent to the use of the fetal tissue, and this request should be made in deference to the woman's wishes and feelings about the disposal of dead bodies. To honor those obligations that a society has to its surviving members, the appropriate moral concerns are the symbolic significance of the fetus to the woman. The fetus is a powerful symbol of humanity, and for that reason alone it should be treated with respect, as several have argued. Steinbock (1992) spoke of the symbolic significance of the fetuses that precludes using them for unnecessary experiments or for purely commercial gain, although she does consider this symbolic value to be less important than the actual interests of life and health of born humans. Elsewhere, she referred to the human fetus as a powerful symbol of humanity which should be treated with respect, and of the embryo (although it lacks moral status) as a potent symbol of human life which deserves respect.

A physician who transplants fetal tissue is responsible to the person receiving the tissue. The source of the tissue, if obtained in a legal manner, is not the proper concern of the physician.

An interesting case is that in which a mother has a child who is incurably ill, but who can be saved by a bone marrow transplant from a genetically compatible individual. Given that the bone marrow cannot be obtained by any other means, the question arises whether it is permissible for the woman to become pregnant, have an infant, and then take the bone marrow from the infant to implant it in her first child. The intent the mother had to conceive this infant is to provide the means to achieve the end of saving the first child. Fox and Swazey (1992), in their book *Spare Parts*, considered the actual case on which this scenario is based to represent an act of love, as well as of science, because the parents made it clear they never considered aborting the fetus if the tissue type did not match that of the first child. I see nothing morally impermissible in the mother's decision, providing the infant who is born for this purpose is then accorded all of the care required to provide him or her a satisfactory life. The bone marrow removal is an invasive procedure but it is not dangerous, and adults who have experienced the procedure have reported that little pain is involved. The benefit to the existing child who will be allowed to pursue a satisfactory life, as well as the satisfactory life that is begun for the donor infant, exceeds the minor cost to the donor, who was unable to make any informed decision in the matter.

The Slippery Slope

We encounter the slippery slope argument in this context. Some have challenged the approval of any research using embryos, because they fear that women will become pregnant to create embryos for research, especially if the fetuses can be harvested for a profit. Even if the profit motive is not operative, they consider it possible that a mother might wish so strongly to help a sick person that she would abort her own fetus to benefit the needy sufferer. It has also been argued that the profit motive would lead doctors to abort fetuses to sell, receiving a fee for both the transplant and abortion procedures. Steinbock (1992) effectively challenged these arguments by pointing out that there is always the danger that physicians of all kinds will recommend procedures inappropriately or act in an unprofessional manner. These types of argument are not raised regarding coronary bypass surgery or plastic surgery, but only abortions. Steinbock (1992, p. 178) concluded, "[T]o suggest that physicians who perform abortions are more susceptible to financial incentives than are other physicians is unsubstantiated and unfair."

The argument that mothers will abort to aid another person is unlikely, given all that we know about maternal behavior. It is doubtful that a mother who chooses to have a child would undergo an abortion, thereby sacrificing a wanted child, or that a pregnant woman who does not want the child would need the further altruistic incentive to decide to abort. Steinbock (1992) wondered whether anyone can seriously imagine that a woman, torn between aborting or having the child, would decide to have an abortion because of the possibility that the fetal remains might be used for transplantation.

As Harris (1992) argued, it is conceivable that a woman who has decided, for whatever reason, to have an abortion might find consolation in knowing that the abortion could help someone in need; I consider such a motivation laudable. The probability that a mother chooses to abort solely for the commercial purpose of harvesting tissue for sick people, although possible, strikes me as vanishingly low.

The scenario in which a woman becomes pregnant and aborts to sell the embryo has a parallel with surrogacy. I find nothing morally impermissible in producing a fetus with the intention of aborting it for therapeutic use and being paid for such a service. The same arguments that were used to justify surrogacy are applicable here. What Walters (1987) called a "liberty-oriented approach" can be applied to this issue. The liberty-oriented approach argues that individuals and managers of commercial sperm or egg banks should be allowed to buy and sell gametes as long as such transactions are regulated to guarantee safety standards. Such a liberty-oriented approach is what is used to regulate blood banks and organ donor centers, and these banks are allowed to receive payment for their services. I see no reason why it is morally impermissible for a woman to engage in the hazardous occupation of producing and selling embryos any more than anyone should be forbidden to engage in any of the other hazardous occupations discussed above.

It was reported in *The New York Times* (April 11, 1993, Sec. A, p. 9) that a California research clinic plans to import fetal tissue from Russia (which has tissue banks in place) to reduce diabetics' dependence on insulin injections. Russian doctors have performed more than 3,000 such transplants and report that patients' needs for outside insulin has been reduced by up to 90%. A California antiabortion group has opposed this arrangement because they say it will encourage abortion.

If it is decided that commercial use of embryos is not legally allowable, then there is no problem with the slippery slope. All that has to be done is forbid commercial sale of embryos by law, and the slope is no longer slippery, a wedge has been placed to stop the slide, or a step has been reached beyond which one cannot descend—whichever metaphor suits you. Those who pursue the slippery slope argument maintain that one should never enter the slippery slope because the initial precedent might be the step that starts the inevitable descent to the unacceptable eventuality. If this argument is taken seriously, then one could never engage in any activity in which there is any conceivable undesirable outcome. Thus, nothing should ever be done for the first time, because there is no certainty that any exploration will have only desirable outcomes. Rather than engaging in hand-wringing about the possibilities of harmful consequences, the question of proper controls can always be considered and mandated. Just because one has begun a course of action, this does not mean that any problems encountered must be allowed to persist, or that the wisdom of the actions cannot be reconsidered. If problems arise, either the first step is no longer permitted or the mode of approach is changed to avoid the harmful consequences that have occurred.

CONCLUSION

One of the take-home messages of Part II of this book is that there is a consistent tendency to view issues regarding reproduction in an almost mystical light. It is common to encounter references to "the miracle of birth" and "the sanctity of life." Part of this mysticism stems from awe regarding the creation of life, as well as a fear of the end of life. Another consistent thread running through many of the discussions is a sexist bias. I have documented throughout the discussion of reproduction and abortion that attitudes, regulations, and laws tend to be punitive or paternalistic when they apply to women only, but are much more evenhanded when they affect both sexes.

Many seem to work from the implicit belief system that it is a woman's duty to reproduce and, as Margo Wilson and Martin Daly (1992) remarked, wives often are valued as a commodity that men own and exchange. Their view, and the one expressed throughout this book, is that the sexual psychologies of men and women have been shaped by a history of natural selection and many of the attitudes and behaviors that were appropriate in the environment of evolutionary adaptation have produced cultural institutions that, given contemporary circumstances, needlessly inhibit a women's sexual autonomy and economic independence. Given the rapid changes in the human condition that have been made possible by technological developments, it is necessary to fashion rational attitudes, rules, and laws to regulate reproduction in order to counteract some of the evolved biological tendencies that work to the disadvantage of women, who constitute a significant portion of human society.

13

Epilogue

This book has two basic parts. Part I considers basic principles in moral philosophy, evolutionary biology, and the cognitive and social sciences. The discussion of these principles involved the presentation of a fair amount of data, much of which was presented in a summary fashion, but all of which was accompanied by an extensive set of references to direct the interested reader to the primary literature. In Part II these principles are applied to issues concerning the beginning of human life, especially questions regarding the moral issues involved in abortion and in the moral dilemmas produced by the development of new reproductive technologies.

Part I began with a discussion of some basic points regarding argumentation that should be considered when attempting to bring information from the sciences to bear on questions regarding moral philosophy. Two fallacies were discussed at some length. The first is the naturalistic fallacy, which I argued is not necessarily a fallacy at all; there is no fallacy involved in describing the *is* and using it as a base to consider the *ought*. The second is the slippery slope fallacy, which I argued is indeed a fallacy unless the causal mechanisms are identified that lead from a first step to the decline, ending in an inevitable and dreadful conclusion. Usually the slippery slope scare is made whenever there are attempts to change the status quo, especially if the changes involve the use of new technologies.

REPRODUCTIVE BIOLOGY

There are at least three levels of theory running throughout Part I. One deals with the biology of reproduction, which I have argued is the ultimate basis, the "glue" if you will, regulating the proximate mechanisms of social cooperation and communication. As we move from realities at the level of evolutionary biology, we must deal—at a quite different second level—with the characteristics that differentiate moral agents from moral patients. It is critical to decide when a developing human should be accorded some moral standing, if not the moral agency that characterizes full moral status. I argue, in Part II, that moral standing begins at the point of birth. It is at this point that the neonate is a public entity and is entitled to the respect that any human moral patient should receive. The moral agents who make up the social community must, from this point on, honor the obligations and duties that make up what I have called a social contract. I presented evidence supporting the argument that the social contract is a biologically mandated one that exists for the members of many species. This contract is forged by experiences during development and its function is to knit the members of the community into a cooperating, self-perpetuating entity. The critical aspects of the contract involve emotional bonding and the development of communicative networks. The ultimate function of these aspects of the contract are to enhance the reproductive success of the members of the community by increasing inclusive fitness. I believe that basing moral standing on the attainment of personhood and separating that standing from the attainment of moral agency, is an important step in the developments of morally defensible social policies.

PERSONHOOD

The onset of these processes define personhood which, as argued in Part II, is based on biological processes involving phenomena similar to those observed in what is called imprinting. These biological processes include a strong emphasis on events in the stimulating environment that the developing organism encounters and will use to form social attachments, and the focus shifts from automatic biological processes to what I discussed as experience-expectant, experience-dependent, and activity-dependent systems.

The general phenomenon of imprinting has been demonstrated in many species (including humans), for many stimuli, and for a wide range of behaviors. For example, the first object experienced by human newborns is almost always the mother, the first animal sounds heard are usually those of the parents (especially the mother), and the first tastes experienced are those of the food-types available in the immediate environment—either taken directly or through feeding of maternal milk. There is a genetic tuning of receptor systems, which increases the likelihood that stimuli with a restricted range of characteristics will be selected and responded to by the developing organism, and attention preferentially will be directed to those stimuli. These early experiences drive the infant toward sensitivities and preferences for certain classes of objects over others, such as a preference for the sight of the mother's face and the sound of her voice, and to respond to faces by smiling.

EVOLUTIONARY PRINCIPLES

I argued that evolutionary principles are relevant if we are to understand the human condition, and focused attention on the mechanisms involved in the development of human speech and the initial stages of language development. These early mechanisms seem to unfold in much the same way as for other, simpler developmental systems of both human and nonhuman animals. A large number of social bonds, especially between the mother and neonate, are cemented almost from the moment of birth. I believe that these bonds are extremely important when considering issues regarding moral status because they mark the entry of an interacting young organism into the social community. It is at this point that the neonate gains personhood and when the organism should be considered to be a moral patient—an individual who does not have the full moral standing of a moral agent. The neonate cannot be considered to be an agent because it is not yet able to reason in such a way that it can understand the nature of moral obligations what the concept of a moral obligation involves, being unable to appreciate the nature of causal relationships.

I defended the proposition that people have a predisposition to adopt a set of moral principles as a result of early experience, and that these principles reflect the coordinated influence of early social interactions and an evolved genome that is biased to enhance the developing organism's reproductive success. I argued that the basic aspects of morality develop in a manner that is analogous to the development of speech: They depend on, and utilize, processes that inevitably occur for almost any neonate that is going to survive.

MORAL AGENCY

A third level of principles emerge if we are to identify the defining characteristics of moral agency. These principles are governed by the cognitive characteristics that make it possible for a person to attain a continuous concept of self, to understand the ideas of causality, and to understand the rules on which ethical systems depend. Moral agents can be held to the duties required by the customs, rules, and laws that society has adopted, they must respect other moral agents as well as look to the welfare of moral patients. These patients neither can be expected to behave in accordance with the societal rules nor be considered culpable when they violate them.

No one level of theory will be adequate to guide the search for the morally permissible. Just as reality involves different principles when viewed at different levels, the theories required to understand these realities have to be framed in qualitatively different, pluralistic terms. Scientific methodologists have argued that, in order to frame a science adequately, converging lines of evidence should be used to establish the validity of constructs based on the evidence at hand. Intersecting lines of theory should be developed at multiple levels that support, rather than supplant, one another and which are adequate to allow the emergent properties of more complex levels to be expressed and appreciated. I consider the development of a pluralistic theoretical approach to be necessary in order to deal adequately with issues in the sciences as well as with those as complex as the morality of reproduction, life, and death.

When I began this book I intended to discuss many more phenomena than I was able to include. The development of the basic theoretical concepts in argumentation, evolutionary theory, cognitive science, and moral philosophy required considerably more space than I had planned. I chose to make the basic arguments carefully, especially those involving the application of evolutionary theory to human behavior, and I presented a wide range of empirical evidence to support the arguments. I attempted to consider issues concerning problems that arise when adopting a naturalistic stance and spoke to problems involving determinism and reductionism.

Rather than declining to discuss the complicated issues in moral philosophy, I read fairly widely in that literature and arrived at a pluralistic position which basically is consequentialist, emphasizes the importance of individual freedom, and stresses what I refer to as rational liberalism. My philosophizing might not meet the standards expected by philosophers of philosophers, but what I bring to the table is a set of sound biological principles and a solid empirical base that seasoned philosophers should consider and bring to bear on the critical issues in morality.

THE EMPIRICAL FOUNDATION

I want to emphasize one critical aspect of this presentation. I have taken pains to relate all of my views to theory and data that come from the biological, cognitive, and social sciences. I believe that one of the most important contributions I can make to the ongoing discussions regarding issues in law, society and policy is to focus careful attention to the network of scientific theories and facts that relate to the issues under consideration. As a scientist I appreciate the fact that the conceptual framework I have developed here is only one of many that could be applied and that, even if the overall framework is essentially correct, it will have flaws that need to be removed and, even, downright errors that need to be corrected. I consider this state of affairs not to be a weakness, but to be one of the essential strengths involved in using objective data to support a conceptual framework. We know that all existing theories are flawed and much of what has been proposed will be falsified. However, it is also true that, with every theoretical revision, there is likely to be a movement in the direction of a stronger verisimilitude—a better and better approximation of "truth-likeness." My intention is to develop arguments in an objective manner in order that it will be easier to find the gaps, and to present a naturalistically based target toward which further argumentation can be directed.

I believe the presentation of empirical data regarding the organization of human moral intuitions included here represents an important step, due to the fact that it provides a more solid foundation on which to base argumentation than is possible when there is complete reliance on the outcome of armchair theorizing or the results of thought experiments. The empirical methodology presented here can be developed further and can be used to analyze some of the basic dimensions that were found to be important; this analysis can be done at a deeper and more sophisticated level than we have achieved to this point. One major advance would be to use these methods to gain some understanding of the critical question of how the concept of value can be developed. A central problem that confounds much consequentialist thinking is how to establish the relative importance and strength of what are often incommensurate values when decisions are to be made regarding what should be done in specific instances, especially when legitimate conflicting interests exist. I believe this issue is one that needs careful attention and that measurement and scaling methods are available to obtain a clearer picture of what communities of people value and what policymakers should take into account when establishing public policy.

A critical step involves showing that basic evolutionary ideas can be used to help us understand the human condition. The first step involves a rejection of the argument that the complex characteristics of we, the people, are so emergent that we have transcended the basic rules that govern other organic systems. Do we have an essence that, although it might have evolved, has become free to manifest itself through cultural rules that are uniquely independent of biology?

I documented the fact that few deny the existence of such basic pro-

cesses as habituation, selective sensory mechanisms to detect certain classes of stimuli, and tendencies for animals to have biases toward efficient
learning of those things that are crucial to survival. It is also accepted that
humans have automatic attention mechanisms that increase the salience of
stimuli presented in certain displays in such a way that the stimuli are
quickly and accurately detected. It has been argued that these mechanisms
would have undergone strong selection and would have resulted in a
survival advantage in the environmental of evolutionary adaptation.

PRINCIPLES OF SOCIAL COGNITION

In addition to these simpler processes, a body of evidence has been
developed that challenges the Standard Social Science Model, which assumes that basic cognitive processes involve general purpose mechanisms
that apply similarly in a wide variety of circumstances. This Standard
Model is based on the assumption that a general, culturally driven learning process is sufficient to explain the development and functioning of
human cultures and social norms. The typical strategy is to describe how
some learning explanation can be devised that will explain a given phenomenon. The problem is that different mechanisms tend to be offered to
account for different phenomena. The causal processes that are considered
to be generally involved, and to lead different societies to display different
cultural traditions, are seldom specified. The distinct advantage of the
evolutionary models is that a set of unifying principles are used to consider
all instances in which organisms are coping with one another and with the
demands of the environment. The evolutionary perspective leads to a
deeper understanding of what seem to be inexplicable variations in proximate processes, and permits us to relate them to the ultimate causal
mechanisms driving the process of reproduction on which evolutionary
stability and change depend.

The evidence indicates that there are content specific learning mechanisms involved in the acquisition of many complex processes. The acquisition of speech and language are among the best understood of these
processes. In addition, there seem to be content-specific tendencies to solve
problems that involve social cognition in contrast to when the problems do
not involve social exchange, even though the formal steps required to
solve the problems are the same. In fact, if the identical problem is posed
in such a way that a person is asked to take the perspective that a cheater
is to be detected, then the problem is solved easily. However, if the perspective taken is one in which the person is only searching for the rule that
is involved, it is solved with difficulty.

A large body of literature was discussed that supports adaptational explanations of more complex social behaviors, and it is this evidence that distresses traditional humanists and social scientists the most, and against which they have offered the strongest objections. I consider the most compelling evidence to be provided by indications that the evolved psychologies of men and women are quite different in those aspects of behavior that are related to reproduction. It has been found that there are different patterns of jealousy shown by men and women, there are sex differences in the age and status preferred for mates, and in the different reproductive strategies employed by men and women in terms of a potential partner's reproductive potential. It seems that the adaptive logic of men and women is different when pursuing short- versus long-term mating strategies, with both being more similar when seeking a mate who would be a good parent. Patterns of homicide support expectations that result from employing the principles of inclusive fitness, and the structure of legal principles is compatible with expectations of evolutionary mechanisms that further reproductive success. It seems that many of the aspects of human societies are structured to enhance reproductive success, even though the specific details differ given the structure of the ecology with which the particular society had to cope during the period of evolutionary adaptation. The segment of the gene pool that is represented in the founding population will also be a factor producing different proximate solutions of the problems involved in the ultimate evolutionary adaptation.

THE ABORTION DEBATE

After devoting considerable space and energy to these basic conceptual developments, I have, in Part II, brought the argument to bear on issues involved in the abortion debate. The treatment of abortion issues required a more extensive consideration than I had planned initially because it is necessary to consider evidence ranging from neurophysiology, through ethological mechanisms, the biological bases of personhood, issues in cognitive science, and going as far as considerations regarding constitutional law.

The abortion argument involved several critical steps. The first was the one discussed above to establish the point at which personhood begins. Arguments that personhood should be based on quickening, viability, or neurophysiological criteria were considered and all were rejected. One basic argument was that all aspects of the situation surrounding the reproductive episode should be considered rather than focusing exclusive attention on the fetus. These other aspects include the woman and the social community. The woman is an existing person with the full status of moral agency in the eyes of the community, while the fetus is but a potential person, and known directly only to the woman. The argument was developed that the interests of an existing moral agent always trump those of a potential person. This argument was used to justify the permissibility of abortion until the point of birth. At the point of birth the neonate becomes a public member of the social community and must be regarded as a moral patient.

The restrictive and permissive positions regarding the morality of abortion were discussed in order to highlight some of the existing points of dispute, some basic policy considerations were identified, and a set of policy recommendations were made. The research literature supports the conclusion that the level of mortality and the incidence of psychological distress seem to be less for legal abortions than for normal childbirth. Many of the arguments used to support the regulation of reproduction and to determine family law can be argued to have a strongly sexist bias: Those attitudes and laws that affect both men and women seem fairly even-handed, while those that affect women alone are often punitive or paternalistic. It also seems to be the case that family law discriminates against the young and the very old.

REPRODUCTIVE TECHNOLOGIES

An interesting set of issues has arisen as a result of the new developments that have taken place to assist people who have fertility disorders to conceive and bear children. The techniques of artificial insemination and in vitro fertilization, as well as the use of surrogate mothers, bring several moral issues to the fore. A consideration of these issues helps to identify some of the underlying values that society uses to drive policy decisions. It seems that whenever the creation of life is concerned a deep-seated mysticism often is brought into play, and people appeal to a different set of principles than those involved in other matters regarding similar formal concerns regarding moral and commercial issues. The same level of emotionality can be seen when people discuss the Human Genome Project and when they consider the possibilities of genetic screening, cloning, and manipulations of the genome.

The task remains to extend the principles that I have developed here to consider issues and policies that relate to the end of life: The defining characteristics and moral implications of death, suicide, and euthanasia; the debate regarding the permissibility of organ transplants; the potential and the hazards involved in the aforementioned Human Genome Project.

A consideration of these topics requires a discussion of medical ethics, which leads to a general discussion of the practical and ethical issues involved in developing a national health care system. These considerations are now ongoing, and these issues are yielding to the analyses I have begun here.

If the principles I have outlined are comprehensive and universal enough to extend to all organic systems they should also prove sufficient to consider issues and policies pertaining to the status of nonhuman animals, as well as the human relationship to the overall ecology within which we operate and for which we have responsibility. These issues, too, seem to be yielding to the overall conceptual framework developed here.

Finally, I hope that the theory and data brought to bear on critical issues in social policy will be of some value to those who are charged with the responsibility to develop policies relating to the profound moral issues facing our society. I have stated previously that I consider it the responsibility of biological and social scientists to bring their peculiar talents and skills to bear on the solution of practical problems. I have done what I could toward achieving that goal.

References

Adler, N. E., David, H. P., Major, B. N., Roth, S. H., Russo, N. F., & Wyatt, G. E. (1992). Psychological factors in abortion: A review. *American Psychologist, 47*, 1194–1204.

Alexander, R. D. (1979). *Darwinism and human affairs*. Seattle, WA: University of Washington Press.

Alexander, R. D. (1987). *The biology of moral systems*. New York: Aldine de Gruyter.

Alexander, R. D. (1993). Biological considerations in the analysis of morality. In M. H. Nitecki & D. V. Nitecki (Eds.), *Evolutionary ethics* (pp. 163–196). Albany, NY: State University of New York Press.

American Medical Association, Council on Scientific Affairs. (1992). Induced termination of pregnancy before and after *Roe v Wade*. *Journal of the American Medical Association, 268*, 3231–3239.

Anand, K. J. S., & Hickey, P. R. (1992). Pain and its effects in the human neonate and fetus. *The New England Journal of Medicine, 317*, 1321–1329.

Anderson, J. R. (1990). *The adaptive character of thought*. Hillsdale, NJ: Erlbaum.

Andrews, L. B. (1987). The aftermath of baby M: Proposed state laws on surrogate motherhood. *Hastings Center Report, 17*(5), 31–40. (Reprinted in R. T. Hull (Ed.). (1990). *Ethical issues in the new reproductive technologies*. Belmont, CA: Wadsworth, pp. 186–210.)

Angier, N. (1994, May 17). Genetic mutation tied to father in most cases. *The New York Times*, Sec. B, p. 9.

Annas, G. J., & Elias, S. (1992). The major social policy issues raised by the human genome project. In G. J. Annas & S. Elias (Eds.), *Gene mapping* (pp. 3–17). New York: Oxford University Press.

Baker, R. R., & Bellis, M. A. (1988). "Kamikaze" sperm in mammals? *Animal Behaviour, 36*, 936–939.

Baker, R. R., & Bellis, M. A. (1989). Elaboration of the Kamikaze sperm hypothesis. *Animal Behaviour, 37*, 865–867.

Baker, R. R., & Bellis, M. A. (1992). Number of sperm in human ejaculates varies in accordance with sperm competition theory. *Animal Behaviour, 37*, 867–869.

Baker, R. R., & Bellis, M. A. (1993a). Human sperm competition: Ejaculate adjustment by males and the function of masturbation. *Animal Behaviour, 46*, 861–885.

Baker, R. R., & Bellis, M. A. (1993b). Human sperm competition: Ejaculate manipulation by females and a function for the female orgasm. *Animal Behaviour, 46*, 887–909.

Barkow, J. H., Cosmides, L, & Tooby, J. (1992). *The adapted mind.* New York: Oxford University Press

Barringer, F. (1992, December 19). U.S. ratio of abortions is lowest since late 70's. *The New York Times*, Sec. A. p. 1.

Bartholomew, G. A. (1953). Behavioral factors affecting social structure in the Alaska fur seal. *Transactions 18th N. American Wildlife Conference*, 481–502.

Bayles, M. D. (1984). *Reproductive ethics.* Englewood Cliffs, NJ: Prentice-Hall, pp. 33–51. (Reprinted in R. T. Hull (Ed.). (1990). *Ethical issues in the new reproductive technologies* [pp. 241–258]. Belmont, CA: Wadsworth).

Beck, J. (1994, January 5). Over-the-pill motherhood shouldn't be ethical worry. *The Oregonian* Sec. C, p. 9.

Becker, L. C. (1973). *On justifying moral judgments.* London: Routledge & Kegan Paul.

Beckner, M. (1974). Reduction, hierarchies and organicism. In F. J. Ayala & T. Dobzhansky (Eds.), *Studies in the philosophy of biology.* Berkeley: University of California Press, pp. 163–177.

Belkin, L. (1993, June, 19). Planned Parenthood starting to train doctors in abortion. *The New York Times* Sec. A, p. 1.

Bellis, M. A., & Baker, R. R. (1990). Do females promote sperm competition? Data for humans. *Animal Behaviour, 40,* 997–999.

Bellis, M. A., & Baker, R. R. (1992). *Human sperm competition: Ejaculate manipulation by males.* Paper presented to The Human Behavior and Evolution Society Meetings, July 26. University of New Mexico, Albuquerque, N.M.

Benn, S. I. (1973). Abortion, infanticide, and respect for persons. In J. Feinberg (Ed.), *Abortion.* Belmont, CA: Wadsworth, pp. 92–104.

Betzig, L. L. (1986). *Despotism and differential reproduction.* New York: Aldine.

Bickerton, D. (1990). *Language and species.* Chicago: University of Chicago Press.

Bloom, P. (In Press). Recent controversies in the study of language acquisition. In M. A. Gernsbacher (Ed.), *Handbook of psycholinguistics* (pp. 000–000). San Diego, CA: Academic Press.

Bolles, R. C. (1970) Species-specific defense reactions and avoidance learning. *Psychological Review, 77,* 32–48.

Boorse, C., & Sorensen, R. A. (1988). Ducking harm. *Journal of Philosophy, 85,* 115–134. (Reprinted in J. M. Fischer & M. Ravizza (1992). (Eds.), *Ethics: Problems and principles* [pp. 77–91]. New York: Harcourt, Brace Jovanovich.)

Bowlby, J. (1969). *Attachment.* New York: Basic Books.

Boyd, R., & Richerson, P. J. (1985). *Culture and the evolutionary process.* Chicago: University of Chicago Press.

Brandt, R. B. (1980). *The concept of a moral right and its function.* Paper presented at Virginia Polytechnic Institute and State University. (Reprinted in R. B. Brandt (Ed.). (1992). *Morality, utilitarianism, and rights* [pp. 179–195]. Cambridge, U.K.: Cambridge University Press.)

Brandt, R. B. (1987). Public policy and life and death decisions regarding defective newborns. In R. C. McMillan, H. T. Engelhardt, & S. F. Spicker (Eds.), *Euthanasia and the Newborn*, pp. 191–208. Dordrecht, Holland: D. Reidel. (Reprinted in R. B. Brandt (Ed.). (1992). *Morality, utilitarianism, and rights* [pp. 354–369]. Cambridge, U.K.: Cambridge University Press.)

Brink, D. O. (1992). Mill's deliberative utilitarianism. *Philosophy & Public Affairs, 21,* 69–103.

Brooke, E. H. (1994, April 12). Latin American abortions may outpace those in U.S. *The New York Times*, Sec. B, p. 10.

Brown, D. E. (1991). *Human universals.* New York: McGraw Hill.

Brown, L. M., & Gilligan, C. (1992). *Meeting at the crossroads*. Cambridge, MA: Harvard University Press.

Brunswik, E. (1952). The conceptual framework of psychology. In *International encyclopedia of unified science* (Vol. 1). Chicago: University of Chicago Press, pp. 1–102.

Brunswik, E. (1956). *Perception and the representative design of psychological experiments*. Berkeley: University of California Press.

Burnstein, E., Crandall, C., & Kitayama, S. (In Press). Some Neo-Darwinian decision rules for altruism: Weighing cues for inclusive fitness as a function of the biological importance of the decision. *Journal of Personality and Social Psychology*.

Buss, D. M. (1989). Sex differences in human mate preferences: Evolutionary hypotheses tested in 37 cultures. *Behavioral and Brain Sciences, 12*, 1–49.

Buss, D. M. (1994). *The evolution of desire*. New York: Basic Books.

Buss, D. M., & Schmitt, D. P. (1993). Sexual strategies theory: An evolutionary perspective on human mating. *Psychological Review, 100*, 204–232.

Caplan, A. L. (1986). The ethics of in vitro fertilization. *Primary Care, 13*, 241–253. (Reprinted in R. T. Hull (Ed.). (1990). *Ethical issues in the new reproductive technologies*. Belmont, CA: Wadsworth, pp. 96–108.)

Caplan, A. L. (1988). New technologies in reproduction—New ethical problems. *Annals NY Academy of Sciences, 530*, 73–82.

Caplan, A. L. (1992a). Introduction. In A. L. Caplan (Ed.), *If I were a rich man could I buy a pancreas?* Bloomington, IN: Indiana University Press, pp. xii–xvii.

Caporael, L. R., & Brewer, M. B. (1991). Evolutionary psychology. *Journal of Social Issues, 47*, (3), 1–195.

Chan, W-T. (1963). *A source book in Chinese philosophy*. Princeton, NJ: Princeton University Press.

Chira, S. (1994, January 2). Of a certain age, and in a family way. *The New York Times* Sec. 4, p. 5.

Chomsky, N. (1986). *Knowledge of language: Its nature, origin and use*. New York: Praeger.

Clarke, A. L., & Low, B. S. (1992). Ecological correlates of human dispersal in 19th century Sweden. *Animal Behaviour, 44*, 677–693.

Collins, J. A. (1994). Reproductive technology—The price of progress. *The New England Journal of Medicine, 331*, 270–271.

Collis, G. M. (1981). Social interaction with objects: A perspective on human infancy. In K. Immelmann, G. W. Barlow, L. Petrinovich, & M. Main (Eds.), *Behavioral development* (pp. 603–620). Cambridge, U.K.: Cambridge University Press.

Cook, R. (1991, June 18). Perspective on the abortion pill: Is a flat ban ethical? *Los Angeles Times*, Sec. B, p. 7.

Corea, G. (1986). The subversive sperm: "A false strain of blood." In G. Corea, *The mother machine* (pp. 34–48). New York: Harper & Row. (Reprinted in R. T. Hull, (Ed.). (1990). *Ethical issues in the new reproductive technologies*. [pp. 56–68] Belmont, CA: Wadsworth.)

Cosmides, L., & Tooby, J. (1987). From evolution to behavior: Evolutionary psychology as the missing link. In J. Dupre (Ed.), *The latest on the best: Essays on evolution and optimality*. Cambridge, MA: MIT Press, pp. 277–306.

Cosmides, L., & Tooby, J. (1992). Cognitive adaptations for social exchange. In J. H. Barkow, L. Cosmides, & J. Tooby (Eds.), *The adapted mind* (pp. 163–228). New York: Oxford University Press.

Cronk, L. (1993). Parental favoritism toward daughters. *American Scientist, 81*, 272–279.

Crow, J. F. (1988). The importance of recombination. In R. E. Michod & B. R. Levin (Eds.), *The evolution of sex: An examination of current ideas*. Sunderland, MA: Sinauer, pp. 56–73.

Daly, M., & Wilson, M. (1984). A sociobiological analysis of human infanticide. In G. Hausfater & S. B. Hrdy (Eds.), *Infanticide: Comparative and evolutionary perspectives* (pp. 487–502). Hawthorne, NY: Aldine.

Daly, M., & Wilson, M. (1988). *Homicide.* New York: Aldine de Gruyter.

Daly, M., & Wilson, M. (1990). Is parent-offspring conflict sex-linked? Freudian and Darwinian models. *Journal of Personality, 58,* 163–189.

Damasio, H., Grabowski, T., Frank, A., Galaburda, A. M., & Damasio, A. R. (1994). The return of Phineas Gage: Clues about the brain from the skull of a famous patient. *Science, 264,* 1102–1105.

Daniels, N. (1979). Wide reflective equilibrium and theory acceptance in ethics. *The Journal of Philosophy, 76,* 256–282.

Darlington, C. D. (1969). *The evolution of man and society.* New York: Simon & Schuster.

Darwin, C. (1859). *On the origin of species by means of natural selection.* New York: D. Appleton.

Darwin, C. (1871). *The descent of man.* New York: D. Appleton.

Darwin, C. (1887). *The autobiography of Charles Darwin.* London: John Murray.

Davis, N. (1993). The abortion debate: The search for common ground, Part 2. *Ethics, 103,* 731–778.

De Caspar, A. J., & Spence, M. J. (1986). Prenatal maternal speech influences newborns' perception of speech sounds. *Infant Behavior and Development, 9,* 133–150.

Degler, C. N. (1991). *In search of human nature.* Oxford: Oxford University Press.

Devine, P. E. (1978). *The ethics of homicide.* Cornell: Cornell University Press.

Diamond, J. (1992a). Our phantom children. *Natural History, 101,* 18–23.

Diamond, J. (1992b). *The third chimpanzee.* New York: HarperCollins.

Dickey, K. (1992). Why I may count the numbers. In J. M. Fischer & M. Ravizza (Eds.), *Ethics: Problems and principles.* NY: Harcourt, Brace Jovanovich, pp. 244–250.

Donagan, A. (1972). *The theory of morality.* Chicago: University of Chicago Press.

Donceel, J. F. (1970). A liberal catholic's view. In R. E. Hall (Ed.), *Abortion in a changing world,* (Vol. I). New York: Columbia University Press. (Reprinted in J. Feinberg (Ed.). (1984). *The problem of abortion* [pp. 15–20]. Belmont, CA: Wadsworth.

Dworkin, R. (1989). The original position. In N. Daniels (Ed.), *Reading Rawls* (pp. 16–53). Stanford, CA: Stanford University Press.

Dworkin, R. (1993). *Life's dominion.* New York: Knopf.

Ellis, H. D. (1992). A wise child: Face perception by human neonates. *Behavioral and Brain Sciences, 15,* 514–515.

Emde, R. N., & Gaensbauer T. (1981). Some emerging models of emotion in human infancy. In K. Immelmann, G. W. Barlow, L. Petrinovich, & M. Main (Eds.), *Behavioral development* (pp. 568–588). Cambridge, U.K.: Cambridge University Press.

English, J. (1975). Abortion and the concept of a person. *Canadian Journal of Philosophy, 5,* 233–243. (Reprinted in J. Feinberg (Ed.). (1984). The problem of abortion [pp. 151–160]. Belmont, CA: Wadsworth.)

Espmark, Y. (1971). Individual recognition by voice in reindeer mother-young relationship. Field observation and playback experiments. *Behaviour, 40,* 295–301.

Etcoff, N. L., & Magee, J. J. (1992). Categorical perception of facial expressions. *Cognition, 44,* 227–240.

Fahn, S. (1992). Fetal-tissue transplants in Parkinson's disease. *New England Journal of Medicine, 327,* 1589–1590.

Faludi, S. (1991). *Backlash: The undeclared war against American women.* New York: Crown Publishers.

Feinberg, J. (1980). Potentiality, development, and rights. In T. Regan (Ed.), *Matters of life and death.* New York: Random House, 1980. (Reprinted in J. Feinberg (Ed.). (1984). *The problem of abortion* [pp. 145–150]. Belmont, CA: Wadsworth.)

Feinberg, J. (1986). *Harm to self.* Oxford: Oxford University Press.

Feinberg, J. (1989). Rawls and intuitionism. In N. Daniels (Ed.), *Reading Rawls.* Stanford, CA: Stanford University Press, pp. 108–124.

Feingold, A. (1992). Gender differences in mate selection preferences: A test of the parental investment model. *Psychological Bulletin, 112,* 125–139.

Fernald, A. (1992). Human maternal vocalizations to infants as biologically relevant signals: An evolutionary perspective. In J. H. Barkow, L. Cosmides, & J. Tooby (Eds.), *The adapted mind* (pp. 391–428). New York: Oxford University Press.

Fetzer, J. H. (1992). *Ethics and evolution.* Paper presented at The Human Behavior and Evolution Society Meetings, July 25, University of New Mexico, Albuquerque, NM.

Figueredo, A. J. (1992). *Preparedness and plasticity: A stochastic optimality theory.* Paper presented at The Human Behavior Society Meetings, July 23. University of New Mexico, Albuquerque, NM.

Fischer, J. M., & Ravizza, M. (1991). *Thomson and the trolley.* Department of Philosophy, University of California, Riverside.

Fischer, J. M., & Ravizza M. (1992). *Ethics: Problems and principles.* Orlando, FL: Harcourt, Brace Jovanovich.

Fisher, R. A. (1930). *The genetical theory of natural selection.* Oxford: Clarendon Press.

Fleischman, L. M. (1990, March 18). What abortion debate is really about: When is killing permitted? *The Los Angeles Times,* Sec. M, p. 1.

Ford C. S., & Beach, F. A. (1951). *Patterns of sexual behavior.* New York: Harper & Row.

Forer, L. G. (1991). *Unequal protection: Women, children, and the elderly in court.* New York: W. W. Norton.

Fox, M. A. (1986). *The case for animal experimentation.* Berkeley, CA: University of California Press.

Fox, R. C., & Swazey, J. P. (1992). *Spare parts.* Oxford: Oxford University Press.

Frantz, W. (1991, June 20). Perspectives on the "abortion pill": Should we remove restrictions? *The Los Angeles Times,* Sec. B, p. 7.

Freed, C. R. et al. (1992). Survival of implanted fetal dopamine cells and neurologic improvement 12 to 46 months after transplantation for Parkinson's disease. *The New England Journal of Medicine, 327,* 1549–1555.

Gallistel, C. R., Brown, A. L., Carey, S., Gelman, R., & Keil, F. C. (1991). Lessons from animal learning for the study of cognitive development. In S. Carey & R. Gelman (Eds.), *The epigenesis of mind: Essays on biology and cognition.* Hillsdale, NJ: Erlbaum, pp. 3–36.

Garcia, J., & Brett, L. P. (1977). Conditioned responses to food order and taste in rats and wild predators. In M. Kare (Ed.), *The chemical senses and nutrition* (pp. 277–289). New York: Academic Press.

Gewirth, A. (1993). How ethical is evolutionary ethics? In M. H. Nitecki, & D. V. Nitecki (Eds.), *Evolutionary ethics* (pp. 241–256). Albany, NY: State University of New York.

Gibson, J. J. (1950). *The perception of the visual world.* Boston: Houghton Mifflin.

Gibson, J. J. (1986). *The ecological approach to visual perception.* Hillsdale, NJ: Erlbaum.

Gifford, D. (1990). *The farther shore.* New York: Atlantic Monthly Press.

Gigerenzer, G., & Hug, K. (1992). Domain-specific reasoning: Social contracts, cheating, and perspective change. *Cognition, 43,* 127–171.

Gigerenzer, G., & Murray, D. J. (1987). *Cognition as intuitive statistics.* Hillsdale, NJ: Erlbaum.

Gillespie, N. C. (1977). Abortion and human rights. *Ethics, 87,* 237–243. (Reprinted in J. Feinberg (Ed.). (1984). *The problem of abortion* [pp. 94–101]. (1984). Belmont, CA: Wadsworth.)

Gillett, G. (1993). "Ought" and well-being. *Inquiry, 36,* 287–306.

Gilligan, C. (1982). *In a different voice.* Cambridge, MA: Harvard University Press.

Gilligan, C., & Attanucci, J. (1988). Two moral orientations: Gender differences and similarities. *Merrill-Palmer Quarterly, 34*, 223–236.

Glasier, A., Thong, K. J., Dewar, M., Mackie, M., & Baird, D. T. (1992). Mifepristone (RU 486) compared with high-dose estrogen and progestogen for emergency postcoital contraception. *New England Journal of Medicine, 327*, 1041–1044.

Goddard, G. V. (1980). Component properties of the memory machine: Hebb revisited. In P. W. Jusczyk & R. M. Klein (Eds.), *The nature of thought*. Hillsdale, NJ: Erlbaum.

Goodman, E. (1992, May 5). Ownership over frozen embryos latest absurdity. *The Oregonian*, Sec. B, p. 9.

Goodman, P. (1972). *Little prayers and finite experience*. New York: Harper & Row.

Gould, S. J. (1977). *Ontogeny and phylogeny*. Cambridge, MA: Harvard University Press.

Greenfield, P. M. (1991). Language, tools and brain: The ontogeny and phylogeny of hierarchically organized sequential behavior. *Behavioral and Brain Sciences, 14*, 531–551.

Greenhouse, L. (1992, June 30). High court, 5-4, affirms right to abortion but allows most of Pennsylvania's limits. *The New York Times*, Sec. A, p. 1.

Greenhouse, L. (1993, Feb. 23). Supreme Court roundup. *The New York Times*, Sec. A, p. 8.

Greenough, W. T., Black, J. E., & Wallace, C. S. (1987). Experience and brain development. *Child Development, 58*, 539–559.

Grice, P. (1991). *The conception of value*. Oxford: Oxford University Press.

Gruson, L. (1993, Feb. 16). A mother's gift: Bearing her grandchild. *The New York Times*, Sec. B, p. 1.

Hack, M., & Fanaroff, A. A. (1989). Outcomes of extremely low-birth-weight infants between 1982 and 1988. *New England Journal of Medicine, 321*, 1642–1647.

Haig, D. (1993). Genetic conflicts in human pregnancy. The *Quarterly Review of Biology, 68*, 495–532.

Halliday, T. (1980). *Sexual strategy*. Chicago: University of Chicago Press.

Hamilton, W. D., Axelrod, R., & Tanese, R. (1990). Sexual reproduction as an adaptation to resist parasites (A review). *Proceedings National Academy of Sciences, U. S. A., 87*, 3566–3573.

Hammond, K. R. (1966). *The psychology of Egon Brunswik*. New York: Holt.

Hardin, G. (1972). *Exploring new ethics for survival*. New York: Viking.

Hare, R. M. (1975). Abortion and the golden rule. *Philosophy and Public Affairs, 4*, 201–222.

Hare, R. M. (1989). Rawls' theory of justice. In N. Daniels (Ed.), *Reading Rawls*. Stanford, CA: Stanford University Press, pp. 81–107.

Harris, J. (1992). *Wonderwoman and superman*. Oxford: Oxford University Press.

Hebb, D. O. (1949). *The organization of behavior*. New York: Wiley.

Herman, L. M. (1988). The language of animal language research: Reply to Schusterman and Gisiner. *The Psychological Record, 38*, 349–362.

Herman, L. M., Kuczaj II, S. A., & Holder, M. D. (1993). Responses to anomalous gestural sequences by a language-trained dolphin: Evidence for processing of semantic relations and syntactic information. *Journal of Experimental Psychology: General, 122*, 184–194.

Hills, P. J. (1991, April 6). Fetal tissue use: Personal agony in medical first. *The New York Times*, Sec. A, p. 1.

Hilts, P. J. (1994, May 17). Reliable and politically sensitive. *The New York Times*, Sec. A, p. 8.

Hochberg, J. (1988). Visual perception. In R. C. Atkinson, R. Herrnstein, G. Lindzey & R. D. Luce (Eds.), *Stevens' handbook of experimental psychology* (2nd ed., pp. 195–276). New York: Wiley.

Holmes, S. A. (1991, May 12). U.S. set to change abortion policies. *The New York Times*, Sec. A, p. 11.

Howe, M. L., & Courage, M. L. (1993). On resolving the enigma of infantile amnesia. *Psychological Bulletin, 113*, 305–326.

Hrdy, S. B., & Hausfater, G. (1984). Comparative and evolutionary perspectives on infanticide: Introduction and overview. In Hausfater, G. & Hrdy, S. B. (Eds.), *Infanticide* (pp. xiii–xxxv). Hawthorne, NY: Aldine.

Huebner, A. M., & Garrod, A. C. (1993). Moral reasoning among Tibetan monks. *Journal of Cross-Cultural Psychology, 24,* 167–185.

Hull, R. T. (1990). *Ethical issues in reproductive technologies.* Belmont, CA: Wadsworth.

Immelmann, K., & Suomi, S. (1981). Sensitive phases in development. In K. Immelmann, G. Barlow, L. Petrinovich & M. Main (Eds.), *Behavioral development* (pp. 395–431). Cambridge, U.K.: Cambridge University Press.

Jacobs, B., & Raleigh, M. J. (1992). Attachment: How early, how far? *Behavioral and Brain Sciences, 15,* 517.

Johnson, K. (1992, August 17). Child abuse is ruled out in mother's use of cocaine. *The New York Times,* Sec. B, p. 1.

Joshi, V. (1992, October 10). Scientists announce a birth-control vaccine. *The Oregonianddditive fallacy. Ethics, 99,* 5–31.

Kalil, K. E. (1989). Synapse formation in the developing brain. *Scientific American, 264,* 76–85.

Kamm, F. M. (1992). *Creation and abortion.* Oxford: Oxford University Press.

Kaufman, S. A. (1993). *The origins of order.* Oxford: Oxford University Press.

Keller, E. F. (1992). Language and ideology in evolutionary theory. In E. F. Keller (Ed.), *Secrets of life, secrets of death.* New York: Routledge.

Kellert, S. R., & Wilson, E. O. (1993). *The biophilia hypothesis.* Washington, DC: Island Press.

Kenrick, D. T., & Keefe, R. C. (1992). Age preferences in mates reflect sex differences in human reproductive strategies. *Behavioral and Brain Sciences, 15,* 75–91.

King, P. A. (1980). The juridical status of the fetus: A proposal for the protection of the unborn. In C. E. Schneider & M. A. Vinovskis (Eds.), *The law and politics of abortion* (pp. 81–121). Lexington, MA: D. C. Heath. (Reprinted in J. L. Garfield & P. Hennessey (Eds.). (1984). *Abortion: Moral and legal perspectives* [pp. 57–80]. Amherst, MA: University of Massachusetts Press.)

Kitcher, P. (1985). *Vaulting ambition.* Cambridge, MA: MIT Press.

Kleinig, J. (1991). *Valuing life.* Princeton, NJ: Princeton University Press.

Knauft, B. M. (1991). Violence and sociality in human evolution. *Current Anthropology, 32,* 391–428.

Kohlberg, L. (1971). From is to ought: How to commit the naturalistic fallacy and get away with it. In T. Mischel (Ed.), *Cognitive development and epistemology* (pp. 151–235). San Diego, CA: Academic Press.

Kolata, G. (1992, September 1). Linguists debate study classifying language as innate human skill. *The New York Times,* Sec. B, p. 6.

Kolata, G. (1992b). Defect detected in embryo just days old. *The New York Times,* Sec. A, p. 1.

Kolberg, R. (1993). Human embryo cloning reported. *Science, 262,* 652–653.

Kraemer, G. W. (1992). A psychobiological theory of attachment. *Behavioral and Brain Sciences, 15,* 493–511.

Kroodsma, D., & Baylis, J. R. (1982). Appendix: A world survey of evidence for vocal learning in birds. In D. E. Kroodsma & E. H. Miller (Eds.), *Acoustic communication in birds* (Vol 2, pp. 311–337). New York: Academic Press.

Kuhl, P. K., Williams, K. A., Lacerda, F., Stevens, K. N., & Lindblom, B. (1992). Linguistic experience alters phonetic perception in infants by 6 months of age. *Science, 255,* 606–608.

Lader, L. (1966). *Abortion.* Boston: Beacon Press.

Lamb, M. E., Thompson, R. A., Gardner, W. P., Chornov, E. L., & Estes, D. (1984). Security of infantile attachment as assessed in the "strange situation": Its study and biological interpretation. *Behavioral and Brain Sciences, 7,* 127–171.

Lancaster, J. B. (1986). Human adolescence and reproduction: An evolutionary evolutionary perspective. In J. B. Lancaster & B. A. Hamberg (Eds.), *School-age pregnancy and parenthood: Biosocial dimensions* (pp. 17–37). Hawthorne, NY: Aldine.

Lashley, K. (1958). Cerebral organization and behavior. *Proceedings of the Association for Research in Nervous and Mental Disease, 36*, 1–18. (Reprinted in, F. A. Beach, D. O. Hebb, C. T. Morgan, & H. Nissen (Eds.). (1960) *The neuropsychology of K. S. Lashley* [pp. 529–543]. New York: McGraw-Hill.)

Lau, D. C. (1963). *Lao Tzu: Tao Te Ching.* New York: Penguin Books.

Leary, W. E. (1993, April 23). Maker of abortion pill reaches licensing pact with U.S. group. *The New York Times*, Sec. A, p. 18.

Lettvin, J. Y., Maturana, H. R., McCulloch, W. S., & Pitts, W. H. (1959). What the frog's eye tells the frog's brain. *Proceedings of the Institute of Radio Engineers, 47*, 1940–1951.

Lewin, T. (1994, May 20). When the death of a fetus is murder. *The New York Times*, Sec. B, p. 14.

Lewontin, R. C. (1994). Women versus the biologists. *The New York Review of Books, 41*(7), 31–35.

Lieberman, P. (1990). "Not invented here." *Behavioral and Brain Sciences, 13*, 741–742.

Lin Yutang (1938). *The wisdom of Confucius.* New York: Random House.

Locke, J. (1993). *The child's path to spoken language.* Cambridge, MA: Harvard University Press.

Lomasky, L. E. (1982). Being a person—Does it matter? *Philosophical Topics, 12.* (Reprinted in J. Feinberg (Ed.) (1984). *The problem of abortion* (pp. 161–172). Belmont, CA: Wadsworth.)

Lorenz, K. (1935/1970). Companions as factors in the bird's environment. *Journal of Ornithologie, 83*, 137–213. (Reprinted in K. Lorenz, (1970). *Studies in animal and human behaviour,* [Vol. 1, pp. 101–258]. Cambridge, MA: Harvard University Press.)

Macklin, R. (1984). Personhood and the abortion debate. In J. L. Garfield & P. Hennessey (Eds.), *Abortion: Moral and legal perspectives* (pp. 81–102). (1984). Amherst, MA: University of Massachusetts Press.

Mahowald, M. B., Silver, J., & Ratcheson, R. A. (1987). The ethical options in transplanting fetal tissue. *Hastings Center Report, 17*, 9–15. (Reprinted in R. T. Hull (Ed.). (1990). *Ethical issues in the new reproductive technologies* [pp. 259–271]. Belmont, CA: Wadsworth.)

Marler, P. (1970). A comparative approach to vocal learning: Song development in white-crowned sparrows. *Journal of Comparative and Physiological Psychology, 71*, 1–25.

Marler, P. (1976). Sensory templates in species-specific behavior. In J. C. Fentress (Ed.), *Simpler networks and behavior.* Sunderland MA: Sinauer, pp. 314–329.

Masters, R. D. (1982). Is sociobiology reactionary? The political implications of inclusive-fitness theory. *The Quarterly Review of Biology, 57*, 275–292.

Mayr, E. (1980). Prologue: Some thoughts on the history of the evolutionary synthesis. In E. Mayr & W. B. Provine, *The evolutionary synthesis: Perspectives on the unification of biology* (pp. 1–48). Cambridge, MA: Harvard University Press.

Mayr, E. (1982). *The growth of biological thought.* Cambridge, MA: Harvard University Press.

Medical Task Force on Anencephaly. (1990). *The infant with anencephaly.* New England Journal of Medicine, 322, 669–674.

Meier, R. P. (1991). Language acquisition by deaf children. *American Scientist, 79*, 60–70.

Mill, J. S. (1859). *On liberty.* London. (Reprinted in M. Warnock (1947). *John Stuart Mill* (pp. 126–250). New York: Meridian Press.

Miller, N. E. (1983). Understanding the use of animals in behavioral research: Some critical issues. *Annals NY Academy of Sciences, 406*, 113–118.

Milner, P. (1957). The cell assembly: Mark II. *Psychological Review, 64*, 242–252.

Modgil, S., & Modgil, C. (1985). *Lawrence Kohlberg: Consensus and controversy.* Philadelphia: Falmer.

Moore, G. E. (1903). *Principia ethica.* Cambridge, U.K.: Cambridge University Press.

Murdock, G. P., & White, D. R. (1969). Standard cross-cultural sample. *Ethnology, 8,* 329–369.

Murray, T. H. (1987). Moral obligations to the not-yet-born: The fetus as patient. *Clinics in Perinatology, 14,* 329–343. (Reprinted in R. T. Hull (Ed.). (1990). *Ethical issues in the new reproductive technologies* [pp. 210–223]. Belmont, CA: Wadsworth.)

Nagel, T. (1979). Death. In T. Nagel (Ed.), *Mortal questions.* Cambridge, U.K.: Cambridge University Press, pp. 1–10.

Nelson, L. J., & Milliken, N. (1988). Compelled medical treatment of pregnant women: Life, liberty, and law in conflict. *Journal of the American Medical Association, 259,* 1060–1066. (Reprinted in R. T. Hull (Ed.). (1990). *Ethical issues in the new reproductive technologies* [pp. 222–240]. Belmont, CA: Wadsworth.)

Neumann, P. J. Gharib, S. D., & Weinstein, M. C. (1994). The cost of a successful delivery with in vitro fertilization. *The New England Journal of Medicine, 331,* 239–243.

Newport, E. (1991). Contrasting conceptions of the critical period for language. In S. Carey & R. Gelman (Eds.), *The epigenesis of mind.* Hillsdale, NJ: Erlbaum, pp. 111–130.

Nozick, R. (1983, November 27). About mammals and people. *New York Times Book Review,* p. 11.

Parker, G. A. (1982). Why so many tiny sperm? The maintenance of two sexes with internal fertilization. *Journal of Theoretical Biology, 96,* 281–294.

Pascal, L. (1980). Judgement day or the handwriting on the wall. *Inquiry, 23,* 242–251. (Reprinted in P. Singer (Ed.). (1986). *Applied ethics* [pp. 105–123]. Oxford: Oxford University Press.)

Pear, R. (1992, October 26). Fertility clinics face crackdown. *The New York Times,* Sec. A, p. 7.

Petitto, L. A., & Marentette, P. F. (1991). Babbling in the manual mode: Evidence for the ontogeny of language. *Science, 251,* 1493–1496.

Petrinovich, L. (1972). Psychological mechanisms in language development. In G. Newton & A. H. Riesen (Eds.), *Advances in psychobiology* (Vol. 1, pp. 259–285). New York: Wiley.

Petrinovich, L. (1973a). A species-meaningful analysis of habituation. In H. V. S. Peeke & M. J. Herz (Eds.), *Habituation: Behavioral studies* (Vol. 1). New York: Academic, pp. 141–162.

Petrinovich, L. (1973b). Darwin and the representative expression of reality. In P. Ekman (Ed.), *Darwin and facial expression.* New York: Academic, pp. 223–256.

Petrinovich, L. (1974). Individual recognition of pup vocalization by Norther Elephant Seal mothers. *Zeitschrift fur Tierpsychologie, 34,* 308–312.

Petrinovich, L. (1976). Molar reductionism. In L. Petrinovich & J. L. McGaugh (Eds.), *Knowing, thinking, and believing.* New York: Plenum, pp. 11–27.

Petrinovich, L. (1979). Probabilistic functionalism: A conception of research method. *American Psychologist, 34,* 373–390.

Petrinovich, L. (1981). A method for the study of development. In K. Immelmann, G. Barlow, L. Petrinovich, & M. Main (Eds.), *Behavioral development.* Cambridge, U.K.: Cambridge University Press, pp. 90–130.

Petrinovich, L. (1988). The role of social factors in white-crowned sparrow song development. In T. Zentall & B. G. Galef (Eds.), *Social learning: Psychological and biological approaches* (pp. 255–278). Hillsdale, NJ: Erlbaum.

Petrinovich, L. (1989). Representative design and the quality of generalization. In L. W. Poon, D. C. Rubin, & B. A. Wilson (Eds.), *Everyday cognition in adulthood and late life* (pp. 11–24). Cambridge, U.K.: Cambridge University Press.

Petrinovich, L. (1990). Avian song development: Methodological and conceptual issues. In D. A. Dewsbury (Ed.), *Contemporary issues in comparative psychology* (pp. 340–359). Sunderland, MA: Sinauer.

Petrinovich, L., & O'Neill, P. (1995). The influence of wording and framing of questions on moral intuitions. *Ethology and Sociobiology.* (In press.)

Petrinovich, L., & O'Neill, P. (1994). A cross-cultural study of moral intuitions. Unpublished manuscript.

Petrinovich, L., O'Neill, P., & Jorgensen, M, (1992). *An ethogram of moral intuitions.* Paper presented at The Human Behavior and Evolution Society Meetings July 23. University of New Mexico, Albuquerque, NM.

Petrinovich, L., O'Neill, P. & Jorgensen, M. (1993). An empirical study of moral intuitions: Toward an evolutionary ethics. *Journal of Personality and Social Psychology, 64,* 467–478.

Piaget, J. (1932). *The moral judgment of the child.* London: Paul.

Pinker, S. (1994). *The language instinct.* New York: Morrow.

Pinker, S., & Bloom, P. (1990). Natural language and natural selection. *Behavioral and Brain Sciences, 13,* 707–727.

Plomin, R. (1981). Ethological behavioral genetics and development. In K. Immelmann, G. W. Barlow, L. Petrinovich & M. Main (Eds.), *Behavioral development.* Cambridge, U.K.: Cambridge University Press, pp. 252–276.

Poizner, H., Klima, E. S., & Bellugi, U. (1987). *What the hands reveal about the brain.* Cambridge, MA: MIT Press.

Proctor, R. N. (1992). Genomics and eugenics: How fair is the comparison? In G. J. Annas & S. Elias (Eds.), *Gene Mapping* (pp. 57–93). New York: Oxford University Press.

Profet, M. (1992). Pregnancy sickness as adaptation: A deterrent to maternal ingestion of teratogens. In J. H. Barkow, L. Cosmides, & J. Tooby (Eds.), *The adapted mind* (pp. 327–365). New York: Oxford University Press.

Quinn, W. S. (1989). Actions, intentions and consequences: The doctrine of double effect. *Philosophy and Public Affairs, 8,* 334–351. Reprinted in J. M. Fischer & M. Ravizza (Eds.) (1992). *Ethics: Problems and principles* (pp. 179–190). New York: Harcourt, Brace Javanovich.

Rachels, J. (1986). *The end of life.* Oxford: Oxford University Press.

Rachels, J. (1990). *Created from animals.* Oxford: Oxford University Press.

Rakic, P., Bourgeois, J.-P., Eckenhoff, M. F., Zecevic, N., & Goldman-Rakic, P. S. (1986). Concurrent overproduction of synapses in diverse regions of the primate cerebral cortex. *Science, 232,* 232–235.

Ratzinger J. C., & Bovone, A. (1987). *Congregation for the doctrine of the faith. Instruction on respect for human life in its origin and on the dignity of procreation: Replies to certain questions of the day.* Boston: St. Paul Editions. (Reprinted in R. T. Hull (Ed.). (1990). *Ethical issues: The new reproductive technologies* [pp. 21–39]. Belmont, CA: Wadsworth.)

Rawls, J. (1971). *A theory of justice.* Cambridge, MA: Harvard University Press.

Regan, T. (1983). *The case for animal rights.* Berkeley: University of California Press.

Regelson, W. (1992). RU 486: How abortion politics have impacted on a potentially useful drug of broad medical application. *Perspectives in Biology and Medicine, 35,* 330–338.

Reynolds, V. (1991). Socioecology of religion. In M. Maxwell (Ed.), *The sociobiological imagination* (pp. 205–222). Albany, NY: State University of New York Press.

Richards, R. J. (1987). *Darwin and the emergence of evolutionary theories of mind and behavior.* Chicago: University of Chicago Press.

Richards, R. J. (1993). Birth, death, and resurrection of evolutionary ethics. In M. H. Nitecki & D. V. Nitecki (Eds.), *Evolutionary ethics* (pp. 113–131). Albany, NY: State University of New York Press.

Riding, A. (199, November 17). New catechism for Catholics defines sins of modern world. *The New York Times,* Sec. A., p. 1.

Riding, A. (1994, January 5). French government proposes ban on pregnancies after menopause. *The New York Times,* Sec. A, p. 4.

Rimer, S. (1993, March 31). Abortion clinics search for doctors in scarcity. *The New York Times*, Sec. A, p. 7.

Robertson, J. A. (1983). Surrogate mothers: The case for and against. *Hastings Center Report*, 13, 28–34). (Reprinted in R. T. Hull (Ed.). (1990). *Ethical issues in the new reproductive technologies* [pp. 156–166]. Belmont, CA: Wadsworth.)

Robey, B., Rutstein, S. O., & Morris, L. (1993) The fertility decline in developing countries. *Scientific American, 269,* 60–67.

Rodd, R. (1990). *Biology, ethics and animals.* Oxford: Oxford University Press.

Rowe, D. (1994). *The limits of family influence.* New York: Guilford Press.

Ruse, M. (1979). *Sociobiology: Sense or nonsense?* Dordrecht, Holland: D. Reidel.

Ruse, M. (1993). The new evolutionary ethics. In M. H. Nitecki & D. V. Nitecki (Eds.), *Evolutionary ethics* (pp. 133–162). Albany, NY: State University of New York Press.

Ruse M., & Wilson, E. O. (1986). Moral philosophy as applied science. *Philosophy, 61,* 173–192.

Russell, B. (1977). On the relative strictness of negative and positive duties. *American Philosophical Quarterly, 14,* 87–97. (Reprinted in J. M. Fischer & M. Ravizza (Eds.). (1992). *Ethics: Problems and principles* [pp. 122–133]. New York: Harcourt, Brace Jovanovich.)

Schonfeld, M. (1992). Who or what has moral standing. *American Philosophical Quarterly, 29,* 353–362.

Scrimshaw, S. C. M. (1984). Infanticide in human populations: Societal and individual concerns. In G. Hausfater & S. B. Hrdy (Eds.), *Infanticide: Comparative and evolutionary perspectives.* Hawthorne, NY: Aldine, pp. 439–462.

Seelye, K. Q. (1994, May 17). Accord opens way for abortion pill in U.S. in 2 years. *The New York Times,* Sec. A, p. 1.

Seger J., & Hamilton, W. D. (1988). Parasites and sex. In R. E. Michod & B. R. Levin (Eds.), *The evolution of sex: An examination of current ideas.* Sunderland, MA: Sinauer, pp. 176–193.

Shatz, C. J. (1992). The developing brain. *Scientific American, 267,* 60–67.

Shepard, R. (1987). Evolution of a mesh between principles of the mind and regularities of the world. In J. Dupre (Ed.), *The latest on the best: Essays on evolution and optimality* (pp. 251–275). Cambridge, MA: MIT Press.

Shuster, E. (1992). Determinism and reductionism: A greater threat because of the human genome project? In G. J. Annas & S. Elias (Eds.), *Gene mapping* (pp. 115–127). New York: Oxford University Press.

Simpson, J. A., & Gangestad, S. W. (1992). Sociosexuality and romantic partner choice. *Journal of Personality, 60,* 31–51.

Singer, P. (1975). *Animal liberation.* New York: Avon Books.

Singer, P. (1990). *Animal liberation* (Rev. Ed.). New York: Avon Books.

Smart, J. J. C. (1973). An outline of a system of utilitarian ethics. In J. J. C. Smart & B. Williams (Eds.), *Utilitarianism: For and against* (pp. 1–74). Cambridge, U.K.: Cambridge Univerity Press.

Smith, E. A. (1987). Optimization theory in anthropology: Applications and critiques. In J. Dupre (Ed.), *The latest on the best: Essays on evolution and optimality* (pp. 201–249). Cambridge, MA: Harvard University Press.

Smothers, R. (1992, May 2). Court gives ex-husband rights on use of embryos. *The New York Times,* Sec. A, p. 1.

Snarey, J. R. (1985). Cross-cultural universality of social-moral development: A critical review of Kohlbergian research. *Psychological Bulletin, 97,* 202–232.

Snell, G. D. (1988). *Search for a rational ethic.* New York: Springer-Verlag.

Sober, E. (1984). *The nature of selection.* Cambridge, MA: MIT Press.

Sober, E. (1987). What is adaptationism? In J. Dupre (Ed.), *The latest on the best: Essays on evolution and optimality* (pp. 105–118). Cambridge, MA: Harvard University Press.

Sosa, D. (1993). Consequences of consequentialism. *Mind, 102,* 101–122.

Spencer, D. D., et al. (1992). Unilateral transplantation of human fetal mesencephalic tissue into the caudate nucleus of patients with Parkinson's disease. *New England Journal of Medicine, 327,* 1541–1548.

Stebbins, G. L. (1971). *Processes of organic evolution* (2nd Ed.) Engelwood Cliffs, NJ: Prentice-Hall.

Steinbock, B. (1992). *Life before birth.* Oxford: Oxford University Press.

Studdert-Kennedy, M. (1990). This view of language. *Behavioral and Brain Sciences, 13,* 758–759.

Sulloway, F. J. (1979). *Freud: Biologist of the mind.* New York: Basic Books.

Sumner, L. W. (1981). *Abortion and moral theory.* Princeton, NJ: Princeton University Press.

Taurek, J. (1977). Should the numbers count? *Philosophy and Public Affairs, 6,* 293–316. (Reprinted in J. M. Fischer & M. Ravizza (Eds.). (1992). *Ethics: Problems and principles* [pp. 215–227]. New York: Harcourt, Brace Jovanovich.)

Terry, D. (1993, December 15). Illinois fight on Caesarian pits mother against fetus. *The New York Times,* Sec. A, p. 11.

Thomson, J. J. (1971). A defense of abortion. *Philosophy and Public Affairs, 1,* 47–66.

Thomson, J. J. (1976). Killing, letting die, and the trolley problem. *The Monist, 59,* 204–217. (Reprinted in J. M. Fischer & M. Ravizza (Eds.). (1992). *Ethics: Problems and principles* [pp. 67–77]. New York: Harcourt, Brace Jovanovich.)

Thornhill, N. W. (1991). An evolutionary analysis of rules regulating human inbreeding and marriage. *Behavioral and Brain Sciences, 14,* 247–261.

Thorpe, W. H. (1961). *Bird-song.* Cambridge, U.K.: Cambridge University Press.

Tooby, J., & Cosmides, L. (1990a). On the universality of human nature and the uniqueness of the individual: The role of genetics and adaptation. *Journal of Personality, 58,* 1–67.

Tooby, J., & Cosmides, L. (1990b). Toward an adaptationist psycholinguistics. *Behavioral and Brain Sciences, 13,* 760–762.

Tooby, J., & Cosmides, L. (1992). The psychological foundations of culture. In J. H. Barkow, L. Cosmides, & J. Tooby (Eds.), *The adapted mind.* New York: Oxford University Press, pp. 19–136.

Tooley, M. (1980). An irrelevant consideration: Killing versus letting die. In B. Steinbock (Ed.). *Killing and letting die.* Englewood Cliffs, NJ: Prentice-Hall (1980). (Reprinted in J. M. Fischer & M. Ravizza (Eds.). (1992). *Ethics: Problems and principles* [pp. 107–111]. New York: Harcourt, Brace Jovanovich.)

Tooley, M. (1983). *Abortion and infanticide.* Oxford: Oxford University Press.

Trammel, R. (1975). Saving life and taking life. *Journal of Philosophy, 72,* 131–137. Reprinted in J. M. Fischer & M. Ravizza (Eds.). (1992). *Ethics: Problems and principles* (pp. 116–121). New York: Harcourt, Brace Jovanovich.)

Treisman, A. (1988). Features and objects: The fourteenth Bartlett Memorial Lecture. *Quarterly Journal of Experimental Psychology, 40A,* 201–237.

Trevarthen, C. (1992). Emotions of human infants and mothers and development of the brain. *Behavioral and Brain Sciences, 15,* 524–525.

Tribe, L. H. (1990/1992). *Abortion: The class of absolutes.* New York: W. W. Norton (Rev. Ed. 1992).

Trivers, R. L. (1972). Parental investment and sexual selection. In B. Campbell (Ed.), *Sexual selection and the descent of man.* Chicago: Aldine, pp. 136–179.

Trivers, R. L. (1974). Parent–offspring conflict. *American Zoologist, 14,* 249–264.

Trivers, R. L., & Willard, D. E. (1973). Natural selection of parental ability to vary sex ratio of offspring. *Science, 179,* 90–92.

Unger, R. K., Draper, R. D., & Pendergrass, M. L. (1986) Personal epistemology and personal experience. *Journal of Social Issues, 42*(2), 67–79.

Vicedo, M. (1992) The human genome project: Towards an analysis of the empirical, ethical, and conceptual issues involved. *Biology and Philosophy, 7,* 255–278.

Vom Saal, F. S., Grant, W. M., McMullen, C. W., & Laves, K. S. (1983). High fetal estrogen concentrations: Correlation with increased sexual activity and decreased aggression in male mice. *Science, 220,* 1306–1309.

Walker, L. J. (1984). Sex differences in the development of moral reasoning: A critical review. *Child Development, 55,* 677–691.

Walker, L. J., de Vries, B., & Trevarthen, S. D. (1987). Moral stages and moral orientations in real-life and hypothetical dilemmas. *Child Development, 58,* 842–858.

Walters, L. (1987). Test-tube babies: Ethical considerations. *Clinics in Perinatology, 14, 271–280. (Reprinted in R. T. Hull (Ed.). (1990). Ethical issues in the new reproductive technologies* [pp. 109–119]. Belmont, CA: Wadsworth.)

Walton, D. (1992). *Slippery slope arguments.* Oxford: Oxford University Press.

Warren, M. A. (1973). On the moral and legal status of abortion. The Monist, 57, 43–61. (Reprinted in J. Feinberg (Ed.). (1984). *The problem of abortion* pp. 102–116. Belmont, CA: Wadsworth.

Warren, M. A. (1977). Do potential people have moral rights? *Canadian Journal of Philosophy, 7,* 275–289.

Warren, M. A. (1982). Postscript on infanticide, February 26, 1982. In J. Feinberg (Ed.). (1984). *The problem of abortion.* Belmont, CA: Wadsworth, pp. 116–119.)

Waterman, A. S. (1988). On the uses of psychological theory and research in the process of ethical inquiry. *Psychological Bulletin, 103,* 283–298.

Werker, J. F. (1989). Becoming a native listener. *American Scientist, 77,* 54–59.

Werker, J. F., & Lalonde, C. E. (1988). Cross-language speech perception: Initial capacities and developmental change. *Developmental Psychology, 24,* 672–683.

Wertheimer, R. (1971). Understanding the abortion argument. *Philosophy & Public Affairs, 1,* 67–95.

White, G. (1789). *The natural history and antiquities of Selborne. in the county of Southampton.* London: Benjamin White.

Widner, H. et al. (1992). Bilateral fetal mesencephalic grafting in two patients with parkinsonism induced by 1–methyl-4–phenyl-1,2,3,6–tetrahydropyridine (MPTP). *New England Journal of Medicine, 327,* 1556–1563.

Wilkerson, I. (1993, March 31). Couple is told to return girl to biological parents. *The New York Times,* Sec. A, p. 11.

Williams, G. W. (1975). *Sex and evolution.* Princeton, NJ: Princeton University Press.

Williams, G. W. (1992). *Natural selection: Domains, levels, and challenges.* New York: Oxford University Press.

Williams, G. W., & Nesse, R. M. (1991). The dawn of Darwinian medicine. *The Quarterly Review of Biology, 66,* 1–22.

Williams, P. A. (1993). Can beings whose ethics evolved be ethical beings? In M. H. Nitecki, & D. V. Nitecki (Eds.), *Evolutionary ethics* (pp. 233–239). Albany, NY: State Univeristy of New York Press.

Willke, J. (1990, March 3). the fetus is life itself. *Los Angeles Times,* Sec. B, p. 6.

Wilson, E. O. (1975). *Sociobiology: The new synthesis.* Cambridge, MA: Harvard.

Wilson, M. (1987). Impacts of the uncertainty of paternity on family law. *Univ. of Toronto Faculty of Law Review, 45,* 216–242.

Wilson, M., & Daly, M. (1992). The man who mistook his wife for a chattel. In J. Barkow, L. Cosmides, & J. Tooby (Eds.), *The adapted mind* (pp. 243–276). New York: Oxford University Press.

Wolfe, L. (1994, January 4). And baby makes 3, even if you're gray. *The New York Times,* Sec. A, p. 15.

Zaner, R. M. (1984). A criticism of moral conservatism's view of in vitro fertilization and embryo transfer. *Perspectives in biology and medicine, 27,* 201–212. (Reprinted in R. T. Hull (Ed.). (1990). *Ethical issues in the new reproductive technologies* [pp. 137–147]. Belmont, CA: Wadsworth.)

Zimmer, H. (1956). *Philosophies of India.* New York: Meridian Books.

Zuk, M. (1992). The role of parasites in sexual selection: Current evidence and future directions. *Advances in the Study of Behavior, 21,* 39–68.

Author Index

Subject Index